ACTIVITIES 1914–1919

The Collected Writings of John Maynard Keynes

Maynard Keynes about 1920

THE COLLECTED WRITINGS OF
JOHN MAYNARD KEYNES

VOLUME XVI

ACTIVITIES 1914-1919

THE TREASURY AND
VERSAILLES

EDITED BY
ELIZABETH JOHNSON

© The Royal Economic Society 1971

All rights reserved. No part of this publication
may be reproduced or transmitted, in any
form or by any means, without permission

Published by
MACMILLAN AND CO LTD
London and Basingstoke
Associated companies in New York Toronto
Dublin Melbourne Johannesburg and Madras

SBN 333 11253 9 (hard cover)

Library of Congress catalog card no. 76-133449

Printed in Great Britain
at the University Printing House, Cambridge
(Brooke Crutchley, University Printer)

CONTENTS

GENERAL INTRODUCTION

This new standard edition of *The Collected Writings of John Maynard Keynes* forms the memorial to him of the Royal Economic Society. He devoted a very large share of his busy life to the Society. In 1911, at the age of twenty-eight, he became editor of the *Economic Journal* in succession to Edgeworth; two years later he was made secretary as well. He held these offices without intermittence until almost the end of his life. Edgeworth, it is true, returned to help him with the editorship from 1919 to 1925; Macgregor took Edgeworth's place until 1934, when Austin Robinson succeeded him and continued to assist Keynes down to 1945. But through all these years Keynes himself carried the major responsibility and made the principal decisions about the articles that were to appear in the *Economic Journal*, without any break save for one or two issues when he was seriously ill in 1937. It was only a few months before his death at Easter 1946 that he was elected president and handed over his editorship to Roy Harrod and the secretaryship to Austin Robinson.

In his dual capacity of editor and secretary Keynes played a major part in framing the policies of the Royal Economic Society. It was very largely due to him that some of the major publishing activities of the Society—Sraffa's edition of Ricardo, Stark's edition of the economic writings of Bentham, and Guillebaud's edition of Marshall, as well as a number of earlier publications in the 1930s—were initiated.

When Keynes died in 1946 it was natural that the Royal Economic Society should wish to commemorate him. It was perhaps equally natural that the Society chose to commemorate him by producing an edition of his collected works. Keynes himself had always taken a joy in fine printing, and the Society, with the help of Messrs Macmillan as publishers and the Cambridge University Press as printers, has been anxious to give Keynes's writings a permanent form that is wholly worthy of him.

The present edition will publish as much as is possible of his work in the field of economics. It will not include any private and personal correspondence or publish letters in the possession of his family. The edition is concerned, that is to say, with Keynes as an economist.

Keynes's writings fall into five broad categories. First there are the books which he wrote and published as books. Second there are collections of articles and pamphlets which he himself made during his lifetime (*Essays in Persuasion* and *Essays in Biography*). Third, there is a very considerable volume of published but uncollected writings—articles written for newspapers, letters to newspapers, articles in journals that have not been included in his two volumes of collections, and various pamphlets. Fourth, there are a few hitherto unpublished writings. Fifth, there is correspondence with economists and concerned with economics or public affairs.

This series will attempt to publish a complete record of Keynes's serious writing as an economist. It is the intention to publish almost completely the whole of the first four categories listed above. The only exceptions are a few syndicated articles where Keynes wrote almost the same material for publication in different newspapers or in different countries, with minor and unimportant variations. In these cases, this series will publish one only of the variations, choosing the most interesting.

The publication of Keynes's economic correspondence must inevitably be selective. In the day of the typewriter and the filing cabinet and particularly in the case of so active and busy a man, to publish every scrap of paper that he may have dictated about some unimportant or ephemeral matter is impossible. We are aiming to collect and publish as much as possible, however, of the correspondence in which Keynes developed his own ideas in argument with his fellow economists, as well as the more significant correspondence at times when Keynes was in the middle of public affairs.

Apart from his published books, the main sources available to those preparing this series have been two. First, Keynes in his will made Richard Kahn his executor and responsible for his economic papers. They have been placed in the Marshall Library of the University of Cambridge and have been available for this edition. Until 1914 Keynes did not have a secretary and his earliest papers are in the main limited to drafts of important letters that he made in his own handwriting and retained. At that stage most of the correspondence that we possess is represented by what he received rather than by what he wrote. During the war years of 1914–18 Keynes was serving in the Treasury. With the opening of the 1914–18 records, many of the papers that he wrote have become available. From 1919 onwards, throughout the rest of his life, Keynes had the help of a secretary —for many years Mrs Stevens. Thus for the last twenty-five years of his working life we have in most cases the carbon copies of his own letters as well as the originals of the letters that he received.

There were, of course, occasions during this period on which Keynes wrote himself in his own handwriting. In some of these cases, with the help of his correspondents, we have been able to collect the whole of both sides of some important interchange and we have been anxious, in justice to both correspondents, to see that both sides of the correspondence are published in full.

The second main source of information has been a group of scrapbooks kept over a very long period of years by Keynes's mother, Florence Keynes, wife of Neville Keynes. From 1919 onwards these scrapbooks contain almost the whole of Maynard Keynes's more ephemeral writing, his letters to newspapers and a great deal of material which enables one to see not only what he wrote, but the reaction of others to his writing. Without these very carefully kept scrapbooks the task of any editor or biographer of Keynes would have been immensely more difficult.

The plan of the edition, as at present intended, is this. It will total twenty-four volumes. Of these, the first eight will be Keynes's published books from *Indian Currency and Finance*, in

1913, to the *General Theory* in 1936, with the addition of his *Treatise on Probability*. There will next follow, as vols. IX and X, *Essays in Persuasion* and *Essays in Biography*, representing Keynes's own collections of articles. *Essays in Persuasion* will differ from the original printing in two respects; it will contain the full texts of the articles or pamphlets included in it and not (as in the original printing) abbreviated versions of these articles, and it will have added one or two later articles which are of exactly the same character as those included by Keynes in his original collection. In the case of *Essays in Biography*, we shall add various other biographical studies that Keynes wrote throughout his life.

There will follow three volumes, XI to XIII, of economic articles and correspondence, and one volume, XIV, of social, political and literary writings. We shall include in these volumes such part of Keynes's economic correspondence as is closely associated with the articles that are printed in them.

The further nine volumes, as we estimate at present, will deal with Keynes's *Activities* during the years from the beginning of his public life in 1905 until his death. In each of the periods into which we propose to divide this material, the volume concerned will publish his more ephemeral writings, all of it hitherto un-collected, his correspondence relating to these activities, and such other material and correspondence as is necessary to the understanding of Keynes's activities. The first four of these volumes are being edited by Elizabeth Johnson; the later volumes will be the responsibility of Donald Moggridge. It is their task to trace and interpret Keynes's activities sufficiently to make the material fully intelligible to a later generation. Until this work has progressed further, it is not possible to say with exactitude whether this material will be distributed, as we now think, over nine volumes, or whether it will need to be spread over a further volume or volumes. There will be a final volume of bibliography and index.

Those responsible for this edition have been: Lord Kahn, both as Lord Keynes's executor and as a long and intimate friend of Lord Keynes, able to help in the interpreting of much that would otherwise be misunderstood; Sir Roy Harrod as the author of his biography; Austin Robinson as Keynes's co-editor on the *Economic Journal* and successor as secretary of the Royal Economic Society. The main editorial tasks in the first four of these volumes have been carried by Elizabeth Johnson. She has been assisted at different times by Jane Thistlethwaite, Mrs McDonald, who was originally responsible for the systematic ordering of the files of the Keynes papers, Judith Masterman and Susan Wilsher, who in turn have worked with Mrs Johnson on the papers.

EDITORIAL FOREWORD

This volume, together with volume xv, form the first of a group of nine or more which will make available Keynes's more ephemeral writings, his letters and contributions to the newspapers, his memoranda while employed in the India Office and in the Treasury in two wars, and such correspondence as is directly related to the events about which he is writing or is necessary to the understanding of the documents that are published.

For his published contributions to the press, the main source is the series of scrapbooks which, as explained in the General Introduction, his mother indefatigably maintained throughout his working life. (Keynes, knowing that she was doing this, helped by sending her copies of all he published.) For the periods in Whitehall, first in the India Office and subsequently in the Treasury, dependence has been primarily on the files that are now available in the Public Record Office. In some cases, however, Keynes had himself retained an earlier draft of a memorandum that he had written. Almost all of the correspondence that is here published is among his surviving papers. At points the diaries of John Neville Keynes—Maynard Keynes's father— serve to illuminate Keynes's thoughts or state of mind at important moments.

This volume, like that which precedes it, has aimed to publish as much as possible of Keynes's writing of the period covered. In this early period there was none of the duplication in his contributions to the press, syndicated in different parts of the world, that sometimes is to be found in his later years. For the two Civil Service periods it has been necessary to be somewhat more selective and to confine publication to what is both clearly Keynes's work and of more than routine interest. During the later war years, for example, he wrote at intervals appreciations of the position regarding inter-allied finance, rehearsing much the same arguments about much the same problems in the light of progressively changing figures. We have selected for publication those examples of such memoranda which best illustrate a particular problem or best show his analytical handling of them.

It has been necessary, in order to make this material intelligible to a generation which did not live through the events and to whom the participants are unknown names, to provide a minimum of factual background. It has been sought to make this background information sufficient for clarity, but neither obtrusive nor argumentative. The purpose has been to provide the reader with the material from which to make his own judgement of Keynes rather than to attempt to impose the judgements of the editors.

No reader, we think, can fail to be impressed by the immensely detailed mastery which, as revealed in volume xv, Keynes had achieved as a very young man of all the many ramifications of Indian finance. This capacity for mastery of detail remained with him through life. He was never content with a merely superficial understanding of the broad essentials of a problem. We suspect that a reader will find it equally fascinating to contrast Keynes's analysis of the economic problems of war as set out in some of his Treasury memoranda or other discussions of war finance of 1914–18 with the analysis that he developed twenty-five years later in *How to Pay for the War*. Finally, one sees here vividly through his own eyes and in his own words his agonies of despair as a rational handling of the problems of reparations became irretrievably frustrated by political ineptitude.

NOTE TO THE READER

In this and subsequent volumes, in general all of Keynes's own writings are printed in larger type. All introductory matter and all writings by others than Keynes are printed in smaller type. The only exception to this general rule is that occasional short quotations from a letter from Keynes to his parents or to a friend, used in introductory passages to clarify a situation, are treated as introductory matter and are printed in the smaller type.

Most of Keynes's letters included in this and other volumes are reprinted from the carbon copies that remain among his papers. In most cases he has added his initials to the carbon in the familiar form in which he signed to all his friends. We have no means of knowing whether the top copy, sent to the recipient of the letter, carried a more formal signature.

PART I

THE TREASURY
IN THE WAR YEARS

Chapter 1

THE EARLY STAGES, 1914–1915

'I was in the Treasury throughout the war and all the money we either lent or borrowed passed through my hands'—so Keynes, speaking in 1923, airily described his wartime duties. He hardly exaggerated, as he was directly concerned with the strategy of financing Britain's war expenditure and that of her allies, and finally took charge of a division of his own responsible for all of Britain's inter-allied financial arrangements.

He kept a mass of minutes, memoranda, first and second drafts, reports and printed papers documenting this period of his life. By itself, however, the material is incomplete and inconclusive. The records of the Treasury and the Cabinet Office, now made available at the Public Record Office, help in large measure to fill in the gaps and reveal a remarkably influential role for a man between the ages of 31 and 36.

When Keynes entered the Treasury it was a comparatively small group, and the war still seemed a small war. At first he had many jobs, but as the war went on Britain's financial involvement mushroomed, and this national burden became his particular care. The following section does not provide an exhaustive account of his work. The papers reproduced have been chosen to show the different kinds of things that he was doing and his manner of doing them. They are interesting for the light that they throw on his development as an economist or on the similarities and differences in his thinking at this stage and in later years.

Keynes officially joined the Treasury in January 1915, but he made an earlier unorthodox foray into events in the first days of the war. Basil Blackett, who had returned to the Treasury after the report of the Chamberlain Commission, wrote to him 1 August:

> I tried to get hold of you yesterday and to-day but found you were not in town. I wanted to pick your brains for your country's benefit and thought you might enjoy the process. If by any chance you could spare time to see me on Monday I should be grateful, but I fear the decisions will all have been taken by then. The joint stock banks have made absolute fools of themselves and behaved very badly.

Keynes lost no time; he arrived in Whitehall the next day, Sunday, after riding down from Cambridge in the side-car of the motor cycle of his brother-in-law, A. V. Hill.

British banking was in a state of transition. For the past decade or so the joint stock banks had been accumulating large reserves of gold, and their London clearing house was beginning to replace the Bank of England as the central banking institution. Inspired by Sir Edward Holden—whose views on gold Keynes had criticised (*JMK*, vol. xv, pp. 88–90)—the banks argued that the gold reserves were too small in relation to the volume of British business and to the large hoards being amassed by other countries. They thought that the government should take more responsibility for maintaining the gold reserves, and in particular should keep a reserve against the claims of government savings bank depositors.

Early in 1914 this criticism became a demand for a public inquiry. Blackett had been given the task of writing the memorandum embodying the Treasury view, and had sent his paper to Keynes. Keynes's comments, in a letter dated 24 June 1914, with one exception consisted of points of detail. (For example, when Blackett remarked that 'so enlightened an economist as Stanley Jevons' had subscribed to the theory that commercial crises recurred under the influence of sunspots, Keynes observed: 'I am inclined to think there may still be something in Jevons' sunspot theory. At any rate it is not altogether derisory.')

In the last four paragraphs of the letter, however, Keynes took up the question of government responsibility, which was the central problem that the banks posed for the Treasury in their demand for reform. How far did the commercial banker's special interest in maintaining high gold reserves for the benefit of his own financial safety coincide with the interest of the general community, and to what extent should he expect the government to protect his interest at the public expense? Blackett was inclined to think that the bankers expected too much.

From a letter to BASIL BLACKETT, *24 June 1914*

I do not agree that the bankers are the only interested parties in avoiding a panic. In a modern panic it is improbable that the big banks will come to grief, and the main loss which the community suffers arises in rather a different way. This main loss, I should say, is due to forced realisations on the Stock Exchange of international securities. The first effect of a panic is that the banks withdraw accommodation from their weaker clients and these weaker clients are forced to realise securities for what they can get. I believe that we made an enormous profit out of the United States in 1907 by buying stocks from them of securities and goods at bargain prices, and similarly in the autumns of 1911 and 1912 our financiers pocketed a small fortune from the Germans by buying back Canadian Pacifics and other securities for much less than they had sold them for. It may not be good policy to save the weaker clients of banks from their own imprudence, but I do believe that it is the weaker clients rather than the banks themselves who lose most heavily in the next panic. There is I think arising out of this some slight reason why the government as representative of the general public should interest itself in the gold reserve question. It would not be primarily the bankers who would suffer from a bank rate of 10 per cent.

The main questions really at issue appear to me to be three:

(a) The question is not so much, are our gold reserves insufficient, as what parties in the changed circumstances of the present day shall bear the responsibility and burden of the normal increase of the reserves which is from time to time necessary. Now that the Bank of England is altogether overshadowed by the larger joint stock banks, it is quite unable to bear, as it bore formerly, the whole burden. The present controversy, while it appears to be about the magnitude of the reserves, is really about a much more important question—namely, as to where in the future the centre of power and responsibility in the London money market is to lie. You point out, quite correctly, that the gold reserves are probably at the worst only a little inadequate, but this question of distribution of power is a question of first-rate importance, which does deserve very careful consideration on the part of the government as well as on the part of bankers.

(b) Is it worth the government's while to attempt to influence the nature of settlement by putting pressure on the bankers, or by striking a bargain with them? I think it may be. If I were Chancellor of the Exchequer, I should be inclined to bear part of the burden of the increased gold reserves, not because there is any justice in the demand of the bankers that this should be done on account of the [Post Office] Savings Bank, but in order to give me bargaining power with the banking community. At the present moment the bankers are absolutely ripe for accepting some plan or other. If the Chancellor came forward with an offer of some financial assistance he would probably be able to secure the adoption of whichever of the possible plans he decided to favour. It would be far better to obtain a settlement by consent in this manner than to introduce legislation.

(*c*) There remains the question of some legislative change introducing a measure of emergency elasticity into the Bank of England note issue. I regard this as very important, largely for the reason which I explained to you in conversation. The number of bank branches is now so very great that nervousness on the part of bankers, leading them to increase the amount of their till money, might very substantially reduce the Bank of England's reserve. It is important that all the gold should be kept either for export or for show, and that extra notes should be available for making bankers feel quite easy as regards the possibility of a run on them.

A run did in fact materialise, but it was a run by the banks themselves on the Bank of England. During the last week of July the Bank of England paid out an unprecedented amount of gold for home demands, mainly to the joint stock banks. Some of the banks, however, were not willing to pay out gold so freely to their own customers and offered them notes—the bad behaviour mentioned by Blackett in his letter of 1 August.

On 1 August a secret committee of the joint stock bankers, which had been meeting for months, produced an emergency plan proposing the paying in by themselves of a large sum in gold to the Bank of England, the issue of special Bank of England notes in return (i.e. the suspension of the Bank Act), and the suspension of all gold payments outside the country. Lloyd George, who was Chancellor of the Exchequer, was known to be attracted to this plan—which, with its stated intent to lock up gold, was diametrically opposed to the principles held by the Treasury and the Bank of England.

This was the situation when Keynes alighted at the Treasury. At Blackett's instigation he wrote a memorandum on the folly of suspension before such drastic action was necessary. The only copies of the paper were kept as type-scripts in the Treasury files (T 170/14 and T 171/92)—the first with the papers of Sir John Bradbury, the Joint Permanent Secretary to the Treasury, the second with papers from the Chancellor of the Exchequer's office, i.e. Lloyd George's copy. They are dated 3 August (Monday), signed 'J. M. Keynes' and begin with Keynes's short summary of his argument written in his own hand.

MEMORANDUM AGAINST THE SUSPENSION OF GOLD

I deal first with the probable magnitude of the foreign drain of gold.

Next with some of the evils of a suspension of specie payments.

Then with the possible means of preventing an internal drain of gold.

If the foreign drain is not likely to be very large, and the internal drain can be obviated by other means, it is difficult to see how such an extreme and disastrous measure as the suspension of cash payments can be justified.

J.M.K.

Is the suspension of specie payment necessary?

Assuming (a point I deal with later) that internal demands for currency beyond the normal are mainly met by some form of emergency paper currency, the suspension of specie payment by the Bank of England can only become necessary if the probable immediate drawings on foreign account are greater than the Bank can possibly afford to lose. Three factors are involved in the determination of this:

(1) The amount of gold available in the Bank's reserve.

(2) The possibility of replenishments from abroad.

(3) The amount of foreign credits now available in London for the purpose of drawing gold.

(1) We may assume that this amounts to the sum of gold, £28 millions, now in the Bank + approximately £15 millions from the joint stock banks + what they have taken out in the last few days—such amounts as may dribble away into internal use. It is also possible that India may be compelled to un-earmark a certain amount.

(2) We may expect a certain amount of gold from U.S.A. and South America. But undoubtedly it would be sanguine to hope for much from such sources. This arises out of the great difference between war and peace conditions, which has been perhaps insufficiently realised in the past. In peace conditions a 10 per cent bank rate might be expected to draw gold from all kinds of centres, however severe the financial panic. In war conditions we know now that this is uncertain. It is the sudden realisation of this, I believe, which is largely responsible for such degree of timidity as now appears to affect high banking authorities. To an appreciable extent, however, this circumstance is neutralised by other factors to be referred to under (3) below.

(3) The evidence shows that no country is in a position to draw considerable sums of gold, with the exception of France and, possibly (I speak without knowledge respecting this), Russia through France. I put the claims of these countries on one side for the moment. So far from other countries being able to draw from us, the most formidable difficulties which now face the money market arise out of the fact that foreign countries are not able to meet their immediate liabilities to us. Germany, I take it, has more than exhausted her credits here. In the case of India and Brazil, to take two countries which often draw much gold from us, the exchanges are already below the point which normally causes gold to flow from them to us. We cannot rely on this actually bringing gold to us, but we can rely on its preventing a movement in the opposite direction. And in the case of India I should not be surprised if the India Office were compelled to un-earmark, not so much to meet their own disbursements as to enable the exchange banks to remit home the large sums which the phenomenally easy position of the Indian money market makes it possible for them to lay hands on.

In the case of U.S.A. it is rumoured that they have determined to send us no more gold at present. This may well be so. But the balance is against them and there is no appearance at the *moment* of their being able (or desirous) of *taking* gold from us.

I do not believe it is possible to name any country, apart from France, which is *now known* to be in a position to take important amounts of gold from us.

Before turning to the question of France, let me take account of the circumstances which to some extent neutralise our unwonted and unanticipated inability to obtain fresh gold from elsewhere. First (a minor point), the present state of the insurance market raises the gold export point far above (or below, according to your terminology) its normal level. Second, the closing of the stock exchange and the fact that the discount houses have ceased to do business, taken in conjunction with the 10 per cent bank rate, have virtually abolished the power of any foreign country to raise *fresh* credits here. They cannot sell us securities and they cannot discount their bills with us. We only have to take account, therefore, of the credits actually existing.

Now as to France, so far as one can judge from the exchanges, she is in a position if she wishes to take some gold from us. It may be observed that it is unlikely at the present juncture that the Bank of France would wish to embarrass the Bank of England, but I do not propose to take account of this consideration in what follows. The main relevant question is—*how much* gold is France in a position to take from us? What is the amount, that is to say, of France's unexhausted credits with us? High authorities should be able to make some approximate estimate of this. It would be astonishing if it were to exceed an amount of from £10 million to £15 million, and I should expect it to fall considerably short of this.

I see no *present* reason, therefore, for supposing that the foreign drain on the Bank of England is likely to be more than she can support.

One possible objection may be anticipated. It may be urged that we may want all our gold at a later date for making foreign purchases. In reply to this it may be remarked:

(1) in relation to the magnitude of our imports the amount in question is not large;

(2) the mere cessation of new foreign investment on our part enables us, as time goes on, to draw an enormous quantity of goods from foreign countries, so long as trade routes remain open;

(3) the mere fact of the cessation of specie payments and the consequent doubt as to the exchange value of our paper money must greatly impair our purchasing power in international markets.

One consideration never to be forgotten is the following. It is useless to accumulate gold reserves in times of peace unless it is intended to utilise them in time of danger. I have always believed that Continental state banks would realise this as little in the future as in the past, and that in accumulating gold they were making sacrifices to comparatively little purpose. But everyone has supposed that the true maxim, originally popularised by Bagehot, influenced our own authorities, and that the suspension of specie payment by the Bank of England would be a last, and not a first resource.

Reasons against suspension of specie payment

The *future* position of the City of London as a free gold market will be seriously injured if at the *first* sign of emergency specie payment is suspended. A point may conceivably come when such a measure cannot be avoided, but, if it is taken before our resources are obviously overtaxed, it will be said that in future similar suspensions are not very improbable and are indeed to be expected when anything really serious happens. If such things are said or believed in international banking circles, our position and prestige will be very different from what they have been in the immediate past. Putting aside consequences of a general character, the special evils to be anticipated are the following. To an extent which has been increasing largely in recent years foreign countries have been keeping a substantial part of their ultimate monetary reserve (or reserve of free monetary resources) in London. Others were about, or were proposing to do so, e.g. Chile and Brazil. Such business as this is profitable and enormously enhances London's position as a monetary centre. Its existence depends *very directly* on complete confidence in London's unwavering readiness to meet the demands upon her. It happens that at the present time these countries are not in a position to draw on London. If we suspend specie payments in conditions comparatively favourable to ourselves, it will be assumed *a fortiori* that we shall suspend when they are able and desirous to draw on us—thus defeating one of the chief objects of their keeping balances here. What is important is not so much what we actually shall do in future emergencies, as the impression which our present conduct is likely to produce. It appears to me probable that if we suspend now, a marked tendency will set in for the secondary countries to keep a far larger proportion of their free resources in gold at home.

Other important classes of business, as is well known, depend also, though much more indirectly, upon a continuance of this confidence. The existence of this confidence in the past has been one of the most important *differentiations* between London and Paris or Berlin. It ought not to be endangered except for the very gravest cause. That the evils of the suspension of cash payment are very great is not likely, however, to meet with denial.

The internal currency and the connection between suspension of the Bank Act and the suspension of specie payments

These two questions are properly taken together.

It is sometimes supposed that the suspension of the Bank Act and the suspension of specie payments necessarily, or probably, go together. If things are well managed and go properly this is very far from being the case. They have not gone together in the past. Indeed *one* important object of the suspension of the Bank Act is to enable the internal circulation to be filled with emergency paper, in order that all or nearly all our gold may be available for a foreign drain. This object falls to the ground if no gold is to be used for the latter purpose.

The suspension of the Bank Act makes it possible to use emergency paper for internal purposes.

The continuance of specie payments makes it possible to get gold for foreign purposes.

The continuance of specie payments is only incompatible with the object of the suspension of the Bank Act, if it leads to a very heavy drain of gold out of the Bank for *internal* purposes.

It seems to me for the following reasons that it ought to be possible to maintain specie payments while keeping the drain of gold for internal purposes within comparatively narrow limits. So far the public have behaved admirably. The recent heavy drain of gold from the Bank of England has been mainly due to a fit of hoarding on the part of the joint stock banks. This gold will be available again as soon as these banks regain their equilibrium.

But the main point is this. It is possible to maintain specie payments, so as to meet foreign demands, while making it extremely difficult and inconvenient for the ordinary man to get gold. Gold should only be available at the head office of the Bank of England. The joint stock banks should entirely refuse to supply gold over the counter to their customers, but should meet all demands in legal tender paper money of suitable denominations. They should also refuse to be parties to obtaining gold for customers from the Bank of England unless they are satisfied that it is genuinely required for foreign purposes, either for travelling or for remittance. Genuine demands for these purposes should be met immediately. Thus the only way in which the ordinary man, who had no real need for it, would be able to obtain gold would be by going to the Bank of England in person and presenting notes. The position of London as a free market for gold for foreign export would nevertheless be completely preserved.

I believe these measures would be adequate to restrict in a

sufficient degree the internal drain. The evidence of history in other countries and at other times shows that people take very readily to notes. In the greater part of England most people will have no option but to use notes for a time, if the local offices of the joint stock banks provide them with nothing else. They may soon discover that they are quite well adapted to their purpose.

If, however, this proves on experience not to be the case, no more than half measures need even then be taken. The Bank of England might refuse to pay gold over the counter to any casual applicant, while it might continue to make gold readily available to any customer of a joint stock bank who could present a letter from his bank that he had satisfied them that he genuinely needed gold for external purposes. It would be impolitic, with a view to the future, for even these half measures to be taken until experience had proved them to be necessary. But the vital point is that we should not repudiate our external obligations to pay gold, until it is physically impossible for us to fulfil them.

In conclusion it is desirable to consider the relation to the above of proposals to extend the Bank Holiday period for two or three days, and to issue Treasury £1 notes, as distinguished from bank notes.

The first of these measures does not affect the above appreciably. The period can be excused on the ground of mobilisation and on account of the necessity of printing and circulating to banks all over the country £1 and 10s notes. At the end of the period the arrangements outlined above will come into operation—the banks, that is to say, all over the country will cash cheques for notes over the counter, and gold will again be available at the Bank of England.

The issue of Treasury £1 notes, instead of Bank of England £1 notes, appears to me to be a doubtful policy, complicating the situation, somewhat now, and greatly in the future (either if there is danger of inflation *or* if we are seeking to regularise matters again), and without compensating advantages. But the precise form of the internal emergency currency is of secondary importance, and it is not worth while to argue against the above proposals at the present moment.

But if, however, the Bank of England maintains specie payment, it is desirable that some degree of convertibility should attach to the Treasury notes. I am inclined to think that they need not carry on their face the obligation of convertibility into gold on demand. If they are to be issued in the name of the Government it would be safer not. But in addition to their being accepted at face value by Post Office, tax collectors, etc., and being invested by law with legal tender quality, they should in fact be encashable at the Bank of England or some single corresponding centre in London (e.g. the National Debt Office) on the same terms as those prevailing for £5 notes. And it might, I suppose, be a better plan for the Government to lay itself under an obligation always to give at (e.g.) the National Debt Office on demand a £5 bank note in exchange for Treasury notes amounting to an equal denomination. This would ensure a parity between government notes and bank notes, would prevent any appreciable depreciation of the former in terms of gold, so long as specie payment was maintained, and would at the same time interpose two separate personal presentations between them and specie.

It is desirable to add that if I am right in thinking that no large foreign drain is immediately probable, very little can be lost (and a very great deal gained) by keeping open a formal offer to supply gold for this purpose (i.e. foreign remittance).

The evils arising out of the suspension of specie payments (namely the effect on the future position of London and the depreciation of our currency) will be no greater if this step be postponed until we are unquestionably driven to it and no alternative is open to us, than if it be taken immediately in a spirit of timidity or panic.

If the fatal step is taken of suspending specie payments before it is *absolutely* necessary, the questions of how the exchanges will be regulated and how much depreciation of the paper currency in terms of gold is to be faced with equanimity, deserve very serious consideration. The absolute suspension of specie payments necessarily involves the solution of these questions.

J. M. KEYNES

3 August 1914

Lloyd George was given the memorandum to read on 4 August and later that day made the point in a meeting with representatives of the bankers and traders that suspension of the Bank Act and suspension of specie payments did not necessarily go together. According to Blackett's diary, quoted by Harrod, he had 'clearly imbibed much of Keynes's memorandum and is strong against suspension of specie payments'. Much of the bankers' plan was accepted by the Treasury. The banks' gold reserves were paid into the Bank of England. An emergency currency was issued, but since it was brought out by the Treasury and not by the Bank of England, the Bank Act did not have to be suspended. And gold payments abroad were not suspended; England and the United States were the only countries not to stop specie payments at this time.

During these days the Treasury swarmed with activity—Lloyd George summoned bankers and businessmen for consultation from all parts of the country, and public and private officials wearily inscribed minutes at two and three o'clock in the morning. Keynes obviously enjoyed being on the inside. He wrote to Hill (4 August): 'I spend most of my time at the Treasury and this work is very exciting. When not there, there is the press to influence, so I'm very busy.' To his father he wrote:

From a letter to J. N. KEYNES, *6 August 1914*

The bankers completely lost their heads and have been simply dazed and unable to think two consecutive thoughts. [On the contrary, the Treasury papers show that they had a definite plan of action.]

Specie payment by the Bank of England has now been saved— by the skin of its teeth. The points now to concentrate on are saving of the accepting houses (I doubt if a single director of the Bank of England is solvent today) and the settling of the conditions of the £1 note issue.

I've just heard that they consider I played an important part in preventing the suspension of specie payments, as it was my memorandum converted Lloyd George.

He tackled the problem of the acceptance houses in one more memorandum for the Treasury, dated 5 August; a single typed copy survived in the Chancellor of the Exchequer's files (T 171/92). The function of the acceptance houses was to endorse the bills of foreign customers for the discount houses and banks which advanced them money. The war had made it impossible for foreigners to pay their debts, but the acceptance houses were saved from immediate embarrassment by a moratorium, declared 3 August, on bills of exchange. This was the state of affairs when Keynes wrote his memorandum.

THE PROPER MEANS FOR ENABLING DISCOUNT
OPERATIONS TO BE RESUMED

In order that our foreign trade may be conducted in a normal way, it is necessary that as soon as possible the business of discounting bills, which is now suspended, should be re-established.

This is not at present possible because the credit of the accepting houses is for the time being shattered; and the banks and discount houses will not discount bills until they have been accepted by someone in whose credit they can place confidence.

The following are two of the possible alternatives:

I. To rehabilitate the credit of the accepting houses by guaranteeing their *past* engagements; this, if it goes far enough, might give them sufficient credit to enter into new engagements.

II. To guarantee, in whole or part, their *new* engagements only.

I. Let us take the first of these proposals.

It is not quite plain what is involved in the Government's 'guaranteeing the past engagements of the accepting houses'. Two points have to be made plain:

(1) Is the Government merely to guarantee any deficits

16

which may be shown in the affairs of any individual accepting houses, when at some distant date their affairs are straightened out, or is the Government, in some way, to prevent the necessity of any accepting house being wound up at any time on account of past transactions?

(2) Is the Government to meet the outstanding engagements of the accepting houses in cash, or is it merely to undertake to meet them at some undetermined distant date, so that the bills will be, for the banks which hold them, locked-up assets, though eventually good ones?

If the Government takes in each case the lesser alternative, i.e. merely guarantees to meet any deficit shown in the affairs of any individual accepting houses at some undetermined distant date, the main consequence is to guarantee the banks and dis-count houses, who hold the acceptances of the accepting houses, against *eventual* loss. This is no doubt very desirable from the point of view of the banks; but their *eventual* losses under this head are not likely to be more than they can support; and it is not clear that such action will best serve the Government's prime object, namely the facilitation of *new* business. For if the Government merely guarantees such deficit as may exist on past acceptances, *after* the existing assets of accepting houses have been swallowed up, there will (or may) be little or no assets to back *new* acceptances and the credit of accepting houses for *new* engagements will consequently not be particularly good.

If therefore a Government guarantee of past engagements is to do much good it must go *farther* than is proposed above, and must, in effect, *either* involve a gift of undetermined amount, going beyond their past liabilities, to such accepting houses as may eventually be insolvent, or involve the guarantee of their new engagements *as well as* of old ones.

The essential point to observe is that the mere guarantee of any deficit of old engagements, which the accepting houses them-selves are eventually unable to meet out of their capital and reserve, does not make their credit good for new engagements,

17

because it does not, *for certain* leave the accepting houses with a margin from which to meet any deficit on these new engagements.

A proposal on these lines must, therefore, also involve either a guarantee on new engagements, as well as of old, or a guarantee not merely of such part of the loss arising out of old engagements as the accepting houses are themselves unable to meet, but of some larger part of the loss which may arise out of old payments. This would saddle the Government with a very serious liability in the future, at a time when it may not at all wish to add to its existing liabilities.

II. Apart from other advantages or disadvantages the second of the expedients achieves directly the object, for which Government is chiefly solicitous, namely the establishment of a discount market for new business.

This second expedient is only practically feasible if the accepting houses will form themselves into a single body or syndicate with mutual liabilities, so far as new business is concerned. If this could be done the Government, as in the case of insurance, might accept a contingent liability of (say) 90 per cent on account of new bills accepted after August 6th by the mutual association of accepting houses. (The bills would have behind them the credit of the drawer of the bill and of the client on behalf of whom the accepting house accepts, as well as that of the accepting houses themselves; so that the contingent liability of the Government would not be very onerous.) The Government, after giving their names to the bills to the above extent, would probably need to take no further part in the transactions.

This alternative should be combined with a moratorium affecting past acceptances, the period of this moratorium possibly varying with the domicile of the client on whose behalf a given bill was accepted. Thus it would be declared that an accepting house need not meet an engagement of a bill on behalf of a client of domicile A until date x, date x depending, along with other circumstances, upon whether a moratorium still exists in country *A*.

III. A third alternative may be mentioned. Past acceptances, assisted by moratoria of various periods (as proposed above), might be left, for the present to look after themselves. The effect of this is to leave the banks with a certain amount of non-liquid assets. The accepting houses might then be given credit, sufficient to give them a margin of free assets upon the strength of which they would be able to enter into new business, by the Bank of England's giving to a syndicate of them overdraft facilities of suitable amount; the overdraft to be without specific security, but to be an eventual first claim against the total assets of the syndicate of borrowing houses *after* the future acceptances of the syndicate have been met. The 'total assets' of the syndicate for the above purpose to be the aggregate of the eventual surpluses of the houses entering the syndicate after they have met their past engagements, an individual house, which is not eventually able to meet its pre-August 6 engagements, being reckoned as contributing nothing (*not* a negative amount, so that past acceptances are not guaranteed); the Government to be responsible to the Bank for any eventual deficit in meeting the overdraft (and possibly to share in any interest paid to the Bank on account of the overdraft).

I am somewhat doubtful as to the value of this alternative and prefer alternative II. It depends a good deal upon the amount of the overdraft facilities which would be required in order to satisfy those who could discount the acceptances, and on the willingness of the accepting houses to work together in a syndicate.

It may be presumed that in the immediate future a greater proportion of accepting business than in the past will come to the banks instead of to the accepting houses proper.

J. M. KEYNES

5 August 1914

Rehabilitation of the credit of the acceptance houses turned out in fact to be the crux of the matter in restoring the movement of trade. A moratorium on all debts, declared 7 August, froze the assets of the banks and the discount houses. They were provided with new funds by the Government authorising the Bank of England to buy up their pre-moratorium bills. The acceptors were allowed to reaccept bills that they were unable to meet, and later were also furnished with loans by the Bank of England, guaranteed by the Government. Yet the banks were still reluctant to use the money they had been given to enter into new business. The credit of the acceptance houses was not restored, and the situation remedied, until 4 September, when new acceptances were given precedence over the Bank of England's claims on the free assets of the acceptance houses until one year after the war.

It is evident that Keynes hoped for an official Treasury appointment; in his enthusiasm he wrote to the Permanent Secretary offering the names of several Cambridge men eligible for war work. The Treasury, however, was in no hurry to rush into an expansion of staff. Keynes wrote to his father 14 August that he was returning to 'Probability' and was thinking of bringing out 'a small book' in September—a financial history.

He had already composed a short article on the currency measures taken by some of the other belligerent countries, which appeared in the *Morning Post*, 11 August 1914, headed 'from a correspondent'. Mrs Keynes started a scrapbook, the first of many, with a clipping of it, to which she added the initials 'J.M.K.'. Keynes made use of this material in some notes on 'Currency Expedients Abroad' under 'Current Topics', *Economic Journal*, September 1914 (*JMK* vol. XI).

From the Morning Post, *11 August 1914*

CURRENCY MEASURES ABROAD

A certain amount of information is gradually becoming available as to the means which are being adopted in France, Russia, and Germany to husband the use of gold and to supply an emergency currency. All three countries, like England, are, of course, arranging for large additional issues of notes, but none of them is following England's example in maintaining the obligation for conversion of the notes into gold. In France the necessary measures are very simple. At no time is the Bank of France under any legal obligation to redeem her notes in gold, and she is always free to encash them with token silver. Nor is there any rule whatever governing the specie reserve which she need keep against her notes. The only restriction under which she lies at normal times is on the aggregate of notes, whether backed by gold or not, which may be issued. The only important relaxation, therefore, which is required in abnormal times is to raise, by whatever amount is requisite, the limit of the aggregate circulation of notes which is permitted to the Bank. It happened that at the outbreak of war the actual circulation was not far short of the legal limit of £272 million, having risen from £236 million on 23 July to £267 million on 30 July. On Friday last, therefore, the French Chambers authorised an increase in the limit from £272 million to £480 million, thus practically permitting to the Bank of France an unlimited power of note issue. At the same time all obligation to cash the notes, even in token silver, was suspended. In spite of this, however, it is to be expected that the Bank will not permit its notes to fall to a discount of more than 3 or 4 per cent at the most, and will release some part of its enormous stock of gold (£166 million on 30 July) rather than permit the exchange value of the paper franc to fall unduly. The present quotations for French exchange, though still somewhat nominal, do not suggest that any heavy depreciation of the paper money is anticipated. A small depreciation of the notes of the Bank of France is no new thing, having occurred more than once in the last three or four years. It is a recognised part of the Bank's means of protecting itself, and need not be thought to prelude a further break in the exchange.

The legal position of the Bank of Russia, which is a purely government institution, is much more like that of the Bank of England. It has, that is to say, a fixed fiduciary issue, the circulation of notes being allowed to exceed the cash held against them by a certain fixed amount only. The Bank of Russia, however, regards as 'cash' for the above purpose not only the gold and silver in its own vaults, but also deposits held on its behalf in the chief European financial centres. As a matter of fact, in quite recent times the permitted fiduciary issue has not been of practical importance, as the 'cash' held has actually exceeded the circulation of notes. Suspension of the ordinary restrictions in such cases may take the form of allowing the fiduciary issue to increase by an undetermined amount, as in England, or by substituting for the former figure of limitation some new and much higher one. The latter course has been adopted in Russia, the permitted fiduciary issue having been raised last Friday from £30 million to £150 million. Although the 'cash' at the present time is stated to amount to £160 million in gold and £40 million on deposit abroad, the obligation to meet the notes in specie has been nevertheless entirely suspended. It is impossible to predict what the Russian policy will be in the matter of allowing its paper to fall to a discount rather than part with 'cash'. But one would expect that, to start with at any rate, some considerable efforts would be made to maintain the exchange value of the rouble somewhere in the neighbourhood of par.

The steps taken by Germany seem to be of a more complicated description. Ordinarily the Reichsbank works under three restrictions: first, that a tax must be paid when the fiduciary issue exceeds a certain amount; second, that in no circumstances may the note issue rise to more than three times the amount of 'cash' (though the legal definition of 'cash' includes a few, not very large, items in addition to gold and silver); and, third, that the excess of the note circulation over the cash must be backed by commercial bills bearing two approved names. All these provisions have now been removed, and in addition the obligation to cash notes in specie has been suspended. Thus, so far as note issue goes, the state banks of France, Russia, and Germany are all working under what are, in effect, identical systems, namely, a virtually unlimited right of note issue and a suspension of specie payments. The actual depreciation of the forced currency is, of course, likely to be very different in the three cases.

According, however, to one authority a further and much more abnormal step has been taken in Germany. In addition to bank notes, *Darlehnskassenscheine*, or 'loan' notes, of denominations ranging from 5*s* to £2 10*s* are to be issued up to an amount of £75 million. They are to be available as loans to all comers in amounts ranging down to £5, against numerous kinds of securities up to one-half or two-thirds of their assessed value, for periods of three to six months, at a rate as a rule something above the Reichsbank discount rate. What degree of legal-tender quality they are to possess is not clear, but to some extent apparently they are to be accepted as notes. It is impossible to say that such a measure as this is not required. But it appears to increase enormously the dangers of inflation. If the people of Germany can so easily supply themselves with enormous additional stocks of paper money beyond what they usually have and beyond what the Government pays over for mobilisation and military expenses, one would expect prices to rise hugely in terms of this money. If any foreign exchange with Germany were quotable the exchange value of the paper mark would tend to depreciate largely, and the task of preventing this would be infinitely more difficult than it would be found, for example, by the Bank of France. As Germany is as good as cut off from foreign trade for the present, her authorities may regard it as useless to pay much regard just now to the exchange value of the mark. But there will be a heavy reckoning to pay in due course. And, in the meantime, the rise of prices will much increase the sufferings of the lower classes, by way of compensation for such benefits as the middle classes, who have security to offer in exchange for **loan paper**, may thus be able to secure.

'Maynard finds that London in wartime gets on his nerves', Dr Keynes noted in his diary 29 August, and added that his son had gone to Sussex to stay with Leonard and Virginia Woolf. From there Keynes wrote his father letters commenting on the Government's financial policy and took part in a correspondence in *The Economist* about the gold holdings of the banks.

This exchange was prompted by an article ('The Position of the Banks', *The Economist*, 15 August 1914) which estimated the gold holdings of the joint stock banks and the Bank of England at £80 million. The difficulty in making such a calculation was in the vagueness of the official statistics.

The Economist estimated £50 million as the amount of gold coin and Bank of England notes—cash in hand—held by the seventeen leading joint stock banks. (This figure was reached by assuming that the roughly equal amounts of cash in hand and cash at the Bank of England reported by the one bank publishing these figures separately held true for all the others. The seventeen banks' total 'cash in hand and at Bank' was over £111 million.) To this £50 million in gold and notes was added £40 million in gold coin and bullion at the Bank of England, £11,300,000 being subtracted as the amount required to meet notes outstanding above the fiduciary issue—leaving a total of about £80 million. (*The Economist* implicitly assumed the Bank of England notes held by the banks to be covered by the £11,300,000.) Estimating gold in circulation at not less than £20 million, the writer concluded that there was at least £100 million of gold in the country.

This estimate was challenged by a prominent Manchester banker, D. Drummond Fraser, whose own calculations put the amount of gold held by the banks at more than £100 million (letter to *The Economist*, 22 August 1914). Fraser's figures were based on the Mint census of gold coin: to the £70 million of gold coins held by all the banks, including the Bank of England, he added an assumed £30 million gold bullion belonging to the Bank of England—making £100 million in gold coin and bullion. Beyond this he estimated an increase of £20 million in the holdings of the banks in the past year. With the addition of gold received from abroad by the Bank of England, he arrived at a total of £132,656,000.

Keynes attacked Fraser's estimates in a letter in the next week's *Economist*. (He had already questioned the adequacy of the Mint's figures when he reviewed the 1912 Annual Report for the *Economic Journal*, March 1914, and corresponded on the subject with the Deputy Master (*JMK*, vol. XI).) But criticism of Fraser's estimates apart, Keynes seemed chiefly moved in writing the letter to castigate the banks—praised by Fraser—for their habit of window-dressing revealed by the figures in the *Economist* article. During the same week they had been publicly taken to task by Lloyd George for their failure to assist trade in the crisis; *The Economist* in the same issue defended their instinct for self-preservation ('A Plea for Our Banks', 29 August 1914).

To the Editor of The Economist, *29 August 1914*

Sir

The letter from Mr Drummond Fraser published by you last week gives, I believe, a much exaggerated idea of the amount of gold held by the joint stock banks. He mainly relies on the return of gold coin called for by the Mint on 30 June of each year. No return has yet been published for a year later than 1912, but we may accept Mr Fraser's presumed figure of £70 million for 1913. Now this includes gold *coin* held by the Bank of England as well as by the joint stock banks, and no public information is available as to what part of the Bank of England's total gold holding is in British coin and how much in bars and foreign coin. As Mr Fraser estimates (by implication) the bars and foreign coin at £30 million, he is putting the Bank of England's holding of British coin at, say £10 million to £12 million. I do not know on what information he bases this estimate, but it is not likely that the Bank's holding of sovereigns can be nearly so low as this. Mr Fraser then adds £20 million as the addition of the joint stock banks to their gold holdings between 30 June 1913 and 30 June 1914. This figure is purely hypothetical, and can hardly be correct, the total flow of gold coin during the period in question from the Bank of England into the country, for the purposes of the joint stock banks and the internal circulation taken together, being not more than about £12 million. (It may be assumed that the direct coinage carried out by the Mint for the joint stock banks is relatively small.) Mr Fraser's final total of £132,656,000 as representing the amount of gold in the vaults of the Bank of England and the other banks, which he obtains from the various calculations described above, must be from 30 to 40 per cent in excess of the correct figure. £100 million is an outside amount, and I should estimate the figure myself as somewhat lower. It should be added that of the amount held by the joint stock banks by far the greater part is required, until sovereigns are superseded by notes to a far greater extent than at present, as till money. The number of branch banks now exceeds 9,000. A comparatively small amount at each absorbs in the aggregate an enormous amount of cash. If we put at £20 million the gold held by the joint stock banks in excess of till money requirements, we shall not be below the mark.

In your own article on 'The Position of the Banks' in your issue of 15 August you point out that the 'cash in hand and at Bank' shown by seventeen leading joint stock banks on 30 June 1914 amounted to £111 million. You generously estimate that of this sum £50 million was held in gold and bank notes. (This estimate should, I think, include silver also.) £61 million, therefore, ought to have been 'at Bank'. As the normal total of 'other deposits' at the Bank of England, which include, of course, numerous important accounts besides those of the seventeen banks referred to above, may be taken at £43 million, and as even at the end of June 1914 this was temporarily swollen, 'for balance-sheet purposes', not above £54,500,000, we have some measure of the extent to which it has been the practice of the joint stock banks to endeavour to hoodwink the public as to their true normal position.

As things have turned out, with ample and judicious Government assistance, and with admirable calmness on the part of the British depositor, there is every reason for thinking that the position of the banks is, nevertheless, perfectly sound, and that nothing but a little courage and public spirit is required for them to be able to carry on much as usual.

But I suggest that a bad conscience in respect of the matters referred to above may be a part explanation of why, on an occasion when the Bank of England has stood staunch and the other elements in the money market have done their best in overwhelmingly difficult circumstances, the joint stock banks should, with some notable exceptions, have failed, as they so signally have failed, in courage and public spirit.—I am, etc.

J. M. KEYNES

Fraser replied in a letter appearing 5 September 1914, making three points:

(1) His estimate of the amount of gold *coin* held by the Bank of England, published in a paper of his own, had been confirmed by the Deputy Master of the Mint.

(2) His estimate of a £20 million increase in the gold coin held by the joint stock banks between June 1913 and June 1914 was based on the common knowledge of bankers that a greater effort had been made by the banks to amass gold in that year than in any other year since 1907. He also referred to the public knowledge that some of the larger joint stock banks held gold bullion as well as gold coin, and drew attention to the fact that, in reporting the annual increase of gold coin held, account must be taken of the day of the week on which the return was made, gold in the vaults always being at its lowest at the end of the week and highest at the beginning. In 1913, 30 June fell on a Saturday and in 1914 on a Tuesday; with £70 million known to be the amount held in June 1913, he expected the figure to be £90 million in June 1914.

(3) The number of branch banks had increased by not more than 20 per cent since 1907, while the gold *coin* held by the Bank of England and the joint stock banks had more than doubled, an increase of over £50 million.

In addition Fraser accused Keynes of basing his criticism of the joint stock banks on the figures of a single bank. Commenting on Keynes's hostility towards the banks, he remarked: 'If so well known an economist could exchange the comfortable academic armchair for the arena of practical banking, he would find the "notable exceptions" were the unimportant few who "so signally failed in courage and public spirit".'

Keynes in the meantime had been writing his account of the August crisis in an article for the September 1914 number of the *Economic Journal* entitled 'War and the Financial System' (*JMK* vol. XI), in which he was scathingly critical of the banks and commensurately admiring of the Treasury and the Bank of England. In a letter to his father (3 September) he said that he had 'seldom written so industriously'. His reply to Fraser follows:

To the Editor of The Economist, *12 September 1914*

Sir

Where exact figures are not available, and estimates have to be made, controversialists must be content to differ. I suppose the joint stock bankers themselves must know whether Mr. Fraser or myself is nearer the truth, but *we* can only depend on reasonable inferences. I would submit the following remarks in reference to Mr Fraser's letter on the banks' gold holdings in your last issue.

(1) On reference to Mr Fraser's paper in the Transactions of the Manchester Statistical Society for 1911, to which he refers me, I find no confirmation by the Deputy Master of the Mint (who could not have confirmed or denied without a breach of confidence) of Mr Fraser's view that the normal holding of sovereigns by the Bank of England at the end of June does not exceed £10 million to £12 million. The Deputy Master did not go further than to say that £113 million was the best estimate he could make of the total number of sovereigns within the country in 1910. Mr Fraser's elaborate inference from this, that not more than £12 million of this amount is held by the Bank of England, is entirely his own. I submit that it is palpably contrary to good sense to suppose that the Bank of England normally starts the autumn season with no more than £12 million in sovereigns, an amount less than what she may have to pay out within a short period in connection with the autumn drain, and less than she actually paid out in the fortnight ending 7 August 1914. Is it Mr Fraser's belief that on that day the Bank of England was virtually at the end of its sovereigns, and had nothing but bullion and foreign coin? It is hard to see what the Bank of England would have to gain by so rash a policy, and one so contrary to its ordinary methods of precaution.

(2) I said that the banks are in the habit of 'window-dressing' for balance-sheet purposes, and that they claim in their annual statements much more 'cash in hand and at bank' than they normally hold. Every banker knows this to be so. The only questions in doubt are as to the precise scale of the practice, and as to whether it is increasing or diminishing. I quoted figures, based not on the returns of one bank, as Mr Fraser suggests, but on those of the seventeen leading banks, to show that it is probably large.

(3) I said that, at the beginning of the crisis, the banks certainly did not hold more than £20 million in excess of till money

requirements, and doubted whether they held as much. Whether this estimate is right or wrong (the bankers must know which), Mr Fraser cannot successfully counter it by building up hypothesis on hypothesis, several improbable and not all explicitly stated, on the basis of the Mint returns of Imperial gold coin.

Mr Fraser, who can presumably speak for Manchester, maintains that the joint stock banks are, and have been, able to carry on for their customers 'much as usual', and you, Sir, corroborate their view for London and the country generally, so far as your information goes. It is a source of great satisfaction to learn from such high authorities that this is so, and I certainly have no information, so far as the present is concerned, to justify me in denying or even qualifying it.

My remarks, written on 26 August, referred to the early and middle parts of August. It is certain that during that period the banks took every precaution on their own behalf of which they were capable, and abstained from every form of bold or definitely public-spirited action. Whether this course is better described as showing a lack of courage and public spirit, or as showing a proper degree of caution, partly depends on the view to be taken as to how intrinsically desperate the situation really was; and partly on what is the right view as to the proper relation of the banks, who were the objects of special government assistance, to the financial system of this country as a whole. Personally, I believe that the financial situation on the outbreak of war was amenable to courageous action, and that the responsibilities of the banks to the financial community are large.   I am, etc.

J. M. KEYNES

Fraser had a last, rather angry, word (*Economist*, 19 September 1914), in a letter making four points:

1. The confirmation of the Deputy Master of the Mint had been given in a private letter.

2. In arguing that £10 million to £12 million in gold coin was not sufficient for the needs of the Bank of England, Keynes had confused what were the June figures of four years ago with the autumn drain. Here Fraser was correct.

3. Repeating that in adopting *The Economist*'s figures Keynes had based his accusations of window-dressing on the returns of only one bank, Fraser stated that window-dressing could only be detected in the 'other deposits' balances of the Bank of England. The excess of the Bank's 'other deposits' in the weekly statement nearest 31 December (presumably over its normal level) did not amount to more than £20 million—only two per cent of the total deposit liability of all the joint stock banks. This comparison, however, is irrelevant to the argument; what Keynes was complaining about was the relative extent to which the banks overstated their cash reserves, not the ratio of the overstatement to the total deposits.

4. Keynes's statement that the joint stock banks did not hold more than £20 million in excess of till requirements was disproved by the annual Mint census of gold coin, '*unless* Mr Keynes's theoretical estimate of till requirements is enormously in excess of that held by the practical banker!'

Keynes's two main criticisms of Fraser's figures—that they set the Bank of England's holding of bullion too high, and made the joint stock banks' increase in gold holdings too large, for credibility—may have been valid; however, they do not seem sufficiently strong to reduce £132 million to £100 million. According to the Mint reports eventually published, the gold coin held by all the banks, including the Bank of England, on the last weekday of June 1913 (a Monday) totalled £69,524,127 and on the last day of June 1914 (a Tuesday) totalled £82,794,963. While Fraser's projected increase of £20 million was thus proved too high, the actual increase was greater than Keynes's argument on this point would imply. Perhaps the chief interest of Keynes's two letters is his antipathy towards banks and bankers.

Writing to Alfred Marshall about his *Economic Journal* article, he said (10 October 1914):

From a letter to ALFRED MARSHALL, *10 October 1914*

... It was impossible to do justice to the question of the behaviour of the banks in the early days of the war without going into personalities, which was not possible in the *Journal*. —— and —— were the spokesmen of the bankers and the men whom the Treasury looked to as their leaders. [Their names were deleted from the only version of this letter available, which is published in R. F. Harrod, *The Life of John Maynard Keynes*.] The one was cowardly and the other selfish. They unquestionably behaved badly, and it is not disputed that they pressed strongly for suspension of cash payments by the Bank of England. By no means all of the other bankers either trusted —— and —— or agreed with their immediate proposals; but they were timid, voiceless and leaderless and in the hurry of the times did not make themselves heard. I think, however, that, taking a long view, the banks themselves are to blame for this. They are too largely staffed, apart from the directors, on what in the Civil Service is called a second division basis. Half of their directors, on the other hand, are appointed on hereditary grounds and two-fifths, not on grounds of banking capacity, but because they are able, through their business connections, to bring to the bank a certain class of business. Naturally when the time comes they find themselves without a leader of the right kind. And no one but themselves is to blame. Parker, here, tells me that the meetings at the Treasury took place before the Board of Barclays had an opportunity to meet. Of course they did. In crises you must have a few men at the top capable of taking wise decisions immediately. Fortunately we had a few such—but not amongst the joint stock bankers.

At least that is my view of what happened.

'Your experience goes on similar lines to that which I had on the Labour Commission: the preponderance of heavy minds in the management of businesses that can be reduced to routine is a great evil', was Marshall's comment (12 October). 'The minds of leading working men seemed often more elastic and strong.'

The *Bankers' Magazine* heartily commended Keynes's *Economic Journal* article to its readers, noting that it had been the only one to deal with events critically ('The Crisis—III', *Bankers' Magazine*, November 1914). While admitting that some criticism was justified, the writer of this editorial thought it too early to declare a judgment on such a difficult matter. To him, as to Fraser, Keynes's analysis seemed 'to lack a little of what may be termed the human element . . . a closer and more practical touch with financial affairs would have left upon Mr Keynes's mind a clearer impression of just what was involved in the sudden outbreak of war . . .'.

Keynes heard that Felix Schuster, chairman of the Committee of London Clearing Banks and of the Central Association of Bankers, was very angry about the article. Evidently Schuster suggested an interview and was able to make Keynes see the bankers' conduct in a more favourable light. At any rate, when Keynes wrote a sequel, 'The Prospects of Money', for the December 1914 *Economic Journal* (*JMK*, vol. XI), he added a final paragraph in which he admitted that 'In one or two respects . . . imperfect knowledge caused me to describe the action of the clearing banks, as distinguished from some other banks, with less than fairness.' His complaints, Keynes said, had been 'those of a true lover' of the banking system. Marshall wrote approvingly of this modified view. His letter (14 December), worrying about the possibility of a German invasion, expresses the apprehensions that made him sympathetic to the bankers. '. . . Many people will go mad with terror; and demand gold to bury in their gardens etc. Until the danger of such mad and senseless terror is over past (perhaps it nearly is now) I do not want the Old Lady's stocking to be thinned out.'

Keynes appears to have been restless before settling down to the Michaelmas term. He wrote to his father, 25 September, that he was putting a plan for dealing with German debtors into a memorandum directed at the Treasury, and, 1 October, that he had sent it to Sir John Bradbury. There is no trace of this among his papers or the Treasury files. He sent a copy of his first *Economic Journal* article on the banks and the war to E. S. Montagu, Financial Secretary of the Treasury, and was invited to lunch. Before returning to Cambridge, he contributed the following piece on German financial expedients to *The Economist*, published as a letter— with a sting in its tail for official censorship.

To the Editor of The Economist, *10 October 1914*

Sir

An examination of German newspapers which have come to hand brings to light fuller details respecting the new currency arrangements in Germany than, so far as I am aware, have been available in this country hitherto. A brief summary may be interesting to your readers.

Specie payment was suspended by the Reichsbank on the morning of 1 August. But the Reichsbank authorities have not found it necessary to avail themselves of the abolition authorised at the same time of the ordinary rules governing the cover for the notes, except as regards the payment of the tax on excess issues. At the same time, as we already know, credit institutes were opened in all parts of Germany under the authority of the Government, acting through the agency of the Reichsbank and its branches, for the issue to all comers of loans against security, in amounts varying according to the character of the security from 40 per cent of its value up to 70 per cent in the case of Imperial and State debt. The loans are given 'at something above bank rate' for periods of from three to six months. But cautious persons who have pointed to the short currency of these advances when urged to obtain them for the purpose of subscribing to the National War Loan have been reassured as to the probability of renewal. The credit institutions were authorised in the first instance to lend up to an aggregate of £75 million. But for some time much less use seems to have been made of this offer of accommodation than had been expected. Up to 15 September the aggregate amount lent was about £12,750,000. By 23 September this had risen to £16 million. I have no later figures, but the Reichsbank returns suggest that there was a considerable further increase between 23 and 30 September.

The loans provided by these credit institutes are made in notes of a special kind, known as *Darlehnskassenscheine* or loan notes. These notes have the same limited legal tender quality that the Treasury notes (*Reichskassenscheine*) have always had; they must be accepted, that is to say, by all Government institutions, but cannot be forced on private persons. To a large extent, however, these loan notes have not remained in circulation, but have been sent in to the Reichsbank and exchanged for bank notes. On 15 September £7,370,000, out of £12,750,000 issued, were held by the Reichsbank, so that only £5,380,000 were in circulation. The loan notes in circulation have been largely used to correct the great lack of small change in Germany, having been issued from the outset in denominations down to 5 marks, and after 31 August in denominations of 1 and 2 marks.

The loan notes in the hands of the Reichsbank have been treated by them exactly on the same footing as the Treasury notes. They reckon, that is to say, equally with gold as cover for the Reichsbank's own notes, and are included in the totals given for the Treasury notes in the Reichsbank's weekly returns as published by the English newspapers. The great increase shown under this head for 30 September, from £7,460,000 to £16,820,000, is probably due to increased issues of loan notes to intending subscribers to the Imperial War Loan.

The demand for small change in Germany during August was remarkable. Apart from the loan notes of small denominations referred to above, a considerable volume of Treasury notes of 5 and 10 marks went into circulation. On 7 August £1,750,000 in Treasury notes were issued from the Government's War Reserve, and the holdings of Treasury notes by the Reichsbank fell from £3,275,000 on 23 July to £425,000 on 15 September. And, further, £15 million in silver coin was issued during August. In spite of these measures the shortage during the early days of the war was so great that Königsberg and one or two other towns in East Prussia issued municipal notes of 1 and 2 marks. These were withdrawn at the beginning of September.

The Reichsbank's holding of gold has steadily increased since the suspension of specie payment on 1 August. At first there was a considerable accretion of £10,250,000, which was transferred to the Reichsbank in gold on 7 August from the Government's War Reserve. Since then a certain amount seems to have been recovered week by week from the circulation, perhaps £7 million altogether between 23 July and 30 September, of which £2 million came in during the last week. If the authorities receive a certain amount of gold and only pay out paper, a gradual addition of this kind is to be expected. The process may have been helped, however, by a newspaper campaign during August calling on patriotic citizens to exchange their gold for notes. A Berlin official, for example, was given a paragraph for having collected £190 in gold coin from his friends and acquaintances to be exchanged at the Reichsbank for notes. Or, to take another instance, it is recorded that £200 in gold was collected in a small village near Berlin and taken in triumph to the Reichs-bank.

The Reichsbank's holdings of Treasury notes (*Reichskassen-scheine*) and of loan notes (*Darlehnskassenscheine*) are given below:

	Treasury notes £	Loan notes £	Total £
23 July	3,275,000	nil	3,275,000
30 July	1,670,000	nil	1,670,000
7 August	1,330,000*	3,500,000*	4,830,000
15 August	1,000,000*	5,335,000*	6,335,000
22 August	925,000	5,000,000	5,925,000
31 August	490,000	8,660,000	9,150,000
7 September	430,000	7,585,000	8,015,000
15 September	425,000	7,370,000	7,795,000
23 September	—	—	7,465,000
30 September	—	—	16,825,000

* Estimated and only approximate.

In addition to the official credit institutes (*Reichsdarlehnskasse*), a great number of war credit banks (*Kriegskreditbanken* or *Kriegsdarlehnskasse*, or *Kriegshilfskasse*) have been founded all over Germany under semi-official or unofficial auspices. The capital of these banks, which are not all on the same model, has been provided partly by the states (as in Saxony), partly by the municipalities (as in Frankfort and Charlottenburg), and partly by private individuals, financiers, joint stock companies and corporations (as, for example, a bank founded by a syndicate of insurance companies, or a bank jointly supported by the municipal authorities, the Chamber of Commerce, and the Bankers' Union, as in Leipzig). The capital thus obtained is not large, ranging from £200,000 downwards to quite small sums, and is, I gather, of the nature of a guarantee fund, on the strength of which working funds can be obtained from the Reichsbank. These local war credit banks have no power to issue notes, and their object is to help small people generally—small tradesmen and small industrialists—with loans on personal security up to, say, £150, or on their stock, or on the guarantee of two respectable citizens.

3-2

But the methods and the scale on which these institutions propose to work vary a good deal. How important their practical activities have been so far, I am not able to say.

The four private note-issuing banks of Bavaria, Baden, Würtemberg, and Saxony have made no increase in their normal circulation.

May I add that, having had occasion for the above purpose to consult German newspapers which came into my hands by good fortune, I have been strongly impressed by the unwisdom of our own government's present policy of making difficulties about the admission of German newspapers into this country? A few privileged members of our Press are allowed to receive copies, but it appears that customs officials have orders to confiscate copies brought in by travellers, and private persons may not receive them by post from neutral countries. The privileged copies can only be studied by a few, and the necessarily brief extracts published in our own Press are sometimes devoted to quoting the more absurd and extravagant of the German comments on the situation. It is not clear what advantage our government hope to gain by keeping us in a state of ignorance about the internal affairs of Germany. Not only is it desirable that we should be able to form some judgement from time to time on the economic and financial position of the country. But a correct estimate of the novel and psychological factors is of such importance that it will do us no good in the end to run the risk, by limiting the possible channels of news, of resting under widespread misapprehension as to the ideas, true or false, which are influencing the minds of the German public, and as to the spirit in which the German nation is waging this war. There is much sober and instructive news to be found in the German Press, even amongst misstatements and exaggerations. Anybody in England who wants to study it ought to be able to do so.

I am, etc.,

J. M. KEYNES

The publication of a current Reichsbank return gave Keynes an opportunity for some detective work. His conclusions were printed as 'From a Correspondent' by the *Morning Post* and marked 'by Maynard' in his mother's scrapbook.

From the Morning Post, *16 October 1914*

THE COST OF WAR TO GERMANY

The Reichsbank return of 7 October, published herein on 14 October, allows us for the first time to catch a glimpse of the methods by which the German government is financing its war expenditure. At the beginning of the war we may safely assume that the expenses of mobilisation were defrayed out of the War Reserve—as had always been intended. We know that the constituents of this reserve—£10,250,000 in gold, a large amount of silver, and some Treasury notes—were transferred in the first week of August to the government's credit at the Reichsbank, an amount of from £25 million to £30 million altogether.

This, however, would not do much more than pay the expenses of mobilisation, and, apart from any other ways in which the Government may have financed itself, it was soon necessary to borrow from the Reichsbank. We have had little or no clue to the amount of such borrowing, because the Treasury bills or other security given the Reichsbank against temporary advances to the Government have been concealed in the Reichsbank return under the item 'Bills Discounted'. This item increased in the first fortnight of the war by about £184 million, and was another £16 million up by 23 September. But until now it has been impossible even to guess how much of this increase was due to the discount of genuine trade bills and how much to government borrowings. The figures, week by week, suggest that at first the increase was largely due to the discount of trade bills, and that as time has gone on and these have matured they have been increasingly replaced by government bills.

With the receipts from the first instalments of the new War

Loan, however, it is likely that the Government was in a position, by the beginning of October, to pay off the whole or a part of these advances; and accordingly in the Reichsbank return for 7 October the item 'Bills Discounted' is diminished by the huge amount of £73 million. The probability of this explanation is increased by the consideration that trade bills do not run off in huge amounts simultaneously, and that a moment when the instalments of a war loan are being paid up is not one at which the public and the banks are likely to be in a position greatly to reduce the amount of accommodation obtained from the Reichsbank. It is not impossible, on the other hand, that the holding of trade bills may have increased and that the Government may have paid off more than £73 million of temporary advances. Whether the whole of the Reichsbank's advances to the Government have yet been paid off it is impossible to say. The item 'Bills Discounted' still stands as high as £165 million, nearly £130 million above the normal. It would not be surprising if this included another £30 million or so of government borrowings.

Including the War Reserve, the German government's expenditure on the war up to the beginning of October may be put, therefore, at not less than from £100 million to £130 million. This agrees very well with an estimate, which has sometimes been put forward on other grounds, of about £2 million a day. No allowance has been made, of course, for expenditure ordered or incurred but not paid for.

The Reichsbank return also throws light on the means by which the German public have paid up the first instalments of the War Loan. A shrinkage in the return of 7 October of £14,600,000 in the circulation of bank notes and of £21,800,000 in the Reichsbank deposits shows how part of the payment has been made. Nearly £40 million, however, is to be accounted for by an increase of this amount, during the fortnight ending 7 October, in the Reichsbank's holdings of the new loan notes (*Darlehnskassenscheine*), which are now entered in the Reichsbank's weekly returns under the heading 'Treasury Notes'.

These notes are the outcome of an elaborate trick by which the German government is issuing large quantities of inconvertible paper money. The trick is so elaborate that it may have some effect in keeping up for a time the confidence of the public. Investors are encouraged to borrow loan notes against all kinds of security, gilt-edged and otherwise. To a large extent the loan notes so obtained are exchanged at the Reichsbank for bank notes. The Reichsbank suffers this with equanimity because, by a recent change of the law, it is allowed to reckon these loan notes as absolutely equivalent to gold for the purpose of its reserve. The bank notes thus obtained are then used by a patriotic public to subscribe towards a war loan, and thus put at the disposal of the Government. The Government thus has good bank notes wherewith to pay its debts to the Reichsbank or to meet current expenses. It is easy to forget that these bank notes are not only inconvertible, but are issued against all sorts and kinds of absolutely fixed and non-liquid security.

Such expedients were all very well in a short war when they were only required to be adopted once, but they were dangerous to adopt twice, Keynes told the Newcastle Economic Society early in November in a talk on 'The Effect of War Upon Finance'. He believed that England would be better able than Germany to stand the strain of a prolonged war.

He kept in touch with the Treasury. A letter to Sir John Bradbury, dated 24 October 1914, enclosed a note '(a copy of which I am also sending to Montagu), which brings together the result of my reflections on the War Loan question since our conversation'. The letter went on to discuss the probable amount of debts owing to Britain from Germany and Austria on account of the Indian trade; Keynes had inquired 'from some big Indian shipping firms, the heads of which I know personally'.

The 'Note on Government Loans', 23 October 1914, has survived in the Treasury records among Bradbury's papers (T 170/31). Something like Keynes's strategy of dividing prospective lenders into three classes was adopted in the second War Loan of June 1915 when for the first time the Government appealed to investors of limited resources and offered to take subscriptions of £5.

NOTE ON GOVERNMENT LOANS

The banks, the ordinary investor, and the small investor are three distinct sources of supply, deserving separate attention.

I. The banks, after their recent experiences, are likely to attach much importance to a due date. They might be best catered for by something of the nature of exchequer bonds of from five to ten years currency, say in the first instance for £50 million or £60 million altogether. By this arrangement (i.e. series) no unmanageable amount would fall due at any one time.

II. The ordinary public would no doubt like a due date, but not sufficiently, I believe, to make up in the price for the very grave disadvantages which such an arrangement brings, in the case of a very large loan, from the point of view of the State. There are weighty arguments against either drawings, series, or a single due date.

On the other hand the investor certainly attaches much importance to protection against early conversion. An issue in the neighbourhood of par must not be redeemable at the sole option for Government for a considerable period, if it is to be popular.

Consols at 62 (e.g.), whatever the date of optional redemption, give a certainty of an annual income of £4 until the rate of interest has fallen below $2\frac{1}{2}$ per cent; and in that event there is a large increase of capital value.

4% Consols at 100 do not carry any part of this advantage, unless the date of optional redemption is very remote.

Investors in trustee stocks, looking more to a certainty of future income than to anything else, are probably willing to pay a good deal in the way of reduced interest for insurance against conversion. I do not know of any stock which tests the degree of this feeling. But Colonial $3\frac{1}{2}$% stocks below par were dearer than the same 4% stocks near par by more than the value of the due date redemption.

I suggest it would be unsafe to issue a loan in the neighbour-hood of par with optional redemption earlier than 1945 at the earliest, and a much longer run than this might be desirable. If the Government, in issuing a 4 per cent loan, attaches great importance to the possibility of early conversion, they must, I believe, fall back on a due date (with all its risks). Redeemability, both early and optional, is giving the investor, as distinguished from the patriotic citizen, too little.

III. An issue of £5 and £10 bonds free of income tax through the Post Offices, a selling and, possibly, a buying price (with a fairly wide turn—say 2 per cent) being announced weekly, could be made *experimentally*, by putting them on sale without offering any definite amount.

The effect of this on the [Post Office] Savings Bank could then be gauged before the Treasury were committed to the issue of a large quantity. They *might* be a great success and tap a new public. (It must be remembered that, if Consols are to be at 4 per cent, it will not be practicable to keep Savings Bank interest at its present rate much longer.)

Possible future complications, arising out of their freedom from tax, would have to be guarded against by giving Government an option of redeeming them at a very early date—say five years. This option would balance the immunity from tax.

A £5 4% bond would receive 1s a quarter interest, payable on demand at Post Offices where the bonds would be stamped on payment.

Issues of exchequer bonds (under I above) might be made gradually in the future, the policy governing them to be con-sidered from time to time in conjunction with that of Treasury bills.

Issues of 4% stock (under II above) might be offered for sub-scription up to £150 million *at once*.

Small bonds (under III above) might be put on sale shortly

with no definite limit of amount—to be retailed by Post Offices gradually. It may take some time to get them understood.

23.10.14   J.M.K.

If Keynes was striving to be noticed during these months, the new year brought results. Dr Keynes entered in his diary, 6 January 1915:

> Maynard writes, 'I have been offered a position in the Treasury alongside of Paish for the period of the war. No time for details, as I have a very heavy piece of work to do for them by Friday when L. G. (private) sails for France.'

He capped this news with the announcement that 'the Governor of the Bank of England has been reading my works and has asked me to come and visit him at the Bank' (letter to his father, 6 January).

The heavy piece of work was the following 'Notes on French Finance,' finished 6 January 1915 and kept in the files of the Chancellor of the Exchequer's office (T 171/107). Keynes's footnote to the title explains the circumstances: he had made the trip to France to visit his brother Geoffrey who was serving as a medical officer in a hospital at Versailles. Fifteen pages of handwritten manuscript show that the part which was dictated (Keynes first wrote 'put together') starts in mid-paragraph, p. 49, from 'There is only danger, that is to say . . .'

NOTES ON FRENCH FINANCE[1]

The leading characteristics of the financial position in France have been:

(i) The extraordinary completeness of the breakdown of credit up to November 1914 and the marked inactivity of the Government and the Bank of France in the matter of finding a way out up to December 1914. Only now are matters beginning to become at all normal.

(ii) The embarrassments of government finance through the too great delay of the pre-war loan, the insufficiency of its

---

[1] These notes have been hastily dictated out of material partly obtained during a visit to Paris in the middle of December, and collected for the purpose of a fuller treatment than this. The sources of information are those available to an unofficial enquirer, and for the section on Public Finance M. Ribot's recent exposé has been drawn on freely. [Alexandre Ribot was Minister of Finance at this time.]

amount, and the fact that only a part had been paid up when war broke out.

(iii) The determination of the Government to avoid a funded loan, and the fact that they have been enabled to live mainly on advances from the Bank of France in virtue of the huge volume of notes which is now hoarded by the public. These hoards, so long as they remain hoards, constitute a loan to the Government without interest.

(iv) The favourable position of France as measured by the foreign exchange.

I. *Private finance*

During the last days of July and before the outbreak of hostilities the run on the banks had already reached very grave dimensions. The Bank of France's commercial portfolio rose *at once* from about £61,500,000 to £123 million, and had reached £158 million by 6 August. The withdrawals by depositors from the Sociétés de Crédit (i.e. the banks) in the few days preceding the moratorium have been estimated at £120 million. The funds by which these withdrawals were met were mainly raised by rediscounting as above at the Bank of France.

On 6 August the Bank of France suspended specie payment and ceased to issue weekly bank returns; and the limit of note issue was raised from £272 million to £480 million.

In virtue of a law passed in 1910 the Government issued a series of moratorium decrees, beginning on 31 July with a decree relating to bills of exchange. But this law of 1910 only permitted decrees affecting 'negotiable instruments', and accordingly the Government were given wider powers, in virtue of a new law, with effect from 6 August.

By 11 August a series of decrees had made the moratorium of practically universal effect. In particular depositors in banks could draw from their current accounts no more than £10 and 5 per cent of the balance in excess of £10.

From 11 August up to the end of November, a long series of moratorium decrees was issued extending the period and modifying the conditions. They cannot be explained briefly, and, while of the greatest interest as representing an attempt to make a workable affair of a fully operative and effective moratorium, they have no great bearing on present affairs. As time went on, depositors were allowed to draw from their banks larger proportions of their accounts, and the requirements, such as payment of wages, proof of which allowed a further withdrawal, were gradually extended.

By 12 October some of the chief banks voluntarily allowed their customers to draw out more than the prescribed amount. And finally on 1 January 1915 the leading banks withdrew all remaining restrictions.

Debtors generally were divided by proclamations of 30 October and 25 November into two classes—those serving with the colours or domiciled in invaded territory, and the rest. Up to 31 December 1914 there was a moratorium for everybody. After that, the second category of debtors were to be subject to conditions closely analogous to those laid down in our own *Courts* (*Emergency Powers*) *Act*. The precise machinery proposed in France has been subjected to very severe criticism. I have not yet heard whether or how it is working.

In the meantime the Bank of France, so far from coming to the rescue of the banks and the public by relaxing the conditions on which accommodation is normally granted, stiffened them. In an important circular, issued on 10 August, the authorities of the Bank somewhat narrowed the categories of bills admissible to rediscount facilities, greatly restricted the granting of advances against security, the normal conditions of which are very strict (with the affect that no advances were granted in excess of £200 except under rigorous conditions as to the manner of employment of the money), and hindered rather than helped the liquidation of the immobilised foreign bills. This circular was not withdrawn until 27 November.

44

The net effect of these various measures was an almost complete breakdown of credit for the space of at least three months. The banks ceased lending altogether, new post-moratorium bills were negotiated in trifling amounts, and apart from the rediscount of bills, those who were in a position to borrow from the Bank of France were but few.

The exact consequences of this breakdown are very difficult to ascertain. By the end of August the economic condition of France had become exceedingly serious, far more serious than has been generally recognised in this country. The disorganisation of industry was appalling, and unemployment in the urban districts (but not in agricultural employments) was reaching a dangerous level. All of this, however, cannot be put down by any means to the state of credit. It was largely due to the very complete breakdown of transport, of the posts and of means of communication generally; also to the invasion of one of the chief industrial centres of the country and to the disorder arising out of the sudden mobilisation of the acting-heads of businesses, employers etc. Some of these things were very badly managed in France.

It is certain, however, that the state of affairs was much aggravated by the breakdown of credit. In a good many cases unemployment was stated to be directly due to the difficulty of obtaining funds for the payment of wages.

If the seriousness of the position at the end of August deserves emphasis, on the other hand the steady, if slow, recovery since that time also deserves attention. The economic system of France is one of extreme stability. The available information is most scanty, but my impression is that since the beginning of December there has been a very steady improvement and the inherent strength of the country is now more liable to be underestimated than overestimated. But the nerves of the French are not yet in as good order as they might be, and the nastiness with which French finance has become so deeply impregnated in recent years is not to be cured in a day. It must be added that the credit-breakdown has not brought with it the completeness of disorder which a similar breakdown must have occasioned in England, because the credit system of France (as typified, for example, by the extent to which cheques are used) is still much underdeveloped. It is still extremely usual in France both for private persons and for traders to keep astonishingly large sums of money in their own possession. And they are, consequently, much less upset than we should be by a breakdown of banking.

The Government proclaimed, as we have seen, a far-reaching moratorium. But otherwise right up to the beginning of December neither they nor the Bank of France had taken any steps whatever to save the situation or to bring about *la reprise des affaires*. The financial position of France cannot be properly understood without some discussion of the underlying causes of such notable inactivity. I judge them to have been mainly three.

(i) It was *politically impossible* for the Government to come to the rescue of the banks after the English fashion, for the reason that, with a very few distinguished exceptions, they were in disgrace. The story of French banking during the last decade is a long one—sordid, corrupt, disastrous and deeply intertwined with the basest features of French political life. While one or two, the Crédit Lyonnais for example, have persevered on lines perhaps the safest and most conservative in the world, others, even amongst those of supposed high standing, have come to depend more and more for their profits on company promotion and speculative underwriting,[1] and have industriously prostituted their influence with their clients to the end of inducing them to embark their savings in most doubtful enterprises, mines, rubber shares, South American securities of all sorts, nearly all of the second or third order of their kind and taken over at top prices.

[1] The *Sociétés de Crédit* (i.e. the banks) acting as retailers for the *Banques d'Affaires* (i.e. the finance houses).

This had been going on for some time. By the beginning of 1914 the breakdown in Mexico and Brazil had completed the disillusionment of the French investor. His losses have been *prodigious*, and he now knows the true value of the interested eloquence of his banker, to which so considerable part of his current savings has been sacrificed. At the same time recent events had supplied the public, rightly or wrongly, with more definite suspicions as to subterranean connection between doubtful finance and certain political influences.

All this made it impossible for the government to come open-handed to the banks' assistance in spite of some of the most important being absolutely sound and most of them probably solvent. It is as though our government had been asked to help out, let us say, the Investment Registry, or Mr Bottomley [Horatio Bottomley, company promoter, mob orator, editor of *John Bull*, member of parliament, imprisoned for fraud], with the difference that business much unsounder than anything the Investment Registry has ever been responsible for has emanated from institutions of standing corresponding to that of our own clearing banks.

A subsidiary cause has been, undoubtedly, the high relative importance in France of private banks which do not publish balance sheets. In the aggregate these institutions do a good deal of business. It is naturally more difficult for the government to aid private firms, working on private lines, than to aid public companies working in at least semi-publicity.

(ii) The accepting house problem was, in Paris, of very minor importance. But the same essential difficulties presented themselves in a less manageable form. For the foreign bill portfolios of France do not, to the extent that is the case in London, put on the appearance of being home bills by being accepted in Paris. They are largely accepted in the places where the funds are actually being employed, e.g. Vienna. Thus, if the Bank of France had followed the example of the Bank of England, they would have had to accept openly foreign obligations and would have had to do without, in many cases, the interposed guarantee of a French accepting house. For this or other reasons the Bank of France did *not* follow the Bank of England's example. In August they seem to have carried their conservatism to unwise lengths, making impolitic objections to the negotiation of even the best paper of London and New York.

The difficulties of the foreign bill question were somewhat aggravated by the rather high *proportion* (as compared with London) due from enemy countries. The amount thus lent by Paris to Berlin has probably been much reduced in the last few years, but the sums employed at Vienna were large. There was also the large connection with Petrograd.

(iii) The third influence, to which I alluded above, has been the extreme conservatism of the Bank of France, and what appears to some critics to have been their excessive preoccupation with the problem of keeping down to the lowest possible level the figure of their note issue. Compared with the Bank of France, the Bank of England is almost skittish. The very extreme conservatism of the Bank of France has been a potent influence.

Their line seems to have been that the danger of an over-issue was considerable, and more to be feared than alternative dangers, and that as large a part as possible of their available margin of note issue should be conserved for advances to the State. There is a little to be said for this view, and, at the cost of credit-breakdown for three or four months, the Bank of France now finds itself in a technically stronger position than would otherwise have been the case.

Nevertheless many good critics in France, notably M. Fernand Maroni of the *Journal des Débats*, whose judgement deserves much respect, have severely criticised the Bank for its inactivity, its tardiness and its unwillingness to assist the revival of trade and normal finance.

Certainly the authorities of the Bank seem to be showing unnecessary concern about the figure of their note issue. In the first place the proportion of gold reserve to note issue, when once specie payment has been suspended, is of very little importance. In the second place, in so far as notes are hoarded, they do no harm at all, in whatever quantities, and constitute in effect *a loan to the State without interest*. When these notes are ready to emerge from their hoards, then it ought to be possible to reabsorb them by floating a public loan. Danger can only arise if the notes coming out of the hoards are entering the active circulation, and if at the same time the public, though having the money idle, are not willing on any terms to lend it to the Government. [*Handwritten manuscript ends here and typescript begins*]. There is only danger, that is to say, either if the Government delay too long the issue of a loan, or if the Government's credit with its own citizens is quite broken. It is necessary to arrange the finance of war on the contrary hypothesis.

As I have said above, the very conservative policy of the Bank of France, though having its penalties, has left the Bank in a strong position. On 23 July the Bank's portfolio of commercial bills amounted to £61,500,000; by 6 August the figure was £158 million. The maximum, not greatly in excess of this, was reached some time in September. On 1 October the figure was £179 million, and had fallen by 10 December to £154 million. By that date £26 million of pre-moratorium bills had been paid off, and less than £9 million of new post-moratorium bills had been taken.

On the other hand, the advances to the state, which stood at £8 million at the outbreak of war, and had risen to £96 million by 15 October, stood at £144 million on 10 December.

Thus, the diminution of the bill portfolio went some way towards balancing the increased advances to the state. The note issue, which had risen from £236 million on 23 July to £372 million by 1 October, showed but a moderate increase between that date and 10 December, when the total was £400 million.

It is probable that, as time goes on, the bill portfolio will diminish rather than increase, and it is certain that, so long as hoarding continues, the note issue can be safely increased beyond its present figure. There is, therefore, a considerable margin for making additional advances to the state. It is absolutely essential in considering the apparently high figure of note issue to bear in mind the enormous scale on which hoarding is now taking place in France—the hoarding of gold, since notes must take the place of gold in the circulation, being just as effective for the present purpose as the hoarding of notes.

I have said nothing about the position of the stock exchange. It is sufficient to say that nothing was done until December, when the Bank of France agreed to advance 40 per cent of the funds lent on the official exchange or *parquet* against the security of the stocks which were being carried. This transaction was facilitated by the fact that the *agents de change* form a syndicate with mutual liability. Nothing has been done so far for the *coulisse* or unofficial exchange. The money employed on the *parquet* has been estimated by M. Ribot at less than £20 million sterling, and the amount employed on the *coulisse* at about £6 million. The sums involved are, therefore, somewhat trifling. At the beginning of December the Bourse was reopened without the postponed settlement of July having been cleared out of the way. Quotations seem to be more nominal than on our own exchange.

II. *Public finance*

During the early months of the war, problems of public finance in France were much complicated by the fact that the instalments on the loan which had been issued in July had not yet been paid off. It will be recalled that this loan had been a matter of much controversy. It had been too long delayed, and when it came was, in the opinion of many, of insufficient amount, *viz.*: £32 million. It had often been asserted that one of the factors on which Germany had been relying was the controversy in France associated with the name of M. Caillaux [Joseph Caillaux, former minister involved in financial and other scandals]. In this calculation they have not, I think, been altogether disappointed. The bad name of the banks has already been referred to. The inadequacy and inconvenient date of the pre-war loan can be attributed more directly to his influence.

The history of the pre-war loan is as follows:

While the controversy as to its amount and conditions was proceeding, the French banks were not permitted to fund the numerous short-term obligations of the Balkan States and others, which they then held. The banks were exceedingly anxious that the way for their own operations should be paved by a striking public success for the Government's loan. They entered into a conspiracy, therefore, to ensure its subscription forty times over. In this they were successful, but with the result that the loan was taken up by speculators and with borrowed money, and only secondarily by genuine investors. I have heard it estimated that perhaps one-third went to investors proper, one-third was taken up by the *parquet* and the *coulisse*, and the remaining third was taken over by the banks on behalf of their clients, whom they had encouraged to subscribe by offering them loans wherewith to provide the funds for subscription at a low rate of interest, or even at no rate of interest at all. The consequence was that when the war came, speculators could not pay up further instalments, and the banks were unable to provide their clients with the funds they had promised them. By 15 September £17 million out of the £32 million had not been paid up, and the loan which had been issued at 91 had fallen as low as 82·50.

Until this loan could be cleared out of the way it was obviously difficult to issue a new one, and it was, therefore, one of the preoccupations of the Minister of Finance to find some settlement of this problem. He began in September by offering a new advantage to all holders of the scrip who had paid up the remaining instalments within a certain period; this concession was that the scrip of the July loan would be accepted at its issue price of

91 in payment for any new loans to be issued by Government within, I think, the next three years; that is to say, on some future date, since the French government in issuing its eventual loan must issue it at terms satisfactory to the public, the scrip of the July loan is bound to be worth approximately 91 in cash. This concession seems to me to be an ingenious and sound device. It amounts to a guarantee that investors coming forward during the progress of war shall be at least as well off as those who delay their subscriptions until the war is over. In spite, however, of its attractive character, the concession proved inadequate to achieve the desired result. The price of fully paid scrip in the market has now risen to 86·50, but many subscribers were still unable to pay up their instalments. Finally therefore, it was settled that the Bank of France should advance to subscribers to the loan sufficient to pay up whatever was still unpaid. At length last month the incubus of the July loan was cleared out of the way.

We come next to the issue of Treasury bills or 'Bons du trésor'. In ordinary times the Government finance themselves in this way to a certain extent. The permissible maximum of such bills is fixed from time to time, but the amount actually issued is only published at irregular intervals. In June 1914 the maximum stood at £24 million sterling, and the amount issued was supposed to approximate to this. The first instalments of the July loan appear to have been employed towards reducing this total, and at the beginning of August the amount still outstanding was about £17 million. These bills are of short currency. As the war progressed the pre-war bills came to maturity and had to be paid off, while the difficulties of the banking world prevented the subscription of new ones. Thus the volume of Treasury bills outstanding, which had amounted to £24 million in July and to £17 million at the outbreak of war, had fallen to £7 million by 15 December. So far from proving the means of obtaining new money the discharge of the outstanding Treasury bills used up a large part of what was received from the July loan.

Accordingly a new source of money had to be sought for. This was found in the issue of a new form of Treasury bill called 'Bons de la Défense Nationale'. These were put on the market in the middle of September, and were for periods of from three months to a year. They differed from the Treasury bills in that the rate of interest was raised from 4% to 5%, and in that they were not rediscountable at the Bank of France or accepted by that institution as security for advances. These latter conditions were due to the desire of the Bank of France to obtain new money from the public and to avoid the possibility of its having to provide a good part of the money itself by rediscount or advances. As was pointed out at the time, however, this policy overlooked the fact that bills are not necessarily discounted because they are discountable. The new bills, which were peddled out by various government agencies, did not prove much of a success. After three weeks less than £9 million had been subscribed. Accordingly in December new conditions were announced. While the takers of the outstanding bills could renew them at 5%, the rate of interest for bills newly issued was reduced to 4%. On the other hand, the bills were made discountable at the Bank of France, and acceptable there as guarantees against advances up to 80 per cent of their value. The reduction of the rate of interest from 5 to 4% was not, as stated in some newspapers, proof of the Government's improved credit, but was necessitated by the fact that the Bank of France's bank rate now stands at 5%. The authorities of the Bank thought it essential that holders availing themselves of discount facilities should lose a little interest. If the bills were still to yield 5% and to be discountable at 5% this would not be so. Whether on account of the new conditions, or through the gradual revival of normal conditions, the bills seem to have become rather more popular. By the middle of December some £40 million had been placed with the public.

The only other resource of which the French government have made use has been the Bank of France. At the outbreak of war the advances from the bank to the state stood at £8 million; by 1 October this increased to £84 million; and by 10 December to £144 million. The Bank of France has undertaken to raise its advance eventually to £240 million. The Government have succeeded in obtaining this advance on terms very favourable to themselves. For the period of the war and for a year after they propose to pay interest to the Bank at the rate of 1%, and, subsequently, at the rate of 3%, the excess 2% to form a sinking fund.

To sum up; the position in the middle of December seems to have been approximately as follows:

	£ million
Bons de la Défense Nationale	
placed with French public	40
issued in England and the U.S.A.	4
Old Treasury Bills still outstanding	7
Advances from Bank of France	144
Total	£195

The war expenditure up to the end of the year appears to have exceeded £240 million. The balance of this has been financed in various ways, about which it is not possible to particularise, e.g. balance of July loan, a small advance from the Bank of Algeria, savings in civil expenditure, Exchequer balances, etc. Perhaps part of the expenditure has not been disbursed, and is being carried forward as a liability.

M. Ribot estimates his expenses for the first six months of 1915 at not less than £240 million in excess of the proceeds of taxation. He proposes to meet this to the extent of £90 million by further advances from the Bank of France. He hopes that the public may take up £80 million to £100 million more of the Bons de la Défense Nationale. And he leaves from £50 million to £80 million still unprovided for. No hint has been given as to the manner in which he hopes to raise this sum.

The amount of advances from the Bank of France seems to have been fixed at a figure bearing some relation to the figure which has been fixed for the maximum note issue. On 10 December the actual advances to the state stood at £144 million as against a proposed maximum of £240 million, and the note issue stood at £400 million as against a proposed maximum of £480 million. Thus the advances to the state are expected to increase £96 million, and the note issue £80 million, the difference between the two being met by an anticipated diminution in the bank's commercial portfolio. For reasons already given it would probably be perfectly safe to increase the note issue beyond £480 million and to make corresponding advances to the state in excess of what is now proposed. If circumstances force M. Ribot's hand, no doubt this will happen, and however unpalatable to the Bank of France, there seems little reason for thinking that any harm will be done. As stated above, the vital point is to make the issue of a popular loan coincide with the emergence of money from hoards. This is the only possible guarantee against inflationism. In this policy there is virtue, and no virtue at all in the precise figure of £480 million, which happens to have been fixed on. It is not a figure which will obviate inflationism if money comes out of hoards and is *not* reabsorbed by a government loan.

It is also to be noticed that M. Ribot does not propose to invite applications from the public to any funded loan whatever during the period of the war. And, as at present advised, he offers on temporary paper no more than 4 per cent. Nor does he intend to raise anything during the present year by increased taxation. That is why there is still a considerable amount of the expenditure for the first six months of 1915 still unprovided for. It is hard to believe that if pushed he could not raise from the French public with the offer of suitable terms a larger sum than is proposed at present.

III. *The foreign exchanges*

Throughout the war all the foreign exchanges, including our own, have been in favour of Paris. During August the chaos was so great that both the French and our own currency were simultaneously depreciated in terms of the other. For a considerable period Messrs Thos. Cook would only change in Paris actual gold sovereigns at the rate of Frs. 24.50, or a loss of 3 per cent. When such absurdity had come to an end, the exchanges remained in favour of Paris. But, so far as I could ascertain, government transactions apart, the market is a very narrow one, and would be sensitive to any considerable transaction. Nor has the exchange been sufficiently low, although for a long period below the normal gold export point from England, to make the export of gold a really profitable transaction in present circumstances, the extra expenses of shipping gold at the present time in combination with the fact that only sovereigns, and not bar gold, are available has brought the export point down from about 25.182 to 25.045. The exchange has been at times very slightly below the latter figure, but not sufficiently so to tempt anyone to take advantage of it on any scale worth thinking about.

The reasons for the existing state of the exchanges are probably various. It is likely that payments due from New York to Paris are being arranged to some extent through London. And of the current imports into France an unusually large part is on government account, and financed quite outside the exchange market.

There does not seem to be anything in the state of the Paris exchange which requires special explanation.

But the level of the exchanges certainly suggests somewhat strongly that France is by no means at the end of her power of purchasing abroad without assistance, though it is impossible to conjecture exactly how far off this point still is.

The above summary suggests that internal expenses ought, and can be, financed by France herself, and that, in the matter of expenses abroad, whatever may be the case shortly, she is in no obvious difficulties at present so far as appearances go.[1]

[1] She can hardly claim to be in any such difficulties at a time when she is earmarking gold in Ottawa through her American agents. I do not suppose the authorities of the Bank of France, any more than those of the Bank of Russia, have any clear idea *why* it is important for them to get or to keep all the gold they can, or of what good they hope it will do them. They seem to adhere to maxims, the observance of which is recommended as a means of maintaining specie payment, after the end in question has been abandoned.

It has only to be conceded that in present circumstances appearances are deceptive, and do not preclude the possibility of her being somewhat near the end of her foreign resources.

6.1.15   J. M. KEYNES

Keynes started at the Treasury as an assistant to Sir George Paish, who was a special adviser to Lloyd George as Chancellor of the Exchequer. He was temporarily appointed for the period of the war at an annual salary of £600, with the understanding that he would be allowed latitude regarding one day off a week, subject to public emergency, and that he would continue the editorship of the *Economic Journal* in his spare time, not using official materials without Treasury consent. He began work formally 18 January, and 22 January his father recorded:

> Maynard writes, 'After a slack beginning I am now very busy, having become Secretary of a Secret Committee of the Cabinet, presided over by the Prime Minister. First meeting this morning. So I now know exactly what a cabinet meeting is like. This is of course absolutely private.'

The secret committee was a committee to inquire into the rising cost of food. Within a week Keynes was the author of a paper on wheat prices which was printed for the use of the Cabinet (CAB 37/123/51). It carries his initials, with the date 25 January 1915, and has the same air of dashing into things as those early papers that he wrote for the India Office.

WHEAT PRICES

High prices may be due to:

(*a*) Intrinsic conditions—Supply of wheat not equal to demand over a given period, because of crop shortage, or because Government orders and the issue of paper currency so stuffs people's pockets with money that they are not restrained from buying (this factor just now quite as important as the other);

—Supply of transport insufficient over the period in question.

(*b*) The beliefs of the market—which are affected not only by intrinsic conditions, but also by unjustified speculation, manipulation, timidity, governments buying regardless of price, and the various 'bull points' which turn up from time to time.

(*a*) *Intrinsic conditions* can hardly be affected very much by anything this country can do. Two points are worth mentioning:

(i) The supply of wheat could be affected a *little* by making available some part of the Indian old crop which is not allowed for in current estimates (discussed in detail below).

(ii) The supply of transport could be improved in various small ways already discussed. (Yet this is not likely to help wheat a great deal, because it is not practicable specially to divert to South American ports, within the period during which pressure is likely to arise, any large part of what tonnage may be released.)

(The influence of the freight problem, though important in itself, on the wheat-price problem, is, I think, over-estimated. To some extent the high freights are at the expense of the Argentine shippers, and cause the price of wheat f.o.b. at the Plate to be *lower* than it would be otherwise. And if wheat rises to a dangerous level, the rise *beyond* the present level is not likely to be due to freights mainly.)

If intrinsic conditions prove, or are likely to prove, such as to make wheat prices rise dangerously, the only course of interference open to Government appears to me to be to influence prices at home (not to fix them) by buying freely and selling, if necessary, at a loss. Things do not seem to have reached a point yet, which would justify anything so drastic. (There is a different kind of argument, dealt with below, for Government purchases on a comparatively small scale.)

Any attempt to keep down prices *in this country*, before a stock has been secured, would be dangerous because it might divert stocks elsewhere.

(*b*) *The beliefs of the market in their influence on prices.* The period of possible shortage and very high price is expected to be from March or April to May or June. The market price will depend not only on the stocks at that time, but also on market expectations as to the price in the succeeding months. The principal 'bull points'—apart from quite uncontrollable factors, such as the weather in the Argentine—seem to be:

(i) Shortage of tonnage.

(ii) The position of Russian wheat.

(iii) The Indian embargo and doubts as to what policy will be in regard to the new crop.

(iv) Purchases by governments.

(v) Doubts as to what supplies will be coming forward six months hence (this head partly includes the former).

Short of buying and selling at a loss, Government can only influence prices by influencing sentiment on one of these heads.

(i) I have nothing to add on the tonnage question. As I have said, I think there is a tendency to over-estimate its bearing on the wheat question. Certainly enough tonnage can be obtained somehow to bring us the wheat we want, assuming it to be available on the other side, without driving prices to a prohibitive level.

(ii) An undertaking from Russia, which could be made public, that she would permit the export of, say, 10,000,000 quarters, whenever this should become physically possible, would be an important 'bear point' in the market. In any loan transaction with Russia, unrestricted wheat export to the United Kingdom up to a certain amount might be bargained for.

(iii) The Indian embargo is discussed in detail below. So far as the new crop is concerned, market doubts as to what the future policy of the Government of India may be constitute a 'bull point'. But a statement that the new crop would only be available for export within the British Empire might possibly be a bull point also, so far as the world price is concerned. Policy in regard to this new crop is discussed below.

(iv) There is much evidence that the recent rise in price has been largely due to urgent purchases on account of various governments. These governments are less likely to be influenced by reasoned beliefs as to the future course of prices than professionals would be. It is possible, therefore, that prices may drop again when these government operations have been completed.

In this connection it may be remarked:

First, that these wheat purchases on foreign account are very likely being financed to a not unimportant extent *in London*. It has been reported by Mr Granville (who is, perhaps, the most important of the middlemen who buy bills from Anglo-foreign banks, and resell them to the clearing banks) that a considerable quantity of produced bills are being accepted in London on behalf of France, Italy, and Switzerland. He has also said that it is, to some extent, within his power to discourage and discriminate against such bills, and he enquired whether it is the wish of the Treasury that he should do so. It might be worth while to inquire into this. It is quite possible that these countries can only get the means to buy wheat in the Argentine in competition with us, if *we* finance them.

Second, that secret purchases by our Government aggravate the position, so long as they are going on. Secret purchases *on a large scale* might send wheat up to any price.

(v) If a declining tendency for prices is anticipated from June onwards, the market will hurry forward supplies to take advantage of the high prices before that date and will allow stocks to fall below normal. Thus if the Government can secure supplies of wheat for delivery from June onwards, and can sell these from March onwards, they will do almost as much for prices in April as if they were selling for immediate delivery.

The policy which is now in process of being carried out[1] of Government's holding a small secret stock, both for immediate and future delivery, with which to influence and check sudden market fluctuations is a wise one. But in so far as purchases are hurried forward for delivery in this country sooner than is absolutely necessary, the freight trouble is aggravated.

The price of wheat (and, in fact, prices generally) has an

[1] A note of what has been done is given in an appendix to this paper.

important influence, not only on the cost of living to the working classes, but also on our balance of trade. Our foreign-bought wheat may very well cost us in the year £20 million more than before. This is a net loss, and a net diminution to our power of purchasing abroad or of financing the purchases of others. With other imports rising in price also, the question is serious. In present circumstances the offset from higher prices for our exports does not count for very much.

The Indian crop

The Government of India have limited the export of the old crop between 1 December and 1 April to 450,000 quarters. This policy was due not to any anticipated shortage of stocks, but to the high level of bazaar prices ruling at the end of November. It was expected that the embargo, by dashing the hopes of speculators, would cause prices to fall.

The policy was also defended on the grounds—

(i) That the ordinance, permitting the government of India to acquire compulsorily wheat unreasonably held, could not well be enforced so long as exports are permitted; there is no likelihood, however, that this ordinance ever will be enforced.

(ii) That the embargo will make no difference, i.e., not more than 450,000 quarters would be exported anyhow. (See below for an examination of this contention.)

(iii) That the exporting firms raised no objection to the proposed embargo and even welcomed it. This is hardly to be wondered at. The total of 450,000 quarters has been allocated between the different firms concerned in the trade. If the embargo has any effect, it will depress the Indian price, so long as it lasts, below the world price. Every shilling by which the Indian price is depressed below world price puts £22,500 straight into the pockets of the firms in question, out of the pockets of the Indian cultivator and dealer.

There are no recent statistics available in this country to

show what effect the embargo has actually had on local Indian prices.

The shipments of wheat from India have been as follows:

Before embargo
    October   ...   .   450,000 quarters
    November   ...   .   220,000 quarters
After embargo
    December   ...   .   190,000 quarters
    First three weeks of January   ...   110,000 quarters

leaving 150,000 quarters still to be shipped before 1 April under present arrangements.

Is it true that the embargo will make little or no difference to this country?

On 23 October, before there was any talk of an embargo, the Government of India estimated the exportable surplus of the old crop at approximately 2,700,000 quarters for the period from October 1914 to April 1915. 670,000 quarters were exported in October and November, and no more than 450,000 will be permitted for the rest of the period. *If* the Government of India's original estimate was right, the embargo has deprived this country of 1,580,000 quarters. When, in December, they were making for an embargo, they revised their former estimate, chiefly because the export firms (who, it must be remembered, wanted the embargo) supplied them with a lower figure, and partly because the bazaar price was then so high in relation to world price as to discourage export. Since then two things have happened: world prices have gone up and very optimistic estimates of the new Indian crop can now be made with confidence. In ordinary circumstances both these influences would have helped exports, particularly the second. As things are, the embargo *postpones* the benefits of the abundance of the new crop. When prospective abundance has become a matter of fair certainty, India can afford, with advantage both to herself and to us, to run down her stock of the old crop somewhat lower than would be safe otherwise. The embargo puts a stop to any such tendency.

On the other hand trade reports from India suggest that wheat is not now coming on offer in their markets in very liberal quantities.

(The fact that the permissible maximum of export has not yet been reached goes for little, since the exporting firms, having been allotted their quota, have no interest in hurrying forward their shipments.)

While it is not certain that the embargo makes much difference to this country, it appears to me not unlikely that it may, between now and April, make *some* difference.

The following course of action is, therefore, worth considering:

(*a*) The embargo should continue in its present form, so far as private exporters are concerned. But Mr Rew's committee [see Appendix], which is now purchasing 2 million quarters of wheat outside India, should be authorised to purchase up to 1,500,000 within India, in addition to what they are purchasing elsewhere: these purchases to be outside the terms of the embargo.

(*b*) These purchases should be made through the agency of one of the big Indian export firms and, in order to prevent conflict of interest, the quota allocated under the embargo to the firm employed, should, so far as it has not yet been exported, be taken over by the committee on agreed terms.

(*c*) In order not to interfere with the Government of India's legitimate attempts to avoid a dangerous price level for wheat in India, the Government of India should retain the right, if and when the purchasing committee's operations were putting up the price in India unduly, to request the committee not to offer in India a price above some agreed maximum level, and the right to revise at any time the limit of 1,500,000 quarters here proposed.

(*d*) Any net profit made by the purchasing committee in buying and selling Indian wheat should be credited to the revenues of the Government of India.

The quantity of wheat in question is, of course, rather trifling.

But it has the great virtue of being absolutely additional to the stocks which the market is expecting, and it might affect both prices and sentiment out of proportion to its magnitude, if the Government were in a position to throw it on the market in the critical period May to June.

Further, the mere announcement of such an arrangement with the Government of India might affect sentiment immediately, even though the action taken were to be in the end on a very small scale.

But in this connection, as also in others, we must remember the dilemma we are up against—that, if it is believed that Government will do something to keep U.K. wheat prices low, imports on private account will be discouraged. And if the opposite is believed, prices may go on soaring. High prices now are a safeguard against actual shortage later on. It is a tricky business to cure the former without risking the latter.

As regards the new Indian crop, current estimates are exceedingly optimistic. But it will not begin to reach this country until the end of June. It might, however, be worth while for the purchasing committee to buy a certain amount of the *new* crop (in addition to the operations outlined above) for June–July delivery (which will soon be possible), in order that they may be in a position to throw offers of this on the market in May–June. The due influence of the prospective crop on price might be made in this way more fully effective.

A restriction of exports of the new crop to the British Empire might help, but I am rather sceptical. The announcement of, or the fear of, such a policy might raise the price to be paid for purchase obtained elsewhere.

Summary of proposals

The few definite proposals, made above, are all rather trifling. But there does not seem sufficient justification *yet* for a drastic policy on the lines of the sugar deal. In the realm of action the only thing really worth doing is to storm the Dardanelles. That done this particular problem would soon lower its crest.

The proposals aim, therefore, at minor effects, and chiefly at influencing sentiment and controlling it (with the help of relatively small Government holdings of wheat). Sentiment is going to be very important during the next five months.

(i) Some sort of understanding about the Russian crop, in so far as export is possible or may become so.

(ii) Dealings by the purchasing committee, on a moderate scale, in both the old and the new Indian crops.

(iii) Enquiry into the extent to which Continental purchases of Argentine wheat are being financed through London.

J.M.K.

25 January 1915

P.S. I see from to-day's *Times* (26 January 1915) that the publication of the existence of a Cabinet committee on Food Prices had immediately the natural consequence of making British buyers timid. This is confirmed by what Messrs Paul and Rathbone (the agents through which Mr Rew's committee is buying) say as to the state of sentiment in the market. Of course this depresses (or hinders a rise in) prices for the moment, but it means also that less quantity is being purchased for this country than would be purchased otherwise. Everybody will be afraid to buy wheat from abroad with the threat of government action (on heaven knows what lines) hanging over them. Here again is the fundamental dilemma referred to already.

J.M.K.

APPENDIX

The Cabinet Committee on Food Supplies has appointed a committee under the chairmanship of Mr Rew [Assistant Secretary in the Board of Agriculture and Fisheries] to purchase up to 2 million quarters of wheat; 500,000 quarters of this are being obtained by purchase, ostensibly on behalf of the Admiralty and War Office, in excess of requirements. The remainder is to be obtained through the agency of Mr Paul and Mr Rathbone (Messrs Ross T. Smyth, of Liverpool). In order better to preserve secrecy and cover their tracks, and also in order to exert some slight control over prices, these gentlemen have been given discretion to sell as well as to buy.

Between 12 December, when they commenced operations, and 23 December, they bought 651,000 quarters and sold 123,000, leaving a stock of 528,000 quarters. Between 23 December and 22 January they have sold on balance more than they have bought, the stock having sunk by the latter date to 410,000 quarters. They have also chartered freights from the Argentine for another 400,000 quarters. At present prices their operations show a handsome profit up to date—say £150,000.

Their present instructions from the Cabinet committee are to buy no more American wheat at present prices and no more Argentine wheat than is covered by the freights already chartered.

At present India has been definitely placed outside the purview of Mr Rew's committee; and Messrs Ross T. Smyth, though abandoning the rest of their private business, have bargained that they be allowed to continue as usual their private trade in Indian wheat (unwilling, I surmise, to relinquish the hopes of gain which the quota assigned to them by the Government of India may possibly bring).

On Saturday 30 January Dr Keynes copied this letter from his son, written the day before, into his diary:

I *am* to go to Paris, and we start Sunday or Monday. It's a most select party; Lloyd George, Montagu, the Governor of the Bank of England, and me, together with a private secretary. We are to be the guests of the French government. There was another meeting of my cabinet committee today. The amount of things I've got to think about in the next few days, in order to be able to advise at a moment's notice, appals me. I wish I hadn't a cold coming on.

On 1 February Dr Keynes recorded:

> Maynard writes—'We start early on Monday and expect to be away a week or less. I'm dining with Ll. G. tonight to discuss things. My cold is going away.'

The meeting in Paris, 2–5 February, was the first joint financial conference of the allies. In an unprecedented decision it was agreed that England and France would share equally in the support of Russia in the war, and that England, France and Russia would pool their resources to assist their other allies.

Keynes seems to have possessed a Treasury eye from the start. The things he had to think about in order to advise, and his manner of thinking, are illustrated in the next three papers. A particular example is his awareness, from his Cabinet committee, of the existence of the Russian wheat crop, cut off from Europe by the closure of the Dardanelles (which the Cabinet at this time was confidently planning to reopen). More generally, these papers set out clearly the problems in lending to allies that were to bedevil the Treasury through the coming year. The first, a typed carbon dated 30 January, formed part of the file that Keynes kept on the conference. The second and third, undated and in longhand, were preserved only in the Chancellor of the Exchequer's files (T 171/107) and may represent explanations of points dealt with summarily in the first. These explanatory notes follow the first memorandum.

RUSSIA

The following points are worth bargaining for:

1. If the Russians are to be financed with such large sums as have been mentioned, it seems absolutely essential that gold should be shipped under *some* kind of arrangement. (If the moneys are advanced to them for the purpose of payments outside the United Kingdom, the effect on our exchange position is more direct and immediate. But the ultimate effect of purchase on Russian account within the United Kingdom is not as different from that of purchase abroad as is sometimes made out. In considering whether gold ought to be shipped the question of where the loan is to be spent, though of some importance, is only of secondary importance.) [See note p. 71].

67

The Russian authorities in resisting so strongly the export of gold seem to be thinking mainly of their published weekly returns. I think they attach an exaggerated importance to these, and are probably influenced by erroneous ideas on the question of gold reserves. But there is no arguing with such ideas whether well- or ill-founded, and it is desirable, therefore, to propound a scheme which respects these ideas so far as possible. I suggest some such arrangement as the following (I previously suggested this to Mr Blackett, and it is, I think, set forth in some memorandum of his):

Under the law governing Russian note issues, foreign bank balances can reckon as part of their reserves. These are entered, however, under a distinct heading from the cash held at home. Hence a balance of theirs at the Bank of England, so long as it is unspent, remains part of the legal backing for their note issue. If, however, the foreign balance was to be in the form, not of a current account, but in the form of actual gold separately earmarked at the B[ank] of E[ngland] to their account as the Indian gold is, and not appearing at all in the Bank of England return, I fancy such gold would not only continue to count as legal backing but could also appear in the weekly returns under the heading of 'cash', and not under the heading of 'foreign balances'. It is not likely that the Russian law, any more than our own, lays down in what locality the gold must be held, provided that it really is gold and not balances.

Now *we* want the Russian gold, not in order to strengthen our present position or for any immediate purpose. Indeed, it would be exceedingly detrimental to the Bank of England's position to receive, and reckon as part of its reserves, a large amount of gold, for this would only weaken the market rates of discount still further. We want the gold as a safeguard against possible eventualities, and against the more remote reactions of the policy of purchasing and financing abroad freely. It seems to me, therefore, that the objects of both governments would be served if the Russian government were to agree to send the gold which is now the matter of dispute *to be earmarked for their account* at the Bank of England. This gold not to appear in the Bank of England's return, and to continue to appear in the Bank of Russia's return. Only in the event of the gold's being required for the maintenance of our exchange position would it be transferred from the account of the Bank of Russia to the account of the Bank of England.

It is quite possible that this gold will never be wanted. In that event the transaction need never be made public. If, on the other hand, the policy of helping Russian external finance causes embarrassment to our exchange position, the Bank of Russia must, necessarily, admit the justice and expediency of our using some of their gold wherewith to right the position. And, if we are to feel quite safe, the gold should be available at short notice and in all contingencies and must, consequently, be located in London. [See note p. 72.]

II. It has been suggested that a separate loan might be negotiated for the sole purpose of enabling Russian merchants to liquidate their debits in London. An arrangement of this kind has already been made with the Bank of France.

Such an arrangement would be highly politic. From our point of view it would be no more than a funding loan, and would not increase our commitments. For a large part of the money would go towards paying off bills now in cold storage at the Bank of England. On the other hand, it would help the government of Russia's internal finance by the whole amount of the loan, for they would utilise its proceeds to sell exchange in Petrograd, and the funds brought in by these sales would be a net addition to their internal resources. (See a memorandum by Mr Blackett for further details of this.)

III. I believe it might be a good thing to make the loan conditional on some definite undertaking from them as to their policy in regard to the wheat crop. A certain amount of Russian wheat is dribbling out of the country as it is, but not much. It is of the utmost importance to this country that there should be no risk of any embargo on free exports to this country being laid on by the Russian Government, if and when free exports become physically possible. It would be a wise precaution to obtain a definite undertaking from them that they would permit the export of, say, 10 million quarters to the United Kingdom. If it were possible to make a public announcement of this it might exert a favourable influence on price long before it actually became effective.

In this connection it would be reasonable to point out to Russia that if we come to the help of the deficiency of her trade balance, it lies with her to do what she can to prevent this trade balance from being more adverse than is absolutely necessary.

IV. Any tendency on the part of the Russians to make attempts to finance themselves independently in the United States ought to be encouraged.

The policy of issuing all loans in the name of the United Kingdom and then making advances to various parties, has this objection, that the number of different ways in which the investor is to be tempted is unduly limited. By various expedients the Treasury is endeavouring to prevent the savings of the country from flowing into non-necessary uses. But it is idle to suppose that all the money thus realised will flow into War Loans or securities of that description. Many investors do not like gilt-edged securities, and will certainly not be tempted except with higher rates of interest and a dash of risk. If Allied Powers were allowed to float loans on the London market in their own names of a kind which could be taken up by the public, I believe that some sources of funds might be tapped which will never be reached by the issues of our own Government.

The connection of the above with the question of encouraging allies to borrow for themselves in the United States is, perhaps, not obvious. The common point is the great importance of increasing rather more than seems to be the policy at present the variety of wares offered to investors both in this and other countries.

J.M.K.

30.1.15

Reasons why the expenditure in England of money lent to Russia may help to bring about a drain of gold, almost as much as expenditure elsewhere.

1. Although the goods purchased are manufactured in England, the importation of raw material from abroad is necessitated to some extent. The degree to which this is important depends, of course, on what particular commodity is in question (e.g. purchases of tea, rubber, munitions of war, or wool).

2. Except in a very few trades (which Russian purchases are not likely to affect), *the industry of the United Kingdom is already employed practically at its maximum capacity.* Additional orders from the Russian government will have the effect in many cases of diverting home orders abroad, or of diminishing our capacity to get purchasing power abroad by exporting.

This argument depends on the peculiar state of our industry at the present time, and is likely therefore to be overlooked. When, as is usually the case, we have a margin of productive capacity, additional foreign orders do not have the above effect.

Or the question may be looked at broadly this way: The amount of capital which can be raised in the United Kingdom is *limited.* This limit, regard being had to existing obligations, is almost certain to be reached. The balance can only be obtained by the export of gold, the calling in of foreign credits, and actual borrowings abroad (directly or indirectly) by us. When this point is reached there is bound to be a *risk* of an export of gold. Any assistance given to Russia brings this risk so much nearer.

J.M.K.

Is it important for Russia, from her own point of view, to keep all her gold?

Once specie payment has been suspended, it is purely a matter of *appearances*. If appearances can be saved, everything is saved. They talk a good deal of the *proportion* of gold to note issue. This is important if the bank may be called on to encash the notes, because the more notes there are out the more the bank may be called on to encash. But when specie payment has been suspended, the precise proportion of gold loses its former significance.

I do not see that any particular harm would result (e.g. to the acceptability of the notes within Russia herself) if the proportion fell from 50 per cent to 40 per cent.

Only the English have realised that the main use of gold reserves is to be *used*. Elsewhere the gold reserve has become a mere fetish or superstition. But of course it does not follow from this that it is easy or possible to shake the faith of believers.

They think that we want their gold, for the same sort of reason that influences them in retaining it namely to strengthen the Bank of England's position on paper. And our *real* reason, namely the possibility of our having actually to *export* their gold and so *use* it, they look on as little better than a pretext. So different is the attitude of the Bank of England to its gold, from the attitude of the Bank of Russia, that it must be very difficult to make the latter appreciate our real reasons and motives in wanting some of their gold.

J.M.K.

At the Paris conference France and Russia agreed to lend gold to the Bank of England when it was needed, the gold still to appear on their balance sheets as cash held abroad. The Russians were permitted to raise sterling loans on the London and French markets and promised in turn to facilitate the future export of wheat to the allies. The proposal of a loan to be jointly guaranteed by the three allies was not agreed to; Keynes wrote a memorandum on this proposal, an undated carbon copy marked 'after Paris' in his file.

MEMORANDUM ON PROPOSALS FOR A JOINT LOAN

The French and Russian Governments were extremely anxious at the Paris Conference to obtain the consent of this Government to the issue of a loan for a large amount, for the general expenses of the three countries at home as well as abroad, having the joint guarantee of all three powers.

So far as possible, each government would meet its own needs by the issue of the joint loan to its own public, but they would be giving this public the joint guarantee instead of merely their own guarantee.

The obvious argument in favour of this arrangement from the point of view of France and Russia, is that they might be able to borrow a larger amount more cheaply with the joint guarantee than on their own unsupported credit; also that it would facilitate their entrance into the British market; and that the issue of such a loan would produce a favourable impression of solidarity on the public mind.

From the point of view of Great Britain, however, and not only from her point of view, there are the following very strong objections:

(1) The joint guarantee is practically useless to us. We could not borrow on appreciably better terms with it than without it.

(2) On the other hand, we should to some extent *spoil our own credit* by issuing such a loan, and depress the price of our own issues. Even the rumour of such a loan was alleged, last week, to have affected our own War Loan unfavourably.

Both these arguments also apply, in different degree, to France and Russia. Their credit with their own public is not yet so bad that funds exist on any large scale waiting for gilt-edged investment, which their own public are nevertheless unwilling to entrust to their respective governments. Thus the additional amount which a joint guarantee might draw out in France and Russia is probably not, at present, large. At the same time the issue of a joint loan on a big scale would spoil the unassisted credit

73

of France and Russia with their own publics much more than it would ours. It would depress the price of their existing loans, and embarrass them in issuing new ones.

(3) Thus the effect of such a loan would be to give our guarantee for all time for the interest payable on a large part of the national debts of France and Russia, without any compensating advantage to ourselves and without even increasing by any large amount the aggregate capital funds immediately available in the three countries for the prosecution of the war.

(4) The issue of such a loan would make it very much more difficult for us to control the extent to which Russia and France are to have access to our market for the purpose of borrowing. While showing ourselves willing to assist them in this way to the utmost extent compatible with safety, it is of very great importance that we should not relax the completeness of our control over such entries of the allies into our market.

A jointly guaranteed loan would only have substantial advantages in the event of things coming to such a pass that there were large sums awaiting investment in France and Russia, which the public of those countries were unwilling to lend to their own governments on any terms, unless supported by a guarantee from Great Britain. And in this case it might be the best policy for Great Britain to borrow direct and then make advances to the others.

J.M.K.

On 11 February Dr Keynes noted that 'Florence [Mrs Keynes] spent the day in London, and went to the House of Commons, where Asquith delivered a speech, prepared by Maynard. Maynard was himself in the House'. The subject being debated was 'the rise in the price of the necessaries of life'; prices had risen between 20 and 24 per cent since the start of the war and there had been agitation in the press over alleged profiteering.

The prime minister's speech was in effect a report from the Cabinet Committee on Food Prices, of which Asquith was chairman. It was a conciliatory speech, the gist of which was that the rise in prices was not so great, all things considered, prices generally being not so high as after the Franco-

Prussian war, when wages were lower. In the case of wheat, a rise of 72 per cent, he looked for 'an easement of the situation by what I may call a natural process' and rejected the idea of fixed maximum prices—'an experiment which the German government have made with the most disastrous consequences'.

There is no evidence that Keynes actually wrote any of this speech. The style is Asquith's and the substance comes from the papers before the committee—the Franco-Prussian war statistics, for example, from a report by the Board of Trade. Much of it was in Keynes's minutes of a meeting of the day before (10 February) and of his first meeting, 22 January. Presumably he supplied the facts.

Keynes, however, did write two notes on economic points made in the debate that followed. The first rebuts an argument advanced by the Labour leader J. R. Clynes.

MR CLYNES'S ARGUMENT

Mr Clynes in his speech on Thursday argued that the rise of prices must be artificial because the Board of Trade returns of imports showed a large increase in value. There are of course two obvious fallacies in this. In the first place, the figures of import value are higher in part precisely because of the rise in prices. In the second place, in so far as quantities are maintained the figures show that this country has been able to buy as much as usual *in spite of* the high prices. If, as is the case, the available world supply is diminished and Great Britain nevertheless gets as much as usual, there seems to be ground for satisfaction rather than complaint. Mr Clynes's argument suggests that prices in this country are fixed by the amount of supplies which are brought here and not by what importers have to pay for these supplies—which is obviously rubbish.

The second comment is longer and concerns the remarks of two members on the influence of currency inflation on prices. David M. Mason, a Liberal banker and founder of the Sound Currency Association, had called attention to the abnormal increase in the supply of currency in both belligerent and other countries. The resulting depreciation was the most influential cause contributing to the rise of prices, he said. His remedy was for the British government to redeem outstanding paper as quickly as possible. He also urged that Britain should continue to permit investments abroad, lest the assets in question depreciate through the unwillingness of other markets to take them up.

A contrary opinion was put forward by another Liberal member, Dundas White: that prices quoted in paper currency were not 'artificially inflated' since this paper money was not forced on the acceptance of people instead of gold, but circulated at par.

THE RELATION OF CURRENCY INFLATION
TO PRICES

I agree with the general argument of Mr Mason—that the increased volume of legal tender money now available in various countries lies behind the present rise in prices—rather than with the view of Mr Dundas White.

In their influences on prices, bank notes and bank balances, against which cheques can be drawn, are just as effective as gold coins are. In suggesting the opposite Mr Dundas White was certainly wrong.

While, however, the increased volume of legal tender money and bank money *lies behind* the more immediate causes of advanced prices, I believe that the full effect of this increase is being delayed, and that it is not yet of first-class importance. In France for example, a very large part of the increased currency is *hoarded*, and what is hoarded can exert no influence whatever on prices. This is also the case, in varying degree, in many other countries. And in Great Britain the increased volume of bank money available has been left for the most part by the clearing banks at the Bank of England, unused for the creation of further credit. It must also be remembered that the increase of bank notes has been largely offset, up to the present time, by a diminution, or a breakdown, of other forms of credit.

On the other hand, it must be recognised that many of the influences tending towards high prices, to which the Prime Minister called attention, are only possible *because of* the increase of legal tender money available. Let me give three instances.

1. If it were not for the Government's borrowings from the Bank of England, and other loans made by the Bank, which have so greatly inflated bank balances in this country, the Government could not have afforded to purchase on such a large scale or to grant such generous separation allowances.

2. If the Italian Banks of Issue had not greatly increased their fiduciary note issue, the Italian government could not have afforded to buy on so large a scale in the Argentine.

3. If money had not been made so freely available by the changes introduced in the United States by the new Bank Act to which Mr Mason alluded [the Federal Reserve Act of 1913], money would not have been so easy in the New York market and speculators would have found it much more difficult to obtain funds wherewith to speculate for the rise.

It is in these sort of ways that an increased volume of currency affects prices. Every *particular* rise of prices is due to some *particular* trade cause, which may be conclusively connected with supply or demand. But the trade cause in question may itself only have been *rendered possible* by currency changes. Mr Mason, therefore, was not so much giving an alternative explanation of the rise of prices, as going behind the explanations which had been given, and calling attention to one of the more remote influences which had made these explanations possible.

Speaking generally I should say that the *average* rise of prices for all kinds of commodities, such as is shown by one of the index numbers, is due in no small measure to increases in the volume of currency and credit. But the exceptional rise in the prices of certain foodstuffs—with which the House is mainly concerned in this debate—are *not mainly* due to currency influences.

The currency side of the question deserves to be borne in mind, because it is likely to get more and more important as time goes on. I believe there is good reason for expecting a substantial rise in metals, which have so far lagged behind food prices, in the near future. Food prices may possibly reach their highest point this spring, but the *general level* of prices is likely to go on rising for some time to come. How much rise we shall stand before the Allies and the United States feel equal to adopting the regulated gold standard for an unregulated gold standard, it is quite impossible to say.

Mr Mason's own suggested remedies appear to me to be quite useless. To pay off the currency notes, by means of the gold which is now held in reserve against them, would have no effect on prices whatever. The purchasing position of a man with a sovereign in his pocket is precisely the same as the purchasing position of a man with a currency note in his pocket. Nor do I see that the question of permitting investment abroad is particularly relevant to the question under discussion. If, on the other hand, bank credits were to be diminished some real good might be done. From many conversations I have had with the Governor of the Bank I know that he has the importance of this fully in mind. But it is not suggested by Mr Mason.

Keynes was appointed Treasury representative on the inter-departmental Committee on Wheat and Flour Supplies, mentioned in his paper on wheat prices, which was secretly buying for the government. The government of India was anxious to prevent the pressure of world demand for wheat, of which India produced an exportable surplus, from raising the Indian price to famine levels. But a restriction of exports raised the problem that speculation would keep the price up, while a complete embargo on wheat exports threatened to reduce the price so much as to cause acute dissatisfaction among the producers of wheat. The Committee was able to step in and solve the problem by buying the surplus of production over consumption at a price well below the world market price, to the advantage of the British war effort. Many of the details for this scheme of mutual benefit were worked out by Keynes, in consultation with Sir Thomas Holderness of the India Office. The problems that they faced are illustrated in a note written by Keynes 22 February 1915, carrying his initials and marked 'confidential' (Lord Crewe was Secretary of State for India).

Limitation of the *amount* of export on private account cannot have much effect in bringing the Indian prices below the world price, so long as the limit has not been reached. Especially must this be the case, when the price in the near future is expected to be higher than in the more remote future. In order to hurry forward consignments to take advantage of the high world price, Indian exporters will pay nearly the equivalent of this price in India and so keep Indian price linked to world price.

The Government of India are right, therefore, in thinking that the only way of achieving their object, of bringing Indian price substantially below world price, is to prohibit all export on private account for a long period.

Since there is no question of local shortage of supply in India, the purchase of considerable quantities by the Indian government on behalf of the home government is not necessarily incompatible with the above object.

The point may be illustrated as follows. Take the Indian crop at 50 million quarters, the normal price at 35s 6d a quarter (9 seers), and the consumption at this price at 40 million quarters. An increase of price to 46s a quarter (7 seers) might reduce the local consumption to 35 million quarters. On the other hand the price might have to fall below 30s a quarter in order for the whole crop of 50 million quarters to be absorbed by local demand.

If the world market can absorb up to or more than 15 million quarters at 46s a quarter (equivalent, say, to a London price of 60s), India may be led to sell more wheat than she can really afford to sell. Yet though this wheat could be absorbed in the world market at 46s under competitive conditions, it would be worth while for the Indian dealer to sell 10 million quarters for export at, say, 38s, rather than be forced to throw this on the local Indian market.

Thus if the Government of India could persuade the Indian dealer that there is no chance of any buyer for export coming forward and offering more than (say) 40s a quarter (8 seers) within any period over which speculation is likely to extend, Indian price might be forced down to this level and at the same time a large quantity might be bought at this price for export.

The success of the first alternative proposed by Sir T. Holderness (and contemplated in less precise terms by the viceroy) entirely depends on how far it is possible to persuade the Indian dealer in the above sense.

I suggest that, in an attempt on these lines, the following points deserve consideration:

(i) The Government of India would not fix maximum prices. Certainly if the price is now 6 seers (53s 4d), suddenly to prohibit dealings above 9 seers (35s 6d) would be a most dangerous policy and well calculated to produce extreme temporary shortage of supply. Having prohibited export on private account, they should announce a price at which their agents would buy wheat or accept it in lieu of taxes.

(ii) They should begin by fixing a purchase price not too much below the price now ruling; and they should announce at the same time that this price would be lowered every month. E.g., they should offer to buy wheat at 45s in April, 43s in May, 41s in June and 40s in July, subject to a limitation of aggregate quantity purchasable in each month. Further they should announce that from August onwards they will hold themselves free, in accordance with powers they already have, to commandeer wheat at 35s a quarter. This sort of policy, by inducing a belief that prices will fall rather than rise, is the only way to counteract the holding-up of stocks. It will be more efficacious than an heroic attempt, almost certainly doomed to failure, such as that suggested by the viceroy, to force the price down at once from 53s 4d to 35s 6d or even 32s a quarter. If the price could be quickly reduced from 53s 4d to 45s, this would be as much as one could reasonably expect.

(iii) It would be necessary for the success of this scheme to utilise the services of all the wheat-exporting firms in Northern

India and to pay them well. I should expect the native dealers to be more influenced by the words and actions of these firms than by anything Government could say.

(iv) The Government of India should take over all forward contracts already made.

(v) While the Government of India obviously could not be pledged absolutely to purchase 500,000 tons for export before the end of August, the home Government ought to be in a position to make a very strong statement by way of reassuring the market on this side—to the effect that the Government of India is pledged to the export of this amount subject only to the intervention of unforeseen circumstances. The home Government ought also to say that the Indian wheat would not be thrown on the market, but would be sold for what it would fetch through the ordinary channels and in the ordinary way, any profits being credited to the Government of India.

With regard to the political argument, it is hardly possible for anyone outside India to speak. But the Government in India seem to emphasise one side of it, without mentioning at all another side which must plainly have some importance.

These high prices are a very great benefit to a large part of the population of Northern India. The small cultivator, who consumes two-thirds or three-quarters of his own crop and sells the balance for his other needs, has never been so well off in his life. Surely the great Sikh colonies of the Punjab must be proving most infertile ground for the agitator.

On the other hand, the high prices are at the expense partly of the landless labourer and of the dwellers in towns, and partly of the foreign consumer.

The dwellers in towns are doubtless noisy, but whether they are as dangerous as the other classes, referred to above, might become, may be doubtful. The viceroy seems to assume that the vast agricultural interests of Northern India, which comprise some of the most formidable classes in the whole country, are going to submit without a murmur to an operation which will act enormously to their disadvantage and which will deprive them of profits, to the possibility of which they are already fully alive, and to the greedy anticipation of which the present situation may be partly due. High prices for grain, at a time of bountiful crop, in India, where a large part of the population are themselves cultivators, is an evil, in so far as it is not a benefit, of a totally different order from what it would be in this country. I detect no hint in the viceroy's telegrams of this sort of consideration.

J.M.K.

22.2.15

The British government had started buying wheat secretly at the end of 1914 and continued until 4 April 1915 when, after representations from the corn trade, they stopped both buying and selling, awaiting a final decision by the Cabinet Committee on Food Supplies. The following Cabinet paper, written and signed by Keynes, 1 May 1915, gives the opinion of the Wheat Committee that their operations should continue, but it did not carry the day: the Cabinet Committee, which had been touchy from the beginning about interference with business, decided 4 May that the government should buy no more wheat and should rely in future on the trade. Mr Rew, as indicated above, was Assistant Secretary to the Board of Agriculture and Fisheries and chairman of several committees concerned with cereals supplies.

NOTE ON THE WHEAT POSITION OF THE UNITED KINGDOM

I. *The statistical position*

This has been analysed by Mr Rew. The most important figures are the following: Up to the end of the cereal year, 31 August 1915, the requirements of the importing countries of Europe, allied and neutral, are estimated at 21,500,000 quarters. The supplies to meet this demand are only 16,500,000 quarters. The situation is so well recognised that several governments have embarked on purchasing for themselves, in particular, the governments of France and Italy, who have been, and are, buying largely and without much regard to prices. Those who do not get their supplies in good time will not get them at all.

The consumption of the United Kingdom for this period will be 12 million quarters. This cannot be met to the extent of more than 2 million quarters by further depleting home stocks. Such stocks (including farmers' stocks), which were estimated at 9 million quarters at the end of January, had fallen to 6 million quarters by 15 April. And 4 million quarters is the minimum for safety, since, after allowing the bakers and millers what they require for carrying on their business, this figure leaves nothing for the farmers, and only one week's visible supplies at the ports; a visible supply so low as this might provoke panic, and only extreme necessity should induce us to deplete stocks still further.

We must, therefore, import at least 10 million quarters. Whence can these supplies be drawn? The Wheat Committee had secured 2,200,000 quarters before its operations were suspended. The whole of the Indian supply has been secured for this country, and is under the control of a government committee. The Indian Wheat Scheme is proving very successful, and the May wheat is now coming forward for purchase in large quantities. But the amount which can be shipped in May is narrowly limited by the freight obtainable, and in June by the capacity of the ports. Further, the crop is a week or two later than we hoped, and April shipments, instead of reaching 450,000 quarters will be only 350,000 quarters. Consequently Indian wheat will not reach this country in large quantities until after the first week of July, when the June shipments begin to arrive. However, it is hoped that 3,500,000 quarters will have arrived by 31 August. Thus of the total requirements of 10 million quarters, 5,700,000 quarters have already been arranged for and are controlled by the Government.

There remains a balance of 4,300,000 quarters. It is impossible to say with any accuracy for how much of this the trade has already provided. We know approximately how much wheat is on passage and how much freight has been taken for wheat not yet shipped, but there is no knowing how much of this will reach this country. Foreign governments have lately proved much keener buyers than British importers, with the effect that cargo after cargo upon which we reckoned has been diverted to the continent as soon as it reached European waters. Mr Rew thinks that, apart from the Wheat Committee's purchases, some 1,200,000 quarters now on passage may actually be delivered in this country. If this is so, there remains 3,100,000 quarters for the provision of which no steps have yet been taken.

The question of the proper policy in regard to this balance is the subject of the present discussion. It is the equivalent of four and a half weeks' consumption. A large part of it ought to be here by the end of June or soon after, as the lateness of the Indian supplies, which will go a long way towards seeing us through August, makes the middle of July the critical period. The chief source of supply must be the Argentine, and, as this is a five weeks' voyage, and freight not available at a moment's notice the purchases should be arranged within a fortnight from now. The balance must come from U.S.A. The available supply from this source is the most incalculable factor. It is arguable that the figures on which the preceding calculations are based ought to be increased by 2 million quarters and a sanguine statistician might be justified in taking the higher figure. But America is in great danger of over-exporting, and some experts hold that she is within a very few weeks of stopping export of the old crop altogether. Conditions are said to resemble the Leiter year, and there is a real danger of the sellers of the May option being cornered. It has been reported that the French government have already bought 86 cargoes for forward shipment. If this is true, prudence requires this country to act with very little delay. The question is therefore one of great urgency. Someone must take the necessary steps to secure a good part of the wheat in the next two or three weeks.

II. *The position of the trade*

Can this duty be safely left to the trade? From the nature of the case no one, not even members of the trade themselves, can give a precise answer to this question. As the result of hearing a great deal of evidence of one kind or another, I am convinced that it would be running far too great a risk to trust the trade to buy freely in the near future. The chief reasons for this may be summarised thus.

(*a*) At present the price of wheat in the United Kingdom is substantially below world price both for American and for Argentine wheat, both for near positions and for shipment. That is to say, foreign countries have been bidding higher prices than ours for cargoes in European waters; and further the current price of wheat in the Plate and in U.S.A., *plus* freight, exceeds the price here. As long as this is the case, the importing firms admit that they will not bring their cargoes to this country. The importers say that they are prepared to sacrifice a few pence per quarter to bring the wheat here, but that they cannot be expected to refuse any foreign government which offers them a shilling or two more. The continuance or discontinuance of these conditions depends primarily, not on the importers, but on the foreign governments in question and on the millers at home. These are discussed under (*b*) and (*c*) below. A very striking piece of evidence has lately come to hand that there is virtually no buying at the present time for this country in the Argentine. When the Wheat Committee were ordered to discontinue purchasing, they were left with some 60,000 tons of freight on their hands. They have been endeavouring to relet these boats on condition that they are brought to the United Kingdom. Yet it has proved impossible to do this, as there are at present no buyers in the Plate who will take freight which is without Continental options except at a huge reduction of price. According to the latest telegrams we can relet a boat for Australia at 70s, and there are numerous offers for the Continent at 72s 6d;

but for the United Kingdom the boats are so little wanted that no one will give more than 57*s* 6*d*, and even in that case there is no absolute security that the boats will eventually get here. It appears then that it is more than 3*s* a quarter more profitable to ship wheat to the Continent than to the United Kingdom. While these conditions last, little or no wheat can be set in motion for this country; and what is at present on its way will be diverted.

(*b*) The evidence is that the trade have not taken the necessary steps, so far as the near future is concerned, and that at present it is not worth their while to do so. As long as foreign governments are in the market, private buyers in this country have little chance. If our wheat trade only had other private buyers to bid against, I believe they could get us our share. But they, only willing to take trade risks, are met by government competitors who are not thus limited. It is not a matter of chance that the United Kingdom price is below the price elsewhere. Foreign governments deliberately offer for the wheat a shilling or two more than whatever is the United Kingdom price at the moment. The relatively low level of the United Kingdom price is simply a reflection of the fact that buyers elsewhere are more urgent than they are here.

Some of the firms consulted have expressed the opinion that the demands of foreign governments are nearly satisfied. But they were not able to produce evidence for this. The carefully compiled figures of the Board of Agriculture point in the opposite direction. From these it appears that Italy still has a substantial amount to buy, and France a very considerable amount. There is some reason for thinking that France has been hoping until lately to secure from the Black Sea the wheat which Russia has sold her; but she must now realise that the famine in railway trucks on the Russian Southern Railway and the shortage of freight, quite apart from military obstacles, must disappoint her hopes in this cereal year.

(*c*) The millers and the wheat trade generally are less inclined than usual to take risks. After a series of very unprofitable years, the trade has now made huge profits—profits which they badly needed. They are exceedingly disinclined to lose these profits, as they have often lost them before, by being caught on the crest of the wave. The new crop is likely to be much cheaper than the old, so that at some point of time there will be a very heavy fall of price. The chief preoccupation of the trade is not to be caught long of wheat at this moment. They can hardly be blamed for this. But the effect is to cause this country to live from hand to mouth in a year in which, apart from the risks of war, supplies are estimated by the highest authorities to be substantially short of demand—so long as we remain alone amongst the chief importing countries in depending on private importers.

(*d*) The trade are not, and cannot be, in as full possession of the facts as the Government are. They do not know how much is held by the Wheat Committee. They have no exact information in regard to India, whereas the Indian Wheat Committee know from day to day all there is to be known. They have been enormously influenced by false hopes (or fears) of the early arrival of Russian wheat. They have no access to the somewhat full information as to the stocks in the hands of millers, farmers, and bakers, which has been lately collected by the Board of Agriculture. In listening to the views of representatives of the trade, both those who have taken an optimistic view and those who have taken a pessimistic view, I have been immensely struck by the superiority of the information in the hands of the Board of Agriculture.

In short, the reasons for doubting the sufficiency of commercial motive to ensure the necessary supplies of wheat to this country are very strong. Why should the trade plunge in where it is so very difficult to see the way ahead? The fact that the Government stand aside, after dealing in wheat for four months, would indicate that the position is not very serious. The trade have nothing to lose by 'going slow' for the next two months. If they go in heavily they may lose heavily. The hopes of gain are not correspondingly great. If prices were to soar, it is vaguely felt that Government would step in and do no one knows what. And if the trade actually secured great gains, can they feel much confidence that they would escape unmolested with booty, the name of which would be 'war profits'?

III. *The views of the trade*

The opinions which have been expressed to us by the trade are conflicting. The Government's own advisers are unanimous in regarding the situation as extremely serious. Messrs Ross T. Smyth, whom the Cabinet Committee have employed as being the most trustworthy of the big importing firms, speak in the strongest possible terms of the risk involved in our continuing inactive. The representative, whom the Wheat Committee sent out to watch the position on their behalf in the United States, has taken a very much more pessimistic view of the possibility of further supplies from America than I have expressed above. (His informing report is appended to Mr Rew's memorandum.) Mr Saltmarsh, the representative of the Baltic Exchange, who has been acting as one of the Board of Agriculture's confidential advisers, has, I believe, written a memorandum on his own account, to the effect that the risk involved in a policy of inaction is too great. The representatives of the Board of Agriculture, after a very great amount of time spent in discussion and in correspondence with every description of person interested in the trade, are unanimously of opinion that the time has come for the resumption of government action.

On the other side there is to be put the opinion of three big importing firms who have consistently opposed Government action ever since they discovered that they were not to be employed as government agents, who have made charges and complaints in connection with it which proved to be without foundation, who fear that if government intervenes they will lose the business, whose interest is in rising prices, and one of whom has contributed to our present difficulties by selling on a large scale to the Italian government and other foreign destinations cargoes of wheat originally consigned to this country. These firms have expressed the opinion that the trade can be safely left to itself. They have not, however, traversed on substantial points the facts of the situation as set out above, except in respect of the exportable surplus of North America. Mr Springman, who represents one of the most important firms which deal with the United States, put the exportable surplus 4,500,000 quarters higher than it is put by the Board of Agriculture. Whatever may be the value of Mr Springman's intuitions, the statistics on which he bases them will not bear examination. He arrived at his results by taking the official estimate made by the United States government last year in place of that made this March, by assuming that the domestic consumption of that country has been unaffected by the increase of population since 1913, and by allowing for a price level so high as to reduce the carry-forward in U.S.A. to nearly half the lowest hitherto recorded. If Mr Springman's opinion is to have any value, we must assume it to be based, not on the statistics he produced, but on a general feeling that present prices will bring out all kinds of unsuspected supplies. Such a view is very likely well founded. But at the best we must treat it as doubtful. It may be sufficiently well founded to deter a merchant from speculating for the rise, and yet sufficiently doubtful to require a government in time of war to insure against the possibility of its being wrong.

I have referred above to the personal bias of some of the firms. In balancing the opinion of the trade, this should be neglected, because the bias, if any, of Messrs Ross T. Smyth, who may expect to continue to act as the government agents, is clearly on the other side.

It must then be conceded that the opinion of the trade, so far as we have been able to ascertain it, is divided. I would add, however, that in preferring one set of opinions to another, I have been influenced, I think, not merely by numbers but by impressions, formed in the course of many hours' personal contact chiefly in connection with the details of the Indian Wheat Scheme, that the judgement and width of outlook of some members of the trade is superior to that of others. Perhaps this is too vague a thing to mention. But one cannot weigh the diverse evidence of authorities without some such clue; and I think that Lord Lucas and Mr Rew, who have had similar opportunities of observation, agree with me.

IV. *A comparison of the risk with the cost of insurance*

In deciding policy, it is right to be very greatly influenced by a comparison of the magnitude of the risk we run if anything goes wrong, with the ease with which the position can be safeguarded. If it is true that the demands of foreign governments are nearly satisfied, if, after all, some important quantity of wheat gets out of the Black Sea before the middle of June, if all goes well with our Indian venture, if there is promise a month hence of a bumper crop in the United States, if we lose no cargoes through marine or enemy risk, then we may expect to scrape through anyhow with perhaps a week's, even a fortnight's, visible supplies in hand. But there is no margin against contingencies. We should be running a measurable risk of a definite breakdown of the country's supplies, and a much greater risk of an extreme rise of price. It is not necessary to enlarge on the consequences of either the lesser or the greater of these two evils. If the Government postpone action until June, they will have to pay an enormous price and may be unable to get enough wheat in time at any price—for it is not to be lightly assumed that it is always possible if it is necessary, to secure more wheat from the United States.

On the other hand, if the Wheat Committee are authorised to continue on their former lines, they ought to be able, with the experience in buying which the Board of Agriculture now have, to make the position reasonably secure by the end of the month. Last February the problem was not manageable. But now,

5,700,000 quarters out of 10 million total requirements being controlled by Government already, the problem of dealing with the balance presents no insuperable difficulties. The Home Wheat Committee have already dealt in 3 million quarters. The Indian Wheat Committee hope, before they have finished, to deal in 10 million quarters. Authority is now asked for the Home Wheat Committee to deal in 2 or 3 million quarters more.

The financial risk is very moderate. At present prices the Home Wheat Committee have already secured profits of about £500,000. The proposed new operations might add to this profit; but on the other hand they might involve the loss of the present profit and perhaps £500,000 more. On the balance of all transactions, I should put the actuarial risk at nil, and the maximum loss at £500,000.

It is of much importance that it should be recognised that what is proposed is merely a *resumption* of government action. The present position appears to me to be a most foolish compromise between interference and *laissez-faire*. Up to the critical date the Government have interfered, with the effect, according to the trade, of greatly upsetting private importers. This interference has given the trade the impression that the Government have taken responsibility for the national security. It has certainly given them a sufficient excuse if anything goes wrong. We have at present most of the evil effects of interference, and, unless the matter is now carried through, but little of the advantages. The Government have already exposed themselves to the critics of interference. There may have been a good case for leaving the trade entirely to themselves, but it is difficult to see that there is any case at all for the Government's retiring from responsibility at the present stage.

In conclusion, it is worth while to refer again to the present, almost ludicrous, position in the Plate. The Wheat Committee have 60,000 tons of freight ready for wheat. Some members of the trade having objected to the activities of the Wheat Committee, the Wheat Committee desist from purchases to fill this freight. And the trade are told that we look to them to bring along the country's supplies. It is then discovered that the trade left to themselves have no immediate intention of buying wheat for us in the Plate. They refuse to take our 60,000 tons of freight and fill it themselves in our place with wheat for this country; and they are hardly willing to look at our boats unless we give them the option of diverting the cargoes to the Continent.

If action is permitted, the trade must of course be informed, and the Cabinet Committee must be prepared for the responsibility of providing—if it proves necessary when we see our way more clearly—for the whole of the balance required by this country up to the end of the cereal year. For this purpose it would be advisable to employ the services of two or three of the firms. (I suggest Messrs Sanday and Messrs Shipton, Anderson, in addition to Messrs Ross T. Smyth.) But there would be no need to interfere with anything which private importers may care to do on their own account. It is very difficult to predict how they will be affected by an announcement of further government action. It is quite possible that it will make them more bullish and more ready to buy at the present level of prices than they are now.

J. M. KEYNES

1 May 1915

Although Keynes's chief preoccupation during his early months at the Treasury was wheat, he also became involved in the problems of war finance. The following note, surviving among his papers as an initialled carbon of a typed copy dated 12 March 1915, foreshadows a Treasury decision to authorise the Bank of England to issue Treasury bills from 14 April at rates of discount fixed from day to day.

NOTE ON THE MONTHLY STATEMENTS OF THE CLEARING BANKS

For various reasons these returns are not a very reliable foundation on which to base inferences; but the removal of the temptation to window-dress (on account of the large size of the banks' normal balances) may have made them a little less misleading than usual. The leading figures (excluding Coutts, and London and Provincial in order to maintain the continuity of recost) are in £1 million:

	Deposits, etc. (1)	Cash in hand and at Bank of England (2)	Cash at call and notice (3)	Ratio of (2)+ (3) to (1), % (4)	Monthly increase or decrease in assets other than (2) and (3)
1914					
July	604	92	75	27·65	—
August	621	125	70	31·4	−11
September	630	139	72	33·5	−7
October	641	142	75	33·85	+5
November	660	158	74	35·15	+3
December	661	147	60	31·3	+26
1915					
January	666	140	54	29·1	+18
February	670	137	49	27·75	+12
February 1914	562	86	75	28·65	
March 1915	683	135	59	28·3	+5

The big drop in 'cash at call and notice' in the return for December 1914 was probably due to several of the banks transferring non-liquid pre-war loans to the Stock Exchange from this category to some other heading in their balance sheets. The outstanding facts are:

(*a*) The increase of 'cash in hand and at the Bank of England' is now no more than enough, allowing for the increase in deposits, to make up for the decrease of 'cash at call and notice'. The ratio to deposits of cash in hand and cash at call *taken together* is now almost exactly what it was in July and less than it was in February of last year. It looks, therefore, as if the banks will not be anxious to reduce their 'cash in hand and at bank' much below the present level, so long as the shortage of bills and the restriction of Stock Exchange business cuts them off from their favourite employments of funds which must be kept liquid. The bankers have been gradually working back again to their usual ratio of liquid assets to deposits and have now reached it.

(*b*) The bearing of this on the question of how the Bank of England is to recover its control of market rates is rather complicated. If the bankers' balances at the Bank of England were to be reduced by an increase in the Exchequer balances or in any other way, the bankers would try to restore their position by a diminution of their 'other assets', probably by a diminution of their holding of trade bills or Treasury bills. In the former case there would be all the more trade bills for the discount houses, and, as the banks would prefer to have a higher proportion of their liquid assets 'at call' and less 'at bank' than is now the case, the discount houses would have no difficulty in obtaining cheap day-to-day money wherewith to carry the increased supply of bills. There would not be much effect, therefore, on the market rate for fine bills. More bills would be held by the discount market and carried with short money from the banks, and less would be held by the banks themselves: but that would be all.[1] The same point may be put thus. While the banks probably have no more 'cash in hand and at bank *plus* cash at call' than they want, they would like a larger proportion of this aggregate to come under the second head and a smaller proportion under the first head. So long as this is the case, day-to-day money is bound to be cheap. And so long as an expectation of cheap day-to-day money persists, fine bills are bound to be cheap.

(*c*) I conclude from the above that there is not much danger at present of the banks' being tempted to increase to any important extent their loans and investments or other relatively non-liquid assets. But, nevertheless, it will not be easy to raise the market rate for bills etc. And, as long as this rate is as low as it is at present, foreign bankers will keep their balances in this country at as low a level as they can. They will draw money

[1] Not quite all, of course; the temptation to the bankers to increase their loans and advances, in so far as this is a real danger, would be somewhat diminished.

94

away where they are able, to take advantage of the higher rates elsewhere, and they will refrain from sending fresh money to this market. The bearing of this on our gold position is obvious.

(*d*) If the rate for fine bills is to be increased (and this seems to be the centre of the problem) the right way to go about it would be to provide as many rivals to them as possible in the market's affections. Nothing from which income tax is automatically deducted will do. And short-dated Treasuries seem to be what is required. I suppose the discount market would just as soon, or sooner, take short Treasury bills as fine trade bills of the same date. A sufficiently large issue of such bills ought, therefore, to produce the required results—that is to say, an issue of short Treasuries *combined* with action calculated to reduce the bankers' balances (i.e. with measures having the effect of reducing the Bank of England's 'other securities', or, alternatively, of increasing permanently the public deposits).

(*e*) Since November the bankers' deposits have scarcely increased at all—from £660 million to £670 million.

(*f*) From July to September the bankers' assets, other than cash in hand and at call, fell by £18 million. Between October and February they rose by £64 million. By February 1915 they were £83 million above what they were at the same time last year. Allowing for the removal into this category of frozen loans to the Stock Exchange and for the bankers' holdings of War Loan and Treasury bills, the amount of funds employed in other ways cannot be above its normal level.

J.M.K.

12.3.15

The First War Loan of November 1914 had been aimed at attracting the money of the banks and not the surplus purchasing power of the public— a criticism made by Keynes in his *Economic Journal* article, 'The Prospects of Money, November 1914' (*JMK*, vol. XI). The loan was for £350 million, yielding approximately 4%; the special inducement to bankers was a provision that the Bank of England would make advances against the loan scrip at 1 % below bank rate. This had the effect of the banks making use of War Loan stock as call money and deprived the Government of a sum that it could depend on as a long-term loan.

The following memorandum, signed by Keynes and dated 14 May 1915, was circulated as a secret paper. On 14 May he wrote to his father that he was spending the weekend with the governor of the Bank, Lord Cunliffe, 'to hatch out something about War Loan. That's my principal preoccupation just now.'

THE BANK OF ENGLAND IN RELATION TO GOVERNMENT BORROWING AND THE NECESSITY OF A PUBLIC LOAN

The Bank of England was compelled by circumstances to take up about £180 million (net) of War Loan and Exchequer Bonds. Some part of this has been disposed of, and room has been found amongst the Bank's normal investments for some further part by the sale of pre-war securities. By this means the burden, beyond the Bank's normal investments, has been reduced by about £50 million to £130 million.

In addition to the above, there are the Cold Storage Bills [the accepting house bills taken over by the Bank of England]. Hence by the beginning of May, when the last instalments of War Loan had been paid up, something like £200 million had been borrowed from the Bank of England by the Government directly or indirectly for the purposes of the war, this being made up roughly as follows:

	£ million
Cold Storage Bills	60
War Loan and Exchequer Bonds (balance) ...	130
Sundry	10
	200

About £140 million of this was shown in additions to the other securities and to the government securities; and about £60 million had been re-borrowed by the Bank of England from the market (transactions in connection with the American exchange

Maynard Keynes 19..., Portrait by Duncan Grant

being included in this). I include in sundry any securities which may still be held on account of France, Russia, and other allied or friendly countries.

The effects of these transactions, the magnitude of which has been successfully concealed from the public by a masterly manipulation of the Bank returns during March and April, are mainly two—on the amount of what is in effect unfunded debt and on the Bank's control of the money market and the exchanges. I deal in this note with the former—the unfunded debt.

It is obvious that, due account being taken of the peculiar position of the Bank of England in the British credit system, it is absolutely out of the question for the Bank of England to lend a sum approaching £200 million for any appreciable period without endangering our whole system. Probably £50 million (in excess of the normal) is the outside figure for safety, and even this leaves no margin. It would be much better if the figure were brought down to £10 million or £20 million, except for brief periods, or in the event of our being really hard pressed for money. The capacity of the Bank to lend safely to the Government is practically limited by the extra amount which, in time of war, bankers and the Bank's other customers are prepared for long periods together to keep idle against emergencies.

This view has been unhesitatingly adopted by the authorities. They have thought it necessary to neutralise primary borrowings of some £200 million, which have been the result of accident and not of design, by throwing back part of them on to the clearing bankers and part of them on to the Government. Of the £200 million analysed on page 96, some £60 million has been re-borrowed from the market and some £110 million has been carried by holding the Exchequer balances much higher than they need be, leaving some £30 million net to be borne by the Bank of England.

But this has been accomplished by shifts—so that it is worth while to consider whether there is any possibility of a cure.

Shifts and cures together, the alternatives are four:

(1) High Exchequer balances.

(2) Borrowing by the Bank from the market.

(3) The taking over of the Cold Storage Bills by the Government.

(4) The cancellation of the War Loan and Exchequer Bonds held by the Bank.

(1) and (2) can be taken together. They differ in the following respects:

(*a*) In the first case the Treasury bear the expense, in the second case the Bank;

(*b*) The second method is the more elastic in respect of rate and period;

(*c*) The second method is the more secret, and, in virtue of a window-dressing operation by which the Bank excludes what are in effect time deposits from its statement of liabilities,[1] it appears to improve the Bank's ratio.

Difference (*a*) ought not to exist. As for (*c*) I do not think anyone takes much interest in the Bank's concocted ratio. To attach much importance to it is to fall into the same error as that of the governors of state banks abroad to whom the ratio of gold to note issue is all in all, and who then try to persuade themselves or their public that all kinds of things are gold; and as a window-dressing device it is almost as 'frail', to use a phrase of the Governor's, as the arrangement by which the Bank of France is pleased to describe loans to Russia as 'cash held abroad'. Difference (*b*) may be a real convenience. But to convert money at call into money at seven days' notice possesses very slight—except window-dressing—advantages and may easily resolve itself into paying the clearing banks interest on what could otherwise be had from them for nothing.

But both of them are open to the objection that they are

---

[1] The Bank converts current accounts into deposit accounts, and then knocks them out of its balance sheet.

essentially shifts. They are artificial and confuse the financial position. They cannot go on for ever; and the sooner they are tidied away surely the better. They represent a perpetuation of the hole-and-corner methods of finance, into which the failure of the attempt to fund at 4% has driven us.

I turn, therefore, to the alternatives which aim at cancelling the Bank's advances. Those of the Bank's advances which lend themselves most easily to this course are the cold storage bills, because the existence of these is already a matter of public knowledge.

For the Treasury to take them over would require legislation, but could be explained as a natural corollary of the policy of Treasury bills on tap. Such a step seems to be clearly advisable.

We come next to the cancellation of the Bank's War Loan. I believe that there would be much indirect advantage in any arrangement which treated the Bank's holding of War Loan as unfunded debt—which it really is—and secured the Bank against loss on it. This unfunded debt should then be discharged out of the proceeds of the next loan. (I am speaking of the essence of the proposed transaction, not of its technique.)

In any case that part of the War Loan which is held by the Bank of England is to all intents and purposes *not* funded. And to all intents and purposes the Exchequer has in hand at the present moment no funds whatever (or at the most liberal estimate some £20 million) for the prosecution of the war, in spite of its brave showing on paper. For everything which is spent, beyond the proceeds of taxation, has to be met by immediate borrowing either on the part of Treasury, or on the part of the Bank, lest the other deposits should reach a dangerous level.

The unfunded debt at the present time consists, in my opinion, if we reckon Exchequer bonds as funded, at the very least of the Treasury bills outstanding *plus* that part of the War Loan which is carried by the sums borrowed from the market by the Bank of England. I believe that the unfunded debt can safely stand at a very high figure. The limited supply of trade bills and the limited demand for Stock Exchange advances leave the banks, quite apart from the inflation of the other deposits, with large additional sums for employment in this manner. But nevertheless it would be very impolitic, for reasons which are analysed below, to endeavour to finance the war even for two months by unfunded borrowings, on the top of the existing commitments.

I now turn to the arguments for the issue at an early date of a War Loan designed to attract the public.

The Treasury bills outstanding on 8 May amounted to £154 million. Thus the unfunded debt, reckoned as I suggest above it ought to be, already exceeded £200 million on that day. And no further disbursements can be made from the Exchequer on an important scale without adding to it.

Now the usual objections to an excessive volume of unfunded debt are well known and need not be enlarged on. I do not regard them as decisive in present circumstances. If the French Government find that their public prefer the six months *Bons* to the longer termed *Obligations*, I see nothing fatal in constant additions to the oustanding issues of *Bons*.

The fundamental objection to the policy of our financing the war by Treasury bills is of a different kind. It is not that Treasury bills are unfunded—though that is an objection also—but that in existing conditions they mainly employ bankers' and money market money and do not secure directly the money of the public.

It will be worth while to give the grounds of this objection somewhat fully. The Government have borrowed from the Bank of England (as explained above) about £200 million, of which they still hold (and must continue to hold) about £110 million in their Exchequer balances. It is not practicable that they should spend any large part of this £110 million; and the net effect of borrowing from the Bank of England what the Bank of England cannot afford to lend and then salving the position by leaving the money with the Bank is merely to spoil the appearance of the Bank's return and not to increase the resources of the Treasury by a penny. This, however, applies only to the unspent £110 million. The balance of £90 million has been disbursed in excess of the receipts from taxation and from borrowing funded or unfunded. The deposits of the banks and of the money market at the Bank of England, at call and at notice together, are therefore increased by this amount. In order to arrive at the total addition to the other deposits, we have also to take account of the addition of £15 million to the Bank's reserve. Added to the £90 million, therefore, we have a total of £105 million. I will credit (hypothetically) £90 million of this to the banks and £15 million to the Bank of England's other customers.

The addition to the currency of the country outside the Bank of England (gold, silver, currency notes, bank notes) is from £60 million to £65 million. An examination of what evidence is available suggests that about £35 million of this is held by the banks, and from £25 million to £30 million by the public.

The sums left by the public with their bankers on current and deposit account, over and above what was so held at this time last year, cannot be less than £190 million.

I conclude from the above, as is shown by the following balance sheet, that the additional credit created by the joint stock banks is about £65 million. That is to say, they have lent the Treasury £65 million more than the funds released through the net diminution of their holdings of trade bills, loans to money brokers and to the Stock Exchange, and of their pre-war investments and advances to customers.

To sum up, I make out the balance sheet for 1 May 1915, as compared with the previous year, to be approximately as follows:

1. Cash position of the public[1]

	£ million
Increased deposits held with the joint stock banks	190
Increased deposits held with Bank of England by non-banking customers ...	15
Increased cash in hand held with Bank of England by non-banking customers	25
Increase	£230

[1] The term 'public' is used widely in this discussion and covers everybody except the joint stock banks.

II. Position of joint stock banks as compared with previous year

	£ million		£ million
Increased deposits from public	190	Increased deposits with Bank of England	90
		Increased cash in hand ...	35
		Loans to Government in excess of amount by which other assets have been diminished	65
			£190

III (a). The Government's war borrowings[2]

	£ million		£ million
From the Bank of England ...	130	War Loan (net)	330
From the National Debt Commissioners	17	Treasury bills...	140
From the Currency Note Fund	9	Exchequer bonds (net addition)	40
From joint stock banks and the public	344		
	£500		£500

[2] Excluding Cold Storage Bills and sundry advances from the Bank of England on account of foreign countries.

[It will be noticed that the table as here printed does not add precisely. The whole of this paper is reproduced from an uncorrected first proof which Keynes had retained. A correction may have been made later. Alternatively Keynes may have been content with a rounded addition of already considerably rounded components.]

Of this £500 million about £200 million can fairly be described as 'inflation' borrowing (namely, £130 million from Bank of England, £9 million from Currency Note Fund, and £65 million from joint stock bankers not in replacement of other assets). On the other hand £50 million of the Exchequer balances (increase of balances £110 million less £60 million against cold storage bills) ought to be credited against this, if we have regard to disbursements. The 'inflation' spending, therefore, is about £150 million up to date.

It is difficult to say how much of the £344 million taken by the banks and by the public has been taken by each. But the amount taken by the banks cannot be much less than £190 million leaving £154 million for the public—the 'public' it must be remembered including insurance companies and all persons and institutions other than the joint stock banks. This £154 million is wretchedly inadequate.

Table III (*a*) above may now be re-analysed, thus:

III (*b*). The sources of Government loans

	£ million		£ million
Exchequer balances	50	Aggregate war borrowing ...	500
National Debt Commissioners	17		
Joint stock banks in replacement of other assets	125		
The 'public'	154		
Inflation	154		
	£500		

We are now in a position to return to the question why it is essential to raise at an early date a large loan direct from the public. Of the public's increased deposits with their banks, perhaps one-sixth part is represented by new gold. The rest has been lent to the Government and spent. But from the point of view of the public it is still unspent, and even from the point of view of their banks nearly two-thirds is still unspent.

It is necessary either that the public should not spend their surplus funds at all, or that they should spend them on the only thing ultimately held against five-sixths of them, namely Government securities.

The banks having two-thirds of their new deposits in cash or with the Bank of England have individually a feeling of 'liquidity' which from the collective point of view is not justified. The public, other than joint stock bankers, have some £230 million more than they had last year in cash or at the bank. From the individual point of view this money is *unspent*; it is lying idle waiting to be spent or to be invested.

In these circumstances it is not safe to rely on these funds finding no outlet. In so far as they find an outlet, they render the position unsound and compete with the government in obtaining command over the aggregate material resources at home and abroad which are available for the uses of this country.

Just as the consuming power of the people ought to be reduced by taxation so far as is compatible with the maintenance of their productive power, so the power of the people to invest in other than Government securities or in any other form of capital outlay ought to be diminished by securing in good time for the Treasury as large a part as possible of their surplus balances.

Except to the limited extent to which bankers can dispose of assets they held before the war and replace them by government securities, the function of bankers can only be that of temporary intermediaries. They can only lend the Government what the public lend to them: and they can only lend permanently what the public lend them permanently. The public is the only ultimate source of command over the material resources of the country; and direct application to them is the only safe way of securing command over these resources, except for temporary periods and for amounts which are not too large.

The figures analysed above suggest that further direct application to the public has already been delayed too long, and is now urgently necessary.

I do not propose in this note to enter in detail into the principles which should govern the terms of the War Loan, the issue of which is urgently necessary. But there are a few governing principles which emerge from the above discussion.

The first principle is this, that the time has now come to face the facts in the matter of the rate of interest at which the British Government can fund. A gallant attempt has been made to do it at 4% and has failed. The experiment may have been worth while; but the results are certain, and it would be disastrous to allow deception to develop into self-deception. And it is merely postponing the evil day to be deterred by the effect of facing the above facts on the depreciation of other securities.

The next principle is (and I take it next because it is a corollary to the above) that, if the above facts prove only temporary, it may not cost very much to offer the public a handsome rate of interest, provided the Government retains the option of redemption at a very early date. The War Loan should be redeemable at par at the option of the Government, let us say, five or ten years from the date of issue.

The next principle, and a very important one, is that *we do not want the bankers' money*. They should not be encouraged to make applications. Their spare funds can be obtained more safely and conveniently from Treasury bills, and they have no business to be putting large sums into funded debt. On the other hand there should be an advertising campaign on a very splendid scale to induce the public to come in. The new loan should certainly not be on tap, but the lists should be open if necessary for some time, up to a month, and subscriptions should be beaten up until the required total (which need not be announced beforehand) has been obtained.

The fourth principle is that while Consols, etc., may be left to look after themselves, it would be disastrous to leave the recent War Loan to look after itself. It would be inequitable to recent subscribers and might by its effect on sentiment, which counts for a very great deal, much injure the new loan. The first War Loan, therefore, must be accepted at the value of £95 for subscriptions to the new loan.

If this course is taken, it becomes possible to provide for the cancellation of the stock held by the Bank of England. In issuing the new loan, the Treasury would take powers to issue it in exchange for or in cancellation of old War Loan at 95. They need not disclose how much falls into each category.

J. M. KEYNES

14 May 1915

This was written a month ago. The figures are, therefore, not up to date. The position has certainly become a good deal worse during the interval.

J.M.K.

9.6.15

Keynes wrote a brief note for Bradbury, 19 May 1915, setting out terms for a second War Loan—one of many such recipes being concocted in the Treasury and the Bank of England at the time. It appears solely as a single handwritten page among Bradbury's papers (T 170/71), supplementing a joint memorandum by Keynes and Hartley Withers (at this time a member of the Treasury staff), and is only reproduced here for its characteristically succinct manner in coming to grips with a large practical problem.

NOTE ON TERMS OF SECOND WAR LOAN

First War Loan to be accepted in payment of subscriptions at price of issue, and Treasury bills at a suitable discount.

Loan to be redeemable in whole or in part (pro rata) in 40 years or at the option of Government at any time after 10 years (or possibly 5 or 8 years).

Terms of issue	Yield free of tax		
	£	s	d
4½% free of tax at par =	4	10	0
5% less tax at par =	4	7	6
4¼% free of tax at par =	4	5	0
4% free of tax at 97 =	4	2	6
4% free of tax at par =	4	0	0
4½% less tax at par =	3	18	9

The yield free of tax should, I think, be not higher than £4 7s 6d or less than £4 2s 6d. 4¼% free of tax at par may be about the right rate. If a loan free of tax or the fractional 4¼ is objected to, 5% less tax at par would be extremely attractive to the ordinary investor; and with the option of early redemption not unduly burdensome to the Treasury.

The lists to be open for a month, or less at the option of Government. A patriotic campaign to beat up subscriptions, with daily announcements of results.

Amount offered not to be announced in advance. But £250 million exclusive of exchanges of first War Loan but inclusive of exchanges of Treasury bills, to be the sum in view.

Instalments not to be spread over so long a period as in the case of the first loan—another loan on the same terms to follow in three months' time.

J.M.K.

19.5.15

Of course 4% free of tax at par is the *best looking* proposal—
if the yield is enough for the response of the public to be
absolutely certain; it is not worth while to run risks.

In an accompanying letter written one day later, Keynes added:

From a letter to SIR JOHN BRADBURY, *20 May 1915*

The more I think about it, the more I like your proposal of 5%
less tax at par. After all, this is only £4 7s 6d net; and investors
who do not usually go into the gilt-edged market have got to be
attracted. In this case a fairly remote due date could be lightly
given, as the rate of interest is likely to be below 5% in some
quinquennium of the next forty years. With 5% I think the
optional date of redemption might be earlier than Withers'
ten years—say seven or eight . . .

I don't believe that the Governor's 4% tax free is good enough
for anyone but the strictly gilt-edged investor.

The second War Loan was issued 21 June 1915 for an unspecified amount
of stock at par, with interest at 4½%.

Chapter 2

THE ECONOMICS OF WAR, 1915-1916

At the end of May 1915 Asquith formed a coalition government, with Lloyd George taking over the Ministry of Munitions and Reginald McKenna replacing him as Chancellor of the Exchequer. Keynes became a member of the Treasury's No. 1 Division, which was concerned with finance, and almost immediately was assigned to go with the new Chancellor to meet the Finance Minister of Italy, the newest ally, at Nice. 'I am overwhelmed with work (and naturally much excited)', he wrote to his father, 1 June. 'As usual they have given me just 24 hours to get up and write memoranda on a more or less new subject.'

He returned exuberant from crossing the Channel in a destroyer at a speed of 35 miles an hour. The trip had been concentrated hard work; Keynes laboured for thirteen of the twenty-three hours spent at Nice. Dr Keynes wrote, 25 June, that 'Florence hears from young Birrell [Francis Birrell, a friend of Keynes who was the son of Augustine Birrell, a member of the Cabinet] that McKenna speaks extremely highly of Maynard and the work he did at Nice'.

Possibly as a consequence of the strain—or, according to a jocular letter from a colleague, of feasting from Dover to London at Treasury expense— Keynes had to undergo an emergency operation for appendicitis 12 June. Pneumonia followed ten days later. He was convalescent until the beginning of August, although each of his parents took a turn at acting as his secretary and he preceded his return to work at the Treasury by a few days visit with the Governor of the Bank. By 20 August he was in Boulogne with other British and French financial representatives to discuss the raising of a joint loan in the United States.

Since the Paris agreement in January, the Treasury had made further large advances to France and Russia in the United Kingdom and provided credits for them in North America. In July the balance of trade turned against Britain and McKenna had to report to the Cabinet that he was unable to pay the Russian account in New York. The withdrawal of labour from industry to man the army and the expenditure of allied loans within Britain on goods ordinarily sold abroad were having their effect in lowering exports, while at the same time it was impossible to reduce imports of food, munitions and raw materials needed to carry on the war.

The gold hoards of France and Russia were virtually still intact, and the Treasury determined to put them to use in securing the American loan. The argument Keynes took to the financial meeting in Boulogne appears in a note in his handwriting dated 19 August 1915, under the title, 'A Summary of the Gold Position'. After setting out the amounts of gold arranged to be held in London on behalf of allies, and Britain's claims under the Paris agreement to draw on French and Russian gold, if need be, he continued:

FROM 'A SUMMARY OF THE GOLD POSITION'

During the last two years the Bank of France have increased their stock of gold by about £40 million. They could, therefore, export £40 million without their reserve falling below what it was in 1913. A large part of the Russian gold reserve has also been built up in the last few years. Both banks could lose a large amount without being worse off than they were within very recent memory. Apart from the exigencies of the moment there are, of course, very strong reasons why it is to the interest of both France and Russia to use a part of their huge reserves and not wastefully to hoard the whole of them. Germany has probably exported approximately £30 million in spite of her very limited opportunities of making purchases abroad. Once specie payments have been suspended, the right policy—which appears to have been adopted by Germany so far as her opportunities have allowed—is to commandeer the gold, in effect, for government purposes and then *use* it. In present conditions the purchasing power of bank notes in France and Russia will depend almost entirely on the volume of them oustanding and hardly at all on the psychological effect of the gold reserve held against them. As gold no longer circulates, any premium on gold is of but slight importance. In so far as notes are hoarded, a disinclination to hoard them could do little harm, as there are few alternatives available in which to keep savings except government securities. In any case there is but little reason for thinking that a distrust of the notes would be awakened by a diminution of (say) 25 per cent of the gold reserve, but not awakened by a very great depreciation of the notes as measured by the exchanges.

J.M.K.

19.8.15

At Boulogne it was agreed that the Banks of England and France would each hold ready $200 million in gold for export to the United States and would propose that the Bank of Russia should do the same. The gold was to be exported week by week as the loan negotiations, conducted by the British, required and the proceeds of the loan were to be shared in proportion to the amounts of gold provided.

In reporting his financial embarrassment to the Cabinet McKenna had questioned the wisdom of continued recruiting when this absorption of labour was spoiling the country's ability to fulfil her obligations to her allies. The supply of recruits, however, was slackening off and Kitchener did not have the 70 divisions he had asked for; he insisted that the army must be kept at full strength. A Cabinet Committee on War Policy was appointed and throughout August interviewed ministers and generals on how to get both men and money. It appeared that Kitchener's 70 divisions could be maintained only by conscription, a move which Lloyd George and the Unionists supporting him considered inevitable, but which Asquith and like-minded Liberals resisted. Yet according to Walter Runciman, Liberal President of the Board of Trade, the number of men who could be spared from the labour force was only 840,000, less than half those said to be required.

McKenna presented his case to the committee 23 August: it was simply that Britain could not afford at the same time both to maintain an army of 70 divisions and to continue the financial support of her allies. 'One or other of the two tasks we might compass, but not both', related Lloyd George, describing McKenna's, and the Treasury's, stand in his *War Memoirs*. 'The Committee found his arguments ingenious but unconvincing . . .'

The too-ingenious arguments were Keynes's. The memorandum appears in his files as an untitled manuscript, initialled and dated 23 August 1915.

THE ALTERNATIVES

The following memorandum is directed to showing:

(I) the amount of the aggregate contributions of the United Kingdom to the Allied cause, in men, ships, subsidies and munitions, measured in terms of manpower;

(II) that the labour forces of the United Kingdom are so fully engaged in useful occupations that any considerable further diversion of them to military uses is *alternative* and not *additional* to the other means by which the United Kingdom is assisting the Allied cause.

I

(a) The army

The cost of the Army during July 1915 was	£54,250,000
The estimated cost during August is	£62,000,000
The conjectured estimate of cost during September is	£64,000,000

Thus the *daily* of the cost army may be put at £2 million. It should be added that more than half of this cost goes to the employment of civilian labour; in August, personnel and miscellaneous payments will amount to £23,500,000, and payments for clothing, stores, works, etc. to £38,500,000.

(b) The navy

Navy issues during July 1915	£19,000,000
Estimated issues in August	£20,000,000

Thus the present rate of expenditure is well in *excess* of £200 million a year.

(c) Subsidies to allies and colonies

Subsidies paid in money or kind to allies etc. up to 16 August	£124,000,000
Further payments already promised before the end of 1915	£125,000,000
	£249,000,000

It is noticeable that the subsidies required for the last 4½ months of 1915 are equal to the whole amount required during the first year of the war. The other allies, having exhausted their own manpower, are more and more dependent upon subsidies based on ours.

In addition to the above

Subsidies to the colonies up to 16 August are	£64,560,000
Promises up to the end of 1915	21,295,000
	£85,855,000

Thus the total subsidies up to the end of 1915 are £335,000,000 and from now onwards at a rate much in excess of £1 million a day.

The above subsidies are largely, in effect, subsidies in kind. Serbia, for example, has been supplied by us since May last with actual goods to the value of £5 million. A large part of the Russian orders are placed by our War Office, which is liable to the contractors, so that the above promises of money really represent promises to deliver goods.

At the Boulogne Conference M. Ribot estimated that the value of goods which he required to obtain from the United Kingdom, quite apart from his orders to the United States of America, now amounts to £4 million monthly (this has grown from an estimate which M. Ribot gave last May of £2 million monthly); and he asked for an assurance that the British Treasury would undertake to pay for these goods.

The meaning of this, which is only a small item amongst many others, and which does not represent the whole even of the French demands on us, can be illustrated thus. If instead of our supplying the French with goods to the value of £4 million monthly, *they* were to supply *us*, we could afford—reckoning the cost of an additional man at about £200 a year—to put into the field an additional army of 500,000 men.

We have undertaken to subsidise Italy at the rate of £2 million a week; if *instead* they were to subsidise us at this rate, we could afford, since we should be £4 million a week better off, an army of another 1 million men.

Summary

Thus we contribute, *in addition* to that part of our armed forces the cost of which is borne on Army Votes:

At the rate of £20 million a month for the navy representing in manpower (say) 1,000,000;

At the rate of £36 million a month for various subsidies representing in manpower (say) 1,800,000.

In making a comparison with allies, a *subtraction* must be made from the total strength of their armies corresponding to the manpower which, on their standards, our subsidies allow them to withdraw from civil life.

II

The Board of Trade's latest report as to the state of the labour market refers to the middle of July last. Mr Runciman has prepared a paper showing the numbers in each important industry (*a*) already recruited (*b*) already employed on government contracts.

In estimating on this basis the additional number which can be 'spared' from civilian employment, we have to consider:

(i) not only the number of men to be called to the 'colours', but also the additional number in civilian labour and the additional imports which would be required to support these additional men with the colours; since the labour required to clothe, feed, arm, house, train and transport a soldier is far greater than that required to clothe and feed him (in addition to his family, which goes on as usual) when a labourer;

(ii) how far the men recruited, i.e. healthy men in the prime of life, are above the average of efficiency in their trades. In so far as they are, the number which can be 'spared' must be modified accordingly;

(iii) how far the compulsory depletion of men from the less necessary industries leaves things in other respects as they were. This is the vital question.

Let us take Mr Runciman's figures of 840,000 men who could be 'spared'. The labour of these men, since they are employed, satisfies a part of the consuming power of the community. Unless this consuming power is *confiscated*, it will find an outlet elsewhere, either by drawing men from the more necessary industries into the now depleted less necessary, or by increasing civilian demands from the more necessary industries, or by increasing the purchases of imports.

It is not possible to control production without controlling consumption in an equally drastic manner. Thus it is fallacious, in estimating the number of men who can be 'spared', to take a list of industries and then pay attention to the industries not much employed on Government contracts, unless it is intended to control with perfect wisdom not only the activities but also the amount and the nature of everybody's consumption.

Such a method is not the right way of estimating the 'margin' available for recruitment.

This margin can only be measured in the following manner. *After* raising loans in U.S.A. and loans and taxation in the United Kingdom sufficient to meet our existing commitments, which is far from accomplished at present, the 'margin' is measured by

(*a*) the men now unemployed or on short time;

(*b*) the additional loans which can be raised in U.S.A. beyond those required for present commitments, i.e. the amount the allies can hope to raise there in the near future in excess of about £300 million;

(*c*) the amount by which home consumption can be reduced by loans on a scale in excess of those raised hitherto, and by new taxation.

The margin under (*a*) above is now negligible. There is no margin under (*b*) and (*c*) but the possibility already of a deficit as regards existing commitments, unless *either* we cease subsidising allies *or* confiscate private power of consumption on a scale which is quite beyond normal methods of taxation.

N.B. As to the first alternative, there is no question what the answer of the allies would be if we gave them the choice of more men or more money. As to the second alternative, it is so difficult to predict in advance how far it is feasible to carry confiscation that proposals with this object in view ought to precede proposals for an appreciable increase in our armed forces. If, for example, it were thought practicable to divert to the Treasury the whole or nearly the whole of rents and of the profits during the war of all companies or other businesses, the project of increasing our armed forces would take on quite a different complexion.

Our productive powers cannot be further reduced, unless we first resort to a very drastic reduction of the power of private persons to consume. A 'margin' cannot be obtained from any other source. Without a policy for the confiscation of private income, a considerably increased army and a continuance of subsidies to allies are *alternative*.

J.M.K.

23.8.15

This was too doctrinaire, the war policy committee decided. They would continue the attempt to maintain an army of 70 divisions, by voluntary means if possible or by some kind of compulsory service if necessary. With *The Times* and the *Daily Mail* crying for more British soldiers to fight beside their gallant allies, the conscription of men was easier to contemplate than the conscription of wealth.

At 11 p.m., 8 September 1915, Keynes wrote to his mother from his house at 3 Gower Street:

As I write, Zeppelin bombs are dropping all round, about one every minute and a half I should say, and the flashes and explosions are most terrifying. I am much more frightened than I thought I should be. Miss Chapman is sitting with me in the dining room which we have decided is safest—I don't know why. She doesn't seem in the least nervous and spends her time soothing Rex. I daresay we shall find in the morning that the bombs have not been within a mile of us; but it seems very near. I'm extremely busy at the Treasury, but am enjoying the work. Today I have been commissioned by the Chancellor to write an important memorandum, and as usual, have only a day to do it in.

On 1 September he had taken over Blackett's work as second in command to Malcolm G. Ramsay, the Assistant Secretary in charge of matters of banking, currency exchange and allied finance. (Blackett had gone to the United States as a member of Lord Reading's financial mission for raising the American loan.) The important memorandum that Keynes had to write was 'The Financial Prospects of This Financial Year', dated 9 September 1915 and circulated officially as a Cabinet paper over his signature. Lloyd George in his *War Memoirs* scathingly attacked him for the judgements expressed there. These judgements reflected the Treasury view. Keynes's paper was circulated to the Cabinet at the same time as another memorandum on the financial outlook by Sir John Bradbury to similar effect entitled 'Limits of Borrowing Abroad and At Home', together with an introductory statement by McKenna. The fact that in mentioning these 'two dismal papers' Lloyd George chose to heap his scorn on Keynes's as 'more alarming and much more jargonish' was obviously influenced by the chequered history of their relations up to 1933 when the memoirs were published.

McKenna told the Cabinet that he could see the way ahead, with the aid of familiar expedients, as far as 31 March 1916, the end of the financial year, but after that he defined the problem as one of outstaying Germany in providing for Britain's allies as well as for herself. At this time McKenna and some other members of the Cabinet—notably Runciman and Sir Edward Grey, the Foreign Secretary—certainly contemplated the possibility of defeat if the war was prolonged into 1916. 'Mr McKenna's nerve was shaken by these vaticinations of his chief adviser, Mr J. M. Keynes', Lloyd George said. Caricaturing Keynes as he appeared in the 1930s—as a 'volatile soothsayer' who 'dashed at conclusions with acrobatic ease'—he wrote that 'Mr Keynes was for the first time lifted by the Chancellor of the Exchequer into the rocking chair of a pundit, and it was thought that his very signature appended to a financial document would carry weight'.

Lloyd George added that he knew 'it was part of the campaign which the Treasury were waging against my great gun programme'. When the Lloyd George memoirs were published, Keynes protested in a letter to *The Times*, 28 November 1933, against this use of a secret document written by a civil servant (*JMK*, vol. XIX). The memorandum, however, is significant for another reason than that ascribed to it by Lloyd George; it foreshadowed McKenna's first Budget, introduced 21 September 1915, with its steeply increased income tax, Excess Profits Duty, indirect taxes on household commodities, increased postal charges, and the 'McKenna duties' on such luxury articles as automobiles and watches.

The version of the memorandum given here is that of Keynes's manuscript.

THE FINANCIAL PROSPECTS OF THIS FINANCIAL YEAR

The latest estimate of the deficiency for the present financial year, after allowing for taxation and all borrowing up to date (except the net increase in Treasury bills outstanding), is £700 million. Fresh commitments in the course of the next six months will be on the top of this. From April onwards the rate of deficit will be, if commitments to allies and other expenses go on upon their present scale, not less than £120 million a month.

This note is directed to the two questions:

I. How far is it possible to meet this deficiency from 'real resources' as distinguished from 'inflationist borrowing'.[1]

II. What would be the consequences of depending upon 'inflationist borrowing'.

I. By 'real resources' I mean

(i) that part of their current income which individuals and corporations in the United Kingdom do not spend but hand over to the Treasury in taxes and loans;

(ii) that part of the capital-goods belonging to individuals and corporations in the United Kingdom (a) which is consumable, (b) which is saleable outside the U.K., the proceeds of which they hand over to the Treasury in taxes and loans;

(iii) the proceeds of loans obtained by H.M. Government abroad.

These three categories are absolutely exhaustive, and the answer to I depends upon how much can be obtained from each of them.

(i) The course of events during the past year (generous separation allowances, war bonuses, overtime, and the keenness of competition for labour between employers) has had the effect of diverting a greater part of the income of the nation than ever before into the hands of those classes of the population which are

---

[1] The meaning attached to these expressions will appear below.

not much affected by direct taxation and are not accustomed, or likely at any time, to subscribe largely to Government loans. An enormous part of our financial margin over Germany, arising out of our greater wealth, is being absorbed at the present time, not in the expenses of war, but in allowing the great mass of the people, for reasons of humanity, sentiment, weakness or policy, to be rather more prosperous than usual. I agree with the view that, if the richer classes were to be reduced to the position of the corresponding classes in Germany, the Treasury would not obtain from them, in loans and taxation together, much more than £100 million a year in excess of what they will obtain as it is. But if the lower and lower middle classes were to be reduced to the position of the corresponding classes in Germany, the Treasury would benefit to the extent of £400 million to £500 million. Thus, with a continuance of our present methods, Germany is able to make up £500 million to £600 million a year of her financial leeway by universal economy. (I am speaking now, without any regard to questions either of policy or social justice, in order to expose with clearness what the situation is financially.) In the literal sense it is true that Germany has not increased taxation. But in effect she has increased it largely. Her system of forced depreciated currency, made possible by a position of economic isolation, acts, in conjunction with her policy of preventing an increase in wages, as an enormous tax on the working classes. Food prices in Berlin since the beginning of the war have gone up 64 per cent. There is no evidence that wages have gone up at all. Separation allowances are on a lower scale than our outdoor relief to paupers. The advantage to the government of this reduction of consumption is partly direct, and partly indirect by diverting wealth into the hands of landowners and others who are likely to subscribe heavily to War Loan.

These considerations are relevant to the amount of the contribution we can expect from (i).

We must also take account of the reduced national income due to enlistment. Our industrial reorganisation has been extra-ordinarily successful. Twenty per cent of the males employed in industry have been enlisted; but overtime, the absorption of the normal reserve of labour, and the increased employment of women have reduced the net diminution of the industrial labour of the country (men and women together) to about 6 per cent—though as we have now used our reserves, further enlistment will not easily be compensated.

Thus our income from industry is reduced by 6 per cent, and of this reduced income a higher proportion than usual is being earned and *consumed* by the working classes.

One other figure may be mentioned. Nearly one-half of our industrial population is employed, directly or indirectly, by our own and the allied governments. But nothing like one-half of the money income is being taken from the people in loans and taxation together. Hence the deficit.

(ii) The part of our national capital which can be liquidated for immediate use is but a small fraction of the total.

The wealth of the world mainly consists in buildings, railways, roads, and cultivated fields. These things must yield their return gradually.

Apart from current savings, all we can do is to consume stocks of commodities and divert the labour which would ordinarily go to making good depreciation.

This is generally recognised; but it has been maintained that we can sell a large part of our national capital to the United States. This perplexing problem can be best simplified by taking it in connection with the amount of our direct Government borrowing in the United States. If the British government is going to borrow in the United States all it can, it is useless to take account of any part of our invested capital except that part which the United States investor *will take more readily than he will take British government securities.* A large portion of our national investments have no market in the United States and could only be sold there over a long period of time and at prices below their value. On the other hand, because we own these securities and have the reputation of being a rich and trustworthy nation, our national credit is good; and American investors, therefore, will prefer to lend to us direct—against the security, as it were, of our national wealth instead of buying outright this national wealth, which is composed of real goods about the true value of which in detail the American investor is ignorant.

When, therefore, we are considering what we can sell to the United States of America over and above what we can hope to borrow from them direct, it would be foolish to take account of anything except what it is likely they would prefer to buy outright, rather than take British government securities.

It can be safely said that this includes no important item except our gold and our holdings of American and certain Canadian securities; though perhaps it ought to be added that, if we were to be quite regardless of the future, we might be able to sell to the Americans a part of our mercantile marine.

(iii) The amount we can hope to borrow from the United States of America direct it is obviously impossible to predict with accuracy now. We ought to be able to obtain by negotiation a large part of the floating funds of Wall Street. But this does not carry us very far. It is necessary to tap the resources of the country districts and of the West. The investor of these parts has never yet put his money in a foreign security and seldom in anything which he cannot touch and see, if he likes. The demand for new capital in his own vicinity is insatiable, and for loans from his bank on good local security he is accustomed to pay anything up to 8 per cent. In the special circumstances of the time we may hope for some of his money, but it will be a matter of extreme difficulty to get a great deal. If we offer him 5 to 6 per cent he may not be attracted; if we offer him 6 to 9 per cent he will be told we are bankrupt.

It would be fallacious to believe that the trade balance in

America's favour will lead automatically to their investing this balance abroad. The balance in the first instance provides individual Americans with 'money'; this may stimulate a strong tendency to expansion and investment at home, although the real goods which are required for this expansion have been shipped abroad. Investment *ought* to follow the goods; but the complexity of the financial machine allows the goods to precede the investment, and then provides an interval of time in which a different kind of compensation may come into play. The tendency to expansion in the United States of America itself will send up prices there and, in the presumed absence of sufficient investment by Americans abroad, we shall become unable to go on buying there.

Logically an expansion of exports can, apart from an increase in imports, have either of two effects; it may be compensated either by corresponding foreign investment or by a corresponding slump of exports subsequently. That is to say, they *may* lend us money, but equally we *may* be unable to go on buying. There is nothing in the nature of things to compel the former alternative. Blind economic forces are no more for us than they are against us. We have to depend upon our own policy and the temper of the American investor.

To make a balance sheet on the basis of these general considerations and of other available information necessarily involves guesswork.

To obtain, out of the proceeds of (i) and (ii*a*), loans actually paid up before the end of the financial year (including the excess of Treasury bills then outstanding over what was outstanding at the end of the previous year), without the assistance of inflationist devices and improper temporary borrowing from banks, as much as £450 million would be an astonishing achievement. It would be sanguine to rely on more than £350 million.

The maximum for this period under (ii*b*) I should put at £90 million being made up of £50 million gold and £40 million securities, a large part of those of the most easily realisable securities which are in sensitive hands having been already disposed of.

The Joint Allied Loan under (ii) is the most incalculable element. If as much as £240 million is paid up within the next six months, the American mission will have done wonders. Allowing for the French and Russian shares of this, we should obtain £80 million.

These figures, which are all very sanguine, add up to £620 million. To take £500 million would be more in accordance with sound estimating.

We shall presumably depend for the balance of £80 million to £200 million, required to make up £700 million, on methods of 'inflationism'. We ought to be able to do this without producing a catastrophe in the current financial year, provided peace puts us in a position to cancel this inflationism immediately afterwards. Otherwise the expenditure of the succeeding months will rapidly render our difficulties insupportable. This leads us to the meaning of 'inflationism' and the consequences of depending upon it.

II. Methods of 'inflationism' all amount in the end to increasing the stock of fiduciary money, including in the term 'money' bank balances as well as notes.

In this country inflation can take place in two ways:

(1) If the joint stock bankers, relying on the provision by which they can obtain currency notes, lend the Government funds in excess of those with which their customers will permanently entrust them.

(2) If the Bank of England pays the Government's obligations by crediting the payee or the payee's bankers with a book-credit.

No harm is done by inflation so long as the persons, into whose hands the increased stock of money comes, make no attempt to spend it. There is likely to be an appreciable interval between the creation of this money and the spending of it. There would be no temptation to inflate if the lame foot of punishment did not lag behind. Cautiously used, therefore, inflationism may be a useful temporary measure in anticipation of a loan. If when the money comes to be spent it is spent on a government loan, the proceeds of the loan can be used to cancel the inflationism and so regularise the situation. Previous to the issue of the second War Loan there was a large element of inflationism, not far short of £200 million, in this country. A considerable part of the proceeds of the new War Loan have gone towards liquidating this. But steps were only just taken in time, and our recent difficulties with the exchanges are partly traceable to the inflationist methods of the spring and early summer.

The method of temporary inflationism, periodically liquidated by loans, has been pursued with great skill by Germany. But the indications now are that this method will fail her in the near future; and Germany may be expected this winter to pass on to the next financial stage, that of dependence on permanent inflation. The effects of this are briefly discussed below.

France and Italy (the case of Russia must be differentiated— the difficulty she experiences in financing imports is mainly due to other obvious causes) have already passed on to an inflationist basis; if they had not an ally, Great Britain, who comes to their rescue, they would be unable to finance their imports of munitions and food and would be compelled to modify profoundly their methods of warfare.

Our own expenditure on its present scale we are nearly rich enough to support. It is the inflationism, to which the scale of their expenditure has driven our allies, which is breaking our back and bringing us to similar courses.

What would be the probable consequences of inflationist finance this winter on Germany and on Great Britain respectively?

Germany's position of economic isolation, and of comparative economic self-sufficiency, provides her with an automatic safeguard. If the German government lives on banknotes, they place on their people a burden which will ultimately become insupportable, but they do not sow the seeds of an early catastrophe. As long as there are goods and labour in the country the government can buy them with banknotes; and if the people try to spend the notes, an increase in their real consumption is immediately checked by a corresponding rise of prices. Germany is handcuffed to the constable. She cannot outrun him. At every stage she is compelled, whether she likes it or not (apart from the danger of using up stocks of certain commodities, to which her government is alive) to suit her coat to her cloth. Economic exhaustion, therefore, which is a slow and gradual thing, must precede financial catastrophe.

If this country could do without substantial imports and if we ceased subsidising allies, our position would be comparable to Germany's. As it is, the effect of inflation would be quite different and much more disastrous. The attempt to spend the inflationist supplies of cash must soon lead to this fiduciary money reaching the hands of would-be importers. They try to turn it into gold or foreign exchange. There is not enough gold or foreign exchange to satisfy them. Specie payment, that is to say, is expended and it is impossible to buy exchange. Food-importers go out of business and foreign munition contracts must be cancelled. The prices of bread and other imported products rise to an unlimited extent.

At least this is what would happen if we persevered with the supposed policy to the bitter end. And this would hardly happen. For before the final catastrophe was reached it would be obvious to everyone (or almost everyone) where the policy was leading us, and presumably we should abandon it.

The alternatives presented to us are, therefore, alternatives of degree. If by flinging out our resources lavishly we could be sure of finishing the war early next spring, I estimate that they might be about equal to our needs. If, on the other hand, it would be oversanguine to anticipate this, it must be considered whether it is more desirable to average our expenditure, or to be lavish until about next January, and then, having regard to the near future, to curtail rigorously and tell our allies that for the future they must look to themselves.

It is certain that our present scale of expenditure is only possible as a violent temporary spurt to be followed by a strong reaction, that the limitations of our resources are in sight, and that, in the case of any expenditure, we must consider not only, as heretofore, whether it would be useful, but also whether we can afford it.

J.M.K.

9.9.15

Keynes defined the meaning of inflation in more detail in a memorandum the only copy of which was preserved with Sir John Bradbury's papers (T 170/73). It is initialled by Keynes and dated 15 September 1915. In the same file is Bradbury's similar version of the results of inflation.

THE MEANING OF INFLATION

I. In a modern community most payments are made, not in gold or in kind, but with what are, in effect, *promises* to pay. These 'promises to pay' whether in the form of bank notes or bank balances, I shall call 'bank-money'.

II. From motives of prudence and convenience, individuals keep a certain proportion of their resources in the form of bank-money. On the average of the whole community the amount of this is, in normal times, a fairly constant total. Up to the amount of this total it is possible to keep 'promises to pay' in circulation, without running a risk of their materialising in 'demands to pay'.

When the bank-money is put into circulation, valuable goods are received in exchange for it. These valuable goods, or rather the titles to them, constitute the community's banking capital.

III. In time of war the government can absorb a considerable part of this capital, by inducing bankers to take Treasury bills or War Loan in place of such part of this banking capital as they are able to withdraw from its normal employment of financing private trade. The government can obtain further funds by substituting 'promises to pay' for that part of the circulation which still consists of gold. And lastly, owing to the fact that in time of war individuals may be inclined to keep a rather larger proportion of their resources than usual lying idle (idle so far as the individuals are concerned) in the form of bank-money, the government can, through the agency of the banks or otherwise, somewhat increase the volume of 'promises to pay' in circulation without running much risk.

During the early stages of a war, therefore, bank-money—especially in such a country as England where the volume of it normally outstanding is very large—is an extremely valuable adjunct to government finance, and can be used to supplement largely the funds obtained by taxes and loans direct from the public.

The ease and safety with which this operation can be conducted at the start is apt to induce the belief that it can be employed to an unlimited extent. And the fact that this belief can be acted on without instantaneous punishment renders it dangerous.

iv. It is clear from the above that the volume of bank-money, the value of which the government can divert to its own uses, is *limited*. When a government or a state bank put into circulation a greater volume of bank-money than is represented by the proportion of their resources which individuals choose to keep in this form, they are said to *inflate* the currency.

v. When the currency is thus inflated, certain individuals find themselves with an increased volume of bank-money in their possession, without *either* other individuals finding themselves with less *or* an increase in the amount of commodities to be bought. That is to say, on the average of the whole community, the amount of purchasing power in the form of money is increased without any increase in the amount of things to buy.

By hypothesis the community is not disposed to leave this

increased purchasing power lying idle at its banks or in its pockets. The precise consequences of the inflation depend upon the ways in which the habits and opportunities of the community lead them to employ it.

A. The money may be returned to the government in taxes or in loans from its own people and from foreigners into whose hands the course of trade carries it. In so far as this is the case, no harm has been done, provided the government do not again part with the money thus recovered. The inflation has been temporary, and has now ceased to exist. But the extent to which it is prudent to rely upon such a cure partly depends upon what *class* of the community happens to get hold of most of the increase. In so far as the *money*-earnings of the working class are increased, it is probable that the proportion which they lend to the government will be small, and that the proportion which they expend will be large.

B. If the money is not returned to the government, it will be spent, sooner or later, on consumable commodities. People will be prepared to buy more than before and to pay higher prices for what they buy.

(*a*) If they buy *more* than before—and if we assume, as we certainly must assume in the case of the United Kingdom, that the industrial capacity of the country is being fully employed and that the channels of international trade are not closed—the effect upon our balance of trade is almost immediate. Our imports are increased and our surplus available for export is diminished.

(*b*) If they find themselves compelled to pay higher prices, there is a concealed tax—provided the government is able to avoid having itself also to pay higher prices (and in any case the date at which the government is compelled to pay such prices may lag behind). For the government's promises to pay, in exchange for which it has obtained goods, turn out to be not so valuable as they were thought to be when they were accepted. In a country, however, which depends upon international trade, the influence of the inflation in the direction of higher prices is in part just as bad as its influence in the direction of increased consumption; for we have to pay higher prices over the whole of our imports and not only over the increase in them. If an increase of 10 per cent in the demand for meat raises the price of the imported supply by 25 per cent, we pay the increased 25 per cent over the whole amount. Our imported meat, instead of costing us 100, rises, not to $112\frac{1}{2}$, but to $137\frac{1}{2}$.

The effect of inflation, therefore—and in present conditions the effect will not be far behind the cause in point of time—must necessarily be to increase our adverse balance of trade. But foreigners are under no obligation to accept our bank-money in payment. The 'promises to pay' materialise into 'demands to pay', which cannot be met. When this happens in Brazil, Brazil is said to be bankrupt.

J.M.K.

15.9.15

'I doubt if I've ever worked harder than during the last two weeks, but I'm wonderfully well all the same', Keynes wrote to his father, who copied the letter into his diary 18 September.

> The work has been as interesting as it could be. I've written three major memoranda, one of which has been circulated to the Cabinet, and about a dozen minor ones on all kinds of subjects, as well as helping Ramsay with the Vote of Credit and the Budget, and keeping going with routine, and the *Economic Journal* in the evenings. I spent most of Wednesday [15 September] in the H. of C. at the Vote of Credit debate. The P.M. was splendid. (Asquith asked for £250 million in the fourth Vote of Credit of that year and the seventh since the beginning of the war. He brushed over some window-dressing by the Treasury in a matter of repayments to the Bank of England with a call for individual sacrifice to the common cause, while his opponents used the occasion to criticise the government's use of manpower.)

The Russian reaction to the Boulogne proposals for shipping gold to America was to ask for the creation of additional credits in London in return. This request involved a serious misunderstanding of the situation: Russia's use of British credits to finance purchases in America was already straining Britain's capacity to finance her own war effort, and Russian insistence that the use of Russian gold must be matched by additional British credits to Russia would, if yielded to, leave Britain's dangerous position unrelieved.

'Regard being had to the existing economic and political conditions of the allied countries,' wrote Sir John Bradbury, 16 September 1915 (T 170/73), 'it is probably inevitable that the creation of credits on behalf of our allies should be continued until an actual breakdown takes place, but it is of the greatest importance to postpone that breakdown, which I regard as inevitable, as long as possible in the hope that it may be forestalled by the breakdown, which for rather different reasons, is equally inevitable in the case of Germany.'

Bradbury was primarily concerned with the necessity of confining the credits that were provided to the availability of the goods that could actually be supplied, so as to avoid inflationary disorganisation of the internal and external trade of the British economy. He noted that there was already an arrangement by which Russian munitions orders in America were placed through the British War Office. He recommended a similar scheme of supervision for all purchases paid for out of British credits to eliminate wasteful competition between allies.

At present (apart from the Russian munition orders) we have no control over, or even knowledge of, the manner in which the allies are spending their credits. The present rate of expenditure by Russia is at the least double the amount required for the things we know about, and I am not without suspicion that there may be some connection between the mysterious disappearance of a large part of these credits and the recent improvement and present extraordinary steadiness of the Russian exchange.

Keynes was given the responsibility for working out these problems— which were largely political—when the Russian financial representatives came to London. In preparation he wrote a long 'Note on the Finances of Russia', dated 18 September 1915. In this paper he first discussed monetary and price developments within Russia and then turned to the influence that this internal financial situation might be expected to have upon the country's external finance and exchange position. (M. Bark was the Russian finance minister of the day; Count Sergius Witte was a great financial administrator of the previous generation.)

FROM 'NOTE ON THE FINANCE OF RUSSIA'

... On the whole, then, I see no reason why in the near future Russia should experience any special difficulty in financing from internal resources all her internal expenditure. She is in at least as sound a position as anybody else. She may have to pay the penalty some day; but we shall all have to do that.

Before we pass from this aspect of the general problem, there are some psychological considerations which must be regarded.

All the indications (M. Bark's actions and speeches, Mr O'Beirne's memoranda [O'Beirne was a member of the British Embassy staff in Petrograd], and the impression gained from conversation with M. Feodossief at Paris) go to show that M. Bark himself is a strong anti-inflationist, that he has done and will do all he can to keep the volume of bank notes down to a minimum, and that he is unduly nervous on this score rather than the opposite. This is not to be wondered at, when it is remembered that Russia was on an inflationist basis and suffered acutely for forty years before M. Witte reorganised her currency and that M. Bark was brought up as a banker during this period.

His critics on the other hand hold the view that the volume of notes issued does not much matter, so long as a strong reserve (in gold and foreign credits) is held against them. They would not criticise him for inflating the currency, but they would criticise him for anything which weakened the reserve.

The existence of this theory as to the reserve (M. Bark is probably much too sensible to share it himself, but his view is not yet clear) causes the problem of internal finance to react upon that of external finance. It is this that makes M. Bark costive with his gold and causes him to ask for £100 million credit in London, not for use but for reserve. If he is to go back free to expand his note issue, to such an extent as his judgement allows and his necessities demand, without the expectation of criticism, he must, if possible, so arrange his external finance as to increase rather than diminish the Bank of Russia's nominal reserve.

But there is a further question, not altogether disconnected with the above, to which M. Bark's critics also direct attention, namely that of the exchanges. His position in this respect deserves separate treatment.

v. *The exchanges*

The following is an extract from a very recent memorandum by Mr Lindley of the Petrograd embassy:

M. Bark's views on the rate of exchange have been much criticised. This question is a burning one now in Russia, and there are competent outside judges who do not share M. Bark's opinion as to the reason for the fall and violent fluctuations in the price of the rouble. They say that the excess of imports over exports has been more than paid for by money raised abroad and that the real balance of trade has been in Russia's favour this year. These critics declare that the unsatisfactory state of the exchanges is due mainly, if not entirely, to the unskilful handling by M. Bark of the Russian government credit balances abroad. He is said to refuse exchange without cause, sometimes for comparatively small sums, to merchants who have been led to expect it, and that these are then forced to go into the open market and buy sterling at whatever rate sellers choose to demand.

The result is a sudden depression of the rouble, followed in a few days by a sudden rise when M. Bark consents to provide exchange . . . It will be seen that M. Bark's position is not an enviable one. He is probably the most generally criticised man in Russia just now, and it is freely stated that he would have been replaced before this had it been possible to find anyone willing to take over the finances in the condition in which he has placed them.

The critics go on to ascribe such rise of internal prices as has taken place in Russia, not to the volume of notes in circulation (to which they have no objection) but to the state of the exchanges.

The above criticisms are very ill-founded. The published adverse trade balance for 1914 was R. 140 [at that time, roughly £14 million], and for the first six months of 1915 R. 180 [roughly £18 million]. To this must be added interest payments and the large withdrawal of capital from Russia represented by the running off of commercial bills which, in the absence of new trade, are not renewed. M. Bark, although he has sold some commercial exchange and may have adopted a vacillating policy in doing this, has not been able to spare enough to make the account balance.

We have no information as to what proportion of the assistance afforded him in this country has been used so far for supporting exchange and what proportion for Russian government payments. But it seems plain that the urgency of M. Bark's recent demand for a further £30 million, over and above what is required for payments in America, must be chiefly dictated by the desire to be in a position to come heavily to the support of exchange in the future. It is not likely that payments for goods to be exported from this country on Russian government account in the near future can come to nearly as much as this. If M. Bark could bring exchange down 20 points, it might do a great deal to re-establish his authority.

In treating of the Russian exchange, it is necessary to recognise that the opening of the Dardanelles is, after the initial sentimental improvement, as likely to raise the exchange as to lower it. The inflow of urgently required imports may exceed the outflow of exports, especially as the latter are, on the whole, more bulky than the former. Mr O'Beirne expressed this view in conversation with M. Bark, as long ago as last April; and M. Bark concurred in it.

So long, however, as the Dardanelles are closed and the present physical limitation to the volume of imports continues, it might not be very expensive to come to the rescue of exchange.

VI. *Conclusions*

I surmise, therefore, that M. Bark will have two distinct objects:

(i) To provide for Russian government disbursements abroad.

(ii) To revive his prestige in Russia, for dealing with the internal financial situation, by returning from London (*a*) with a sufficient surplus, over and above (i) to enable him to support exchange effectively;

and (*b*) with the nominal reserves of the Bank of Russia as far as possible unimpaired.

We have an interest in (ii) as well as in (i), because, so far as one can judge from outside, M. Bark's financial management has been better than his critics allow, and the internal financial situation is as sound as one can expect.

At present rates Russian requirements under heading (i) ought not to exceed £150 million a *year*, including United States of America. Dealing at present only with (i), I suggest that M. Bark's reasonable demands up to 31 March next would be amply covered by the following, which roughly agrees with the calculation, made above on the basis of his budget statement, as to what his external requirements would be:

1. The £25 million provisionally promised in August pending the conference, of which more than half is still in hand and which M. Bark only began to draw on 31 August, to be confirmed.

2. The £30 million provisionally promised this month, all of which is in hand, to be confirmed.

3. A further £20 million to be granted on similar conditions.

4. A sum of £10 million to £15 million to be furnished by the French government in Paris, for the purpose of meeting Russian government coupons in French hands. (The amount suggested as being required for this purpose is a guess.)

These sums should be granted on the following conditions:

1. They shall be used only for direct government disbursements and not for the support of exchange.

2. They shall cover Russian government disbursements in United States of America as well as elsewhere, and orders in United States of America placed through our War Office, which amount up to 31 March next to about £26 million, shall be a first charge against them. Further, no new orders shall be placed in United States of America except through our War Office.

3. They shall be contingent on the arrangement proposed under (ii*a*) below.

Turning to (ii*a*) I suggest that the Bank of Russia should undertake to set up a credit of £30 million at the Bank of England immediately by shipping gold to that amount. This credit should then be used by the Bank of Russia for the support of exchange. Incidentally this would provide the Bank of Russia with funds in Russia to an equivalent extent.

As regards (ii*b*), the nominal reserve of the Bank of Russia would not be diminished at first, as the credit at the Bank of England would replace the gold; but it would dwindle as the credit is drawn on.

If M. Bark lays great stress on a further credit, not to be drawn on, as a paper support for his note issue, something could probably be devised, preferably in conjunction with the Bank of France. But such an arrangement is *prima facie* undesirable.

J.M.K.

18.9.15

'I'm desperately busy as the brunt of Russian negotiations has fallen on me', Keynes wrote to his mother 30 September. 'I had to do 12¾ hours at a stretch.'

The agreement between the two governments, signed 30 September 1915, provided for the shipment of Russian gold for the support of the American loan, and defined and limited the purposes for which credits to Russia would be spent, including the buying of exchange. An annexe to the agreement set out a procedure whereby all Russian purchases made on British credit would first be examined and approved by Russian and British representatives in London.

'Maynard rather oppressed with his work at the Treasury. He seems to think now in millions', Dr Keynes observed 3 October.

While the agreement with the Russians was an important beginning, the Treasury's troubles with control over allied borrowing remained. Keynes wrote the following confidential paper, 15 October 1915, which was printed for the Cabinet carrying his initials.

EXPENDITURE OF ADVANCES TO ALLIES WITHIN AND WITHOUT THE UNITED KINGDOM

No accurate figures exist of the extent to which British government subsidies to allies and to the dominions are expended on payments within the United Kingdom.

If, however, it were possible to make a sharp distinction between funds so expended and those spent outside the United Kingdom, the distinction would not be a valuable one. The general nature of the purposes for which payments are made by the allies and the dominions within the United Kingdom are sufficiently known for it to be certain that by far the greater part of them operate as much in diminution of our external resources, compared with ordinary times, as if the sums were actually expended abroad. These main purposes are—

1. The purchase of raw materials, such as wool, copper, and rubber, of which this country is the *entrepôt*.

2. The purchase of munitions and other military stores, our production of which is at its maximum, so that the fulfilment of allied orders is liable to cause a diversion of other orders abroad.

3. The purchase of coal, which would otherwise be exported, and so diminish the unfavourable balance of trade against us.

4. The sale of exchange to merchants and other persons in the allied countries, with the effect that these countries can discharge their liabilities here without sending to us their normal volume of exports, and that we have to buy these goods elsewhere and pay for them.

Certain available statistics in the case of the allies are given below.

France

M. Ribot estimated his requirements for payments in the United Kingdom at £2 million a month last April, and at £4 million a month last August. 'Payments in' the United Kingdom are not the same thing as 'goods produced within' the United Kingdom.

Up to the end of August the French Government had purchased in the United Kingdom through the Commission Internationale de Ravitaillement £27,500,000, but they had also placed considerable orders in Paris which required private firms to buy from this country under licence large amounts which are not included in the above.

The published trade figures for the first nine months of the year show:

	1914	1915
Exports and re-exports to France	26,025,000	60,769,000
Imports from France	30,809,000	24,194,000

Thus the trade balance for nine months has gone against France as compared with 1914 to the extent of £41,359,000. This is almost exactly equal to the amount lent by this country to the French government during the same period, namely, £40 million. Thus our increased exports to France flatter our trade returns, without increasing in the least our resources.

Russia

Direct Government purchases in the United Kingdom through the Commission Internationale de Ravitaillement amounted up to the end of August to £11 million. Purchases under licence are additional to this. As explosives, etc., are proportionately larger than in the case of France the trade returns are not useful. But it is certain that the bulk of our advances to Russia, that is to say, at least nine-tenths, has been utilised by them either for selling exchange on London, or for purchasing goods produced outside the United Kingdom.

Belgium

Direct purchases in the United Kingdom through the Commission Internationale de Ravitaillement amounted up to the end of August to £8 million. In the case of Belgium from one-third to one-half of our advances would appear to be nominally expended in the United Kingdom.

Serbia

A large part of the Serbian orders are fulfilled out of army stocks. No useful estimate can be formed of the proportion of their purchases which come ultimately from abroad.

Italy

Here again there are no figures of any value. But there is little doubt that the Italian government are employing by far the greater part of our advances to them outside this country and for the selling of exchange. During July and August (nine weeks) the war cost Italy about £25 million, or at a weekly rate of £2,800,000. Our allowance to Italy is at a weekly rate of £2 million. This is drawn irregularly, however—£9,880,000 in July and August together, and £10,560,000 in September. As we are paying the greater part of the war expenses of Italy, it is clear that a high proportion of our subsidy must be expended elsewhere than in the United Kingdom.

In the present industrial condition of the United Kingdom the distinction between purchases abroad and purchases at home is becoming less and less important. An additional purchase at home is only a relief to our trade position, as compared with a corresponding purchase abroad, if the production of the commodity at home takes the place of an unnecessary or unessential piece of production or if it employs persons or machinery which would otherwise be unemployed. The commodities, which our allies want to buy and which fall under the second heading, are of very small importance. Perhaps cotton goods could be held to come under this category. I cannot specify any other important commodity which falls under it.

J.M.K.

15 October 1915

'I've been experiencing one of the stiffest weeks yet . . .' Keynes wrote his parents 15 October, the day he completed the above. 'On Wednesday I was sent for by Balfour [then First Lord of the Admiralty] for a general discourse, and I am to spend the week-end with the Prime Minister.' At a Cabinet meeting on 17 October Balfour, who previously had taken a half-way position on the compulsory service debate which was continuing, tabled a note setting forth the Treasury's arguments against more recruiting.

Keynes took the Treasury's anxieties week-ending. The first draft of the following note, dated 17 October 1915, was written on letter paper engraved 'The Wharf, Sutton Courtney, Berks.', Asquith's country home. Keynes became a frequent visitor at The Wharf, and a particular favourite of Margot Asquith.

THE ADVERSE BALANCE TO BE MET ABROAD

The following figures refer to the period 13 October 1915 to 31 March 1916. An estimate for the following six months namely April to October 1916 can only be given on the basis of the above. With few exceptions there are no figures on which to base an independent estimate of the more remote period. There is no present reason, however, to anticipate that any of the payments in the earlier period will fall off in the latter period.

13 October 1915 to 31 March 1916

	£ million
Existing British Government contracts in United States and Canada	63
Other disbursements by the British War Office and Admiralty abroad (France, Malta and Alexandria)...	15
Loans to allies	246
Loans to dominions	36
Adverse balance on non-Government account, *net* ...	40
Total £400	

The adverse balance on non-Government account is *net*, and is arrived at by setting off against the adverse trade balance our estimated receipts from abroad on account of interest, freights, services etc.

(In calculating the adverse trade balance the Board of Trade returns are taken as the basis. In these returns practically the whole of our exports to allies and to the dominions are reckoned as exports. But such of these exports as are paid for by loans to allies do not enable us to meet the cost of the imports. Explanation, if required.

The fact that such exports have been already included in diminution of the adverse trade balance is the reason why the whole amount of the loans to allies and dominions, whether expended in this country or out of it, is added in to the balance sheet. If, let us say, £40 million of the £240 million loans to the allies is spent in the United Kingdom, this has been already allowed for; since this £40 million must figure as an export and has been counted in diminution of the adverse trade balance. In other words if we were to take off from the loans to the allies that part spent in this country, we should have to add on a similar amount to the adverse trade balance, with the result that the total of the adverse balance to be met abroad would be the same.)

Resources from which to meet the adverse trade balance

	£
Treasury balances in United States on 13 October	2,000,000
British share of American loan less interest	45,500,000
Portion of French share of American loan to be handed to us towards Russian commitments	9,100,000
Russian gold	20,000,000
British gold from Bank of England and joint stock banks under an arrangement already made	40,000,000
	£116,600,000

This is the whole of the resources already secured. We may, however, reasonably anticipate in addition:

	£
Sale of securities at £2 million a week	48,000,000
Gold exports on private account at £1 million a week *net*	24,000,000
Our share of new loan in U.S.A. before 31 March	75,000,000
	£147,000,000
	116,600,000
	£263,600,000

This leaves us with a resultant deficit on foreign account up to 31 March 1915 of £136,400,000.

At a pinch and by reducing our gold reserve to a minimum we could export a further	£50 million in gold
By a very high bank rate we could call in our banking capital from various parts of the world before 31 March to a further amount of (say)	20 million
A Canadian loan might yield before 31 March	10 million
	£80 million

The deficit is thus reduced to £56,400,000.

By various devices, for short periods and on unfavourable terms we might perhaps raise £40 million temporary bank-money from American bankers and the American money market against the security of our American bonds. ^{Very doubt}

For the remaining £16,400,000 we must trust to the Russians being unable to spend the whole of their loan subject to the conditions we have prescribed.

With skill and luck, therefore, we can get through to 31 March. How do we open the next financial year?

On the one hand, unless we change our policy, our expenses will be undiminished.

On the other, we shall have overdrawn in U.S.A. up to £40 million; we shall have virtually no gold; and we shall have lost the greater part of our better class American bonds.

It would be foolish to assert that we have any reasonable security of getting through the six months April–October 1916 without a catastrophe.

We shall have by then £20 million more Russian gold, and by throwing in our watch chains we can find £20 million more British gold. We might sell £50 million more securities. Total assets £90 million against liabilities £400 million. Who believes that in addition to buying back securities from us at the rate of £100 million a year, North America will also lend to us at the rate of £600 million?

The Americans would have to lend us the *whole* of their annual savings and refrain from building a single house or railroad and from every other form of capital expenditure within their own country. The more prosperous they feel, the less likely are they to do this. The actual course of events is likely to be complicated by a prodigious rise of prices.

There are two alternatives: (1) that the contractors will cease to be able to deliver the goods to us, (2) that we shall be unable to pay for them. I should anticipate partly the one and partly the other.

The difference between extravagance and unsound finance at home on the one hand and economy and sound finance on the other shows itself in the doubtful item 'Adverse balance on non-Government account' on page [138].

If we depend for our home finance on loans from the Bank of England and sales of Treasury bills to the joint stock banks—inflation that is to say—this figure may be much increased.

By drastic taxation and successful internal loans it may be much diminished.

Keynes supplied some notes for the prime minister who called for individual as well as government economy in a speech to the House (2 November 1915). He also collaborated with his mother, a member of the Cambridge local savings committee, on the wording of an appeal to citizens to exercise thrift in their homes. This was published by the Cambridge War Thrift Committee in November 1915.

AN URGENT APPEAL

The war in its later stages will be largely a financial struggle. One of Germany's aims is to ruin us financially, and her statesmen reckon upon the supposed inability of this country to exercise the virtues of thrift and economy which have long been practised in Germany.

The following facts are of vital importance. The expenditure of the Government is approaching £5 million a day. Next year the total expenditure will probably exceed £1,800 million, which, the taxation at its present level, would involve a deficit of over £1,400 million.

The Financial Secretary to the Treasury has stated that this gigantic sum must be drawn *almost entirely* from the pockets of the nation in the form of tax or of loan. The annual national income is normally about £2,400 million, of which £400 million is usually saved. Now instead of saving £400 million we are asked to save and *lend to the Government* or pay in additional taxes £1,400 million a year, leaving £1,000 million instead of £2,000 million to be expended by private individuals and public bodies, i.e. the nation as a whole is asked *to save half of what it usually spends.*

Though very many families cannot possibly save to this extent, yet every family should put by as much as possible, for *no saving is too small to be neglected.*

The *only true* saving at the present time consists *in reducing* our demands for *goods and services.* No borrowing or financial manipulations can meet the case. Such operations merely tend to raise prices.

We must therefore consume less and produce more. Our gardens, like our fields and our factories, must be made more productive. We should spend less on food, drink and tobacco. We must burn less fuel, buy less clothing and household stuff, travel less, keep fewer servants, spend less on amusements. We must give up motoring or motor-cycling for pleasure, and all other extravagant forms of sport. We must, in fact, be content with the necessaries of life.

We need have little fear of causing unemployment. Increasing demands will inevitably be made during the coming months for workers, both male and female, for national ends.

If the allies are to win this war the money *must* be raised 'in the form of tax or of loan'. Motives of self-interest alone, therefore, prompt us to make the effort; for, if the allies do *not* win, most assuredly shall we suffer still more seriously in pocket.

The suspension of gold payments was again suggested as a possible solution to the Treasury's difficulties. Keynes wrote once more against this and other such expedients in a note, the only copy of which was kept as an initialled typescript in Sir John Bradbury's files (T 170/73), with the date 6 November 1915.

A NOTE ON 'SUSPENSION OF SPECIE PAYMENTS' AND OTHER METHODS OF RESTRICTING GOLD EXPORT

A suspension of specie payments by the Bank of England or any other form of limitation on the export of gold would neither diminish the amount of our debts nor enable us to discharge them. It would only allow a discrimination as to which of our debts we chose to meet and which to repudiate. And the extent to which it would allow even this, as is shown below, would be limited.

I. *Methods*

Suspension

In present-day conditions in this country a literal suspension of specie payments by the Bank of England would only be useful after other expedients had been exhausted, and might never prove to be necessary. It is a measure designed to meet the danger of an internal, not of an external, drain. If there were to be a distrust of paper currency within the country and a desire to hoard gold, it might be necessary to absolve the Bank of England from the obligation to cash her notes in gold. But there is no sign of this. Further, such a policy would allow the joint stock banks to export *their* gold freely to what destinations they those. 'Suspension of Specie Payments' has in the public ear, both at home and abroad, a disastrous sound. Our credit depends on words as well as facts. 'Suspension' would involve the maximum of discredit and there are alternative measures which may procure substantially the same result, while avoiding the hated name.

There is only one likely contingency against which suspension would be useful—an increase in the practice of earmarking gold in London on foreign account. Several of the dependencies—India, the Straits Settlements, Egypt and the Canadian banks—employ this method. Two foreign countries—the Argentine on a considerable scale and Switzerland so far on a small scale—have adopted it lately. No limitation of the right to export would strike at this practice; and an increase in the difficulties of export would tend to stimulate its further adoption. The Bank of England could refuse to earmark gold within her own vaults. But this might not prove a sufficient preventive. Only experience can show how dangerous to our gold reserves this practice, which amounts in fact to hoarding on the part of foreign legations or foreign banks, might become.

If export were permanently restricted, suspension would have to follow some day. But there would probably be an appreciable interval of time before this; and by then export might be free again. There is fortunately a great prejudice in foreign countries against earmarking, and they could not be likely to make their initial arrangements for such a policy quickly.

Control of export absolutely or by licence

If, on general grounds, it were thought desirable to limit gold exports, this should be effected in the first instance, without touching the position or the obligations of the Bank of England, by the silent authority of Orders in Council and of the Customs.

In spite of a not uncommon belief to the contrary there is at present no hindrance on the export of gold from this country except so far as is involved by the law relating to trade with the enemy. It would, however, be easy (*a*) to introduce a prohibition of export by private persons, such as already exists in the other belligerent countries, and to restrict export to the Government only; or (*b*) to introduce a modified prohibition by requiring private persons to obtain a licence for export which could be withheld at discretion.

Either plan is feasible technically; and either would excite far less remark than suspension. But it does not follow that they would be advantageous.

At first sight the second alternative of export by licence may appear attractive. It might be held that it is much more necessary for us to meet our obligations in some parts of the world than in others; that, for example, it would be no great misfortune if the Madrid exchanges were to be strongly adverse, and that to allow gold to dribble away to Spain is to waste our resources. Such a policy would refuse licences for export to Spain and grant them to the U.S.A.

It is doubtful, however, whether there is much substance in this. So far, the dribble of gold to miscellaneous destinations has been appreciable but not great enough to be a serious factor in the situation. Some figures are given in an appendix to this note.

But the main objection arises out of the fact that, if the exchanges are maintained in one direction, with the United States for example, persons wishing to remove balances from London for any destination would be free to move them in the first instance to New York and remit them from there to Spain or leave them in New York for the time being. The expenses of the roundabout method of remittance would no doubt have the effect of lowering the Spanish exchange somewhat. But on the other hand the limitation of export, by promoting fears of more complete limitation, would probably stimulate the removal of foreign balances from London. We should in fact not so much diminish our exchange difficulties as concentrate them upon the one centre with which direct exchange was being maintained. We should, therefore, be selling our reputation as a free market for gold for a very small compensation.

Putting on one side the policy of suspension as being premature and dismissing the proposal for limiting export in some directions while permitting it in others as a half-way measure which would do us more harm than good, the alternative policies open to the Government appear to me to be two:

(1) To continue, as heretofore, the free export of gold, with the effect of preventing any of the exchanges from going against us, more than is allowed by the physical difficulties and the insurance cost of moving gold in large amounts at a time. With the diminution of the activities of German submarines our gold reserves are less well protected than they were.

(2) To prohibit the export of gold on private account altogether, allowing the market rate of exchange to fall to whatever level the demand for and supply of remittance may bring about, and to conserve the whole of our gold resources and of any other resources in the hands of Government for the purpose of providing exchange not so much for approved destinations as for approved purposes. I do not believe that adequate control, assuming this to be desirable, over the employment of our national resources abroad can be secured otherwise. For the success of this policy it would be necessary to make the export of securities as well as the export of gold a monopoly of Government.

II. *Advantages and disadvantages*

So far I have chiefly discussed the technical side of the question without entering into the reactions and remoter consequences of the policies under discussion.

The disadvantages of interfering with the export of gold are the following:

(1) Our credit for banking business and as the holders of international balances after the war would be gravely impaired.

(2) Our power of attracting international balances during the war would be almost totally destroyed, and there would be a

constant tendency to draw from us, whenever it were possible, the international balances which are in London already.

The reputation of London has caused large balances to be held in London on foreign account. The power of using these balances has been of the utmost assistance to us up to now. The prohibition of the export of gold would impede the withdrawal of these balances. But unless private dealings in exchange were also altogether prohibited they would certainly be withdrawn gradually and as opportunity permitted with the effect of worsening our international balance.

But, further, with a rising bank rate we may hope so long as our credit as a free gold market is unimpaired, to attract further balances. It is certain, however, that balances will no longer come here on an important scale as soon as the freedom to withdraw them at will has been restricted. To take a concrete example, the fact that Argentine banking is largely run from London allows the accumulating deposits of the customers of the banks in Argentine to be employed in London, with the effect that the exchanges with Argentine are kept much steadier than the balance of trade taken by itself would indicate as possible. But this practice, by which banks in all parts of the world leave surplus balances in London, is essentially dependent on the freedom to withdraw them if necessary.

(3) If the Government were to supply remittance in accordance with the purpose to which it was proposed to put it, they would have to undertake the task of discriminating between different home trades and also to decide whether to give a preference to the allies for whom we are furnishing resources in sterling. For example, the Government would have to support the wheat trade by buying wheat bills at a rate more favourable than that current in the open market.

The advantages are as follows:

(1) We should be able to repudiate for the time being some of our obligations.

(2) If the difficulties under (3) above could be overcome we could control to some extent the expenditure of the public upon imports; and the price of non-necessary imports, being dependent on the market rate of exchange, would be greatly raised. But the extent of this advantage must not be exaggerated. The indirect taxation of the public by a means of a semi-deliberate depreciation of the currency is a proposition which may have some attractions at first, but which will not bear examination. If the Government do not intervene in favour of certain imports, such taxation is in the strictest sense of the word *arbitrary*. It has no relation whatever either to natural equity or to ability to support the burden. And by falling primarily upon foodstuffs, it bears most heavily upon the poorest classes. If, on the other hand, the Government do intervene in favour of certain imports, not only is the fiscal benefit much diminished, but the Government at once become responsible for the price of every single imported commodity and are open to pressure from every quarter. There are present not only the evils of a protectionist tariff, but those of one which fluctuates every day according to the action and the decisions of Government. A depreciation of exchange acts precisely in the same manner as an import duty, except that it affects invisible as well as visible imports. If the depreciation of exchange varies with different commodities and according to the will of Government, the objections and the difficulties are obvious.

I conclude that if there were no expectation of attracting foreign bank balances there would be something to be said for following the example of France, Russia and Germany and of monopolising the export of gold for the use of Government. But as things are, any substantial change from our present policy would diminish our international resources through the loss of actual and potential foreign balances in London, more than it would increase them by reason of the power to repudiate some existing obligations and through the limitation of imports on private account arising out of the fall in the open market rate of exchange.

A limitation on the export of gold may in fact be forced upon this country. We may not be able to help it. But there is little to be said for courting it or for adopting it before the last possible moment.

I have not referred to the general loss of prestige which would be involved. This is evident. And the reactions of such a loss of prestige would be far-reaching.

Suspension of specie payments and the like are the symptoms of a fatal disease. But they are not the cure for it. People sometimes speak as though such measures were undesirable on general grounds and to be avoided if possible; but that, if in the last resort we are driven to them, they will in some way relieve our difficulties. This is not so. Our difficulties will be immeasurably increased by them. The only advantage would be that the symptoms, by proclaiming the presence of the disease to everybody, might stimulate the search for a cure.

J.M.K.

6.11.15

This paper was written in a busy week, as Dr Keynes recorded in his journal:

4 November 1915—Maynard is very hard at work this week—he dined a night or two ago with McKenna and the Lord Chief Justice [Lord Reading, who headed the Treasury's financial mission to the United States]. 7 November—Maynard begins his course of lectures tomorrow. He has had no time for preparation. [These were six public lectures on 'The War Finance of the Continental Powers' given by Keynes at the University College of the University of London during November and December 1915.] 14 November—Maynard's stipend at the Treasury has been raised from £600 to £700.

During November and early December 1915 Keynes was occupied with the negotiations over further loans to the Italians and an attempt to obtain some kind of control over their purchases on British credit similar to that already set up for the Russians. He was worried by rumours that the Italians were buying up very large quantities of wool and jute, far beyond their own present needs, and it was known that in a short time they had bought up a year's supply of wheat in North America. Although the Italians were much less willing than the Russians to accept control—'however gilded', as Keynes put it—he was able to incorporate a clause into the agreement providing for their representatives to act in consultation with British officials to avoid this kind of injurious competition.

'It has been a very hard week,' he wrote to his mother 10 December, 'breakfast to bedtime every day except Monday when I stopt at 8.0 p.m. Ordinary work was held back by one of those awful battles over a big wheat contract which lasted a day and a half and which wear one out more than anything.' Yet he was still able to respond enthusiastically to the prospect of being on a new War Office committee for looking after the remnants of the Serbian army in Albania. 'It's very interesting as it brings me for the first time into direct touch with military affairs.'

Aid in controlling allied purchases appeared in the guise of a severe shortage of freight. To the Treasury this was another aspect of the alternative uses of resources engaging the discussion of the Cabinet. Keynes drafted the following memorandum, dated 18 December 1915, which with some changes, almost entirely verbal, was circulated to Cabinet members two days later over the initials of Reginald McKenna. The version given here is that of Keynes's draft.

THE FREIGHT QUESTION

I

The recent steps which have been taken to mobilise our financial resources, and the freer immediate use of these resources, have temporarily dispersed some of the *symptoms* of distress. But the relief which has been experienced during the last six weeks has also been due to the requirements of the Allies having fallen much below what had been estimated.

The monthly maximum up to which the Allies are entitled to draw was put at £40 million. In October this figure was reached almost exactly. But in November their net requirements were only £19 million and for the first half of December about £13,500,000.

In the case of Russia this falling off has been partly due to an improved system of control which it has been possible to establish in conjunction with the authorities at the War Office, under the new financial agreement. But in the case of France and Italy it is chiefly to be attributed to the inability of these governments to expend the whole of the funds, to which they are entitled, on account of the difficulty of obtaining *freight*. I am informed that this difficulty will be of rapidly increasing importance during the next six months; and that the financial relief, which may be expected from the impossibility of transporting goods which we ourselves and the allies desire to purchase, is likely to be substantial. There has been no difficulty so far in carrying munitions, the deliveries of which are still on a moderate scale, and it has been large quantities of Australian and Canadian *wheat* (to be financed by us), which the French and Italians have been restrained from buying by freight difficulties. But in the next few months this form of relief may be expected to spread to other commodities.

From the financial standpoint the relief is, so far as it goes, a real one. But it is exactly the same sort of relief which our blockade of Germany affords to Dr Helfferich [the German Finance Secretary]. From the material and military point of view it is disquieting.

II

I am not in a position to deal fully or in a technical way with the general question of the shortage of freight. But roughly speaking and without claiming complete accuracy, I think it may be shortly summarised as follows.

In the last few weeks the transport department of the Admiralty has, I understand, been warned of the following new requirements.

(1) The Italian Government have put in a statement that they will require during 1916, 5 million tons from North and South America and 2 million tons from elsewhere, as well as some

further tonnage for coal. After using their own requisitioned and detained vessels, all Italian boats and all foreign tonnage ordinarily engaged in the Italian trade, they ask this country to provide by requisition 4 million tons during the year, and they require the sole use of 100 vessels forthwith.

(2) The French have asked us to provide for them by requisition

(*a*) 200,000 tons *per month* for army grain.

(*b*) 40,000 tons *per month* for pyrites over and above what they can carry themselves.

(*c*) an unknown further amount for coal, munition, and wheat for the civilian population.

(3) Russia will have 450,000 tons to carry from the United States of America to Vladivostok before 30 June next (a round voyage of 6 months), of which she hopes to be able to look after 200,000 tons herself.

(4) Our own munitions department will require

(*a*) an unknown but enormous amount for munitions proper,

(*b*) 500,000 tons of iron ore *per month*,

(*c*) 415,000 tons of pyrites *per annum*,

(*d*) 165,000 tons of nitrate in the course of the next six months.

The above demands come on the top of all existing requirements, and there is virtually no surplus to meet them.

The growth during the past year in the figures of tonnage under requisition by the Admiralty is as follows:

1915	Naval services	Military services	Total (gross tonnage)
1 January	2,301,636	874,415	3,176,051
1 September	2,785,322	2,536,110	5,321,432
1 November	3,020,663	2,826,937	5,867,600
1 December	3,271,581	2,931,294	6,202,875

These figures include prizes and detained ships, oil tank steamers and miscellaneous.

The above figure for January 1915 is what was before the Cabinet during the discussions of February 1915, when the position was already regarded as very serious.

The figure for December 1915 is almost exactly double what it was in January. The effect of the gradual increase of our expeditionary forces is strikingly illustrated. It will be noticed that a further 1,000,000 tons has been taken up since September.

The total for 1 December represents nearly a third of the whole of the tonnage flying the British flag which is now available.

As it cannot be seriously disputed that the surplus not yet requisitioned, over and above what is required to carry over absolutely necessary series, is now inconsiderable, it is certain that the requirements of the Ministry of Munitions and of the allied governments cannot be met in full. After cutting down the above figures drastically to allow for the fact that the allied governments have probably put their requirements at an outside figure and that their reasonable demands could be satisfied by an amount considerably less than what they have asked for, it looks, at a very rough guess, as if upwards of 1,500,000 to 2 million tons at least would be wanted. If there is to be any further increase in the requirements of our expeditionary forces, this has still to be allowed for.

III

The problem presents several aspects which require early consideration:

(1) What steps can be taken to increase the amount of effective tonnage available and to ensure economy in the use of it?

(2) On what principles and by whom are decisions to be made as to which of the various demands are to be met and which refused? Are we to maintain a policy of meeting all British requirements first and leaving the allies to fend for themselves, and be starved of food, coal or munitions if such is the consequence? If all British munitions are *not* to be given a preference over all Russian munitions, who is to weigh the respective claims of each? And whose business will it be to weigh the

claims of railway material for Russia against those of wheat for Italy?

But these are questions of organisation, which, however urgent, are not my special object of attention in this paper.

I am concerned with a more general question of policy, namely the relation of this question of tonnage to our military organisation and to the question of the proper size of the army.

I propose to look at it from two points of view, the conclusions drawn from each being cumulative.

A. When, as with us, it is a case of operating abroad, a certain quantity of shipping (very large if the Mediterranean is in question, not nearly so large for the Western front) is as necessary a complement of each military unit, as are staff and transport and munitions. Each one of these, as well as the number of men available, sets independently an upper limit to the number of divisions we can expect to place in the field.

Now if it is both desirable and practicable to give to the shipping demands of our expeditionary forces, to whatever extent they may grow, a priority over all other demands, we can certainly meet them. But it is no less certain that in that case the other demands must be rejected—we cannot meet both sets. If we are prepared to delay the re-arming of the Russian army, to let slide the completion of the Murmansk Railway, to allow food-shortage in France and Italy, to risk a deficiency of coal and metals in the munition factories of France, or to hang up half-completed some part of the great projects of our own Ministry of Munitions, then let us, so far as shipping is concerned, go ahead with the army. But we ought to realise quite clearly that we have now reached the point when any new project must necessarily be *alternative* and not additional to what we are already doing in other directions. To carry overseas each new division of an expeditionary force is *alternative* to carrying food, munitions or other necessary commodities to the allies or to ourselves. We have to decide not merely that one more division would be useful, but that it would be so useful that it is worth while to incur a deficiency in one of these other directions.

B. Every increase of the army is a further tax on the resources of our shipping: that is one side of the picture. But, further, every increase of the army diminishes the amount of the shipping resources which are available.

The short effective supply of tonnage is due to a variety of obvious causes, several of which are incurable for the present. But one of these, and an important one, is beyond question the shortage of labour. The evidence in the hands of the Board of Trade is conclusive on this point. To a minor degree this shortage affects shipbuilding (the difficulty of filling private orders being mainly, however, of a different kind). But labour difficulties affect in a major degree the rate of discharge at the ports and hence the number of voyages which can be made in a year.

They affect this in at least three distinct ways—dock labour, clearance of warehouses, inland railway transport. All these react on the congestion of the ports. I need not go into details. But in this connection I would point out that to believe (*a*) that within a given industry men can be divided into the necessary and non-necessary; or (*b*) that industries themselves can be so divided; or (*c*) that recruiting governed by these principles cannot do much harm, is simply to be deceived by words.

Within an industry we can safely presume that everyone employed in the industry is useful to it; and the utmost that perfect wisdom could accomplish would be to place those who are employed in the order of their usefulness. As, starting from the bottom, the less useful are removed, the efficiency of the industry is progressively undermined; and labour difficulties produce the gravest consequences, long before a point is reached when it is becoming impossible for the industry to get along at all. While *A*, *B* and *C* may none of them be indispensable regarded individually, efficiency will nevertheless be injured if any of them go and ruined if all of them go.

But further the theory that industries can be sharply divided into the necessary and the unnecessary embodies an essential fallacy. To make the distinction involves a profound knowledge of the interactions of industry; but even when it has been made, labour cannot be safely drawn from the supposedly unnecessary industries beyond a certain point without reacting on the labour market generally. Unless the industries in question are altogether suppressed, which is not practicable, nothing can prevent them from attracting labour which could otherwise be employed in other industries.

I would bring most earnestly to the attention of my colleagues the fact that it is a mere delusion in the present state of the labour market to believe that it is divided up into watertight compartments and that a draft can be taken from one compartment without reacting upon the others. Any further considerable inroads on any part of the labour market is certain to react on the supply in every part and incidentally on the efficiency of every branch of our transport.

The whole question is but another example of the deep-seated fact which now governs all our policy whether we wish it or not, and to which I have tried to call attention on previous occasions in connection with our financial prospects—that, except in so far as resources may be released by a diminished consumption on the part of individual citizens, all (indeed probably more than all) of our resources are now in commission, and every new project is not additional, but alternative, to something we are committed to already.

This fact is now so intrinsic to the whole situation that evidences of it will crop up in directions where no one may have expected them, and it is impossible to say in advance what form the outward manifestations of it are going to take next. A short time ago they were most obvious within the sphere of finance. The most pressing embarrassment, which now serves to remind us that we live in the realm of the finite, is to be seen in the deficiency of sea transport.

J.M.K.

18.12.15

Throughout the autumn of 1915 each successive Vote of Credit in the House of Commons had brought increasing criticism of the deployment of labour and a growing demand for compulsory service. Lord Derby's scheme, a campaign for men of military age to attest their willingness to enlist, was launched and extended to 15 December; yet it failed to produce a sufficient number of volunteers, in spite of an assurance by the Prime Minister that no married man attesting would be called until all available unmarried men had been enlisted. This brought the government to the brink of decision; at a Cabinet meeting 28 December 1915 during which, the minutes state, 'much divergence of opinion was manifested', Asquith proposed that unmarried men of military age who did not satisfy their local tribunals that they had grounds for exemption should 'be deemed to be attested and liable as such'. The majority assented, with reservations from McKenna and Runciman. When the Cabinet met 31 December, it was decided at McKenna's suggestion that the Treasury, the Board of Trade and the General Staff of the Army should confer to co-ordinate their efforts, and the rest of the meeting was spent in considering the drafting details for a military service bill, introduced in Parliament 5 January 1916.

Keynes had strong feelings about conscription. Many of his friends were pacifists—Lytton and James Strachey, Duncan Grant, Bertrand Russell, Gerald Shove, David Garnett and Francis Birrell among his Bloomsbury friends, and at Cambridge Pigou. His own attitude was closer to the Liberal principles of his acquaintance Sir John Simon, who resigned from the Cabinet in opposition to the state taking over the right of individual decision. (Simon then volunteered for military service.) But Keynes was also against conscription for the economic reasons that he had been expounding as a member of the Treasury during the past six months.

'Maynard talks of resigning his post at the Treasury, and we are very much worried about him', his father wrote in his diary 6 January 1916, when the two parents were visiting their son in London. The very same day the *Daily Chronicle* printed a letter signed *Politicus*, the original manuscript of which, in Keynes's handwriting, is to be found with his papers. As a civil servant he was of course not permitted to publish a personal opinion on a controversial political issue.

To the Editor of the Daily Chronicle, *6 January 1916*

Sir,

Those who would introduce compulsory military service in the United Kingdom at the present moment of time, must do so for one of two distinct kinds of reason. They may act, some of them, from motives not connected with military efficiency, as from a desire to persecute a minority who differ from them on the moral aspects of war or on the obligations of citizenship, or from a hope to obtain a new weapon for the subjugation of labour to the will of the governing classes. On the other hand, their reasons may be of a quite different complexion, namely that they are determined to defeat Germany and are persuaded that to expand the British army is a necessary means to victory.

Opinions of the first kind can be combated only by broad moral judgements concerning War and Liberty and the State. Those, who care either for the liberty of individuals or for the liberty of classes, must believe such opinions to be perverted, the offspring of the grosser passions to which a nation at war is liable.

There are certainly persons in this country who hold such views. But they are not a majority. The majority of Englishmen are prepared to submit to compulsory military service, not because they do not hate it for its own sake, but because they have been told that success in the German war will depend on it.

Unlike the other sort of ground, which is mainly moral and therefore hard to argue, this question of the size of the army is purely one of fact, expediency and practical good sense. To this question of fact alone a brief analysis is here directed.

Three great groups of facts, none of which are open to serious dispute, stand out for our attention.

The first relates to the possibility of improvising an army on a yet greater scale. We have proved it possible to take Englishmen from civilian life and to render them, after six or nine months' training, at least the equal of Continental conscripts who are, also from civilian life, recalled to the colours. That is to say the men *can* be improvised. But soldiers tell us that for those in the higher command the practice of arms is, like any other, a profession, and that the power to lead and direct large bodies of troops can only be acquired by a long experience. The generals and the staff and the War Office, that is to say, cannot be improvised. In the lack of a numerous corps of trained officers we, amongst all the belligerents, are alone. The friendly critics of France are absolutely agreed that our material is all that it should be, but that we have already increased our army beyond what we can hope to lead with a reasonable efficiency.

The second relates to the situation of the allies. The governments of Russia, Italy, Belgium and Serbia are mainly dependent on us, and the government of France is partly dependent on us, for such supplies of food and the material of war as they need to purchase from abroad. This is partly on account of their inferior wealth, and partly because they have mobilised with their armies so large a part of their labour supply that they cannot manufacture or raise from the soil what they require themselves or what they can normally exchange for imports. If at the beginning of the war we had immediately mobilised between 3 million and 4 million men, we could not also have financed our allies without suffering by now as great an exhaustion as Germany's; and if we had armed these men, the Russian army must have continued indefinitely to go without. If we had exhausted our resources upon our army, Italy would not have joined us, Russia might have been driven into a separate peace, and France and ourselves might have been overwhelmed by the pressure of the entire forces of the enemy. For, it must be remembered, we should not in that event have placed up to now any more men in the field than we actually have placed. As it is our supply of men has always exceeded hitherto our supply of equipment, and to have ruined industry by recruiting would have further retarded production. Nothing but the fact that we remained content for a considerable time with an army of a reasonable size, has deprived Germany of victory. Nothing but military megalomania on our part can still save her from defeat. For, whether the view of the past, expressed above, is true or not, any army which we now start to create, absorbs resources at once, but cannot take the field for many months.

The third group of facts is the most indisputable of all and the most overwhelming in its effect. It is certain that we have already committed our aggregate resources to the maximum of which they are capable. The figures of our estimated expenditure are fantastic. It is true that we have not yet eliminated all unnecessary expenditure or suppressed unnecessary industries. But this margin of reserve is pledged already. The expenditure, to which we are already committed, *assumes* that the consumption of the whole country is to be restricted as much as it is possible to restrict it. To take a further million men from industry and maintain them as soldiers could hardly cost, in net diminution of our resources, a less amount than £400 million a year. This would bring the expenditure of the Government above 80 per cent of the whole national income. The suggestion is ridiculous, and the figures absurd. To finance another new army is, therefore, *alternative* and not additional, to what we are doing already.

But further, it is believed that the allied governments between them have now ordered *all* the rifles and guns and munitions which can be manufactured in any part of the world within a reasonable period of time. If, therefore, we arm an increased army, some other allied troops must go without.

Lastly, our shipping resources are strained to the utmost. If we transport more armies, the allies must go without the essential commodities of warfare and even of existence.

This, therefore, is *the* governing and essential factor of the present epoch of the war—any new development on our part must be at the expense of and not additional to, what we are doing already. The existing armies of the allies, which, in conjunction with the very great army we ourselves have already created, should be ready otherwise for vast efforts in the coming spring and summer, would be stinted of food, transport, arms and money; for what purpose?—that we may create an improvised army without trained leaders, of numbers vastly inferior at the best to what Russia now has waiting, for use a *year hence*. This is the crowning folly our governors ask us to consummate.

The German government know, and all impartial observers know, that, if Germany does not win within a year, she will never win. Are we going to give her the one chance opportunity leaves open? 'Too late', according to Mr Lloyd George, has been the motto of the policy which he, more than anyone else, has hitherto controlled. His conscript army of 1917 will be too late, if it is antedated by bankruptcy.

No country and no resources can support the present strain for very long. But Germany is six months nearer the edge than we are. Nothing can save her but the megalomaniac folly which would, by the reckless dissipation of resources, bring us level.

Those who believe that the true Englishman is one who throws himself not where he is most efficient but where his personal sacrifice will be greatest, who believe that our duty to the allies is not to help them most effectively but to impress them with the nobility of our self-sacrifice by getting as many of our men killed or maimed as we plausibly can, or who believe that the chief test of patriotism is an eagerness to dissipate the national resources at the maximum possible rate, will find much moral solace in compulsory service. But in the business of war there is no room for such sentimentalities. That is not the way to beat Germany.

Politicus

Keynes accompanied this attack on the proposed conscription bill by formulating amendments to protect the interests of conscientious objectors. These he sent to Philip Morrell, a Liberal member of parliament and personal friend. He wrote to his mother optimistically, 12 January: '. . . Intrigues in high quarters in favour of the C.O.'s are progressing favourably—L.G. and the P.M., as well as McKenna and Runciman, have now been won over to their cause.'

The next day he wrote again to his mother:
Things drift on, and I shall stay now, I expect, until they begin to torture one of my friends. I believe a real split now and a taste of trouble would bring peace nearer, not postpone it; otherwise I'd swallow a great deal. I've

been very busy and with occasional excursions into high life—met the P.M. at dinner on Saturday, refused to dine with the old scoundrel on Sunday, banqueted with the Lord Mayor yesterday.

'Maynard is home today...' Dr Keynes wrote 16 January. 'I am afraid he takes an extreme view of conscription.' But 28 January he was able to say, 'Florence... saw Maynard in London. He is still thoroughly interested in his work, and Florence does not fear his throwing everything up in consequence of the Compulsion Bill.'

At this time Keynes was occupied with the Cabinet inter-departmental committee's attempt to reconcile the conflicting claims of the army, industry and finance. He drafted the Treasury section of their report which was presented 4 February 1916, signed by Asquith, Austen Chamberlain and McKenna (Report of the Cabinet Committee on the Co-ordination of Military and Financial Effort, CAB 37/142/11). The committee concluded that 62 army divisions could be maintained in the field, at a risk to industry and finance, but a risk that could be contemplated for a short period. The Treasury found little opportunity for further economies but saw a kind of temporary salvation in the inability of the army and the allies to carry out their estimated expenditure as rapidly as planned. Keynes's draft of the Treasury part of the report follows.

PART IV. THE FINANCIAL PROBLEM

45. The salient features of the financial situation as explained to the Committee by the Chancellor of the Exchequer, assisted by the Secretary of the Treasury (Sir John Bradbury), are shown in the following tables:

TABLE (J). *Outstanding Debts on 29 January 1916*

	£
Treasury Bills outstanding	418,000,000
Liability to the Bank of England for foreign loans	78,300,000
Total other debt (Consols, War Loan, Exchequer bonds, &c.) ...	1,445,300,000
Ways and Means advances (other than Treasury bills)	27,650,000
Total	1,969,250,000

[NOTE. £69 million of the above debt is represented by uncovered currency notes, mainly circulating in place of gold which was formerly in the pockets of the people, and is now either exported or in the bank reserve.]

TABLE (K). *Financial Year 1916–17*

Estimated receipts		Estimated expenditure	
	£	(a) Expenditure, independent of naval and military policy, on which no further substantial saving is practicable.	£
Tax revenue Loans (Treasury bills, Exchequer bonds, and War Loans) (paragraphs 46 and 48)	1,667,000,000	Charges for debt, including 6 months' interest on the debt to be incurred in 1916–17	134,500,000
Additional amounts set free by special economies in consumption (paragraph 47)	100,000,000	Civil Service Vote	57,000,000
		Post Office	26,600,000
Further assistance from America later on in excess of present maximum rate (paragraph 48)	50,000,000	Local Taxation Account	9,500,000
		Other Consolidated Fund Services	1,700,000
		Customs and Inland Revenue	4,700,000
		Total	234,000,000
		(b) Vote of Credit (dependent on naval and military policy).	
		Navy (paragraph 50)	211,000,000
		Army (paragraph 51)	590,000,000
		Munitions (paragraph 52)	420,000,000
		Dominions and allies (paragraphs 54–6)	500,000,000
		Railways (paragraph 57)	12,000,000
		Other items (paragraph 58)	18,000,000
		Total Vote of Credit	£1,751,000,000
Total estimated receipts	£1,817,000,000	Total estimated expenditure	£1,985,000,000
Estimated deficit	£168,000,000		

46. *Notes on Table (K)*. The estimates of the amounts that can be raised by taxes and from loans are based on recent actual experience. It has been considered preferable to estimate the yield of taxes and loans together rather than separately, as experience shows that when revenue is coming in fast, as in January, for example, less money is obtained from Treasury bills and Exchequer bonds, and vice versa. During the last two months the Treasury have obtained (by virtue of a special arrangement between the Bank of England and the joint stock banks, by which the whole surplus in the hands of the latter has been temporarily lent for Government purposes) practically the *whole* of the

available funds within the country. Other methods, which the Treasury would prefer to adopt, for estimating the maximum available funds over the forthcoming year yield a less favourable result.

47. The additional amount of £100 million represents a sum which might be raised by further national economy in consumption to be effected partly by raising the rate of taxation, and partly by special periodic efforts to induce persons to buy Exchequer bonds or War Loan, thereby voluntarily depriving themselves of the means of expenditure. The reduction of private expenditure, as measured in money, has to be greatly in excess of £100 million in order to make that sum *net* available for the Exchequer, since a considerable proportion of any individual economy is bound to be at the expense of other individuals, who lose profit, rent, or remuneration for skill which cannot be otherwise employed to equal advantage.

48. The above estimate of the maximum yield to be hoped for from war borrowing already makes allowance for funds made available (1) by the sale or loan of foreign securities, and (2) by balances left in London by foreign and colonial banks and financiers for investment there or for employment on the London market. During the period on which the estimate is based, the sale of American securities by individual holders in this country has been at a rate which could not possibly be sustained during the whole year, and is considerably in excess of the present power of the American market to absorb. The Chancellor of the Exchequer believes, however, that the power of the American market to absorb will increase rather than diminish as time goes on, and that, as our stock of American securities becomes exhausted, good South American stocks will become saleable. It is on this assumption that a further allowance for £50 million has been made over and above the present rate of sale by holders in this country. As regards the balances left in London by foreign and colonial banks, the recent rate, which has been assumed in the estimate, can scarcely be maintained, and certainly not

exceeded, recent circumstances having been exceptional (the improvement in exchange having caused great confidence following on period of depression, and their initial balances having been only moderate). Lastly, the whole estimate assumes the maintenance of our credit at a high level.

49. The estimate of expenditure is based on the actual preliminary estimates of the departments concerned, with the one exception that the Chancellor of the Exchequer, on a careful review of probabilities, has substituted for the total liabilities of £600 million to dominions and allies an estimate that the actual disbursements can be kept down to £500 million.

50. The estimate for the navy allows for no contract work on new construction outside the programme already approved.

51. The army estimate is based on Scheme (B) (Part III of this Report), namely, on the assumption that recruiting proceeds up to the end of June as for Scheme (A II) (62 divisions in the field, 5 full divisions at home), but that the cost for the whole year must not exceed that of Scheme (A IV) (54 divisions in the field, 13 weak at home). It is further based on the assumption that the Board of Trade limits are accepted for purposes of recruiting, and that 200,000 men, as explained in paragraph 28, will be released from Home service.

52. The estimate of the Ministry of Munitions, with regard to which the Committee were advised by the Minister of Munitions, accompanied by experts of his department, is drawn up on a broader basis than that required to provide munitions for the 62-divisions scheme. In the first instance it was founded on a War Office requisition for guns and ammunition made on a basis of 67 divisions in the field for heavy guns and 70 divisions for guns of other natures. Moreover, the Ministry of Munitions, in giving their orders, have, in the case of guns of the heavier calibres, added a margin above the War Office demands. The reasons for this are discussed later on in this report (paragraph 76).

53. It is worthy of note that the combined Army and Muni-

tions estimates, totalling £1,010 million for the financial year 1916–17, compare with an estimated actual expenditure of £771,600,000 in the current financial year.

54. The departmental estimate for dominions and allies is based on present commitments, which, assuming that the existing agreements are continued for the whole of the financial year, are as follows:

				£ million per year
For Dominions	...	...	... ...	100
For Russia ...	...	...	25 million a month =	300
For France ...	...	...	4 million[1] „ =	48
For Italy ...	...	...	10 million „ =	120
For Belgium ...	...	...	... ...	30
For Serbia (say)	...	...	... ...	10
Total ...	...	...	... ...	600

[1] The sum recently raised in London as a contribution to the French War Loan absolves us of the necessity for paying the French subsidy for three months. For details of the pecuniary assistance afforded to France see Appendix II.

55. The Russian commitment is unconditional only up to 31 March 1916; after that date it is made expressly dependent upon our being able to find means of payment in America. The present Russian agreement expires on 30 September 1916, and the Italian on 31 December, but if the war continues both will inevitably have to be renewed. A large part of the Russian orders has been placed through the British War Office and Ministry of Munitions in their own name, and for these our liability is absolute.

56. The Chancellor of the Exchequer's reason for cutting down the above estimate of £600 million to £500 million is that experience has shown that in practice the goods cannot be delivered to such large amounts, so that, in fact, the larger estimate is not likely to be realised.

57. The estimate of £1 million a month for railways is a Board of Trade item not included in the estimates of the other departments.

58. The 'other items' of expenditure include such arrangements as the purchase of Roumanian wheat, and advances already promised to Greece and Roumania and other neutral

countries. The Treasury have cut down their original estimate by no less than £20 million, and no allowance is now made for any expenditure other than for liabilities already incurred, such as might arise, for example, from the entry of Roumania or Greece on the side of the allies.

59. The deficit of £168 million for the financial year will have to be met either by increasing receipts or diminishing expenditure, and the Committee have enquired fully into both these possibilities.

The possibility of increasing receipts

60. It is sometimes urged that an increase of expenditure automatically increases receipts, on the ground that the money after circulating in the country eventually returns to the Exchequer in the form of subscriptions to Treasury bills or otherwise. This is undoubtedly the case in so far as the money is wholly expended within the country, and in so far as it is wholly additional to and not in substitution for existing expenditure. But in present circumstances, the greater part would be inevitably spent, directly or indirectly, abroad. And so far as expenditure at home is concerned, we have now reached a point when further increase in it would have to show itself mainly in higher prices and could not be expected to call forth increased efforts in terms of labour to any important extent.

61. A large increase in taxation has been already assumed in the above estimate. The Chancellor of the Exchequer is at present contemplating a tax revenue of £500 million, as compared with £387 million, on the basis of existing taxation. The Treasury hold that any increased taxation beyond this extreme limit would defeat its own object by destroying the sources of revenue and loan through over-taxation.

62. The amount of money that can be expected to be raised by means of borrowing has also been placed at the highest possible figure in the Treasury estimate, and is based on the results of actual experience.

63. Various suggestions for forced loans have been considered. It has been proposed that the Government should compel bankers to hand over to them a certain proportion of their deposits. As these deposits amount to a total of about £1,400 million, a forced loan of, say, 30 per cent, would produce over £400 million. But the adoption of this expedient would shake the very foundations of credit and disorganise commerce and industry. It would lead to an almost immediate withdrawal of foreign deposits, which, within the knowledge of the governor of the Bank of England, amount to at least £100 million, and probably reach a much higher figure. The Japanese government alone has £25 million, and a single American banking institution no less than £8 million. The attempt to withdraw the deposits would result in an immediate collapse of the exchanges and a forced suspension of specie payments. And, as a final objection to this method, it may be pointed out that as bankers have already lent to the government the greater part of their free funds, the government would have to lend back to them almost the whole sum to be raised, before they could meet their liabilities.

64. The Chancellor of the Exchequer attaches decisive importance to the maintenance of specie payments as the only possible condition on which we can hope to prolong our participation in the war. Other belligerents, however, having abandoned the gold standard, it has been urged that this country might follow their example. Two factors are overlooked. In the first place, in contrast to Germany, more than half of our national supplies are now obtained from abroad. In the second place, in contrast to the allies, we have to meet the whole of our own expenditure abroad and, *as a consequence* of their abandonment of specie payment, the major part of theirs. The interval between the loss of the gold standard resulting in the breakdown of the foreign exchanges and final collapse is likely to be a short one.

65. The Committee discussed at some length with the representatives of the Treasury the possibilities of obtaining further

credits abroad by one means or another to meet payment due for goods purchased in foreign countries.

66. A large part of the difficulties in connection with internal finance arises directly out of the imperative necessity for maintaining the foreign exchanges. The addition of vast imports of munitions and supplies of all kinds for the allied armies and peoples (which this country has to finance) to the normal imports, combined with a restriction of exports due to a number of causes, including shortage of labour, congestion on railways and in ports, diversion of industry to the production of war material etc. (all being, in fact, indirect results of the raising of great armies), together with a reduction in 'invisible exports', due to the withdrawal of shipping, and a decreased return from investments abroad, has upset the balance of trade, and great efforts are required to maintain the American exchanges.

67. The method by which the Treasury are now seeking to maintain the American exchange is by paying for all Government purchases out of the proceeds of the recent American loan and the sale of American securities, and by employing, when necessary, banking credits which have been arranged in America for the support of the commercial exchange. It has been suggested that this method might be carried further, and that our great holdings of foreign securities might be sold in other foreign countries to pay for the cost of the war. To some extent this is being done already. Further, a considerable sum has already been placed at the disposal of His Majesty's Government by the government of Canada, and it is hoped that the proceeds of further Canadian loans will become available from time to time. This has been allowed for in anticipation in the estimates given above. There is, however, no indication that any foreign country except the United States is in a position to purchase any considerable amount of our securities. As regards the United States, while our total remaining holdings of United States dollar securities probably do not exceed £300 million to £400 million, the amount of securities which could be absorbed by way of

purchase or as security for advances within twelve months is estimated by Lord Reading as not more than £300 million. The Chancellor of the Exchequer, however, takes a more sanguine view, and estimates the maximum annual absorption at £400 million.

68. It has been suggested that, if this country were to continue to dump foreign securities on the American market, thus depreciating them and jeopardising the financial position in America, the United States government might be compelled in the interest of their own country to step in and take some action to re-establish stability on the stock exchanges. The Treasury consider it more probable that the government of the United States of America would merely apply a 'physical possession' rule, such as we have on our own stock exchange, and which would prevent us from selling indefinitely.

69. The maintenance of the foreign exchange by exports of gold is only practicable over very short periods and to relatively small amounts. The gold reserves of the Bank of England and the Government are about £90 million, and there may be another £100 million in the hands of the joint stock banks and in the pockets of the people. The total gold stocks of this country (including gold deposited at colonial centres) may in the opinion of the Treasury be put at about £186 million. Any large inroad on this would drive us off the gold standard. Assistance has already been obtained by the export of gold from Russia and France, and probably some further help might in an extremity be forthcoming from the same quarters, but only at the cost of a high degree of friction, and then not in sufficient quantities appreciably to affect the exchanges.

70. If we embark on a bigger programme of expenditure than we are in fact able to support, this will show itself in a growing inability to finance and carry our necessary supplies. Except in the event of a suspension of specie payment, we shall probably become aware of the impending scarcity of credits sufficiently early to avoid any sudden or dramatic development. The

stringency will show itself in continual additions to the list of commodities which the Government and their contractors must decide to do without, and in a progressive inefficiency, military and industrial, due to the lack of these commodities. The choice is between some retrenchment now in the less essential forms of expenditure, or a continual forced retrenchment at later dates not in what we need least, but in what bargains or proposed purchases we can most easily cancel. The Chancellor of the Exchequer is emphatically of opinion that we are already spending on a scale which allows of little or no margin for further expansion. The process of forced curtailment is already upon us, and the longer we postpone deliberate retrenchment of Government expenditure, the less will be our range of choice when retrenchment is compulsory.

71. After an exhaustive examination of the whole subject, the Treasury have come to the conclusion that the plan of raising the money by big loans interspersed with short-term borrowing, is the one open to the least objection. The Treasury, however, lay the utmost stress on the fact that they cannot provide for expenditure in excess of the estimate in Table (K) by these or any other means not involving the probability of financial disaster.

The possibilities of economies

72. The Committee are agreed that reduction in the size of the army in the field is the last direction in which economy ought to be sought. They have, therefore, examined into the possibilities of effecting savings in other directions.

73. The Committee are satisfied that no substantial economies can be effected in the group of charges under heading (a) of the expenditure column of Table (K). Any substantial savings, if they are to be found at all, must come out of war expenditure, the principal headings of which are as follows: (1) War Office, (2) Munitions, (3) Admiralty, (4) Allies, etc. Each of these will be now examined in turn.

74. *War Office.* Now that the pressure involved in forming the new armies is slightly relaxed, it may be possible for the War Office to effect certain economies. For example, in the near future it should be possible materially to reduce expenditure on training establishments, since the formation of the new armies has now been accomplished and they have nearly completed their training; thus the services of Senior General Officers employed in supervising training, who have large staffs and live in large houses, driving large motor cars, will be dispensed with. Some considerable economy should also be effected in connection with the 200,000 men already referred to, whom the War Office hope to be able to discharge from Home defence, more especially as many of these men belong to the Veteran Reserve, and are very expensive, owing to the large proportion of married men with dependents. It is possible also that large economies may soon be effected in the sea transport service—a most expensive item. The recent evacuation of the Gallipoli Peninsula ought to produce an effect under this head. The release of shipping is doubly important, for every ship returned to trade becomes an asset instead of a liability. The above are the principal items on which economies are possible in connection with War Office expenditure, but it by no means exhausts the field of inquiry. At the present time there are about 2,750,000 men on the War Office pay list, exclusive of troops from the dominions, and this figure appears to be out of all proportion to the number in the field. There seems to be a possibility that the number of unfit men is unduly high, and it has been suggested that the number of fatigue duties undertaken is in excess of war requirements. These and other matters are under consideration by Mr Long's Committee on Army Expenditure, and there is good reason for hope that economies will result from their enquiries. Credit, however, has been taken for some of these economies in the War Office estimates.

75. *Munitions.* The basis of the estimate of the Ministry of Munitions has already been explained in paragraph 52, where it

was shown that the Ministry of Munitions in giving their orders had added a margin above the War Office demands, which were themselves considerably in excess of the 62-divisions scheme. The extent of this margin, which applied only to guns of the heavier calibres, is as follows:

300 in the case of the 4·5-inch field howitzer (1,918 ordered against 1,618 demanded)[1]

120 in the case of the 60-pounder gun (920 ordered against 800 demanded)

240 in the case of the 6-inch howitzer (880 ordered against 560 demanded)

238 in the case of the 8-inch and 9·2 inch howitzer (644 ordered against 426 demanded).

In the case of the 12-inch howitzer 3 less have been ordered than have been demanded (53 ordered against 56 demanded), and in the case of the 15-inch howitzer the exact number (12) demanded has been ordered.

76. The reasons for these excess orders are:

(*a*) to secure quicker delivery,

(*b*) to obtain a margin for manufacturing, accidents, sabotage, etc.,

(*c*) to allow for a possible increase in War Office requirements, such as has occurred in certain cases.

77. The result of this system of giving orders in excess of actual requirements will, in certain instances, be as follows: as regards 60-pounder guns the rate of delivery in July 1916 will be at the rate of 94 per month instead of 80 per month, which would have been the rate if the number demanded by the War Office had alone been ordered; as regards 6-inch howitzers, the rate of delivery will similarly be 100 per month by July 1916, instead of 68 per month by August; and as regards 8-inch and 9·2-inch howitzers, the delivery in October 1916 will be 69 per month in place of 32.

---

[1] The excess of 300 4·5-inch howitzers will disappear if these extra pieces are handed over to the Russians.

78. The expenditure in connection with guns is a definite commitment. Existing orders cannot be cancelled, but the Committee understand that some of our allies will be glad to take over any surplus guns that may be available after we have satisfied our own wants, and that they will be able to take the actual guns made to our design and calibre. The cost would, of course, for the present be borne by this country, but will be deducted from our existing financial commitments to the allies. This is of great importance.

79. So far as ammunition is concerned, the existing contracts of the Ministry for Munitions come to an end in June, and could be cancelled, or fresh arrangements could be made, provided notice is given in March. After the end of June the Ministry of Munitions hope to be dependent more on national factories and less on American supplies of ammunition.

80. Ammunition is represented to the Committee by the Ministry of Munitions as accounting for more than 80 per cent of their total estimate, and is therefore a far more important item than guns and rifles, and the possibility of effecting economies under the head of munitions would appear to depend mainly upon the decision arrived at as regards the number of divisions to be put in the field, and the dates at which they will come into action. As it appears certain that the number of divisions will be less than the number on which the Ministry's preliminary estimate is based, the Committee believe that if the estimates of the War Office and the Ministry of Munitions were drawn up in conjunction a substantial reduction in the final estimate of the two departments could be secured.

81. *Admiralty.* The Committee have not taken any evidence on the subject of Admiralty expenditure. They suggest, however, for the earnest consideration of the Board of Admiralty, that enquiry should be made as to the feasibility of some temporary reduction in the manufacture of ammunition for the navy. If the Admiralty could see their way to abate their requirements for the next few months they might render a great service to the

army, for the Ministry of Munitions anticipate difficulty in fulfilling military requirements by the necessary dates in the supplies for heavy guns. Any temporary reduction in naval orders for heavy gun ammunition would ease the situation from the point of view of labour, plant, and raw material.

82. *Allies.* As explained in paragraph 56, the Chancellor of the Exchequer has already cut down the estimate of commitments to allies by £100 million, for the financial year 1916–17. It is extremely unlikely that any further economy under this head can be looked for.

83. Both France and Italy are faced with a shortage of supplies, and require large imports from abroad in respect to which they demand assistance from us. Their demands do not always take the form of a loan. At present they are asking for tonnage and expect us to requisition shipping for the purpose. The British government pays for requisitioned tonnage at what is known as the Blue Book rate, which was fixed early in the war by a Commission of which Lord Mersey was Chairman, and which is now about one-quarter of the trade rate. If the British government charges allied governments the trade rate it causes ill-feeling, as they say we are making money out of them; but if they charge the Blue Book rate, our national earnings are diminished by the reduction. Probably some agreed figure between the Blue Book rate and the trade rate will in the end be decided on: but the nation will be out of pocket, and the service rendered will be equivalent, in its effect upon the exchanges, to an increased financial advance.

84. It is to be feared that economic stress in the countries of our allies may, within a few months, be nearly as severe as it now is in Germany. The financial resources of this country are the reserve on which our allies invariably fall back in times of difficulty, and, if our support is withdrawn or reduced, it is impossible to foresee what the consequences may be. The Committee are therefore reluctant to recommend any further reduction in this item, which is probably to a great extent the

mainstay of the alliance. They recommend, however, that a complete financial statement on the lines of that prepared in relation to France (Appendix II) should be drawn up and sent to both France and Russia, and that it should be clearly put to them, first, that this burden is the utmost that we can carry— then only if they help us as far as they can; and, second, that any fresh demands for money or credit involves a corresponding reduction of our armed forces.

85. On a review of this section of the Report, it does not appear that any increase can be made in the estimate of receipts given in Table (K). On the estimates as they stand there is a deficit of £168 million for the financial year 1916–17—with the consequences foreshadowed in earlier paragraphs. We have indicated certain directions in which economies can and ought to be made, but, on the basis of the continued prosecution of the war on its present scale and in so many theatres, they would be insufficient to bridge the gap.

Keynes supplied the following appendix which was printed with others at the end of the report.

APPENDIX II

Details of the pecuniary assistance afforded to France

In 1915 His Majesty's Government lent the French government £40,800,000 in cash, £10 million from the market before June, and £30,800,000 from the Vote of Credit after June. Indirect assistance, in the way of supplying them with freight and coal below market rates, cannot be estimated for the year 1915 above £2 million altogether. But in addition His Majesty's government paid further considerable sums for sundry expenses of our troops in France, and for the use of their railways; these payments constituted for the French government an invisible export many million pounds sterling in value.

For 1916 His Majesty's Government have promised the French government £4 million a month in cash, of which three months' allowance has been already paid in advance in the form of British subscriptions to the recent French War Loan. If, as is now proposed, we carry grain and munitions for them in requisitioned vessels, the Treasury are informed by the Admiralty Transport Department that the best guess that can be made of the pecuniary value of these services is £1 million *per month*. But we do them a further indirect service in the matter of freight by leaving free from requisition vessels which they notify to us as being under charter by them. There may be some 300 or 400 of our vessels (quite apart from anything we requisition) thus left by us in the service of the French government.

By far the greatest assistance which we have afforded them has been, however, by releasing them from the obligation which they undertook at the Paris Conference of February 1915 to share with us equally the burden of advances to present or future allies. At the lowest computation this has led us to take over from them a burden of at least £150 million during 1916.

For 1916 therefore our assistance may be evaluated as follows:

	£ million
Direct cash assistance	50
Assistance in kind	12
Taking over France's share of assistance to allies ...	150
Total	212

If, instead of our doing this for them, they were doing it for us we should be about £425 million per annum better off than we are.

1 February 1916

Yet, while Keynes continued to labour at the Treasury and his letters to his parents were full of a busy social life studded with the names of the Asquiths, the McKennas, Lady Ottoline Morrell and Mr Winston Churchill, his feelings were still engaged with the conscription issue. 'The Tribunal crisis is getting over now,' he wrote to Dennis Robertson 18 June 1916, 'as concessions to the C.O.s are impending. But it has been a foul business, and I spend half of my time on the boring business of testifying to the sincerity, virtue and truthfulness of my friends.'

He himself was protected by his work in the Treasury, but it is clear that he wanted to make a positive stand. The Military Service Act, declaring all single men to have attested their willingness for military service, was passed 27 January 1916. Keynes was given an exemption, initially for six months, by the Treasury, so empowered as a government department by the Act, on the grounds that he was engaged on work of national importance. The covering letter with the certificate noted that he had not attested under the Derby scheme and that it rested with himself to make any representations he wished to put forward to the local tribunal on the grounds enumerated in the Act, i.e., hardship, ill-health, or a conscientious objection to the undertaking of combatant service.

This letter and other documents concerning Keynes's exemption were kept with his Treasury correspondence. From them it appears that he made a special application to be exempted on specific grounds of conscientious objection—in his case, conscientious objection to being conscripted. What is either a draft or a copy of a declaration to this effect has been preserved. It is written in Keynes's own hand on King's College paper, dated 28 February 1916, and signed by him. The declaration has no salutation but refers to 'the Tribunal'.

Kings College,
Cambridge.
28.2.16

I claim complete exemption because I have a conscientious objection to surrendering my liberty of judgement on so vital a question as undertaking military service. I do not say that there are not conceivable circumstances in which I should voluntarily offer myself for military service. But after having regard to all the actually existing circumstances, I am certain that it is not my duty so to offer myself, and I solemnly assert to the Tribunal that my objection to submit to authority in this matter is truly conscientious. I am not prepared on such an issue as this to surrender my right of decision, as to what is or is not my duty, to any other person, and I should think it morally wrong to do so.

J. M. KEYNES

With this statement are to be found a postcard from the clerk to the Holborn local tribunal, giving notice of the hearing of Keynes's claim on 28 March 1916 at 5 p.m., and a letter, dated 29 March 1916, from the same source, informing Keynes that his application for exemption had been dismissed, 'Having regard to the fact that you have already been exempted for six months by the Treasury.' The letter added that he would be entitled, if he desired, to apply again after six months. On 18 August 1916 the Treasury duly issued him a further certificate of exemption, conditional on his remaining in the employment of that department. He does not appear to have made any fresh application to the local tribunal.

Eventually Keynes also obtained a certificate of registration under the National Registration Acts, 1915 and 1918. It is dated 26 March 1918, a time when an obligation on employers to demand a certificate of registration from all male employees was added to the Act. It is possible that Keynes may have neglected—as many did—to register when the Act was first passed (5 July 1915, when voluntary recruiting had begun to slow down) as a kind of protest against a census that would obviously be used as an instrument for the Military Service Act.

The pseudonymous *Politicus* appeared in print once more. Keynes's friend Gerald Shove, who was editing the pacifist monthly *War and Peace*, twice wrote during February 1916 asking for an anonymous article on the conscription of wealth 'on practical patriotic grounds'—suggested title, 'How to Pay for the War'. There is no evidence that Keynes wrote such an article. In April 1916, however, *War and Peace* published a short essay entitled 'Face the Facts' by *Politicus* which has some of the earmarks of Keynes's literary style. No manuscript can be found. The assumption that this is Keynes's work rests on the use of the same pseudonym as for the *Daily Chronicle* letter and in many touches that seem characteristic—among them the opening description of Bonar Law, the remark about Lord Derby's figures, the reference to German professors (see Keynes's review of an article by Professor Jaffé on 'The Economics of War in Germany', *Economic Journal*, September 1915 [*JMK*, vol. XI]), and the fascination with the word 'bamboozle'.

From 'War and Peace', April 1916

FACE THE FACTS

by *Politicus*

In a debate last autumn in the House of Commons on the question of peace negotiations, Mr Bonar Law was the Government spokesman. With that curious naïveté of his which proves such a refreshing contrast to the customary ministerial manner he stated that the time would come when speeches in favour of peace would require to be really answered, but in the meantime they could be merely brushed aside. It is to be regretted that it was Mr Asquith and not Mr Law who replied to the similar debate initiated by Mr Snowden a few weeks ago, for it would have been interesting to see whether he thought the time for a real answer had come. Evidently Mr Asquith did not think so. His speech seemed designed to show that he refused to consider the question seriously. But what did Mr Bonar Law think? Was he not a little uneasy? For the truth is that unless he gives his answer soon, it will be too late, as the course of events is speedily making the case for immediate negotiations unanswerable.

There are two things which the advocates of peace have to show. They must establish the 'deadlock or stalemate' theory; and they must show that an early peace is likely to be durable. They have to show both these things before they can hope to influence any important section of public opinion in this or any of the allied countries. So long as we think that there is a reasonable chance of 'crushing' Germany and 'dictating' terms, there is not the smallest doubt we shall insist on going on. On the other hand, even when we have finally made up our minds that there will be no decisive military victory, we shall refuse and rightly refuse to make peace, if we think it probable that it will be used by Germany for a policy of 'reculer pour mieux sauter'. We could at least hang on and let 'attrition' work for a year or two, until a different result became probable. Pacifists must show that a different result is probable now, and unless they can do that, the most convincing demonstrations of a 'deadlock' are in vain.

This double-barrelled nature of the pacifist case is the chief reason why there are so few people definitely and consciously in favour of an immediate peace. Either proposition alone will find supporters of a weight and number which would startle Mr Asquith. Any day you can come across the man who condemns the folly of these costly offensives, with their enormous losses of men and their trivial gains of ground, who asks what it really matters if we succeed in pushing our trenches forward another mile or two and insists that our true policy is to sit tight and let the Germans do the attacking. There are many indeed who, with Verdun in their minds, are saying, 'Well, if the Germans cannot do it, I'm sure we cannot.' Perhaps these latter are superficial critics, whom the last year of Lord Northcliffe has impressed with an exaggerated respect for German efficiency and contempt for British leadership. But the believers in a deadlock include men of independence of mind, of sober judgement and, as the phrase goes nowadays, 'in a position to know'.

It even seems that many of our professional prophets and military experts are beginning to take the same view. Mr H. G. Wells has definitely avowed himself a convert. Mr Gibson Bowles, the latest favourite of the 'ginger' party, is of a very similar opinion, as the *Daily Chronicle* has been pointing out to the uneasy indignation of the *Morning Post*. Even Mr Belloc's deliberate optimism has shrunk to a faith in the success of 'attrition' based on statistical calculations beside which Lord Derby's figures take an almost scientific air. It only needs Lord Northcliffe, and all Britain will be persuaded.

The opinion in favour of the other proposition is less clear and less confident, but it is considerable and growing. 'No one will ever want another war after this one'—you can hear this said in any club or in any railway carriage, among any group of men who let their imagination touch, ever so momentarily, on the awful dull realities of the present conflict. It represents more than a mood: it is the heartfelt conviction to which men turn irresistibly as to a deeper, more abiding thing from the usual facile speculations and comments about the technique and drama of the war. And the sentiment is universal in its application. 'No one will ever want another war.' The man who says that knows that it is true, not only of Englishmen or of the allied peoples, but of Germans and Austrians too, of all who have passed through the same hideous experience. It is not enough to say that the Germans are not like ourselves, that a generation's systematic indoctrination at school, at the university, in the army, wherever bellicose mystics could get at them, of false ideas of the inevitability and glory of war have made them much more warlike and aggressive. All this is quite true, but the lessons of the war go far beneath such superficial facts. They brush aside all national differences and appeal to the common human nature which no professor or drill-sergeant can ever permanently distort.

The professors have taught very many Germans in the absence of experience to applaud war; but when the experience has been supplied, who would not back it against all the writings of Bernhardi? We know it would be so with us, and we know that the German experience in point of privation and horror and loss must be more sombre than our own. True they can claim victories, such as we cannot claim, which help to keep martial ardour alive for a time; but the bread riots, the picture drawn by the great von Hindenburg himself of the growing distress of families of the small shopkeeper class, whose breadwinners are in the army (for the married men are long since 'called up' in Germany)—their fear that they will be reduced to the position of 'indigent day labourers'—reveal how intense and widespread is the discontent and disillusionment there, which here is only beginning to accumulate.

It is on such signs as these that the believers in 'victory' base their hopes, but surely it is a far safer inference that the German people will be cured for a generation at least of warlike notions and pan-Germanic dreams.

Indeed, most intelligent persons will admit this as regards the German people. But the German people, they say, is not the German government. There certainly lies the danger. And the danger that the German government will pursue its aggressive policy in defiance of popular sentiment is, let it be frankly admitted, not a negligible one.

The man who demands absolute certainty that peace will be

durable before he will make it, will rightly refuse to make peace now: only he will never make it, for absolute security is not the outcome of war. But the degree of likelihood which a wise and responsible statesmanship would require, already exists. It lies in the essential dependence of modern governments, no matter whether they are democratic or autocratic in form, on at least the passive acquiescence of public opinion. The idea that the German government is entirely free from this influence, and can make the people do exactly what it wishes will not bear examination. It is hard to see who can seriously maintain it. Certainly not the sympathisers with any of the anti-German leagues or unions who for months past have been deriding the distinction which won some acceptance in the early days of the war between the wicked German government and the innocent, misled German people. They have insisted that the people were the guilty accomplices of their government, for had it not been so, the government could not have dared to do what it has done.

There is much in what these gentlemen say. Had the will for peace in Germany been wholehearted and strong and really widespread, it would not have been so easy to bamboozle the people in August 1914. It was necessary to bamboozle them as it was. If in the future the German government should try a similar stratagem on a forewarned and more determinedly pacific people, cannot we be reasonably confident that they will experience the truth of Abraham Lincoln's dictum: 'You can fool all the people some of the time, and you can fool some of the people all the time, but you can't fool all the people all the time.' They would be about as likely to succeed as Lord Derby would be if he tried to trip Mr Asquith with another pledge.

The military issue of the war will be a deadlock and, for the future, there is already in all the belligerent countries a deep-rooted hatred of war, before which even Kaisers and Junkers will have to bow. These things men already dimly realise, but are only very vaguely beginning to connect. How long will it be before they find their expression in a conscious demand for peace? How long after that will it be before peace is made? Months certainly, perhaps more than a year. The pride of governments stands in the way, and men do not reason quickly or clearly on a subject on which they are told it is unpatriotic to reason at all.

But it is through this process of reasoning and this facing of reality that the only road to peace lies. If further delay did not involve such an appalling loss of human life, Mr Snowden and his friends could afford to await events with complacency. For be the time short or long, peace will be made in the end as they say it will, and when it is made the world will agree that it might far better have been made today.

The Treasury hung on. Since France had been released from her promise at the Paris Conference to take an equal share in financing the allies, disbursements on the Russian account alone were more than the Treasury's entire revenue before the war. The difficulties are made vivid by Keynes's jotted notes for an evening talk that he gave to the Board of the Admiralty at Balfour's request 15 March 1916.

ADMIRALTY TALK

Aug 1, 1914–Jan 31, 1916 we raised by loan and tax about £m 24 a week, of wh £m 6½ non recurring,—i.e. about £m 17½ net. I put it for the future at £m 30, this being extreme optimism for 12 or 18 months. A small spurt possible for 6 mos. i.e. we can do about 4½ a day perhaps. This is approx. present rate. Estimates are 5½—about 1 per day on the wrong side

Resources		1000	
		+ 500	
			+ Stocks
Expenses	Navy	210 —say	200
	Army	590 —say	600
	Munitions	420 —say	400
	Allies		500
	Debt		say 130
	other		say 130
			———
			1960

These resources cannot be seriously increased except by severe taxing of working classes. If they consumed pari passu with Germany we could save £m 400 and just do it.

Allies

By the middle of 1916 we shall be responsible for the whole of the external expenditure of Italy, for the whole of the external expenditure of Russia (outside France and part of Japan), and for two-thirds of e.e. of France, as well as a half share of entire expenses of Belgium and of Serbia. Whole of subsidies to Roumania and Portugal.
Four-fifths of this spent abroad

America

War Depts have placed orders to extent of about £m 400 of which £m 160 has been paid for, leaving £[m] 240 of wh £m 65 will fall due for payment more than 6 months hence, leaving £m 175 for early payment. [Loans to] Allies in America are estimated at about £m 110 and misc. at £m 15, making £m 300 altogether. We have assets in hand to meet this £m 60; we have every expectation of another £m 90 in course of next months. That is to say assets in sight *half* of liabilities in sight.

Total power of U.S. to lead us at annual rate of £m 300. But this is our expenditure in *half* a year.

Now these figures taken at their face value spell disaster. How —pessimistic as we are at the Tr[easury]—can we preserve our equanimity at all?

First, a permanent factor—after allowing for all seen resources, in such an old established country there are others. Our wealth compared with G[ermany].

Second, something I have learnt since October:

(1) Improvement of our credit since then. Our extreme dependence on good war news. If anything bad was to happen as in June or July—we have no financial reserve against bad news.

(2) Belief that above estimates will not be realised. Last

October we took the spending Depts at their word, and we took the allies at their word. If they had spent all they threatened, we should have been ruined.

Imaginary case of M.M. [Ministry of Munitions] and aluminium. Effect of one order pushing aside another. Russian orders. An idiotic way of going on because we don't get what we want most—freight, e.g. Allies and grain. The things don't exist and can't be carried if they do. These two factors have, financially, saved the situation.

Law of Compensation

Relation between [what] the Americans can lend us and what they can produce. The estimates are nearly £m 12 a week. I do not believe they can produce and ship more than two-thirds of this.

After making all possible allowances on these heads, still reason for grave anxiety. Tendency to swing from one extreme to another. We were so depressed in the late autumn that we are perhaps a little too callous now. I used, four months ago, to think that a critical point would be reached in May or June. I now think we shall get through the summer all right.

But anyhow, I at any rate believe that we are gambling on a fairly early peace—a gamble which the condition of Germany, about which I could speak if I had time, seems to me to favour. We may be able to stand the racket 9 mos. We cannot stand it for 18. The worst of it is that different Gov[ernmen]t dep[art-men]ts are gambling both ways—on a late peace and on an early peace.

If one is seeing details hour by hour this is what impresses one.

One more topic

What will be the consequences if we spend too much? Treasury will see danger sufficiently far ahead *probably* to avert catastrophe

—which if it came would spoil our credit. No, the effects would be gradual:

(1) Most important—allies. We have one ally, France. The rest, mercenaries. If, as looks likely, we hold our alliance together and Germany cannot hold hers, it will be money has done it. Capture of Erzurum and Bagdad may bring T[urkey] to separate peace; but would they if G. could pay on our scale? We bribe whole populations. It is our money which keeps the allies sweet. It is my business to deal with our financial relations to the allies day by day, and to help steer the line between too much and too little. I venture to say that not half of what we give has the smallest direct military significance. The rest is a *douceur*. Food for Italy, pigs for Paris.

(2) Connected with this—our financial methods keep the war popular, much too popular in my opinion, at home. We use our money to make life relatively tolerable both for our people and for the populations of the Allies. How much, in the long run, this will benefit us remains to be seen. Thus without our money the Allies will make peace whether we like it or not. And if the population here or with them is discontented, our bargaining position at the Peace Conference will be immensely reduced.

It is useless for the W[ar] O[ffice] to spend money in preparation for the campaign of 1918, if it means docking the allies.

(3) A steadily increasing military inefficiency. If we can go on giving the army what they want longer than the Germans can do this to theirs, we may *appear* to win by military prowess. But we shall really have won by financial prowess.

If we economise now, we can *choose* the directions.

If we postpone, we cannot.

The great truth which everyone who has to do with this spending of money ought to bear in mind is this—We have reached the point where everything we do is *alternative* and not additional to something else. The difficulty is that the individual can never know to *what* his proposed purchase is alternative. It is not vivid to him. That is the fundamental evil of having several great Depts all spending unbridled ignorant of the point of view of the others.

The best hope is a certain change of heart, and the multiplication of small savings.

Rather than exercising restraint, the war departments in fact increased their American orders, the Russians continued their large demands on exchange, and the French became more and more financially dependent. McKenna drew the attention of the Cabinet's finance committee to these mounting liabilities, 17 May 1916, and urged that only unavoidable purchases should be made in the United States; at a later meeting, 3 July, it was decided that Russian needs in particular should be scrutinised for economy. This gave rise to an accusation by Lloyd George, now Minister of Munitions, that the Russians were being cut short of necessary material, and that the American contractors ought to be willing and able themselves to supply credit for the Russian orders. McKenna's reply, 'Memorandum on Mr Lloyd George's Proposals', printed as a Cabinet paper 5 July 1916 over his initials (CAB 37/151), was substantially Keynes's work.

Its genesis can be traced in his files—from three queries on a card in McKenna's handwriting—to the notes that Keynes provided in answer and then expanded into a draft memorandum. McKenna made a number of verbal changes to the draft, added two minor amendments, and blue-pencilled two passages on the possible stinting of the Russians. The first of these, consisting of two paragraphs blaming the Ministry of Munitions for doing the stinting in favour of the British army, Keynes rewrote into an apologia for the Chancellor of the Exchequer—and indeed for himself, as the Russians had been his special charge.

(Keynes had written to his father 5 June 1916, his thirty-third birthday: 'This year I considered the real celebration took place on Saturday, when I received a deputation from the Holy Synod of Russia in the morning and from the government of Serbia in the afternoon and doled out presents I should have liked myself.'

On 5 June the *Hampshire*, carrying General Kitchener and his party on a mission to Petrograd, struck a mine and sank. Keynes had been working with members of the party and until the last moment had expected to accompany them. Lloyd George had also intended to go, but he was called away by rebellion in Ireland.)

The second passage, which was excised entirely from the last section, reiterated the Chancellor of the Exchequer's position that no new orders could be contemplated and showed that the Treasury was gambling on a short war. It read in part:

> *New* commitments, on an appreciable scale, if they really mature in deliveries and involve cash payments, will involve a risk to our whole financial system so grave...that it ought only to be incurred at the last possible moment and under the stress of overwhelming necessity. If the war is going on well into 1917, we have no financial margin. If it is not going on for so long a period, the greater part of any orders to be placed from now onwards will bear no useful fruit. It is, in fact, only safe to place new orders on the assumption that they will not be delivered until after the war is over.

The memorandum as finally printed and submitted to the Cabinet follows:

MEMORANDUM ON MR LLOYD GEORGE'S PROPOSALS

It is Mr Lloyd George's general contention that new orders in the U.S.A. can be arranged on the basis that the contractors themselves provide the necessary credits.

It is important to be clear as to what is meant by 'the contractors themselves providing the credits'. In order to be useful to us, this must mean that the companies either lend the money out of their own resources or borrow it from their banks *on their own credit*, not on the credit of the British government, since for borrowing from banks on British government credit there would be no object in introducing the companies. While financing the business on their own credit, the companies would require a documentary undertaking for ultimate repayment from the British government. If this were to take the form of some sort of Treasury bill which was immediately negotiable, the companies would not be using their credit but ours, and would be drawing from the same bucket as that from which we must draw to finance existing commitments. The bills to be given to the contractors should, therefore, be of a currency not less than the period of war, and should be non-negotiable for that period.

If Mr Lloyd George is able to arrange new orders on this

basis, it will greatly relieve the financial situation and I shall be most happy to see such arrangements made.

In discussion at the Committee Mr Lloyd George has, I think, gone rather farther than the question of financing new orders, and has suggested that the American companies concerned would be prepared to finance some of the existing orders, if they were enticed by the placing of new orders. As regards this, it would be possible to make an experiment at once. And I suggest that, before placing any further orders for steel products, the Ministry of Munitions should sound the principal steel companies on these lines.

I am doubtful, however, as to the feasibility of any such transactions on a large scale. In isolated cases of highly specialised munition manufacturers, whose products, however, are not those which we now most urgently require, we might succeed. The basis of my doubt is explained in the following notes on certain passages of Mr Lloyd George's memorandum.

1. 'If these orders cease, hundreds of thousands of workmen will be thrown out of employment, for there is hardly any other international business being transacted at the present moment.'

There was some truth in this down to the summer of 1915. But it is now no longer the case. The chance of making terms for credit payments may have existed at that time when the original orders were placed, and when the steel companies were extremely anxious for business. But today and for many months past the steel companies are and have been booked up with orders for months ahead, labour shortage is acute, and American railway development and equipment is being seriously retarded by the munition orders of the allies. I would refer the Committee to the monthly statement (appended) of unfilled orders of the United States Steel Trust, which is the recognised barometer of the prospects of the steel industry. It is not unlikely that we may be faced with an agitation for the employment of American capital and American labour on American development. All advices from America are unanimous as to the rising tide of internal expenditure.

2. 'After all, all the business of America is done on credit. No gold passes in respect of the twenty or thirty thousand millions of manufacturing orders annually executed.'

The word 'credit' is here used in three senses:

(1) For a borrowing transaction, where the borrower gives no immediate return, but only a promise to pay in the future, as in the case of a finance or accommodation bill.

(2) For a transaction in which the borrower possesses goods, the sale of which at an early date will furnish funds for repayment of the loan. This is the case of a trade bill.

(3) For cash transactions carried out for convenience by the intermediary of a cheque or bank note.

Mr Lloyd George seems to be thinking of (3), and it is not legitimate to argue from (3) to (1). But even if he is thinking of (2), there is not only the fundamental economic difference between a 'produce' bill and an 'accommodation' or 'finance' bill, that the one is represented by goods and the other is not, but also in U.S.A. a very important legal distinction. The extent to which American banks are permitted by law to lend against finance paper is strictly and rigorously limited, and the Federal Reserve banks discriminate against it.

It is not adequately realised in this country what a significant factor in the situation the banking law of the United States is. Apart from the willingness of the banks, there is an insuperable obstacle in the Statute Book.

3. 'The only question is whether firms and banks who now do business on the strength of the confidence they possess in the financial stability of private concerns and corporations would refuse to accept profitable business tendered them on the strength of the credit of the three wealthiest countries in the world.'

This is really the same point as that just dealt with. It is, indeed, fundamental to the difference of opinion between Mr Lloyd George and myself. In my view, the loan transactions undertaken by the allied governments are absolutely different from the normal banking business with private *producers*. If, for example, all the business ordinarily done was based on quasi-permanent bank loans, the outstanding loans of the banks in the U.S.A. would increase, to take Mr Lloyd George's figures, by 20 or 30 millions a year.

4. 'I cannot believe that they would prefer to close down their works and to face the great crash rather than make the necessary arrangements to exploit the opportunity thus offered to them.'

This may possibly be true of a few very specialised munition factories, such as those which provide rifles or nitro-cellulose powder. But with the exception of a little of the latter, these are not the things we particularly want—except for early delivery, which is not feasible.

All the recent urgent orders of the Ministry of Munitions have been for metals and steel products. All the Russian requirements mentioned by Mr Lloyd George are of this character. When placing their orders, the Ministry of Munitions have repeatedly informed the Treasury that it was urgent to look ahead, because otherwise prices would rise or other buyers snap up the orders.

The belief that orders are going begging, and that if the manufacturers do not sell to us they can sell to no one, is surely erroneous so far as metals and steel products are concerned.

5. 'The Russians have been deprived of heavy guns, heavy shell, and railway material.'

This statement is so serious that I must be excused for entering into some detail.

When I came to the Treasury in May 1915, no orders, so far as I am aware, for any of the above articles had been placed in

America either by the Russians themselves or on their behalf. An order for 5 million 3-inch shells placed by the Russians with the Canadian Car and Foundry Company in February 1915 has resulted up to date in insignificant deliveries, the company having become insolvent and only kept in being by large additional advance payments to which I have agreed.

During my first three months of office the system of placing British government orders on Russian behalf was first instituted, and I agreed to the immediate placing of orders amounting to about £60 million chiefly on shell and rifles. This expenditure has not yet resulted in approximate deliveries, but should do so shortly. Nothing that I could have done would have affected the position of the Russian army up to date.

In July 1915, the Russian Railway Department commenced to place orders in U.S.A. up to some 70 million dollars. These began to deliver last January, and in every week since then vessels have sailed for Vladivostock carrying the goods, all payments for which I have met. Deliveries on these orders are not yet complete, and have taxed to the extreme the available freight facilities.

Up to October 1915 the Russian government had a free hand in placing orders, and, although they spent much money wastefully, I agreed to meet the whole of their commitments. Since that time they have had a liberal allowance for further expenditure under the guidance of the War Office and the Ministry of Munitions. The recent exhaustion of this allowance is the occasion of the forthcoming conference.

I estimate that orders to be met from British credits have been placed on behalf of the Russian government during just over thirteen months, since I became Chancellor of the Exchequer, to an amount exceeding £300 million, while the orders so placed during the preceding nine months before I assumed office fall short of £50 million.

During the past year the Treasury, in close and daily co-operation with the War Office, and latterly with the Ministry of

Munitions, and with the Russian representatives themselves, has been engaged in enabling the Russian government to replace their former unco-ordinated and inefficient methods by a centralised and efficient machine acting in conjunction with the British war departments. This has not hindered but has immensely increased the capacity of the Russian government to place effective orders. This system and the bulk of the orders placed during my tenure of the present office are only just beginning to bear fruit, and will keep the Russians liberally supplied with the principal munitions of war for many months to come. For this year, anyhow, the Russians will be well supplied from America from existing orders, and our own surplus production will be able to produce heavy guns for them many months before they could be obtained from any other source.

6. 'To stint them of these things because these three great rich countries cannot afford to incur another £100 million indebtedness to America is the height of stupidity.'

This is, indeed, putting the cart before the horse—the picture of the allies refusing loans in America for fear of the subsequent burden of indebtedness! Every Finance Minister is trying to borrow every penny anyone will lend him. The real question is:

Is America *prepared* to lend another £100 million over and above what she will have to lend us as it is to see us through? This question can only be answered by the Americans themselves.

My advisers here and in America do not feel confident that she will. If it can be answered in the affirmative, then by all means let us go ahead.

I have of course several projects on foot for borrowing in America in various forms and to the utmost extent which I think possible. If, however, the War Committee think that we ought to present firstly Mr Lloyd George's proposal to finance new orders on the credit of the manufacturers themselves in exchange for British government securities non-negotiable until after the war, I should be very glad if Lord Reading were invited, as Mr Lloyd George suggests, to proceed to America with full powers to negotiate business on these lines. I am also prepared to place his proposal in a specific form before my City advisers, and I will cable immediately to Messrs Morgan [Britain's financial agents in the U.S.A.] for their opinion upon it.

R. MCK.

5 July 1916

Unfilled orders of Steel Corporation

From 30 June 1914 to 31 May 1916

1914					Tons
June 30	...	...	...	...	4,032,857
July 31	...	...	...	...	4,158,589
Aug. 31	...	...	...	...	4,213,331
Sept. 30	...	...	...	...	3,787,667
Oct. 31	...	...	...	...	3,461,097
Nov. 30	...	...	...	...	3,324,592
Dec. 31	...	...	...	...	3,836,643
1915					
Jan. 31	...	...	...	...	4,248,571
Feb. 28	...	...	...	...	4,345,371
Mar. 31	...	...	...	...	4,255,749
Apr. 30	...	...	...	...	4,162,244
May 31	...	...	...	...	4,264,598
June 30	...	...	...	...	4,678,196
July 31	...	...	...	...	4,928,540
Aug. 31	...	...	...	...	4,908,455
Sept. 30	...	...	...	...	5,317,618
Oct. 31	...	...	...	...	6,165,452
Nov. 30	...	...	...	...	7,189,489
Dec. 31	...	...	...	...	7,806,220
1916					
Jan. 31	...	...	...	...	7,922,767
Feb. 29	...	...	...	...	8,568,966
Mar. 31	...	...	...	...	9,331,001
Apr. 30	...	...	...	...	9,829,551
May 31	...	...	...	...	9,937,798[1]

[1] Highest on record, being 1,448,080 tons greater than the previous high record in 1906.

Draft telegram to Messrs Morgan

'It has been suggested to me that new orders to be placed henceforward by the Ministry of Munitions on behalf of the British and allied governments might be financed by the contractors agreeing to accept in payment British government bills non-negotiable until after the war. It is urged upon me that if it was made plain to the contractors that they could not hope for further orders except on the above conditions, they would be prepared to close with them rather than risk the discontinuance of their present profitable contracts. I shall be obliged if you will advise me as to the practicability of this proposal at an early date, especially with reference to the placing of orders for metals, steel products, and railway material.'

This would have effectively quashed Lloyd George's proposal to rely on borrowing from Britain's American suppliers. But the very next day Lloyd George left the Ministry of Munitions to fill Kitchener's place as Minister of War. The memorandum had later repercussions for Keynes.

During the summer and autumn of 1916 Keynes's letters to his parents alternately described allied conferences and high life. In July a fortnight of meetings in London with the French and Italian finance ministers was sandwiched between a weekend with the McKennas and a visit to 'Ottoline's' and dining 'at the P.M.'s'. His letter of 17 August said that he was going to Paris with the Chancellor of the Exchequer and that he had spent the last weekend 'at the P.M.'s at Bognor'. On 10 September, while having a ten-day holiday with the McKennas, he wrote describing an exhausting conference at Calais with Briand, 'crossing the Channel twice in the day and getting only five hours sleep in forty'. On 7 October he wrote from the Asquiths' where he was weekending, and on 19 November his father's diary noted that he was again with the Asquiths.

By the autumn of 1916 Britain's black list of American firms dealing with Germany and her censorship of cables and her shipping blockade on the one hand, and the United States government's Direct Profits Tax on American firms taking war contracts on the other, had led to a tense situation between the two countries. Congress threatened reprisals and, although the British embassy in Washington thought the probability of their application remote, the Foreign Office called together an interdepartmental committee to consider 'how far this country is dependent commercially and financially on the United States and to what extent measures of reprisal by the United States could effectively be met by commercial or other forms of retaliation...'. Keynes represented the Treasury on this committee and his statement on behalf of his department, dated 10 October 1916, was unambiguous.

THE FINANCIAL DEPENDENCE OF THE UNITED
KINGDOM ON THE UNITED STATES OF AMERICA

Of the £5 million which the Treasury have to find daily for the prosecution of the war, about £2 million has to be found in North America.

There is no prospect of any sensible diminution in this amount without a radical change in the policy and activities of the war departments both of this country and of the other allies.

During recent months about three-fifths of the sums required have been obtained by the sale of gold and securities, and about two-fifths by loans. The former resources are nearly independent of any action that the American execution is able to take, except that the Assay Office could put practicable difficulties in the way of the sale of the gold at a sufficient rate. But the extent to which such resources can be used in the future will be greatly inferior to what it has been recently, and they cannot be relied on to supply more than one-fifth of the total requirements during the next six months.

Thus to the extent of four-fifths of their needs the allied powers must depend upon the issue of public loans. A statement from the United States executive deprecating or disapproving of such loans would render their flotation in sufficient volume a practical impossibility and thus lead to a situation of the utmost gravity.

It is not necessary, however, that matters should go so far as an overt act of the executive, in order that the financial arrangements of the allies should be prejudiced. Any feeling of irritation or lack of sympathy with this country or with its policy in the minds of the American public (and equally any lack of confidence in the military situation as interpreted by this public) would render it exceedingly difficult, if not impossible, to carry through financial operations on a scale adequate to our needs. The sums which this country will require to borrow in the United States of America in the next six or nine months are so enormous, amounting to several times the entire national debt of that country, that it will be necessary to appeal to every class and section of the investing public.

It is hardly an exaggeration to say that in a few months time the American executive and the American public will be in a position to dictate to this country on matters that affect us more nearly than them.

It is, therefore, the view of the Treasury, having regard to their special responsibilities, that the policy of this country towards the U.S.A. should be so directed as not only to avoid any form of reprisal or active irritation but also to conciliate and to please.

J.M.K.

10.10.16

These alarming conclusions were presented in more detail in a secret Cabinet paper, 'Our Financial Position in America' (CAB 24/2/87 and CAB 37/157/40), consisting of an introduction initialled by McKenna followed by an extract from a report by the British members of a joint Anglo-French financial committee. It appears that Keynes both prepared the introduction and as secretary to the committee was responsible for the report. (In a letter to his mother, 22 October 1916, he mentioned staying in London over the weekend in order to write 'a state paper' for McKenna.)

The introduction, dated 24 October 1916, is given here followed by the complete report, the first three sections of which were omitted in the Cabinet paper. The report, dated 18 October 1916, was signed by Lord Reading, Lord Chief Justice; Sir Robert Chalmers, joint permanent under-secretary of the Treasury, and Brien Cokayne, deputy governor of the Bank of England, and by Keynes as secretary.

OUR FINANCIAL POSITION IN AMERICA

On 4 February 1916 the Cabinet Committee on the Co-ordination of Military and Financial Effort reported that our financial resources were only equal to the effort then called for by the Army Council by the adoption of financial expedients which would endanger the maintenance of our national credit, and could in any case only be continued for a short period. A reduction in the programme first proposed has in fact been made. On 19 May 1916, I laid a statement before the Finance Committee of the Cabinet who considered that the facts disclosed a danger of our being unable to meet our liabilities in America, and that it was a matter of the first importance that future commitments should be restricted within the narrowest possible limits. In this paper I estimated our expenditure in America from the middle of May to the end of September at 795 million dollars; our actual expenditure for this period was 985 million dollars. It is only to the American side of our problem that I now wish to direct attention.

The above conclusions were reached by committees of my colleagues, of which I was a member. The most recent survey of the situation, which is printed below, has been undertaken by an outside committee of great weight, in whose deliberations I have taken no part, and I prefer to add nothing in detail to their significant statement of the facts.

On the broader aspects of the position, however, I wish to call attention to considerations, which recent events have brought home to my own mind very forcibly.

What, after all, are the financial stakes we are risking? I am not sure that the most obvious are the most important. Granted that essential civilian supplies will always be obtained somehow, and that the military authorities are prepared, with their eyes open, to take the chance of being stinted later on, provided they can have all they want for the present; Are these the only important risks involved? My experience in the administration of my own office suggests some other possibilities.

There are two sets of circumstances, and in my opinion two only, which may deprive us of the liberty to fix for ourselves the time and terms of peace. One is the inability of a principal ally to continue. The other is the power of the United States to dictate to us.

1. In the course of the last three months I have spent more

hours than I care to recall in the company of the finance ministers of our allies. Two conclusions have emerged. There is no likelihood of their furnishing us with any considerable quantity of gold beyond what is already promised. To obtain the secret gold reserve of £100 million[1] mentioned in the following report, I had to exercise pressure which went dangerously far. I doubt if any further pressure could enable me to repeat the gold agreements of August and September last. On the other hand, the Ministers did not conceal that lavish and increasing financial assistance was a necessary condition of their continuance.

None of the existing agreements run beyond next March, and I believe that I have made no promises so far which we cannot fulfil. But when the time comes early next spring for a further batch of financial conferences, what will my position be if our assets in sight are already completely pledged? So far as prolonged conferences have enabled me to judge of the atmosphere, I do not believe that large economies in our subsidies will be accepted by our allies. But if all our liquid resources are exhausted by our own military commitments, drastic reductions in these subsidies will be the consequence.

2. At all times we have been very dependent on the goodwill of the United States. But up to now I have always been able, if necessary, to last out financially any temporary wave of adverse sentiment or unfriendly executive action. If the President had deprecated publicly the issue of loans to belligerents, I should have been disconcerted but not helpless, because of our considerable liquid resources in the form of gold and securities. I am still to some extent in this position. Our stock of American securities is much depleted, but our gold would enable us to last three months *if necessary* without a public issue in America. After the end of this year we shall never be in that position again. At the same time, the degree of our dependency makes a great deal of difference. We ought never to be so placed that only a

[1] I ought to add that I have had to spend £20 million of this in the last fortnight as the result of a temporary break in the American exchange rate and to prepare the way for the new American loan.

public issue in America within a fortnight stands between us and insolvency. Yet we are quickly drifting in this direction. I call special attention to the passage of the following report, in which it is pointed out that, while in recent months we have depended on loans for only two-fifths of our American expenditure (and, I may add, on public issues in the United States for only one-quarter of it), we shall require henceforward to meet from this source five-sixths of an increased total. If things go on as at present, I venture to say with certainty that by next June or earlier the President of the American Republic will be in a position, if he wishes, to dictate his own terms to us.

R. MCK.

24 October 1916

REPORT TO THE CHANCELLOR OF THE EXCHEQUER OF THE BRITISH MEMBERS OF THE JOINT ANGLO-FRENCH FINANCIAL COMMITTEE

1. With our French colleagues, Monsieur Homberg, Monsieur Sergent and Monsieur de Peyster, we held a first session of six sittings from 3 October to 10 October, Mr John Morgan, Mr Davison, Mr Grenfell and Mr Harjes also attending a considerable part of the proceedings on behalf of Messrs J. P. Morgan.

2. Our French colleagues, having explained their own financial position, urged that the allowance of £25 million a month from the British government for external payments by France, promised under the Calais agreement, will be by no means adequate to their needs, their expenses abroad and particularly in America showing 'une augmentation constante et sensible', and filling Monsieur Ribot with sentiments of the gravest despondency and alarm. Further examination, however, showed that the moneys provided under the Calais agreement would probably prove adequate for the present. While, therefore, expressing the greatest sympathy with the difficulties of our French colleagues and taking care to say nothing that could be construed as

a refusal of further assistance, we indicated that in view of our own situation we could not recommend the Chancellor of the Exchequer to increase the credits under the Calais agreement at the present moment, and arranged to meet them again in Paris towards the end of November.

They estimated their deficit, after allowing for the credits under the Calais agreement, at £40 million to £50 million for the six months ending 31 March 1917. As they regard the export of gold, in addition to what will be forthcoming under the Calais agreement, as out of the question and as they are now altogether devoid of other external resources, they looked either to us or to the United States to fill the gap. Failing further assistance from us, they urgently insisted upon the immediate issue in America of an unsecured Anglo-French loan, of which they would receive their share, or of a further issue of $100 million by the French government on the same conditions as their previous issue. Both these courses, as explained below, were declared by the representatives of Messrs Morgan to be impracticable or inadvisable. But we may be certain that at the Committee's next session the French members will renew their pressure on the British government to assist them further, and will ask us to make ourselves responsible for the whole adverse balance of France whether on government or civil account.

3. The next business of the Committee was to obtain the agreement of the French representatives to certain steps required in the immediate future to deal with the situation in America. All the members of the Committee would have approved the issue immediately after the Presidential election of an unsecured Anglo-French loan of $500 million. But the advice of Messrs Morgan in a contrary sense was so decided and, in the opinion of the British members of the Committee, so well founded, that the Committee as a whole, though with the greatest reluctance in the case of the French members, agreed on the issue early in November of a British loan of $250 million or, if possible, $300 million secured by collateral. The Committee also agreed unani-

mously to recommend the adoption of a proposal of Messrs Morgan to form a syndicate, in conjunction with a limited number of powerful American houses, for the purpose of strengthening the position of the existing Anglo-French loan in the American market. This proposal is now being carried into effect, and Messrs Morgan expressed the hope that, after due preparation of this kind and in conjunction with arrangements for conversion favourable to the holders of the existing loan, they might be able to issue an unsecured Anglo-French loan early next year. Upon the realisation of this hope our financial position next spring mainly depends. Such a loan would be advantageous to us by enabling us to conserve our collateral; but by exhausting the available supplies of money it would compel us to postpone alternative financial operations for the time being.

4. The most important results of the Committee's deliberations arose, however, out of a prolonged and detailed examination which they undertook, in consultation with the principal members of the firm of Messrs J. P. Morgan, into the financial position and prospects of the allied powers, and more particularly of the United Kingdom, in the United States of America.

The situation disclosed by this examination is of so serious a character that we desire to record the following conclusions as deserving the immediate attention of His Majesty's Government.

5. In the five months May to September, 1916, the expenditure of the British Treasury in America has amounted to $1,033 million, being at the rate of $207,500,000 a month. This expenditure has been met to the extent of three-fifths by the sale of gold and British-owned American securities, and to the extent of two-fifths by loans.

6. A conservative estimate of the coming expenditure for the six months October 1916 to March 1917 gives a total of $1,500 million, being at the rate of $250 million a month. This estimate makes no allowance for further orders now in course of arrangement or in contemplation by the Ministry of Munitions. Further,

the experience of the last few weeks (though it must be remembered that we are now at the worst season of the year) has shown that the allowance included in this estimate as required for the support of the commercial exchanges may be below the mark to the extent of $100 million or even more. And lastly, the estimate assumes that there will be no further diminution in the capacity of this country to furnish its own products and manufactures to the other allies and that the latter will continue to be pressed to place any orders, which are to be financed out of British credits, here rather than in America.

It must, however, be added that increased expenditure *anywhere*, including this country, by ourselves or by the allies tends to affect the American exchange adversely, inasmuch as the sums so paid in London are likely in present circumstances to be remitted to New York to pay for goods purchased from the United States, if not by ourselves, by those neutrals to whom we owe money. As we are supporting the American exchanges at a level relatively higher than that of the other principal neutral exchanges, the entire adverse balance of trade of the British Empire and the allies tends to be settled over New York.

7. Assets to meet this expenditure can in the main only be found from the sale of British-owned American securities, from gold, and from loans (this term including bank credits and the proceeds of bills).

The first of these resources, which has yielded $300 million in the last five months, must be regarded as negligible for the future. The small amount of American securities still in hand or to be obtained will be more fruitfully employed to render palatable to the American investor a much larger proportion of non-American securities, as our collateral for ensuing loans.

Including the promises recently extracted from France and Russia, the Treasury have built up a secret reserve in gold amounting to nearly £100 million. We should regard it as very imprudent to exhaust this ultimate reserve, which cannot be replaced, until the end of the war is in sight. On the other hand it will not be practicable, even in favourable circumstances, to retain more than half of this reserve by 31 March next; and we must expect to disburse at least £50 million (or $250 million) to the United States in the course of the next six months.

8. This leaves a deficit of $1,250 million to be met by the issue of loans in America. That is to say, five-sixths of our current expenditure in America henceforward must be met out of American loans, as compared with two-fifths during the past five months. Or to take aggregate figures, we have to borrow $1,250 million before 31 March 1917, as compared with actual borrowings of $400 million in the past five months, being at the rate of more than $200 million a month as compared with $80 million a month.

Yet to obtain $80 million a month has required the most persistent efforts.

9. A loan of $50 million has been already promised by the government of Canada; and we must hope that a further $50 million may be obtained from this source in the spring. There remains $1,150 million to be borrowed in the United States.

10. Our French colleagues expressed great concern at the possibility of our being required to provide collateral security against the whole sum to be borrowed. But even in this contingency, which we hope may be avoided, we do not on this score see any ground for special anxiety. Our French colleagues are influenced by a more vivid appreciation of the limitations of their own resources in this kind than of the abundance of ours. Provided the American lenders will be satisfied with a smaller proportion of American securities than hitherto, an event which we have reason to anticipate, we can continue to supply collateral security of a high class to meet our requirements up to 31 March at least. When our existing American securities are exhausted, the hope would be that we might satisfy the American investor by non-American collateral supported by a very ample margin. It is not, however, so much in this direction that we look for the most immediate danger as in that indicated in §13.

11. We exposed to the representatives of Messrs J. P. Morgan our need for $1,500 million before the end of next March, and Mr John Morgan and Mr H. P. Davison were closely interrogated on every relevant aspect of it. This figure was communicated to them for the first time, and they did not conceal their dismay. Mr Davison had been aware that the aggregate figures had grown very large, but he had not realised that so much would be required in so short a time. 'Your confidential information as to requirements of Allied governments is staggering. It is far from clear how they can possibly be met . . .', was cabled by their New York house on 10 October. 'The money required', said Mr Davison, 'is more than or as much as, exists. We must get at the business any way and every way which is credible and will bring money. Every possible device has got to be availed of.' The following dialogue at the close of our discussion with Messrs Morgan perhaps, indicates the position more exactly than any formal statement:

Lord Reading (to Mr John Morgan)   Do you see your way to financing this $1,500 million by March 31st?

Mr John Morgan   No. I don't see the way. But we are taking too long a view of this thing. We don't have to pay it all now.

Lord Reading   No. But we have also to look beyond March 31st. I am not asking exactly how it is to be met. But in your own minds, with every possible expedient, do you see your way to carrying us through to March 31st?

Mr Morgan   That's an awful question.

Lord Reading   May I change the question? In your judgement do you think that somehow or other the money will be found by March 31st?

Mr Morgan   Yes. It will be found somehow or payments will be sufficiently postponed (meaning, by temporary bank overdrafts).

Mr Davison   On the first day of April the allies will not be in a discredited position and will still be paying their way.

Mr Morgan   All devices must be used.

Mr Morgan added that the problem of meeting the situation must be left largely in the hands of his firm, in view of the amount to be obtained within a brief period.

12. If our expenditure were coming to an end on 31 March, such a statement would be comparatively satisfactory. But as we have to provide beyond 31 March even for existing commitments, it is disquieting. Our financial agents tell us, in effect, that by the use of every available device and possibly at the cost of postponing payments by bank overdrafts we shall still be solvent on 31 March. They cannot tell us how this result is to be achieved but they hope and believe it will be possible. As time goes on the American market may grow more accustomed to digest foreign loans and we may also hope for assistance to our credit from an improved military situation. But nevertheless we shall start the next half year with our devices exhausted, the American market congested with our issues, our account in debit, and our gold reserves diminished by one-half at least.

13. This leads us to the principal and dominating conclusion which as the result of our recent conferences overshadows in our minds all other considerations.

The problem of paying our way in America is mainly one of the possible *pace of borrowing*. In its practical aspect it is not a question of our credit, or of our capacity to put up security, or of the confidence of the Americans in the success of the allies or of their sympathy with us—though without any one of these favouring influences we should be in great difficulties. On these heads we must take any risk that may exist.

The question is whether the money can be turned over in America and brought back to us in the form of loans as fast as we are spending it. Between each loan and the next we live on an overdraft with our bankers. Each time the overdraft grows heavier and the longest interval which we can spare between the successive loans grows less. The maximum overdraft we can secure is limited by the financial capacity of New York and by the peculiar banking laws of the United States. A time will come when the overdraft has reached its maximum before it is by any means practicable to secure the issue of a further loan.

Given time, we could probably borrow all we want. The question is whether the rate at which our commitments are falling due will give us time.

14. We considered the suggestion that the industrial and financial world of America is now so deeply committed to the allied cause, that it cannot afford to let us fall into difficulties. There is force in this contention. But it must not be pushed too far. We believe that this factor will enable us to obtain *some* supplies and will prevent us from being left entirely and absolutely without resources even when we cannot find means of immediate payment. But if pushed beyond this point it is fraught with the gravest danger. We cannot expect that these influences will induce the United States to finance anything approaching the total requirements of ourselves and our allies.

Our financial requirements have got far beyond any total which can be met by the great capitalist interests, whose liquid resources are much less than in this country, and who are not all of them good friends of ours. We have to look far beyond these interests to the great investing public, not only on the Atlantic seaboard but in the middle and far Western states where the European war is a distant and unrealised adventure. Those upon whose money we must depend are not only or even chiefly the same as those with whom we place our orders. The New York capitalists can provide only a fraction of what we require. The problem is whether the general public can be induced to subscribe to our loans at a *pace* equal to our expenditure. To raise the interest payable would not serve us, as such action by provoking suspicion of our credit might diminish the proceeds of our loans and could not materially increase them.

15. Large sums are at present expended by the Treasury in maintaining the purchasing power of the £ sterling in terms of the dollar. This expenditure is the pivot of our whole financial policy and the foundation of our credit in all parts of the world.

By supporting the American exchange we limit the possible depreciation of all the other neutral exchanges. And, as the exchanges of the other allies on London are also supported, the purchasing power of every member of the alliance is maintained in all parts of the world. If this policy was suspended, such suspension involving as it must a prohibition of the export of gold, with the consequent demoralisation of all our exchanges, nevertheless some funds would still be forthcoming in America and other neutral countries at a price. It is not to be supposed that a country of the wealth of the United Kingdom can ever become in any literal sense bankrupt. But there is a great difference between being able to obtain moderate sums at a high price and being able to satisfy successfully the unexampled demands which the efficient prosecution of the war by the alliance as a whole now entails. The latter position is only possible so long as our credit is unquestioned and we can maintain the appearance of having at our command a sufficiency of liquid resources.

16. In short, desperate expedients may always keep us supplied with *some* resources. But they certainly will not yield to us or our allies all we want.

Without venturing to prophesy the exact term for which we can hope to meet the present rate of expenditure, we believe that the problem of how long our immediately available resources will hold out and consequently of how they can be utilised most wisely is now one of pressing, practical importance.

The seriousness of the situation as it is now developing cannot be more vividly illustrated than by the statement that out of the £5 million which the Treasury have now to find daily for the prosecution of the war, nearly £2 million has to be found in America.

A crisis came at the end of November. The Federal Reserve Board, alarmed by an extraordinary influx of gold and the continuing demands of foreign governments for loans, advised the American banks to curtail their lending abroad. In deference the Chancellor of the Exchequer and French Minister of Finance immediately withdrew their Treasury bills from sale. The London bankers took fright and once again wanted to suspend specie payments, but the Treasury stood firm. During the first week of December, however, they paid out $76 million in support of the exchange, as compared with their estimated weekly allotment of $12 million, and during the three weeks ending 16 December an average of $107 million. ('Another ten days of this, and we should have been finished', as Keynes remarked in another talk at the Admiralty 15 February 1917.) Keynes recalled the emergency in some 'Notes on Exchange Control' that he wrote at the beginning of World War II (24 September 1939), from which the following is an excerpt.

FROM 'NOTES ON EXCHANGE CONTROL'

1. In the last war there was no exchange control as such, apart from import licences, restrictions on foreign investment etc. The procedure adopted was analogous to that of the Exchange Equalisation Fund just before the war. That is to say, there were free dealings over the exchange at a rate which was 'pegged' by the Treasury, unlimited dollars being supplied at this rate. The only difference was that the pegging was done in New York and not in London, the dollars being supplied by Morgans as our agents. E. C. Grenfell would come round to the Treasury each morning with a pink cable in his hand, showing what had been paid out on the previous day.

Complete control was so much against the spirit of the age that I doubt if it ever occurred to any of us that it was possible. But the absence of it made my task of preparing a monthly budget of the dollar position very precarious. I used to obtain each month an estimate from the various departments and from the allies both of their total outstanding dollar commitments and of the amounts which they expected to mature in each month. To this, if I remember rightly, I added my own estimate of the probable requirements of the 'free exchange'. On the other side, our dollar assets, actual and prospective, were set out in the shape of gold and securities and the proceeds of loans. But the requirements of the 'free exchange' would come irregularly in great rushes, just like the demands on the Equalisation Fund, largely depending on the nature of the war and political news. I remember in particular a terrific run at the end of 1916, when the daily requirement (if my memory is correct) ran for a short time in excess of $5 million, which in those days we considered simply terrific. Chalmers [Sir Robert Chalmers, with Bradbury Joint Permanent Secretary of the Treasury] and Bradbury never fully confessed to ministers the extent of our extremity when it was actually upon us, though of course they had warned them, fully but unavailingly, months beforehand of what was coming. This was because they feared that, if they emphasised the real position, the policy of the peg might be abandoned, which, they thought, would be disastrous. They had been brought up in the doctrine that in a run one must pay out one's gold reserve to the last bean. I thought then, and I still think, that in the circumstances they were right. To have abandoned the peg would have destroyed our credit and brought chaos to business; and would have done no real good. I recall an historic occasion a day or two after the formation of the second coalition government at the end of 1916. The position was very bad. We in the Treasury were all convinced that the only hope was to pay out and trust that the drain would suddenly dry up as it had on previous occasions. But we had no confidence in the understanding of Ministers. Chalmers went over to Carson's room [Sir Edward Carson was a member of the War Cabinet] (my memory tells me that it was in the War Office; but was it?) to report to the newly formed War Cabinet. 'Well, Chalmers, what is the news?' said the goat [Lloyd George]. 'Splendid,' Chalmers replied in his high quavering voice, 'two days ago we had to pay out $20 million; the next day it was $10 million; and yesterday only $5 million.' He did not add that a continuance at this rate for a week would clean us out completely, and that we considered an average of $2 million very heavy. I waited nervously in his room, until the old fox came back triumphant. [This was the first meeting of Lloyd George's new War Cabinet after he succeeded Asquith as prime minister. According to the official minutes of

9 December 1916, 'Sir Robert Chalmers...[was] able to congratulate the War Cabinet on the fact that the amount required daily had dropped in the last two days from 17 million dollars—first to 8 million and then to 4 million dollars.' (CAB 23/1).] In fact the drain did dry up almost immediately and we dragged along with a week or two's cash in hand until March 1917 when U.S.A. came in and that problem was over. So far as I know, the Germans were totally unaware of our financial difficulties. But the American government, of course, knew them. It has been an important part of the case of the recent Nye Committee for denying credits to belligerents that Mr Page cabled to his government as follows on 5 March 1917: 'I think that the pressure of this approaching crisis has gone beyond the ability of the Morgan financial agency for the British and French governments. Perhaps our going to war is the only way in which our present prominent trade position can be maintained and panic averted.'

On the other hand, my monthly estimates were saved by the fact that, as a result of delays in deliveries, the departments and the allies never succeeded anywhere near in spending up to their forecasts. At the end of the war quite a significant part of the orders placed by Ll. G. and Russia in the summer of 1915, were still undelivered; and there were still hundreds of millions of dollars of these old orders outstanding when we were cleaned out in March 1917 and the American Treasury had to foot the bill.[1]

2. These reminiscences are not meant to be wholly irrelevant. It is true that in one important respect our problem then was different. Foreign balances in London were insignificant and were greatly outweighed by what foreigners owed us on acceptance credits. The financial crisis of 1914 was due, not to our being unable to pay what we owed abroad, but to foreigners being unable to pay us. It was not sterling which crashed in that month, but the dollar (which went temporarily over 6 to the £). But by

---

[1] I have depended wholly on my memory unrefreshed by documents in writing the above, and it is probably inaccurate in detail.

1916 the difference between the position then and the position now was not so fundamental.

It is, therefore, well to remember that we did get through after a fashion without blocking the exchanges; and this policy was not without considerable advantages of simplicity and efficiency.

Our international position is so totally different from Germany's that their technique does not offer a good model for us. I have not reached a decided opinion on the point. But there is much to be said against blocking up *all* the loopholes and crevices. Not all the money which slips through is 'lost'. There is a good deal of business which does us no harm and is better allowed which, nevertheless, one cannot make into a precedent by giving it official approval. There is a case for controls which those in charge know to be imperfect and incomplete and deliberately leave so; especially in England. It is far more trouble than it is worth to be too logical about controls. (I remember how the day after I had established the principle that the Russian credits should be for munitions only, M. Routkowsky came round for my initials to a Bond Street bill for a Grand Duchess's underclothing; and there was the case of the beeswax for the Little Fathers.)

I am, therefore, doubtful if it is practicable or advisable to close down too completely the black exchange. It has its uses within limits. One could see to it that it did not cost too much *net*. I can even imagine occasions when it might be worth the while of the Treasury to give it covert support. It is probably on a relatively small scale and is a useful safety valve. It is not advisable to render literally impossible all those transactions which the Treasury cannot afford formally and publicly to approve.

I suggest, therefore, that the main transactions should be canalised and that the rest should be left to themselves. My main criticism of the measures put into force too quickly by the Board of Trade etc. is that they seem to flow from the belief that there is no middle course between complete *laissez-faire* and complete totalitarianism. I feel that it would be more in accordance with the traditions of the Treasury to be cautious and cagey with its control system, and to cultivate turning a blind eye with the other one wide open . . .

Keynes went on from these reminiscences to discuss what he considered should be the aims of exchange control in 1939. This will be printed in full in a later volume.

Chapter 3

INTER-ALLIED FINANCE, 1917-1918

Exchange—the dollar exchange—was to be Keynes's overriding care during the next two years. At the start of 1917 the Treasury again faced the eventuality of being forced to abandon the gold standard; he again upheld the case for its support in the paper that follows. The only copy to be preserved of this memorandum, signed and dated 17 January 1917, was kept in the miscellaneous files of the Chancellor of the Exchequer's office (T 172/643).

MEMORANDUM ON THE PROBABLE CONSEQUENCES OF ABANDONING THE GOLD STANDARD

I. In ordinary times the power to convert sterling into foreign currencies is guaranteed by the right to turn sterling into gold for export. This facility has already been abolished in all but name, the last withdrawals of gold from the Bank of England's reserves for export on private account having taken place at the end of June 1916. Its place is now taken by the official sale of dollars, in exchange for sterling, *to all comers* at a minimum rate which has been fixed for many months past at $4\cdot76\frac{7}{16}$. This arrangement provides directly for the conversion of sterling into dollars; but indirectly it also has the effect of stabilising all the other exchanges, inasmuch, as gold exports being still permitted from the United States, sterling can be converted at a price into any other foreign currency by first purchasing dollars and then using these dollars to obtain the foreign currency required.

In practice, therefore, to abandon the gold standard means to abandon the present policy of selling dollars to all comers at a fixed price not far removed from the parity.

II. If this policy were to be abandoned tomorrow, the first result would be a complete collapse of the exchanges on all neutral countries not only as regards this country but also

215

as regards all the allies and all parts of the empire except Canada.

While a few speculators might be tempted in by the high prices offered for foreign currencies in terms of sterling, it is probable that this would be on a small scale, certainly at first, and that exchange quotations would not only fall heavily but would become nominal—that is to say, there would for the moment be no exchange offering at any price and business would be at a standstill.

This state of affairs would express itself concretely by importers into this country, allied countries, Australasia, India and South Africa, being unable to sell their bills in the country of export for the local currency required by them to pay for the goods they were exporting. The bill on London would have become unsaleable. Vessels would be delayed in port, shippers being unable to obtain delivery of the goods without paying for them.

The initial disorganisation would be very great, and remedial measures would doubtless be taken to deal with it. These would presumably take the form of the prohibition of private dealings in exchange, of the concentration into the hands of an official body of all our foreign cash resources however arising, and of the doling out of monies by this official body from the funds at their disposal to meet such foreign expenditure as was considered essential.

Some such action would be so obviously inevitable that we may presume that the prohibition of private dealings in exchange would be decreed simultaneously with the cessation of sales of dollar exchange to all comers. The policy under consideration, that is to say, would take the form (in addition to the prohibition of the private export of gold) of prohibiting private dealings in exchange and of instituting the official sale of exchange for approved purposes.

It is the effects of such a system which we have to examine.

III. The sale of foreign exchange for approved purposes only would involve an organisation to determine and put into effect an order of priority, not only as regards imports, both on private and on Government account, into this country, but as regards the source and amount of importation into the allied countries and into all parts of the empire except Canada (the currency system of which is not based on sterling). The exchange authority would become a body of the most far-reaching importance, having to determine the channels of consumption and expenditure, private as well as public, of the alliance and of the empire.

To take one instance, Australasia: various British government departments have purchased practically the whole of the exportable produce of those countries—wheat, meat, wool, cheese, gold, ores—and have bargained to pay for these goods in sterling. Australia can only import from the rest of the world by exchanging this sterling for other foreign currencies. One of the incidental duties of the exchange authority would, therefore, be to decide what allocation of exchange and on what conditions should be made to Australia.

The setting up of the necessary organisation, especially if it had to be done in a hurry, and the business of issuing the necessary decisions (which would involve every kind of political and diplomatic issue as well as great technical knowledge on the side of supply) would obviously be a matter of the greatest difficulty and trouble upon which no one would embark for its own sake. We have to consider, therefore, what would be the effect of such a system (i) upon our liabilities and (ii) upon the means we have to meet them.

(i) The exchange authority would undoubtedly be a powerful body for effecting economies with a bludgeon. Various government departments and committees already exist for the purpose of effecting economies, of dispensing with unnecessary imports, of prohibiting wasteful consumption and the like. In practice it is found very difficult to get rid of all unessential expenditure without striking at necessary services. The exchange authority could only effect additional economies if it proved, in the exercise of its multiple functions, to be a more efficient body, all rolled into one, than the War Office, the Admiralty, the Ministry of Munitions, the Food Controller, the Shipping Controller, the Director of Man-Power, the Import Restriction Committee etc., etc. The only obvious advantage it would possess over these bodies would be a more powerful and pervading sense of the need for economy. In short, the abandonment of the gold standard might effect some economies by striking terror into the hearts of the spending departments through the tremendous stir and consternation which it would produce in the Press and in the City, a terror which cannot be produced by quieter methods.

This is as regards consumption in this country. As regards the allies, it is not clear how the change could effect any diminution in their calls upon us, except in so far as the visible signs of our distress might cause them to moderate their demands. In fact, what is said above about the spending departments might also be applied in some degree to the allies. Apart from this, there would be no new factor. What the allies require for the prosecution of the war and what we promise them is purchasing power in various parts of the world. We already endeavour to limit our promises to their necessities. If we were to give them paper which could not be exchanged into such purchasing power, it would be doubtful whether we were keeping our promise and certain that we were not helping them to prosecute the war.

As regards Australia, India and South Africa, the probable consequences are obscure. We might be in a position to enforce on these countries economies which they would not adopt voluntarily. But if so, we should have obtained this power by a species of fraud, having enticed them into selling us goods for pieces of paper instead of purchasing power. We should have to exercise our authority with very great discretion.

So far, then, as our liabilities are concerned, the policy under examination would only diminish them (*a*) by frightening the spending departments and the allies, and (*b*) by rendering necessary and unavoidable (just as our blockade does in Germany) economies not only in the unessential (which is what we aim at at present) but also in services which are now judged essential for the effective prosecution of the war.

(ii) The effect on the means we have to meet our liabilities is the next question to investigate.

(*a*) If the exchange authority offered to buy foreign currencies in exchange for a high price in sterling, the sterling proceeds to be irremoveable until after the war, such an operation would be tantamount to borrowing at a very high rate of interest and some speculators might be tempted to invest. It is impossible to predict on what scale this would occur. The experience of allied countries, in which the rate of exchange is very greatly depreciated, seems to be that the amount to be obtained in this way is not large, the evident risk being a greater deterrent than the hope of gain is an incentive.

(*b*) Foreign balances now in London could be immobilised by the refusal to furnish exchange for their removal. It would be necessary also to prohibit the use of such balances to pay for exports from this country, if the policy was to be effective. If it were the case that foreign balances were tending to diminish (which is not the case at present) some immediate financial advantage might be obtained in this way, though at the cost of what would be regarded by all neutrals as a breach of faith.

(*c*) There are cases in which foreigners have sold goods forward in terms of sterling without any guarantee of the exchange. If they were kept to the terms of their bargain and then refused exchange when they sought to remove the sterling, we should have obtained the goods without paying for them. This is not, however, a practice which could be repeated.

The above are the only means by which our assets could be augmented. There remains one very important respect in which they would be diminished. The consideration about to be discussed is generally (and rightly) given a position of high importance in discussions of this subject and has been regarded by many good authorities as a conclusive ground for the maintenance of our existing policy:

(*d*) Great Britain is in a unique position financially as being the banker of the world. As a result of the primacy attained by the bill on London combined with other complex causes, a very large part of the financial business of the world is settled over London, and for this purpose all countries maintain balances here. When the liquid resources of the world are increasing, the balances tend to accumulate in London and this country enjoys the use of them for the time being. At the present time when difficulties of freight and so forth hamper neutrals in the expenditure of their surplus funds, this is especially the case. The material does not exist on which to estimate the exact benefit we have thus derived. But the London resources of the neutral European countries and the United States have increased in the four months ending 6 January by £23,500,000,[1] apart from balances held here on account of the East, Canada, South America, Africa and other parts of the world, for which we bank. It is indeed probable that this factor has been of the most vital assistance hitherto in enabling this country to bear her prodigious financial burden.

But no one will send balances here unless they are free to take them away again, should they desire to do so. That is of the essence of banking. A bank which has suspended payment does not receive fresh deposits. Not only would a blow have been struck at the post-bellum position of the City of London. We should also have thrown away a great financial asset for immediate purposes. And further, any existing balances out of those now held here which could find some means of evading our system of repudiation as proposed under (*b*) above would escape from us. An official control of exchange can be introduced at Petrograd and even at Berlin without serious consequences; but for this country to follow suit is to evacuate a position of unique advantage.

---

[1] These are the only balances of which statistics are at present available.

IV. Closely connected with the above but deserving, nevertheless, a separate discussion, is the effect upon our credit and reputation generally.

It has been suggested above that some advantages in the direction of economy might be derived from the profound sensation which would be caused by so grave a step as the open abandonment of the gold standard, a step which would be interpreted in all circles as indicative of deep-seated distress. But these advantages would have their counterpart. Our credit would be impaired in all neutral centres and if foreign balances in London were immobilised (which would be a practically inevitable consequence) our good faith would be widely impugned. The prospect of neutral loans without collateral would disappear. Vague doubts would have been awakened which might spread far beyond their origin.

Lastly there is the effect on the mind of the enemy. There are doubtless officials in Berlin whose sole duty it is to watch and report upon our financial position and embarrassments. They suspect our difficulties in America and can probably make a good guess at the position all round, just as we can about their food difficulties. But there is all the difference in the world between making a good and shrewd guess in such cases and having some absolutely tangible evidence. The rulers of Germany may in the past have been over-encouraged by the views of their financial experts as to our embarrassments, and while they listen to what is told them they do not now care to build too much on estimates.

But I believe that the encouragement and corroboration of their hopes which they would discover in our abandonment of the gold standard would be enormous and even exaggerated beyond what would be justified. Germany would have at last received a solid foundation on which to base her policy of *aushalten und durchhalten*. 'If England has gone off the gold standard, she can't last six months more', is what everybody would say, *whether it is true or not*.

This element in the situation deserves a good deal of emphasis. In the past we have made a fetish of the gold standard. We have taken immense pride in it and constantly proclaimed to the world that it is the cornerstone of our policy. To point out the depreciation of the German exchanges and the stability of our own has been our favourite form of propaganda in all parts of the world. We have urged the neutral world month after month that this is to be taken as the criterion of financial strength. It would be imprudent to believe that all this can be swept on one side without far-reaching reactions in the minds of neutrals. Yet we shall still require to borrow abroad between a third and a half of our total expenditure on the war.

v. To summarise: The abandonment of the gold standard does not afford the means to discharge a single liability; it does not furnish a new instrument of economy except through the consternation it creates; it diminishes our assets by involving the abdication of our position as the world's banker; it is gravely injurious to our credit; and it affords encouragement to the enemy. It is not so much a possible policy for deliberate adoption, as the symptom, if it occurs, of a grave disease.

J. M. KEYNES

17.1.17

Andrew Bonar Law replaced McKenna as Chancellor of the Exchequer in the new Cabinet. Lloyd George's accession to power also brought about a further change at the Treasury for Keynes.

He wrote to his mother:

From a letter to MRS KEYNES, *11 February 1917*

... There's very little news, except the following which may interest you—but on all accounts keep it quite private and mention it to no one at all. I was approved and included in the final list to get a C.B. this honours list. But when Lloyd George saw it he took his pen and struck my name out—an unheard of proceeding. Purely revenge for the McKenna War Council Memoranda against him, of which he knows I am the author. Chalmers is very angry and has been very nice about it. I can't say that I care appreciably. But you won't see my name in tomorrow's list. However (partly I suspect to cancel the above) I have got a much more solid advantage in these last few days, having been properly constituted head of a new department, with a staff behind me, to deal with all questions of external finance. It will be an enormous advantage to have a staff of my own, whom I can organise according to my own ideas. I have been given some very good men and I hope before long to devolve a great deal of work, which is now entirely in my own hands, and to get much freer. I was told that I could have more pay if I asked for it. But I didn't . . .

He had the C.B. as well, four months later. In a letter to his parents which Dr Keynes recorded 30 May, Keynes wrote that he owed it 'to the kindness of Chalmers [Sir Robert Chalmers, Joint Permanent Secretary] who exerted the strongest possible pressure through the Chancellor of the Exchequer and made mine the sole name put forward by the Treasury'.

Marshall took great pleasure in this honour. After a first brief note of congratulation, he wrote again 13 June:

My dear Keynes

I do indeed hope that you will not abandon science for administration. But you have a better chance than any economist has ever had in this country of rendering high services to the State on critical occasions: for you will know more of economics than any professional statesman has ever done; and you will know more of Whitehall difficulties—whether founded in the nature of things or in bureaucracy—than any professional economist has ever done. So when you are K.C.B. and are yet thinking out your best thoughts to their foundations, and from your foundations, you are to suppose that my shade is hovering over you, and dropping an ethereal wreath from Elysian fields on your head.

Yours till then, and after

ALFRED MARSHALL

As the head of 'A' division Keynes reported directly to Chalmers and to Bonar Law as Chancellor of the Exchequer. Towards the end of the war his staff numbered seventeen; among his assistants were Andrew MacFadyean,

Frank Nixon, Dudley Ward, O. T. Falk, Geoffrey Fry and Rupert Trouton. The miscellaneous files of the Treasury are the main sources for documenting this period of his career; his work can be traced almost day by day in hand-written drafts of telegrams for the Treasury's representative in Washington, Sir Hardman Lever. The drafts were submitted for Chalmers' approval, and if they were very important for Bonar Law's, before transmission.

With the pound pegged to the dollar, the 'external finance' of 'A' division meant financial relations with the United States, which was now being inexorably drawn into the war. The new government of President Wilson was well disposed towards the allies and the new Governor of the Federal Reserve Board, W. P. G. Harding, was seeking ways and means to reverse the pronouncement of the previous November and encourage American investment abroad. The timing of this came not a moment too soon for the British Treasury. France, which formerly looked to Britain only for loans to cover purchases in sterling, had become dependent on British financing for all her purchases in North America and for the support of her exchange. This burden, added to the large loans for the same purposes already supporting Russia and Italy, was rapidly reducing the Treasury's American resources to a dangerously low point. Assuming a weekly expenditure of $75 million, Keynes reported 22 February 1917 that the available resources would not last 'for more than four weeks from today'. Three weeks later (17 March) he again found resources that would last 'nearly four weeks' by dint of reducing the weekly rate to $65 million.

The Treasury saw the American entry into the war as salvation. They suspended their own dollar borrowing in order to free the American market for the launching of the first United States government loan and scraped through by increasing their overdraft at Morgan's. In a letter to his mother 30 March Keynes mentioned spending 33 hours at the Treasury in three consecutive days of conferences with both the French and the Italians. (All the same he managed to get away to the Asquiths' for Sunday.)

The United States declared war on Germany on Good Friday, 6 April 1917. 'I went off on Good Thursday evening hoping for four clear days,' Keynes wrote his mother 15 April, 'but the usual telegram of recall arrived on Saturday and I maintained my unbroken record of never being allowed to be away for four days running.'

In the same post Keynes sent his father a copy of *England's Financial Supremacy*, an anonymously edited translation of a series of articles from the *Frankfurter Zeitung* of November 1915, which had just been published in a limited edition by Macmillans. He and Dudley Ward had collaborated in its production. The 'Translators' Introduction' is characteristic of Keynes.

TRANSLATORS' INTRODUCTION TO *ENGLAND'S FINANCIAL SUPREMACY*

The series of articles here translated and presented to English readers appeared in the *Frankfurter Zeitung* during the month of November, 1915, and were later republished by that journal in pamphlet form. It is claimed by their German author that they represent an impartial study of the English money market; of the causes which led to its supremacy before the war; of the probable effect upon it of the struggle on which we are now engaged; and of the methods by which Germans may hope in the future to diminish or destroy the supremacy of the City of London.

The claim to impartiality cannot be admitted in its entirety, although the references to the past are on the whole correct. There are inaccuracies of fact and of inference as to events since the outbreak of war which may or may not be due to a lack of information as to war conditions in England, and there are adventures into prophecy—some already proved false by the event—which show that the writer had not always in view an impartial forecast of the future, so much as a desire to encourage his countrymen or discourage the enemy. On the whole, how-ever, the writer shows a close acquaintance with the London money market, and makes an attempt to present his facts fairly, while his views on the war itself and on after-war conditions are valuable as the opinion of one of the ablest and best informed of German critics.

It is for these reasons that it has been thought useful to make these articles accessible in English. It is lawful to learn from the enemy. It is also imprudent not to be aware of what he says and thinks.

The original intention was to issue the translation without comment. But this method appearing open to misrepresentation, some of the author's inaccuracies are indicated below. No attempt is made to deal with every statement of fact or expression of opinion, and the reader is asked to remember that an absence of comment must not be taken to imply that the text is not open to criticism.

Yet the English reader may learn a good deal from these articles. Some of the dangers to British financial supremacy, to which the writer calls attention, are real, and the advice which he gives to his fellow-countrymen seems well founded. One feature of them is reassuring. We may be certain that their author has done his best to paint the prospects of England in the blackest possible colours and to give all the consolation and encouragement he can to his German readers. And yet we can see that even in the eyes of this acute German the only real risk to the City of London lies in the possibility on our part of weakness, sloth or prejudice. By foresight, energy and freedom it is possible to meet and overcome all the dangers with which he threatens us. We have still a long start in finance, and it is not to Germany that the war is giving the opportunity to gain on us.

Keynes finished the following 'Note on the Financial Arrangements between the United Kingdom and the Allies' (T 172/422) on 9 April 1917 (Easter Monday). Copies went to the Chancellor of the Exchequer and to Lord Cunliffe, the governor of the Bank of England, who with A. J. Balfour, now Foreign Secretary, was about to make an official visit to the new ally. It shows how Keynes and his colleagues were expecting the United States to slip into Britain's role of chief cashier.

NOTE ON THE FINANCIAL ARRANGEMENTS BETWEEN THE UNITED KINGDOM AND THE ALLIES

1. *Belgium*

The expense of supporting the government of Belgium is shared equally by the British and French governments (the Russian government accepting an ultimate liability for a one-third share). Joint loans of £20 million (francs 500 million taken at par of exchange) are granted from time to time and are reckoned to be sufficient for six months, although the Belgian government now claim that as a result of the rise of prices this sum is not now sufficient for more than five months. The total sums so advanced by the United Kingdom since the beginning of the war have been:

1914–15	1915–16	1916–17	Total
£12,000,000	£17,000,000	£21,000,000	£50,000,000

The French government is believed to have advanced a practically equal amount. The loans are paid to the Belgian government in cash at the Banks of England and France.

The above sums include payments to the American Commission for Relief. The British government enters into no direct financial relations with the commission but agrees to the Belgian government making a monthly payment of given amount out of the above subsidies. Up to November 1916 the monthly payment was £1 million; it was then raised to £1,500,000; the commission is now pressing for a further increase to £2 million or £2,500,000.

This payment is the largest item of expense and being for foodstuffs a considerable part is expended in the United States. Of the balance a large part is spent in France, the government and army being situated there and the greater part of the munitions being supplied from France. Expenditure in the United Kingdom, United States and other parts of the world is directed from London and previous approval by the British Treasury is required for any purchase of importance. It has been necessary to enforce this with special strictness in the case of purchases from America. The principal classes of expenditure outside France are boots, clothing, horses, oats, sugar, oil and rifles.

The Belgian Government have always shown themselves economical and it has not been necessary to enforce nearly so strict a supervision as in some other cases.

There is nothing in the existing machinery which would cause a difficulty if the subsidy in whole or in part were to be taken over by the American government. Very few forward contracts for orders intended for Belgium have been placed in the name of the British government.

II. *Italy*

The financial assistance required by Italy is supplied entirely by the United Kingdom, France bearing no part.

The money is provided by the discount at Bank of England rate of Italian government sterling Treasury bills renewable for varying periods up to as much as six years after the conclusion of peace. Up to now a loan of gold has been deposited in London by the Bank of Italy equal to 10 per cent of the bills discounted, but this is not to be required for the future. The total amount of bills so discounted is as follows:

1915/16	1916/17	Total
£49,500,000	£107,500,000	£157,000,000

At first the money was expended by the Italian government independently of the British government. As time has gone on an increasingly large part of the orders has been placed through British government departments. Independent purchases are still made in France and Switzerland out of British credits and to a certain extent in the United States, the last-named being limited by the independent resources which the Italian government have been able to raise in New York. Orders elsewhere, including the great bulk of the North American purchases, are placed, as a rule through British government departments, and only after previous approval by the British Treasury.

As a result of this system considerable forward orders have been placed in America on Italian government account in the name of the British government and these should be a first charge on any credits made available for that government in America.

The latest arrangements made between the Chancellor of the Exchequer and the Italian Minister of Treasury on 22 March last were of an ad interim character. They provide for credits not exceeding £8 million in any one month to meet commitments elsewhere than in North America, £3,000 monthly to provide for the sale of sterling exchange by the Bank of Italy and a lump sum of $30 million to cover further commitments in North America. Commitments have already been incurred against a considerable part of this sum of $30 million. As regards the monthly subsidy for the support of exchange a considerable part of this, probably more than half, is required in reality to support the Italian-American exchange rather than the Italian-London exchange, the former being supported at present by arbitrage over London. It would seem proper that a part of this sum should be defrayed in future out of the credits to be received by the Italian government in America.

The questions which arise are, therefore, the following:

(1) To ensure that existing commitments entered into in America by the British government on Italian government account are defrayed out of the new American credits to Italy.

(2) To secure that a share of the burden of supporting the exchange is borne on these same credits.

(3) To consider the machinery to be employed for future Italian government orders in America. This is dealt with separately below.

III. *France*

Up to six months ago France did not receive credits from the United Kingdom to any large amount except to pay for supplies furnished from this country. Excluding three loan operations on the London market the direct financial assistance received by France during 1915/16 amounted to the discount of bills to the face value of £20 million. Latterly, however, France has required financial assistance not only for purchases in this country but for purchases in America and for the support of exchange. As a result bills discounted in addition to one flotation on the London market during 1916/17 amounted to £171 million. Over and above this the Bank of France borrowed £72 million from the Bank of England, making a total of £243 million, the greater part of which fell in the second half of the financial year. It should be added that France supplied a considerable quantity of gold as against these payments.

It is understood that for the future France will not be dependent on British credits for any part of her North American expenditure. She will look after her direct American commitments herself and she will repay us in dollars for any purchases, such as for wheat and maize, made through British government departments. In addition she will support her exchange, at any rate in part, by means of credits in New York. That is to say, she will ask this country only for credits for expenditure in the British Empire and, perhaps, in South America.

This involves few or no practical difficulties. Apart from grain, the forward contracts of the French government have been placed in their own name and the British government have exercised no supervision or criticism over them. No change of system, therefore, is required by reason of the fact that a greater part of her credits than formerly are arranged in New York.

IV. *Russia*

At the Paris Conference of February 1915, France and Great Britain agreed to share equally the financial assistance to be afforded to Russia. This arrangement broke down almost at once. In practice France has financed only the expenditure of the Russian government in France itself and the United Kingdom has furnished funds for Russian government expenditure in all other parts of the world. The Russian government Treasury bills so discounted by the British government have been as follows:

1915/16	1916/17	Total
£174,000,000	£226,500,000	£400,500,000

Owing to the very large sums of money involved and the rather reckless action of the Russian government in placing orders in the early days, leading to considerable waste of money and to much fruitless competition between the allied governments, a very complete and elaborate machinery has been established for the purpose of supervising and criticising Russian demands. As time has gone on an increasing number have actually been placed through British government departments. At the present time in the case of practically every article of importance the appropriate British government department buys jointly for the British and the Russian governments securing for the latter the full benefit of British organisation and for both parties freedom from competition. The elaboration of such a system has been a matter of considerable difficulty. But it is now working well upon the whole. No order is now placed on behalf of the Russian government, with certain exceptions specified below, which is to be financed out of British credits, except with the prior approval of the British Treasury.

In order to moderate the harshness of the system of supervision thus introduced an arrangement was made a year ago by which the Russian government were given a monthly credit to be at their free disposal without supervision or criticism of any kind, the understanding being that this sum would be devoted partly to the support of exchange and partly to the purchase of commercial articles which were not necessarily required purely for military purposes or in the case of which no inconvenient results were likely to follow from a system of independent purchase. This monthly sum has been fixed lately at £4 million a month, of which £1,500,000 is to be used for the support of exchange and the balance for other purposes. Lord Milner's mission thought that it might be appropriate for a short period at any rate to increase somewhat the allowance for the support of exchange. They advised, on the other hand, that the monies for other purposes might be reduced, as no freight was available for the articles to be so purchased except at the expense of military stores. As a result, the total figure has been kept at £4 million for the month of April with the understanding that as much of this as they choose may be directed to the support of exchange. No definite arrangement has yet been made for the period subsequent to April.

The organisation established in London is dealt with in somewhat more detail below.

The governing factor in the Russian position is, however, that of freight. The Russian government have always desired to place orders for much larger quantities of material than could be carried into Russia by the available routes. The growing shortage of shipping has further accentuated the natural difficulties. When Lord Milner's mission visited Petrograd in February they found that the demands of the Russian government amounted, with existing orders, to some 13 million tons of materials. The experts decided, however, that the maximum port capacity over 1917 would be 4,431,000 tons and even this figure was considered by both the British and the French officers to be excessive. The tonnage which can be supplied by the Admiralty, including what Russia can do for herself cannot exceed 3,400,000 tons at the maximum. Recent events have made it improbable that this total can be reached. Lord Milner's mission agreed, however, in order to be on the safe side from the Russian point of view, to work up to a programme of four and a quarter million tons for the present calendar year, so far as the placing of orders is concerned. The Russians agreed accordingly to an allocation of tonnage to different classes of materials on this basis.

A Cabinet committee under the chairmanship of Lord Milner has now been set up in London to endeavour to carry this programme into effect. So far as can be calculated at present existing orders together with coal and allocations of heavy artillery which have been promised to the Russian government will occupy practically the whole and possibly more than the whole of the tonnage referred to above. It is necessary, therefore, to exercise the most careful supervision if purely wasteful orders are to be avoided. The Russian government have never taken the freight figure seriously and do all in their power to secure the placing of orders far in excess of the agreed total. It is most earnestly to be wished that the American government will not enable the Russian government to act independently of considerations of freight. And it is difficult to see how the requisite information for criticism of their demands can be secured except by the utilisation of the existing machinery. Perhaps it would be possible to secure American representation on Lord Milner's committee.

The problems which arise are, then, the following:

(1) Existing orders for the Russian government in America fall into the following groups:

(i) *Orders placed by the Russian government in their own name prior to October 1915.* Originally these were for a large amount but the greater part has now been cleared off. With the exception of a large rifle contract about which full information can be obtained from the Anglo-Russian sub-committee in New York, no considerable payments are likely to fall due. Presumably payments on account of these contracts will be made in future out of American credits.

(ii) *Orders placed by British government departments on Russian government account in the name of the British government through Messrs J. P. Morgan.* The amount of these now outstanding is $115 million. This figure may be reduced by cancellation of late deliveries.

(iii) *Contracts placed by the Russian committee in America but signed by Messrs Morgan on behalf of the British government in order to secure the advantage of British credit.* The total of these which is not very large is not available at the moment but could be obtained in New York.

(iv) *Orders placed by British government departments as British government orders out of which allocations have been approved to the Russian government.* This class of order is chiefly for such things as metals, where a large order is placed in America by the Ministry of Munitions to cover the requirements of several of the allies, allocations being made to each of the allies at a later date.

The exact figure of such orders is not available, as it partly depends on the exact allocations to be made. But it certainly does not exceed $100 million. It is necessary that (ii), (iii) and (iv) as well as (i) shall be a first charge on Russian–American credits.

(2) As regards the support of exchange and the 'free' credit, it is impossible to determine accurately what part relates to American expenditure. It is suggested that as in the case of Italy, the burden should be borne equally by the British and American governments.

(3) The question of how future orders in America should be placed for Russian government account as a result of the deficiency of freight. As explained above for the present at any rate these ought to cost the American government very little. What is chiefly essential is that the question of approving purchases for Russia should not be divorced from the organisation for making arrangements for carrying them.

Nothing is more certain than that the Russian government would like to return to the happy old days when they had credits amounting to large sums at their absolute disposal and could send buying agents, some honest and some less so, buying everywhere whatever a department in Petrograd had in mind to regardless of wider considerations. It is entirely a matter for the American government as to how much restriction they will wish to place on Russian purchases. But it is only fair to tell them that our experience indicates the absolute necessity of a rigorous system of co-operation and control. If such a system is to be employed it is clearly desirable that it should not be separate from the British government system which would be continued so far as relates to purchases still to be met out of British credits in parts of the world other than North America. It is impossible to say whether an order could prudently be placed in America unless it is known what is already on order and what is to be supplied from elsewhere.

v. In the case of the governments referred to above with the exception of France, it has been stated that orders have to receive the prior approval of the British Treasury. The machinery through which Treasury control is exercised is as follows.

A new government department has been established known as the Commission Internationale de Ravitaillement. The officials of this department are responsible to the British government. But each of the Allied governments has attached to this commission a number of delegates representative of each of the principal departments of supply. The principal allied delegates are under a head appointed by the allied government and the financial agent of the allied government in London is associated with them. The Russian committee in particular is very highly organised and has a staff of more than 100. Thus it is possible to centralise all applications and for the experts of the British government supply departments to deal direct with experts appointed by the allied governments. It is the business of the British members of the commission to protect the interests of the allied delegates, to collect information required by them and by the British government departments and to put them in touch with the corresponding British experts. The British staff of the Commission Internationale de Ravitaillement includes experts for each of the principal branches, who act in close co-operation with their allied colleagues.

When, for example, the Italian or Russian governments desire to place an order to be financed out of British credits they refer the order to their representatives on the Commission Internationale de Ravitaillement. These delegates inform the British members of the Commission Internationale de Ravitaillement and inquiries are set on foot as to the possibility and date of supply, the price, etc. and the arrangements for transport. After preliminary enquiries have been made the order is referred to the finance branch of the Commission Internationale de Ravitaillement, who forward the details to the British Treasury. The order is then examined and criticised on the general principles of Treasury control and further information sought for if it seems necessary. When a good case has been made out for placing the order, Treasury approval is accorded and the necessary steps are then taken to place the order in question. Originally the organisation was very imperfect and delays were likely to ensue. It is now generally possible for the Treasury to deal with the applications on the day on which they are received according to principles which the course of experience has established as sound. There have, of course, been some cases of friction. But on the whole the system has worked with much greater smoothness than might have been anticipated.

In early days orders were placed by the allied delegates themselves. But by far the greater part of them are now placed through British government departments.

When the time for payment comes allied Treasury bills are discounted by the Treasury up to a cash value sufficient to meet the orders approved, when they have been placed by the allied governments themselves. When, on the other hand, they have been placed by British government departments, an account of the sums due is rendered from time to time and the debit is cleared by the deposit of Treasury bills to an appropriate discounted value without any cash passing, the funds required to pay the manufacturers having been disbursed in the first instance from British funds.

In the case of Russia the Cabinet committee lately set up under Lord Milner to a certain extent takes the place of the Treasury in the above arrangement. All orders pass through the Treasury as before, but difficult cases are referred by the Treasury to the committee for advice and decision.

Russia and Italy both have delegations in New York somewhat similar to their delegations in London, but on a smaller scale. The Italian delegation does not now place any orders which are to be financed out of British credits, all Italian orders so financed being placed through British government departments. The Russian delegation, on the other hand, is in much closer touch with the British authorities and a good deal of authority has been delegated to a sub-committee of this delegation on which British representatives also sit. The Russian commission in New York, however, is not allowed to place any order until it has been examined in London and approved in the manner set forth above. When an order is so approved for placing in America, a cable is despatched by the president of the Russian commission in London to his New York colleague and at the same time a cable is addressed on behalf of the British government to Messrs J. P. Morgan, confirming and authorising them to make the necessary financial arrangements on behalf of the British government.

It should be added that the above organisation refers only to orders to be placed on behalf of the allies. But it is not to be assumed that the orders of British government departments escape a similar criticism by the Treasury. In their case control is mainly exercised through committees of the departments concerned which meet at the Treasury at frequent intervals and bring forward their proposals as to purchase in America.

VI. Assistance to other allies is of secondary importance. The figures up to date are as follows:

	1914–15	1915–16	1916–17	Total
	£	£	£	£
Serbia	2,000,000	5,000,000	5,000,000	12,000,000
Roumania	—	7,250,000	5,250,000	12,500,000
Montenegro	—	19,000	75,000	94,000
Portugal	—	—	2,000,000	2,000,000
Greece	—	684,000	—	684,000
(Provisional government)	—	—	367,000	367,000
Congo	—	—	900,000	900,000

As regards Serbia (to whom France has furnished equal assistance) the figure for the future should be about the same. As regards Roumania, Portugal and the provisional government in Greece, expenditure during the current year may be on a somewhat larger scale.

The total assistance furnished by Great Britain to her allies since the commencement of the war, including assistance granted through the Bank of England and loans on the open market, amounts to about £950 million.

VII. During the six months October 1916 to March 1917, the average *weekly* expenditure in the U.S.A. (excluding Canada) was about $67 million. This expenditure was roughly divided as follows:

	$ million
British government and minor allies	20
Advanced to France	11
Advanced to Russia	10
Advanced to Italy	6
For the support of exchange[1]	20

[1] $25 million less an allowance for allied government wheat purchases, paid for by commercial bills but included in preceding figures.

The money expended on the support of exchange has been for the benefit of the alliance as a whole and a considerable part of the dollars so supplied have been supplied in exchange for sterling credits placed at the disposal of the allies, although the exact amount cannot be identified.

J.M.K.

9.4.17

Congress promptly authorised a loan of $3,000 million for the support of the allies. Both Britain and France received large advances and it was agreed that France would gradually reimburse earlier British expenditure on her behalf. The Treasury hoped that the same procedure would be extended to the other allies. 'Please . . . impress on American authorities', Keynes cabled Lever in the name of the Chancellor of the Exchequer 19 April 1917 (T 172/423), 'that we are still financing day by day not only our own requirements in U.S. but also those of all the other allies except France. In the absence of loan operations this is a serious burden. It would considerably ease matters, if you could obtain an assurance that all expenditure by us in

238

America on allied account since 1 April will be regarded as a first charge for reimbursement on any credits or preliminary advances to be granted by U.S. government to these allies.'

At first it appeared that the Americans accepted the principle of charging earlier British commitments against new loans. Keynes wrote his mother 6 May that negotiations were going 'extremely well. If all happens as we wish, the Yanks ought to relieve me of some of the most troublesome of my work for the future.'

This heartening beginning proved to be the start of a long train of mis-understandings and disappointments. Often what were interpreted by the British as firm undertakings were intended by the Americans simply as general expressions of goodwill until they had been signed and sealed in a document. The new Democratic government was strongly pro-ally and pro-British (as long as they felt that they were dealing with the Liberal and not the Tory British), but they could not be sure of carrying Congress and the rest of the country with them. There was the abiding distrust of England— and admiration of France—which had persisted since revolutionary times, and pro-German and 'America First' elements were still active in some quarters. The British Treasury's choice of J. P. Morgan and Company as its financial agents in the United States was particularly unfortunate. Morgans belonged to the opposition Republican party, they operated as agents charg-ing a commission, and their connections with the steel and munitions indus-tries made them seem all too interested in wartime profits. With so much emotion in the air, the newly appointed officials of the American Treasury felt very vulnerable in confronting Congress, and although the British repre-sentatives in Washington and New York were convinced of their good intentions, their behaviour seemed exasperatingly vacillating and unreliable to their opposite numbers in London.

The Americans were to discover that they had taken on much more than they had expected. 'The monthly sum we require seems enormous to Americans, who are not used to these figures', reported Lord Northcliffe, who was serving as a financial envoy in the United States (T 172/434). The American public wondered why Britain asked for so much compared with the other allies, particularly France. The effect of British censorship—as it must have given Northcliffe a sardonic pleasure to remark—was that while the exploits of the French army were celebrated, little was known about the British.

'You might take opportunity to point out to U.S. Treasury that credits absolutely required by us will not seem so large relative to those accorded other allies if only they will take early steps as follows:' stated a telegram for Lever from Chalmers, drafted in Keynes's hand, 31 May 1917 (T 72/427)

'(1) repayment of our dollar advances on Russian account since 1 April;

(2) ditto Belgium;

(3) ditto balance still due from Italy;

(4) grant Russia and Italy free exchange credits on stipulation that similar credits from us are reduced. All these steps would obviously reduce urgency of our claims. Disproportion of our credits bound to excite comment, if U.S. government let it be supposed that they have taken off our backs whole burden of allies so far as dollars are concerned, whereas this is really far from being the case. Surely it is better from every point of view and will not add to net burden of U.S. Treasury if facts are brought into accordance with professions...'

American advances were intended only for the purchase of American goods. Congress was especially suspicious of the large sums required by Britain for the support of exchange and was convinced that these figures concealed other purchases. Even the American Treasury officials felt that the British regard for maintaining the rate of $4.79 \frac{7}{16}$ was a sentimental exaggeration of its real importance.

All these elements of possible misunderstanding were dramatised in the exchange crisis which took place during June and July 1917. The first warning of a dangerous situation was a telegram from Lever anticipating unusually large shipments of North American wheat, with a resulting heavy drain on dollar resources. Keynes wrote the minute which follows, addressed to Sir Robert Chalmers and suggesting a course of action. It is dated 30 May 1917 (T 172/427).

Sir R. Chalmers,

Sir H. Lever's telegram No. 1353 of 25 May (below) estimates June wheat shipments at £27 million and expresses great anxiety as to our ability to carry this amount.

The position is as follows:

(1) On 13 April the War Cabinet instructed the Wheat Commission and the Shipping Controller to take steps 'to ship as much wheat as possible at the earliest moment'.

The Wheat Commission tell me that they are acting on an instruction from the War Cabinet to ensure 13 weeks' supply in this country by the end of August. This decision, they state, was communicated to them by the Food Controller. No record of any decision has been found in precisely this form. But the statement is evidently based on the following minute of 29 March: 'The Imperial War Cabinet took note that steps would be taken as soon as possible, as a most urgent war measure, to accumulate a reserve supply for 13 weeks.'

(2) This at any rate is the origin of Sir H. Lever's anxiety. In pursuance of the above the Wheat Commission propose to ship 1 million tons of cereals from the United States during June, which together with shipments from other sources will represent between two and three times our maximum rate of consumption.

(3) It is further hoped to ship 200,000 tons on French account and 50,000 tons on Italian account.

(4) At £20 a ton these shipments would represent £25 million which is roughly Sir H. Lever's figure—his estimate being probably based on more exact statistics.

(5) The cost of the French and Italian shipments will be reimbursed to us in dollars. The net burden on our own resources is, therefore, about £20 million.

(6) We have as yet no information as to how much the United States government will let us have in June. Our expenses *exclusive of wheat* should be about $200 million, or $300 million *altogether*. As regards assets, we shall start the month with a balance of about $50 million, assuming that we pay off no part of the overdraft. There are problematical repayments from Russia and a little from Italy and France apart from their payments for wheat already allowed for. If, as is proposed, we pay off the exchange loan in gold, our available gold will be reduced to about $80 million. Sales of securities might yield $10 million.

(7) *If*, therefore, the United States government give us $200 million, and if there is no run on the exchange, we ought just to get through the month including the wheat. Thus the situation may be described as anxious but not by any means desperate.

I submit that the following steps should be taken as a precaution:

(1) We should renew our instructions (telegram No. 1543 of 7 May) that wheat should be paid for in dollars and not by sterling bills, thus keeping the transaction off the exchange. By this means we keep better control and know where we are.

(2) The Cabinet should instruct the Wheat Commission to allow a somewhat larger proportion of the June supplies to go to France and Italy. These countries are being kept very short and are clamouring for more. I gather that the Wheat Commission think that it might be politic on general grounds to take this course and that they would be able to obtain adequate compensation for such favours later on. The advantage from the financial point of view would be that the French and Italians would in this event furnish us with the necessary dollars.

(3) We do not generally speaking have to finance the wheat at the time of purchase but only at the time of shipment. At any rate we can make arrangements with the Corn Exchange Bank of New York for them to finance up to $50 million of unshipt wheat.

It seems highly desirable, therefore, that actual shipment should only take place with the approval of Sir H. Lever. If things were going badly, wheat shipments could be temporarily postponed. Unless the change of plan was made too suddenly, this should not involve waste of tonnage as the boats which are to take the wheat have been diverted from British and Russian munitions and could be returned to that service. As the wheat is only wanted as a measure of precaution, it would seem foolish to risk an exchange crisis by continuing shipment regardless of the financial exigencies of the moment.

(4) Probably about half the wheat emanates from Canada. We might telegraph to Sir H. Lever and Mr Balfour now in Ottawa to exert all possible pressure to obtain a grain loan of $25 million to replace the loan of $20 million just paid off.

Of the above (2) and (3) would require a Cabinet instruction to the Wheat Commission.

J.M.K.

30.5.17

In passing this on to the Chancellor of the Exchequer Chalmers asked him to lay the matter before the War Cabinet 'who will be aware that we are by no means out of the wood yet and that, having no resources of our own available for immediate use (except the above small stock of gold), we cannot afford to get on to bad relations with the States by demands in excess of their convenience. (I apprehend that the U.S.A. government are only beginning to realize what a financial burthen they are assuming, and that we may look soon to be rationed in things and money.)'

The Cabinet maintained that it was important to move the wheat in June. Keynes drafted the necessary precautionary communications instructing Lever and asking the Bank of England to ship gold and Balfour to arrange a Canadian loan. Unfortunately this heavy strain on the exchange position coincided with a massive withdrawal of sterling from London caused by the American banks moving money home to invest in the Liberty Loan—in effect removing from Britain more than $100 million of those very American funds which the Liberty Loan was intended to provide for the allies.

'Continue to protect exchange by all means at your disposal', Lever was instructed in a telegram originating from Keynes 20 June (T 172/427). At first Lever used gold, then he applied to the Americans. British representatives had assumed advances similar to those received in April and May would be forthcoming in June, but they found themselves able to obtain them only piecemeal and with the greatest difficulty. The suspicion that Britain intended to use these funds for support of the exchange rather than for purchases of American manufactures inspired charges in Congress and the Senate that the administration had entered the war to protect moneylenders and munitions-makers. The Secretary of the Treasury, W. G. McAdoo, held that the support of sterling did not fall within his authorisation of providing for American national security and the prosecution of the war. He released the balance of the funds expected only at the eleventh hour (on 28 June Lever cabled to ask what payments he should stop first)—after Balfour and Northcliffe had won the intercession of Colonel House [President Wilson's confidential adviser].

Keynes drafted the formal diplomatic request, on which McAdoo insisted, in a telegram to the British ambassador in Washington for communication to the American government. The cable (with Keynes's draft, T 172/427) was sent in Balfour's name after he and Bonar Law had interviewed the American ambassador in London, Walter Hines Page, 29 June. Bonar Law made a few diplomatic changes in the wording of Keynes's draft which lowered a slightly emotional overtone. For example, 'The attitude of the officials of U.S. Treasury seems to indicate that they are under profound misapprehension as to true position. Their action has produced a situation in which the capacity of the British government to maintain solvency until end of next week is jeopardised' (Keynes) became 'I think the United States Treasury cannot realise the true position which is that the capacity of the British government to make payments in United States after this week is jeopardised' (Bonar Law). 'U.S. government have given us no warning that they were about to withhold necessary financial support' (Keynes) was changed to 'We have had no fear that the United States would not give the necessary financial support' (Bonar Law).

This telegram (29 June) made a formal request for (1) reimbursement for Russian and Belgian expenses in the United States since 1 April 1917, (2) a definite settlement of the amount of financial assistance to be given to the British during July and August, and (3) Britain's $400 million overdraft with Morgans to be repaid during July out of the proceeds of the Liberty Loan. Items (1) and (3), the telegram added, merely formalised what was understood to be the declared intention of the United States government.

In instalments, and at the last possible moment, the British were tided over with the balance of the $185 million that they had requested for June. Then on 3 July Morgans caused consternation by unexpectedly demanding immediate repayment of the $400 million overdraft. Mistakenly they had thought to strengthen Britain's hand with the Americans, but the result was exactly the opposite: McAdoo said that he did not propose 'to allow New York bankers and their allies to use the British government as a club to beat the United States Treasury with'.

McAdoo denied in an official note to Ambassador Page that he had made any binding engagement concerning the overdraft; in fact he had only asked for more detailed information—which had not been furnished—he said. He implied that the United States was being asked to assume the whole financial burden of the war. In answer to the British request he could promise nothing definite beyond July until the allies had reached an agreement on an inter-allied council for determining their relative needs and priorities for American aid.

British telegrams from Washington warned that McAdoo was rapidly coming to the end of his congressional grant and explained the political difficulties that he would have to face in asking for a further loan. The Treasury was highly alarmed. Far from the United States having taken over from Britain the financial burden of supporting her allies, '. . . during past four months our assistance has been on as great a scale as hitherto.

We are still supporting whole burden including United States expenditure of Russia and Belgium and aid required from us by Italy and France has not diminished in spite of aid given by United States government owing to their growing financial exhaustion especially France. During past three weeks we have had to furnish France with £1 million a day to support her exchange and other expenditure here.

These words were Keynes's contribution to a message to the British ambassador in Washington, Sir C. Spring Rice, 17 July 1917 (T 172/428). The message, which had been circulated to the Cabinet, went on to state that Britain was at the end of her resources for payments in America and that if these purchases could not be financed by the United States government there would be a breakdown of the whole financial fabric of the alliance.

McAdoo's note, communicated by Ambassador Page, finally spurred the Treasury to confide some of its figures to the United States. Since this matter was the exclusive province of 'A' division, Keynes may be assumed to have drafted the Chancellor of the Exchequer's reply to the note, which follows, elaborating on a fairly specific outline by Bonar Law. The copy in the Treasury files (T 172/434) is marked 'Handed to Mr Page 20.7.17' in Keynes's writing.

NOTE FOR MR McADOO

The Chancellor of the Exchequer has seen Mr Page's memorandum of 14 July and would be much obliged if Mr Secretary Balfour would cause the following note in reply to be communicated to Mr Page.

1. The Chancellor of the Exchequer, of course, accepts Mr McAdoo's statement that 'at no time, directly or indirectly, has the Secretary of the Treasury, or anyone connected with his department, promised to pay the Morgan overdraft'. In any event this question of past misunderstandings is of small importance as compared with the question as to whether the financial interests of the alliance make this repayment necessary or advisable at the present time. But in view of what passed at the Chancellor of the Exchequer's interview with Mr Page, the Chancellor of the Exchequer thinks it right to quote the actual words received by cable from Sir C. Spring Rice on 9 April which were the foundation of what he said on that occasion:

'Sir R. Crawford [British financial representative] desires the following to be communicated to the Chancellor of the Exchequer. I told the Secretary of the Treasury *last night* that you

appreciated and concurred in his proposals. He was very grati-
fied and asked me to convey his compliments. I mentioned to
him the four considerations referred to in paragraph two of your
telegram.

(*a*) He agreed that repayment of overdraft of some $400
million should be a first call on the loan. (Here follow remarks on
three other distinct topics)

(The telegram continues:)

'*This morning* Governor Harding called at the request of
Secretary and confirmed the views expressed by the latter on
the above points . . .

'*This evening* I went over the matter again with the Councillor
of the State Department who fully concurred that our overdraft
should be a first charge.'

2. There are several indications in Mr McAdoo's note that he
desires above all a fuller and freer communication of facts on
our part. We have never desired or intended to keep any reserves
from him as to our financial position. On the other hand, it has
been our preoccupation to bring home to him exactly what that
position is. Any specific question we will answer. In the meantime the following figures are presented in the belief that they
are the figures most relevant to present issues:

(*a*) Mr. McAdoo points out 'that America's co-operation
cannot mean that America can assume the entire burden of
financing the war'. How much less than this is in fact asked of
her is exemplified in the following table of assistance rendered
to the European allies by the United States and the United
Kingdom respectively since the date of the entry of America
into the war.

The Chancellor of the Exchequer gratefully acknowledges that
the United States Treasury have advanced $685 million to this
country in addition to the above sums to the other allies.

But he invites Mr McAdoo's particular attention to the fact
that even since America came into the war the financial assistance

Financial assistance from 1 April to 14 July 1917

	By United Kingdom	By United States
	£	$
France	56,037,000	310,000,000
Russia	78,472,000	nil[1]
Italy	47,760,000	100,000,000
Belgium (including Congo)	8,035,000	15,000,000[2]
Minor Allies	3,545,000	2,000,000[3]
Total	£193,849,000	$427,000,000 = £90,000,000

afforded to the other allies by the United Kingdom has been *more than double* the assistance afforded them by the United States, and that the assistance the United Kingdom has afforded these other allies much exceeds the assistance she has herself received from the United States.

(*b*) The United States Treasury have so far limited their assistance to expenditure incurred by the Allies within the United States, rightly recognising that such assistance involves a much less onerous burden than financial assistance abroad. The United Kingdom have been unable to adopt this attitude towards their allies, but have supported the burden of their expenditure in all parts of the world. Without this support the allies would have been unable to obtain the supplies of food and munitions which have been essential to their prosecution of the war.

To such an extent has the above been the case, that up to the present time the United Kingdom is still financing the expenditure of Russia in the United States.

(*c*) The total expenditure out of the British Exchequer between 1 April 1917 and 14 July 1917 amounted to £825,109,000, of which £131,245,000[4] was met from loans raised in the United States.

---

[1] Russia has been promised $100 million. But it is understood that she has not yet received any cash instalments.

[2] For Belgian relief—total amount promised $45 million.

[3] Serbia—total amount promised $3 million.

[4] Both these figures relate to expenditure and income *brought to account* on 14 July.

(*d*) The financial burden upon the Exchequer of the United Kingdom did not begin, however, on 1 April last.

The total expenditure between 1 April 1914 and 31 March 1917 amounted to £4,362,798,000 which, added to the expenditure of £825,109,000 since 1 April 1917, makes a total expenditure of £5,161,471,000. It is *after* having supported an expenditure of this magnitude for three years that the United Kingdom ventures to appeal to the United States of America for sympathetic consideration in financial discussions, where the excessive urgency of her need and the precariousness of her position may sometimes import a tone of insistence to her requests for assistance which would be out of place in ordinary circumstances.

A statement is appended at the end of this note for Mr McAdoo's information showing precisely how this sum of £5,000 million has been financed up to date. The proceeds of the overdraft in New York are included under the heading of ways and means advances. This statement includes several particulars which have not been communicated to Parliament and is to be regarded, like all the other figures cited in this note, as being only for the confidential information of the United States government.

(*e*) The following statement shows the expenditure and receipts of the British government in New York from 1 April to 14 July 1917.

	$ million
Payments out of the Treasury account in New York for the purchase of commodities and interest due	602
Purchase of exchange (e.g. the cost of all wheat purchases for allies is included in this figure *inter alia* during the greater part of the period in question) ...	529
	$1,131
Loans from United States government	685
British Treasury notes (sundry munitions contracts)	27
Repayments by French and Italian governments	134
Gold	246
Sale of securities	58
Miscellaneous	19
	$1,169

(f) It will be seen from the preceding statement that gold and securities were realised during the period in question (for the most part during June) to the extent of $304 million. The impossibility of the United Kingdom's continuing to supplement American government assistance on this scale is shown by the following facts.

Gold. We have exported to the United States since the commencement of the war (including gold lately earmarked for the New York Federal Reserve Bank) a sum of £305 million in actual gold. This has all been sent on behalf of the United Kingdom but a considerable part has been borrowed or purchased from the other allies. In addition a fairly substantial amount has been despatched to other destinations. This represents an enormous effort, of which the reserves of the United States have obtained the benefit.

The United Kingdom now have left about £50 million in the Bank of England's reserve, £28,500,000 in the currency note reserve, and an unknown amount estimated at a maximum of £50 million with the joint stock banks. In addition there is a sum of about £10 million at the disposal of the Treasury but not included in any published reserve. This makes a total of about £140 million. There is virtually no gold in circulation. This is about 6 per cent of our banking liabilities and considerably less than a quarter of the gold in the United States.

The amount of this gold which we could part with without destroying the confidence upon which our credit rests is inconsiderable.

Securities. Before the Treasury initiated their official mobilisation of dollar securities, large amounts were disposed of through private channels and also by the Bank of England who were systematically engaged on the disposal of dollar securities in New York.

The following figures relate only to the Treasury schemes:

	$ million
Value of securities purchased	770
Value of securities obtained on deposit as a loan ...	1,130
	$1,900

The above have been disposed of as follows:

Sold in New York	750
Deposited as security against loans	600
Deposited as security against call loan	400
Still in hand	150
	$1,900

(All figures approximate)

We have now obtained virtually all the dollar securities available in this country and in view of the penalties now attached it is believed that the amount of saleable securities still in private hands is now of very small dimensions.

The balance in hand can only be disposed of gradually, and is not, in any case, of an important amount.

3. In short our resources available for payments in America are exhausted. Unless the United States government can meet in full our expenses in America, including exchange, the whole financial fabric of the alliance will collapse. This conclusion will be a matter not of months but of days.

The question is one of which it is necessary to take a large view. If matters continue on the same basis as during the last few weeks, a financial disaster of the first magnitude cannot be avoided in the course of August. The enemy will receive the encouragement of which he stands in so great need at the moment of the war when perhaps he needs it most.

4. Mr McAdoo suggests that the settlement of joint allied purchasing arrangements must precede any promises from him of financial support in August. His Majesty's government do not know how to interpret this statement. They are doing what they can to promote the establishment of such arrangements and at the end of June prepared a detailed scheme, on lines which they had been given to understand would commend themselves to the United States government, for submission to the other allies. But the settlement depends upon the progress of events in America and the acquiescence of the other allies concerned. They will, however, instruct Sir C. Spring Rice to communicate the details to the United States government immediately without

Exchequer Receipts and Issues (net) 1914–15, 1915–16, 1916–17, 1917–18 (to 14 July)

RECEIPTS

		£
Balance 1 April 1914		10,435,000
	£	
Revenue: Tax	1,115,136,000	
: Non-Tax	163,151,000	1,278,287,000
Treasury bills (excluding bills bought as collateral, shown below)		647,160,000
3½% War Loan (Net)		189,149,000
4½% War Loan		592,345,000
4% and 5% War Loans		944,277,000
3% Exchequer bonds		20,449,000
5% and 6% Exchequer bonds (net)		546,957,000
War Savings Certificates		85,300,000
War Expenditure Certificates		23,561,000
American Loan 1915		50,820,000
Other debt		
In United States (net)		314,213,000
	£	
In Canada	53,410,000	
Add collateral		
Treasury bills (net)	20,549,000	
		73,959,000
In Japan		10,527,000
For French gold		53,320,000
For Russian gold		60,000,000
	£	
Treasury bills (Dutch)	14,819,000	
Scandinavian collateral	14,760,000	
		29,579,000
Miscellaneous (in Colonies and loans without interest)		4,502,000
Ways and Means advances (net)		226,631,000
		£5,161,471,000

ISSUES

		£
National Debt services		273,417,000
Other Consolidated Fund services		39,368,000
Supply services (including £80,400,000 for Army and Navy in 1914–15)		365,283,000
Notes of Credit		4,439,467,000
	Expenditure	5,117,535,000
Exchequer bonds 1910 paid off		16,395,000
Miscellaneous issues (Old Sinking Fund a/c) net		2,703,000
Balance 14 July 1917		24,838,000
		£5,161,471,000

waiting for the replies from the other allies. H.M.G. cannot believe that, if these or other natural and unavoidable causes of delay are operative for reasons altogether out of their control, financial support will be withheld and a catastrophe precipitated?

5. As regards Mr McAdoo's concluding passage, the Chancellor of the Exchequer desires to say that Lord Northcliffe is the duly authorised representative of His Majesty's government to conduct all financial negotiations on their behalf. Lord Northcliffe has, however, suggested that someone with political experience, such as an ex-Cabinet minister, should be asked to cross to the United States for the purpose of dealing with the financial situation. If this is the desire of the United States government, His Majesty's government would gladly comply with it.

The allied purchasing arrangements had been under discussion for some time. As British representatives in Washington took pains to explain, McAdoo needed some kind of official body to establish needs and priorities as a means of convincing Congress that these gargantuan sums of money were being economically used for genuine war purposes. Keynes was concerned lest the Treasury lose the control over allied spending that he had established in the past, fearing that when an ally claimed to be supplied from outside of the United States, it would be impossible to know whether similar claims were not being made within the United States at the same time. This eventuality was provided for, but he remained jealous and watchful for the Treasury's prerogative. Regarding American proposals for the constitution of the new council, he telegraphed to Lever on behalf of the Chancellor of the Exchequer (T 172/443):

From Telegram to SIR HARDMAN LEVER, *21 July 1917*

. . . It appears that the Council comprising representatives of each principal European ally would be entrusted with duty of making recommendations as to disposal of available freight and finance. No provision is made for what is to happen in event of divergence of opinion between different allies. But in any event we could not tolerate a situation in which Italy, France and Russia could forward authoritative recommendations as to disposal of our tonnage to which we ourselves did not agree.

Just as we must deal with each ally separately in allocating our own tonnage, so United States must continue to deal with each ally separately in allocating dollars.

We are prepared to substantiate our own claims before United States Treasury, but it seems out of the question that we should substantiate them before all the other allies, each of whom would be chiefly engaged in making good their own case.

The British insisted that the United States be represented on this council in order to decide the relative merits of competing claims, and the matter was finally decided by having an American chairman. In the meantime the allies agreed to the council in principle, giving McAdoo the political weapon that he needed against congressional attacks.

The threatened catastrophe of the past month now stared the British Treasury in the face and unless help was forthcoming the decision to abandon support of the exchange would have to be made within a week. A special memorandum was prepared with Cabinet approval, originally for presentation to President Wilson and at the last moment more tactfully addressed to McAdoo. Keynes appears to have been the author of this appeal, from the minor corrections in his hand to be seen in copies in the Treasury files (T 172/443). The memorandum was ready as early as 26 July but the Treasury postponed its despatch until the weekend of 30 July in order to guard as much as possible against the leakage of rumours which would mean the removal of large blocks of American balances from London and the dissipation of Britain's remaining gold.

While the Treasury waited Keynes wrote the following minute to Chalmers, initialled and dated 28 July 1917 (T 172/443).

Sir R. Chalmers,

I understand that the Memorandum on Exchange for the President is not to go off until after the week-end. We cannot, therefore, expect a definite reply just yet. When the reply comes it is not very likely to be of a perfectly clear-cut character one way or the other. We shall be given a certain amount of encouragement but no definite undertakings.

253

I submit, therefore, that the only safe policy is the following:

(1) To instruct Sir H. Lever that he is to support the exchange as long as he has any dollars in his account, these dollars being derived from the United States government, repayments of allies and miscellaneous sources other than gold.

(2) That he is in no circumstances to order more gold from Ottawa [for the purpose of supporting the exchange; the bankers had warned that to use it before support was abandoned would start rumours].

(3) That if on any day he has no dollars in his account available for the support of exchange and has been unable to obtain any, after making representations to the United States Treasury, he should forthwith suspend the further purchase of sterling through Messrs. Morgan.

The above is a cut-and-dried policy consistent with the expectation of hesitating answers from the United States government and calculated to maintain the position as long as possible, to throw the onus of responsibility in the last resort on the United States government and to protect our final reserves of specie.

28.7.17

J.M.K.

Chalmers added a note to the Chancellor of the Exchequer:

>After discussion, Mr. Baldwin [Stanley Baldwin, M.P., then Financial Secretary to the Treasury] and I concur in the three positive suggestions hereunder; but we feel, and Mr Keynes agrees, that we ought to tell the USA of this policy beforehand, i.e., that it should be intimated *pari passu* with the long exchange memo.

This suggestion was incorporated into the last two sentences of the memorandum which were added by Bonar Law. They are indicated with square brackets in the memorandum that follows which was sent by the Foreign Office as a message from the Chancellor of the Exchequer to Secretary McAdoo (T 172/443 and CAB 23/3).

*Telegram approved by War Cabinet for despatch to
British Ambassador at Washington*

Foreign Office to Sir C. Spring Rice
*Please communicate following message from Chancellor of the
Exchequer to McAdoo:*

The memorandum which was handed to Mr Page on the 20th July last at the instance of the Chancellor of the Exchequer stated in clause 3 that, 'unless the United States government can meet in full our expenses in America, *including exchange*, the whole financial fabric of the alliance will collapse. This conclusion will be a matter, not of months, but of days.'

That memorandum was intended to set forth, for the information of the United States government, the extent of the financial effort which His Majesty's government have already made and the approaching exhaustion of their resources. It did not deal with the question of exchange in particular. As, however, this form of assistance is at the same time most vital to His Majesty's government and most difficult to render clear to the government of the United States it is dealt with here:

1. The growth of the existing system for supporting the exchange.

2. The cost of it.

3. The consequences of withdrawing it.

4. It is pointed out that His Majesty's government must now learn how far the United States government will be able to give them the necessary support. A point has now been reached when a definite decision must be taken within the next few days, and His Majesty's government trust that the government of the United States will agree with them as to the necessity of putting an end to the present state of uncertainty.

1. At the commencement of the war the balance of trade with America was in favour of this country. That is to say, there were, on balance, purchasers of sterling in New York. We were able, therefore, to finance our war purchases from America—as also

from the rest of the world—by the sale of sterling exchange. In the summer of 1915 large amounts of dollars were required to finance advance payments on shell and rifle contracts placed for the Russian government, with the result that the British Treasury were no longer able to provide themselves with all the dollars they required by the sale of sterling in New York, as hitherto. A break in the exchange took place, and it became necessary in the course of the autumn of 1915 for the British Treasury to finance their munition purchases by other means than by the sale of sterling in New York. By the beginning of 1916 they had to go a step further, and to come to the support of the commercial exchange by making a standing offer through their agents in New York to purchase sterling from all-comers at a fixed minimum rate of 4·7676.

The Anglo-French loan of 1915, the mobilisation of dollar securities for sale and collateral security of loans, and the export of gold to the United States were the chief sources of the funds required for these two purposes.

This arrangement provided a direct means for the conversion of sterling into dollars, by which British purchasers of American goods could reckon on financing them at a fixed rate, while the allies and dominions who received sterling credits could turn them into dollars to meet their American payments. Indirectly, also, it stabilised in some degree all the other foreign exchanges, since sterling could, if necessary, be converted into any other foreign currency by first purchasing dollars, and then using these dollars to obtain the foreign currency required.

As time went on this system developed into one by which the nervous centre of the allied financial system was as much in New York as in London. While gold was occasionally exported to other destinations, the bulk of it was reserved for America. By furnishing America with unprecedented quantities of specie we ourselves provided the basis of the credit she required to finance her sales to us.

At first the adverse balance was relatively small. In fact, up to

April 1916, we were still able to supplement our other resources by the sale on balance of a certain amount of sterling. From May 1916 the balance has been progressively adverse.

In November and December 1916 we were faced with the first serious exchange crisis since the summer of 1915. As shown in a table below, the average weekly requirements for the support of the exchange amounted in December 1916 to 44,600,000 dollars.

Since that date high prices, increased expenditure, the growing exhaustion of the allies, the depletion of British financial reserves in all parts of the world, and the progressive destruction of our export trade by diversion of manpower into other channels, have combined to raise the figures, taking one month with another, far beyond those of 1916.

The past seven months have accordingly required a lavish employment of our ultimate liquid reserves. The conclusion of the third year of war finds us with these reserves at a level which will be entirely exhausted in a few weeks if the present drain on them is to continue.

2. The appended table shows the average weekly expenditure of the British Treasury in the United States for each month since April 1916, the first column representing the purchase of commodities and the transfer of dollars to allies, and the second the support afforded to the dollar exchanges. While the figures in the second column have fluctuated widely it will be seen that the average weekly requirements during the past three months have worked out at rather more than 40 million dollars.

The fluctuations are mainly due to the movement of American banking funds to and from London. It is obvious that when American bankers are increasing their London balances the exchange benefits, and, conversely, that when they are withdrawing balances the normal burden on the exchange is aggravated. In the course of the present year cash balances and bills held on American account in London have been as high as £53,500,000 (14 April) and as low as £22,500,000 (23 June).

Average weekly expenditure in the United States of America
(thousands of dollars)

Month	Treasury Account	Exchange Committee	Total
1916			
April	26,969	5,156*	21,813
May	33,033	9,824	42,857
June	35,377	12,608	47,985
July	20,225	5,592	25,817
August	36,267	14,348	50,615
September	37,300	14,073	51,373
October	46,958	19,712	66,670
November	33,588	31,728	65,316
December	34,313	44,600	78,913
1917			
January	31,112	12,125	43,237
February	41,826	35,051	76,877
March	61,856	11,952	73,808
April	42,152	16,717	58,869
May	39,558	40,402	79,960
June	38,072	61,275	99,347
July (3 weeks to 21st)	49,919	21,606	71,525

* Sale of sterling.

Allowing for the fact that the figures of the past three months have been abnormally inflated by the withdrawal of American balances, and that they include the cost of allied wheat purchases, which will be paid for in future otherwise, the average cost of supporting exchange, assuming that American balances in London remain stationary, is not likely to be less than 25 million dollars a week, or 100 million dollars a month.

3. The above summary of past events will have shown what a central place the support of the dollar exchange has come to take in the financial system of the alliance. The funds which we have placed at the disposal of the allies and the dominions have been mainly sterling, the purchasing power of which, in all parts of the world, has been maintained by this means.

To estimate the consequences of withdrawing support from the sterling exchange in New York we must consider the purposes now served by supporting it. The following analysis refers in each case to the balance unprovided for after allowing for

America's ordinary trade obligations to ourselves and the allies:

(*a*) Exports on private account from America to this country for commodities not yet under government control of which cotton is chief.

(*b*) Similar purchases by the allies, who have not yet controlled so many commodities as we have.

(*c*) Purchases from America by the British dominions and by India, only a small part of whose trade is under government control.

(*d*) The cost of neutral exchange arbitraged over New York, that is to say, those allied purchases in neutral markets which are being financed at present out of the resources of the United States.

Of these the United States government will probably wish to inquire most closely into the magnitude and character of (*d*). The amount involved is fairly substantial, but we have no reliable information on which to estimate it.

If the policy of supporting the exchange were to be abandoned tomorrow, the collapse not only of the allied exchanges on New York, but also of their exchanges on all neutral countries, is to be expected. The allies and all parts of the empire, except Canada, would be affected equally. It is likely that exchange quotations would not only fall heavily, but would become nominal, that is to say, there would for the moment be no exchange at any price, and business would be at a standstill.

The consequences of such a state of affairs are partly material and partly psychological.

(i) On the *material* side, exporters from the United States to the United Kingdom, other allied countries, Australasia, India, and South Africa would be unable to sell their sterling bills on London. New business would be interrupted at the source, and vessels would be delayed in port by reason of shippers being unable to obtain delivery of goods without paying for them.

From the American point of view this would involve a break-down for the time being of the mechanism of a great part of her export trade, the paralysis of business and the congestion of her ports. From the point of view of this country and of the other allies it would represent the cessation for the time being of supplies such as cotton, which, while still left in private hands, are nevertheless essential to the conduct of the war. It must be remembered that practically no trade takes place except in commodities of national importance, considerations of freight, quite apart from finance, having already cut off the greater part of what is dispensable.

At the same time American bankers would see their London assets locked up for the period of the war at least, and also heavily depreciated.

How long this state of affairs would last would depend upon the success of our remedial measures. The initial disorganisation must be distinguished from the permanent results. It is possible that even the initial disturbance would be somewhat less serious than indicated above. But whatever the degree of initial disturbance, the eventual result, if the estimate of 100 million dollars a month is correct, would be that the foreign purchases of the alliance would have to be diminished by at least this amount monthly.

This sum, however, would not represent the whole effect. The destruction of British credit abroad would cut us off from certain sources of income which we now possess. So long as existing foreign balances in London remain immobilised, we could not expect foreign countries to increase them. At present we pay in sterling for numerous foreign purchases. Difficulties of freight and supply prevent the neutral countries from spending this sterling forthwith. In the meantime they leave it in London, and payment is thus deferred.

Allowing, therefore, for losses arising out of the injury to our credit, the economies we should have to effect would largely exceed the 100 million dollars monthly.

Pending reorganisation of trade and finance, the loss would, as pointed out above, extend beyond this to commodities which, after things had settled down, we might hope to pay for.

On the material side, therefore, the breakdown of the exchanges must gravely impair our capacity to carry on the war; but, by itself, it need not prove disastrous. We could, if necessary, effect economies on the scale indicated above and still carry on.

(ii) Turning to the *psychological* consequences, the results would be plainly disastrous. The open abandonment of the support of the exchanges is a step which would be interpreted in all circles as indicative of deep-seated distress. Not only would our credit have been impaired in all neutral centres, but vague doubts would have been awakened which might spread far beyond their origin.

Chief of all there is the effect on the mind of the enemy. There are doubtless officials in Berlin whose duty it is to watch and report upon our financial position and embarrassments. They must suspect our growing financial difficulties, and can make a good guess at our position just as we can with their food difficulties. But there is a world of difference between a shrewd guess and a piece of tangible evidence.

The encouragement and corroboration of their hopes which they would discover in our abandonment of the exchanges would, therefore, be enormous. Germany would have at last received a second hope added to that of the submarine on which to base her policy of endurance. It would be said, whether it is true or not, that with the collapse of their exchanges the alliance cannot endure six months more.

We have openly attached hitherto the utmost importance to the position of our exchanges. We have constantly proclaimed to the world that it is the cornerstone of our policy. To point out the depreciation of the German exchanges and the stability of our own has been a favourite form of propaganda in all parts of the world. We have urged the neutral world month after month that this is to be taken as the criterion of financial strength. It would be imprudent to believe that all this can be swept on one side without a far-reaching reaction.

4. The memorandum handed to Mr Page on the 20th July

will have shown to the government of the United States to what a low level our liquid reserves have now fallen. In the event of the exchanges being allowed to fall and of our having to undertake the reorganisation of our affairs thus made necessary, we must do so with a certain amount of liquid resources still in hand. We cannot therefore deplete them further, and must look to the United States government for the future.

We must therefore know, if possible, immediately, whether the government of the United States can give us the financial assistance we need.

In asking this we do not overlook that we are asking them to moderate two conditions which they have hitherto regarded as essential.

In the first place, to provide funds for the exchange is to defray uncontrolled expenditure for undefined purposes. We can only say that we have already extended the sphere of government control far beyond what would have been believed possible a short time back. But the complexity of the world's trade is too great to allow the whole of it to become amenable to a centralised control. This limited continuance of private commerce is represented financially by the commercial exchange.

In the second place, the support of the exchanges involves in part the employment of American funds to finance the purchases of the allies outside America. America must be the judge of how great a burden she can support. At the present stage of the conflict her resources are greater than ours. She has not only her own pre-war resources, but more than £200 million additional in actual gold with which the allies have furnished her in the past three years. It is necessary for the allies to make purchases in neutral countries in excess of what they are themselves able to finance. Within comparatively narrow limits they look to the United States to augment these resources out of her exports of goods and of gold to neutral countries so far as her capacity allows. She cannot render a more valuable service.

His Majesty's government trust most earnestly that they may

learn within a few days' time the general attitude of the government of the United States to this most vital question. [*Addition by Bonar Law:* This is necessary, because it is only by the assistance of the United States government that the support of the exchange can be continued, and at any moment the demand for exchange in New York may be so great that our representatives there may be compelled to cease to support it if they cannot rely upon funds from United States government for the purpose. If any further information is desired it will be at once supplied, and Lord Northcliffe, who is familiar with the whole situation, would gladly discuss it with you.]

The exchange memorandum had good results. The American Treasury understood the importance of Britain's maintenance of the exchanges; their difficulty, as they confided to the British, was in justifying payments for that purpose to Congress—how to explain to the public, who saw only that the American dollar was at a discount in neutral capitals and that American gold was leaving the country, that this in a larger context was not contrary to the welfare of the United States and the conduct of the war. McAdoo could promise no immediate help but made it clear that the United States Treasury was seeking expedients that avoided asking specifically for support of the exchange, for example by arranging for certain British dollar purchases to be taken care of from the monthly advances. The Americans were also exploring ways to help Britain reduce the debt to J. P. Morgan and Company. Taking advantage of pro-French sentiment, it was arranged for France to borrow more than her actual needs from the United States in order to pay back debts to Britain, thus supplying sums which could be applied to the overdraft.

It was a summer of prolonged tension '. . . I have been living in a continual crisis for the last two or three weeks, the worst series I can remember since the war began,' Keynes wrote to his mother 10 July. On 28 July he wrote again, 'I have had a most fearful gruelling for the last five weeks, the worst on record, nine to thirteen hours a day . . .'.

Financially, all was not going well for the enemy. A mimeographed copy of a Foreign Office telegram to the British representative in Rio de Janeiro crossed Keynes's desk, suggesting that the fall of German credit and heavy depreciation of the mark provided an opportunity for promoting a want of confidence in the solvency of German banks abroad. This drew an explosive comment in his handwriting at the top of the page:

Sir R. Chalmers

I submit that this kind of thing is the foolishest policy in the world, very unlikely to be successful and if discovered lending colour to a charge of our complicity in a sort of iniquity which we publicly allege to be the peculiar prerogative of the enemy. This Dept. has not been consulted in the matter.

23.8.17

J.M.K.

In September Keynes accompanied Lord Reading, the Chief Justice, to the United States on a financial mission for closer discussion of the questions that had occupied the summer. (*The Times* coupled his name with Reading's in a leader.) It was not intended for Keynes to stay long but Reading made a special request to keep him for an extra ten days and in all he was away from London for about six weeks. In a letter to the Chancellor of the Exchequer marked 'Very Confidential' Reading wrote from New York 3 October 1917:

I am parting with Keynes with the greatest reluctance—he has been my mainstay here in finance and has given me most valuable assistance—his knowledge of the situation with the allies is remarkable and I can well understand how difficult it was for you to spare him and why you want him back—and you will appreciate why I wanted to keep him if possible— I am I think capable of much work and strain but it has been very heavy since I have been here and now that Keynes is going it will be worse ... I have talked to Keynes quite freely and mean that he shall be fully informed of my views, so that he may convey them to you, on all matters of finance and representation.

Keynes did not seem to leave such a good impression with the Americans, however. To Americans in London he appeared 'rude, dogmatic and disobliging', Blackett wrote confidentially from Washington to H. P. Hamilton, the Chancellor of the Exchequer's private secretary, 1 January 1918, and added, 'he made a terrible reputation for his rudeness out here'. Hamilton, replying later, said that he thought the Americans may have modified their views (25 January 1918); like Blackett, he was referring to other members of the Treasury as well as Keynes. Certainly on both sides of the Atlantic men worked under great tension; 'the cumulative strain on the cash resources and on the nerves of the [United States] Treasury authorities is very severe', Reading remarked in a telegram 17 October 1917.

Keynes arrived back in England 22 October. While he was in the United States he had begun arrangements for the Americans to receive rupee credits to buy Indian jute. On his return he had a series of interviews with the India Office,

> persuading Sir L. Abrahams last Friday, the Finance Committee last Tuesday and the Acting Secretary of State last Thursday. This occupied time. But the I.O. at last agreed (on Thursday) to send a telegram on very generous lines which I have reason to think will be acceptable to the U.S. administration.

This is taken from a note to Hamilton, dated 27 October, which appears on a file copy of a telegraphic inquiry from Lord Reading as to progress (T 172/437).

Bonar Law wanted Keynes to return in order to participate in a meeting with the French which was postponed on this account until after he came back. At an allied conference in Paris he represented the British government in the company of Balfour, Reading and Northcliffe. During December he was occupied during 'rather a bad week with endless hours absolutely wasted in a newly established monkey house called the Inter-Ally Council for War Purchases and for Finance', as he described it to his mother 15 December 1917. (This was McAdoo's long-awaited official body to placate Congress; Keynes was the Treasury representative.) 'I should imagine the only possible analogy to government by Inter-Ally Council is government by Bolsheviks, though judging by results the latter are far the more efficient. I can't believe these things happen at Potsdam. . . .'

After another trip to France and successive weekends with the McKennas and the Asquiths, he wrote to his mother:

From a letter to MRS KEYNES, *24 December 1917*

My Christmas thoughts are that a further prolongation of the war, with the turn things have now taken, probably means the disappearance of the social order we have known hitherto. With some regrets I think I am on the whole not sorry. The abolition of the rich will be rather a comfort and serve them right anyhow. What frightens me more is the prospect of *general* impoverishment. In another year's time we shall have forfeited the claim we had staked out in the New World and in exchange this country will be mortgaged to America.

Well, the only course open to me is to be buoyantly bolshevik; and as I lie in bed in the morning I reflect with a good deal of satisfaction that, because our rulers are as incompetent as they are mad and wicked, one particular era of a particular kind of civilisation is very nearly over.

I wonder how long your Cambridge queues are. If we put prices low enough and wages high enough, we could achieve the most magnificent queues even in peace time. There never has been anything like enough caviare to go round. How soon do you expect piano queues?

$$\text{Length of queue} = \frac{\text{wages}}{\text{prices} \times \text{supplies}}.$$ If w constantly increases while p and s diminish, q tends towards infinity.

'. . . I am terrified at the prospects of meat rationing and feel that I shall require frequent trips abroad to get a square meal' (he wrote to Mrs Keynes 10 February 1918). 'The proposed rules seem to me appalling—calculated to dry up the food supply on the one side and starve me on the other. Besides they will drive the population on to cereals which is at bottom a far more serious problem than the meat problem which latter by no means deserves to be treated so tragically.'

The new year brought Keynes some offers of public recognition which for various reasons he saw fit to decline. Sidney Webb wrote 14 January 1918 asking if he would allow himself to be nominated as the Labour candidate for Cambridge University:

I venture to hope you will not dismiss the idea. If you do not peremptorily do so, some Cambridge people will put in hand a requisition to you, which we are sure would be very numerously signed by the younger men. Of course, we are not expecting you to be returned! But you would certainly poll a very respectable minority; and it would do a great deal of good to the atmosphere!

The Labour Party's 'War Aims' are known to you. I enclose a new draft 'Report on Reconstruction'. But no Labour candidate need commit himself to anything in particular.

Two years earlier Keynes had also been asked to stand for election as the member of Parliament for Cambridge University under the new Franchise

Bill of that year 'to represent the younger and less Tory section of the academic world' (letter of 27 April 1916).

Writing 22 February 1918, he told his mother that he had been offered a decoration by the Provisional Russian Government; 'Being a Bolshevik, however, I thought it more proper to refuse.' It was just as well that he did, as a few months later duty required him to act severely towards the Russian government committee which was dilatory in liquidating its British affairs (T 172/829).

In March he refused a Belgian decoration on the advice of Chalmers. 'If people come to you with a decoration in one hand and a request for a million pounds in the other, the position is a little delicate; and in the peculiar position in which I stand to the Allied gentlemen I must I think maintain perfect independence of them. Besides the whole thing is rather humbug' (letter to his mother 3 March 1918).

On 30 January 1918 Keynes wrote—or probably dictated as the letter was typed—a long epistle to Blackett. Keynes marked it at the top 'Very private' and added the last two paragraphs in his own hand.

To BASIL BLACKETT, *30 January 1918*

Dear Blackett,

I am a hopeless, indeed a non-existent correspondent. But that does not mean that I have not very much enjoyed your letters of 16 November and 30 December. They have circulated round the office and have been very useful to us.

The stress of work in A.D. however makes me put off and put off, and I am only brought back to dutifulness by the special opportunity of sending a letter by the hand of Swinton, who will turn up in the gay garb of a Maj. Gen. [Major General Ernest Swinton, assistant secretary to the War Cabinet, who as Colonel Swinton had accompanied Keynes and Reading to the United States in September.]

I give you a few general impressions.

The whole question of American purchases is now supervised in great detail by the American Board. Austen Chamberlain is chairman, [Lord] Buckmaster a member, McFadyean secretary, and I Treasury representative. Munitions, Food, War Office,

Admiralty and Shipping are represented, so that the treatment we deal out to each department is in the presence of all the others. By a Cabinet decision food has been given a practical priority for the time being and munitions are suffering somewhat severely. They would kick more than they do were it not for the fact that the Shipping Controller is, in practice, curbing them even more than we do. Anyhow, the position is fairly clear at the moment, as we took it to the Cabinet a week or two ago and got the above policy definitely confirmed in writing. Our trouble with the food people, a trouble you have also, is the utter unreliability of their statistics. As you will have found from our cables, they insist on our setting aside for bacon and the like a quite impossible quantity of dollars, that is to say, a quantity quite impossible for them to spend in the time. But with increased experience they will doubtless improve.

After the demands have been scrutinised by the American board we take them to the Inter-Ally Council on War Purchases and Finance, which sits alternately in Paris and London under the chairmanship of Crosby [Oscar T. Crosby, formerly Assistant Secretary of the United States Treasury and before that Director of the Commission for Relief in Belgium]. There has been a considerable doubt as to whether this Council should be run primarily as a British or as a French organisation. In the end the matter has been fairly compromised. But Crosby's bias is always in the French direction, and if he had his way he would drag the whole lot of us over to Paris every two or three weeks. As it is at present constituted, the Council is a mere talking shop. A vast number of us sit round a table in a gilded palace to listen to the eloquence of Crosby—equally torrential in either language [his wife was French]. The French also talk a great deal, and we, who are terribly bored and exasperated by the whole business, only join in when we can help it. The upshot of this is that a great deal of steam has been blown off and Crosby has persuaded himself that it is he who is really directing the war.

The examination of the details of the allied programmes by

such a body is of course quite impossible. But we are given to understand that at the end of the proceedings he feels himself in a position to cable advice to Washington.

Tiresome as the whole business is, and much time though it wastes, I am not sure that it has not its uses. Our policy is to lay all our cards on the table and to furnish every scrap of information as to which any member of the Council has expressed the least curiosity. As a result the whole tendency is, I think, to increase confidence all round and to convince the principal parties that all is above board and conducted with reasonable efficiency. Further, Crosby, in spite of talking so much, is often very shrewd, and strengthens our hands in curbing departments whose demands are seriously open to criticism. Austen takes the whole business very seriously and is getting on excellently as a sort of deputy Chancellor of the Exchequer—flourishing the name of Crosby with great effect in the faces of recalcitrant buying departments. While we all suffer a good deal from Crosby's way of doing business, we are by no means at cross purposes with them, and really get on surprisingly well. He has an extraordinary mixture of considerable gifts and intelligence with petty faults. Our great standby however is Cravath [Paul D. Cravath, American advisory counsel to the Inter-Ally Council], who is perfectly admirable in every way and the saviour of all difficult situations. The cause of the allies owes a great deal to his wise, upright and straightforward character.

There has, of course, been a good deal of discussion about exchange. But things have really not got much further. I think we have persuaded Crosby that the element of arbitrage is much smaller than he used to suppose and what there is of it is almost entirely due to the assistance we give to the allies.

I enclose a copy we had drawn up of our balance of trade, omitting allied payments for the three months July to September. This shows that apart from assistance given to the allies, we could have got along on our own resources and it created a considerable impression.

This led to the line of thought that if only we were relieved of the financing of France and Italy we could look after the exchange without American help. Some informal discussion has taken place on the lines of the enclosed brief statement. [This appears to have been a proposal for the United States to take over Britain's financing of Italy and France, in return for which Britain would no longer ask American help in supporting her exchange with one exception in the case of cotton purchases.] It will be of enormous advantage to us if this doctrine could be made acceptable in Washington. I believe Reading means to push it if the atmosphere seems at all favourable. It would have great financial advantages for us, as is obvious, and at the same time considerable political advantages both for the U.S. and for the alliance as a whole.

Meantime I am working very hard at securing as large an amount as possible of reimbursements of our allied expenditure, as you will have seen from the amounts we have succeeded in recovering from them. Our general principles, which are, after all, very reasonable, are now more or less accepted and the whole business goes more smoothly than it used to do.

I don't think there is much Treasury gossip to amuse you. One or two extra people have been got in and my organisation in A.D. is now so much stronger than it was that it can run by itself when I have to go to Paris or elsewhere, McFadyean, Ward and Nixon bearing the brunt. Wright is now private secretary, having succeeded McFadyean. Bradbury is largely occupied on special committees and on reconstruction topics. In particular, he is chairman of a committee to go into the whole question of the staffs of the new offices, with Leith Ross as Secretary. Chalmers is trying to get back Upcott from the Ministry of Reconstruction. I think the permanent secretaries are beginning to realise that the office is hopelessly understaffed.

Current talk is chiefly about Food and Peace. The former is an increasing muddle, partly through general shortage, but quite as much through unsound maximum prices and an increase of wages which allows people to eat much more than they ever had before. We rather suspect the French of having got rather more than their fair share of tonnage and food. On the other hand, Italy probably has less than her share. As regards peace, things seem to be moving very quickly. Everyone agrees that there is no hope of a favourable military decision before 1919. But it gets clearer and clearer that it may be other factors which will give the finishing touch. The favourable elements are (1) a genuine improvement in the campaign against submarines; (2) great improbability that Germany can get any appreciable quantity of food out of Russia this year; (3) a rapid dégringolade of Austria. On the other hand German manpower on the West will be alarmingly great and so also, according to our experts, will be their supply of munitions, though I have considerable doubts about this. In spite of the great tonnage cut, our own munitions supply will be extremely satisfactory, provided we don't mind trenching during 1918 very severely upon our accumulated stocks. There has been nothing much in the way of air raids[1] lately; but it is not unlikely that there may be attempts on a serious scale in the near future.

Peace talk abounds in all quarters. The Labour Party is hardening in the direction of peace, is more united within itself, and has a constantly increasing following. Everyone is fed up with the war and would like it to come to an end if only this could be decently arranged. In fact the will to continue is rapidly weakening, according to my belief, in every belligerent country. Even the Cabinet, especially Milner, George and Bonar, would like to bring things to an end if only they could do so on reasonably decent terms. But things move very fast, and I daresay all this will be out of date by the time my letter reaches you. If the enemy insists on going on, I believe time will prove that it was not worth his while. I see no hidden canker in our policy of organisation which is likely to bring us to any unexpected grief, whereas I suspect more than one in theirs.

[1] Two, however, since I wrote this

As regards matters on your side, it looks as though vast extravagance was on foot on the part of the U.S. War Departments and also as though their organisations were breaking down visibly. I suppose matters will end, as with all war governments, in the Democrats becoming partially discredited and some sort of coalition taking their place. Wilson's position in public opinion over here remains enormously powerful.

[The rest of the letter is added in Keynes's own hand.]

I am sending under separate cover the whole proceedings of the American Board up to date. This is very noble of me, as (there being no spare copy) I am sending you my own file in original. I have asked McFadyean to send both you and Lever weekly copies in future.

Please show this letter to Lever but otherwise treat it as strictly private. I should be grateful if you would burn it when he has read it. No document is safe in a foreign country.

Give Lever my love.

Yours ever,
J. M. KEYNES

'We are certainly going to have the whole question of reimbursements up again', wrote Blackett 25 February 1918, in a reply started on the 22nd.

The U.S. Treasury is only just discovering what Lord Reading's letter of 17 September [1917] meant as concerns wheat and the more it understands the less it likes the position. Its periodic impulse is to try and get British obligations for as much as possible of what it lends, and I do not think it will at all cotton to your idea of taking the allies off our hands in return for relief from the liability to lend us money to support exchange . . .

McAdoo had already cabled to Crosby, 14 February, 'I fear that Great Britain is computing claims against the allies on a basis that we cannot approve . . .'

The British claim was for reimbursement in dollars for wheat that they had supplied to Italy from Argentina. Dollar credits had been advanced by the United States to Italy, France and Britain to buy wheat in North America. The Wheat Export Company, successor to Keynes's Wheat Committee, which supplied the allies, had bought up the whole North American export crop, as well as Indian and Argentinian wheat, and in order to make the most efficient use of shipping had furnished the United Kingdom with the North American wheat, paid for with dollars, and the allies with wheat from elsewhere, paid for with sterling for which the Treasury asked dollar reimbursement. France had already complied. The objection of the United States Treasury to this transfer of payments was that dollars were being spent on non-American goods. While American advances were not legally tied to American purchases, Treasury officials regarded it as a political necessity that purchases in other countries were to be provided by free credits or funds supplied for the purchase of exchange, while dollar credits were for purchases in the United States.

The new Inter-Ally Council for War Purchases and Finance set up a special committee, on which Keynes represented the Treasury, to reconsider methods of purchasing and financing cereals. Keynes's proposal was embodied in the committee's recommendations of 20 March 1917: that after a general settlement of cereal accounts with the British Treasury, wheat purchases should henceforth be financed and paid for through the agency of the British Export Company by the dollar credits of the allies.

The thinking behind this proposal was set forth in a telegram to Reading from the Chancellor of the Exchequer, of which Keynes was the author. The version given here is Keynes's original draft as it exists in his own hand. Marked 'Urgent 4 copies (more to follow)' it appears to have been produced in hurried instalments. The draft contains a first proposal, 'of a very drastic character', and a second, compromise, proposal to be offered if the first was not accepted.

The telegram which was actually sent to Reading gave only the first proposal, finishing at the end of the draft section 6. This official version dropped several contentious sentences and repetitive passages. A copy of the telegram in Keynes's files shows the date 25 March 1918. Apparently it was prepared earlier and there was some delay in transmission; another telegram to Reading from the Chancellor of the Exchequer despatched in code 24 March (T 172/445) assumed, 'You will have received my lengthy reply en clair . . .' (This also was probably drafted by Keynes as it speaks characteristically of the 'essential reasonableness of our position'.)

This cypher message of 24 March contained Keynes's alternate proposal, to be put forward only if adoption of the first policy was judged to be out of the question. An early decision in favour of the proposal, the Chancellor mentioned, would be 'of greatest help to me in Budget statement as it would enable me to reduce my estimates of expenditure by £300 million'. He added that it might be worth pointing out to the United States authorities, 'that they could confer this great boon on us with its consequent improvement in our credit without adding a dollar to their own expenditure or their own liabilities.'

Following for Lord Reading from Chancellor of Exchequer

Your telegram no. 1105—Dollar reimbursements for wheat

I quite agree that we should not keep the U.S. Treasury to the letter of an arrangement which it is evident they did not fully understand at the time it was made. Let this matter be settled afresh in the full light of fact. But I am not perfectly satisfied from the report of your interview with Mr Leffingwell [Robert C. Leffingwell, Assistant Secretary of the United States Treasury] that the fundamental principles of the position have yet been made as clear as they might be.

This question really raises in a most fundamental manner the nature of the relationship between the British and American Treasuries in their capacity of joint paymasters of the alliance. It must be settled in a spirit of mutual understanding on broad principles of equity and efficient action in view of all relevant circumstances. I am sure that you and Mr McAdoo will agree with me that it would be useful that he and I in the light of the experience of the past year shall have a frank interchange of views with the object of establishing for the coming year an agreed basis of policy. Starting out, therefore, from the particular case of wheat, I set forth below the elements of the situation as a whole.

1. The U.K. is able to obtain a large part but not the whole of the cereals which she herself requires from the sources of supply, mainly within the British Empire, where she is able to arrange payment out of her own resources. France and Italy are not in this position. They must be fed, therefore, either by the U.K. or by the U.S. or partly by the one and partly by the other. As the U.K.'s own resources are not enough to feed herself and as she is in any case partly dependent on the U.S., she has no

supplies out of which to help the other allies. If she gives them any such help, this simply serves to increase by an equal amount her own dependence on the U.S. It happens, however, that much tonnage can be saved if the British Empire wheat is put mainly to France and Italy and the U.K. is mainly fed from the U.S.

The principle, therefore, upon which we have been acting hitherto has been that as we have no surplus of cereals for the Allies the latter must look to the U.S. for the greater part of their imported supplies, exchanging with us whenever this course will save tonnage but financing wholly out of the credits they receive from the U.S. Treasury.

It is to the logical consequences of this principle that the U.S. Treasury now take exception, on the grounds I understand that while they were prepared to support a large part of the burden of feeding France and Italy, they were not prepared to undertake so large a part as the above would actually throw upon them. They feel justly that they would be open to political criticism on the ground that by allowing the British Treasury to impose on them an ingenious formula the precise working of which was difficult to predict they had taken on themselves undue sacrifices not justified by the circumstances.

If any such thing was to happen, the relations between the British and U.S. Treasuries would have been placed on a thoroughly false footing. But I am so certain that the principles in question are not open to these charges that I think there must still be some misunderstanding as to what it is we are proposing. If the U.K. were in a position to secure by her own resources a surplus of wheat beyond her requirements, the U.S. Treasury would have ground for complaint if the arrangements in force led her to pay the U.K. for such surplus as U.K. was handing over to the other allies. Equally they might complain if the U.K. had surplus resources in the U.S. available for financing a suitable part of the supplies required by the other allies. But neither of these hypotheses are fulfilled. It is certain that the U.K.

can only support a large part of the advances to the allies if the U.S. lend her additional dollars for this purpose.

In short the application of our principle would not alter by a dollar the aggregate amount of the advances made by the U.S. Treasury to the allies as a whole. It would only affect the proposition in which these advances are divided between France, Italy and the U.K. The position then is as follows. The U.K. requires for her own consumption the equivalent of all the cereals she can purchase out of her own money and she requires in addition a certain amount for which she has to borrow from the U.S. She suggests therefore that the U.S. Treasury should finance the cereal supplies to the other allies. As the U.K. has anyhow no financial resources available for this purpose, the only possible alternative is that the U.S. Treasury should lend money to the U.K. for the U.K. to re-lend to France and Italy.

Thus the difference between the two alternatives is that in one case the U.S. Treasury obtain a large amount of the obligations of France and Italy and a correspondingly smaller amount of the obligations of the U.K., whereas in the other case the proportions are reversed. The only solid objection of the U.S. to the first alternative, when once the position has been made quite clear to them, must arise out of the fact that the obligations of France and Italy may be regarded as having inferior financial security to those of the U.K. and that it is only fair in view of this for the U.S. Treasury to insist on the U.K. backing a suitable proportion of the allied obligations which the former is to accept.

I see no clear indication in your telegram that the U.S. Treasury in fact base their objection on this ground. I am also doubtful whether this is the case, not because such an attitude is not from our point of view perfectly intelligible, but because of the stress laid in your telegram on possible *political* criticism. I could understand financial criticism for the above reason. But I have always understood hitherto that political criticism was to be feared not on the ground that U.K. was receiving too small a share of the U.S. Treasury's advances but that we were receiving too large a share. The American public felt a not unnatural willingness to show greater generosity to the allies who relatively were financially weak, and were more inclined in giving assistance to have regard to the sacrifices an ally had suffered than to the financial security it could offer. It is, however, worth while to make some observations on the assumption that the above is the ground of their objection, because this is the only possible objection they could raise when once the issue has been made quite clear to them.

2. If the problem is thus shifted to the question of the fair and proper proportion in which the U.K. should guarantee to the U.S. the capital and interest which the latter are lending to the allies as a whole, it is right that the following considerations should be kept in mind.

(*a*) So far the sums advanced by the U.S. to the U.K. have been very much greater than those advanced to any other ally and amount indeed to nearly one-half of the total advances. Even if the principle now under discussion were pushed to its extreme length, it would be a long time before the total advances to any of the other allies equalled the figure of the advances to the U.K. The proposal is not, therefore, that the total advances to the U.K. should be made much less than those to other allies but that a factor should be introduced tending to diminish their present great excess. It must be added that the relatively large advances received hitherto by the U.K. have not been due to our being more exhausted financially than France and Italy nor primarily to our war effort being on a greater scale than theirs. It has been due to our requiring large sums for the purpose indirectly of handing them on to the other allies.

(*b*) Not only are the obligations held by the U.S. largely British. It is also true that we hold amounts of the obligations of the other allies substantially exceeding the amounts held by U.S. As Mr McAdoo is already aware we hold such obligations up to an amount of six and a half billion dollars of which about three billion are due to us from Russia. More than one-third of this aggregate has been taken over by us since the U.S. entered the war.

(c) The principle of lending to one ally through the intermediary of another is not what we have ourselves practised in the period before the entry of the U.S. into the war. There are ten striking cases in exemplification of this.

At the conference held at Paris in February 1915, the first inter-ally financial conference ever held, it was formally agreed first that France and the U.K. should share equally the burden of such financial assistance as might be required by Russia and second that France, the U.K. and Russia should bear in equal thirds the financial assistance required by the other allies or by any other powers which might enter the war subsequently on the side of the Entente.

This agreement has never been formally abrogated and was for a short time operative. After six months, however, France was clearly unable to bear her full share of the growing assistance required by Russia unless we lent her the money for the purpose. In the circumstances it did not seem to us right to insist on this course with the result that it was arranged in September 1915 that French assistance to Russia should be limited to the expenditures of the latter in France itself and that we should furnish the rest without any backing for the Russian bills from the French government.

Nine months later the same problem presented itself on the entry of Italy into the war. As France was already borrowing from us, we decided not to ask her to participate in any way in the financing of Italy and apart from minor items furnished by the French government in kind we bore the whole cost of financial support to Italy without asking from France any participation in the ultimate liability.

The only remnant of the original Paris Agreement has been in the case of loans to Belgium and Serbia which were made without interest on the basis of equal ultimate liability between Russia, France and ourselves.

I earnestly invite the attention of Mr McAdoo to the above facts which may be new to him to show that we have ourselves practised the principle I recommend to him.

(*d*) The effect on the figures of our expenditure and of our liabilities of a system by which we are simultaneously borrowing large sums from one ally and lending large sums to others is exceedingly serious. The loans we make appear as expenditure. The loans we receive appear as liabilities.

I do not know if Mr McAdoo is aware that we have actually lent a slightly larger sum to France and Italy in the year since the U.S. entered the war than we did in the preceding year. The House of Commons has more than once expressed disappointment that the entry of the U.S. has not had more effect on the amount of our advances to the allies. I can hardly reply that the U.S. Treasury prefers the financial security of our obligations over those of the other allies and therefore insists that we should act as the conduit pipe of a substantial part of the advances which she makes to the allies as a whole.

3. The above will have served to show that the question at issue can only be settled by reference to broad considerations and to the situation as a whole.

The whole system of exchange of cereals and of dollar reimbursement for certain types of expenditures made by us on allied account has been and has been intended to be a sort of compromise between two opposite extremes. Before the U.S. came into the war we had made ourselves almost wholly responsible for the foreign financing of the alliance. This was fast exceeding our capacity and would soon have landed us in bankruptcy but for the timely intervention of the U.S. and their prompt and generous assistance. But the effects of our having carried the main responsibility persisted. Elaborate arrangements had been set up by which in the case of many important commodities we had made ourselves the purveyors for the whole alliance. World supplies were pooled and arrangements for purchase, shipment and finance were organised from London.

These arrangements continued after the entry of the U.S. with the result that the financial burden continued to fall mainly on our shoulders in the first instance while we threw forward onto the U.S. largely in the form of the assistance we had to ask from them to support the sterling exchange, such part as we were unable to carry ourselves. This had the effect of making us the conduit pipe for America's assistance to the alliance without any definite policy to this effect on the part of the U.S. Treasury and to an extent which they have probably not realised.

It was with the object of partially moderating this natural tendency that we established the system of exchange and of dollar reimbursement which now perplexes the United States Treasury. Without some such system we should have become the conduit pipe to an extent which would have been altogether unjustifiable and would have led to an apparent disproportion in the amount of assistance given by the U.S. to us as compared with the other Allies which must have excited widespread adverse comment in the U.S. itself and in the countries of the Entente. The other and more logical extreme would have been for the U.S. to have taken off our shoulders the whole burden of the assistance to France and Italy, reducing their advances to us by a corresponding amount. The system actually followed has been, as stated above, in the nature of a compromise, and, I must add, a compromise by no means favourable to us: for in spite of it our advances to the allies have continued on as large a scale as before.

4. As matters have turned out, this compromise is becoming increasingly unsatisfactory. In the first place its operation involves complicated machinery difficult to understand and difficult to explain, with inevitably resulting doubts as shown in recent discussions as to whether it is really working fairly. In the second place it still leaves us in the position of conduit to an extent which I cannot think justifiable. In the third place it leaves untouched a large debatable ground in which the division between the assistance to be given by us and that to be given by the U.S. Treasury is left uncertain and arbitrary. The first two points

require no further emphasis. But the third is becoming an increasing obstacle to efficiency and deserves to be enlarged upon.

Broadly speaking, the existing principle is that the U.S. Treasury pay for supplies to France and Italy if they are drawn from the U.S. while the British Treasury pay for them if they are drawn from elsewhere. Thus it is to the interest of the U.S. Treasury to press the allies to place their orders outside U.S. and to the interests of the British Treasury that they should place them within the U.S. These conflicting interests are increasingly opposed not only to one another but to the efficient conduct of the war. There are innumerable cases in which the paramount interest of saving tonnage is opposed to the interests of the British Treasury and we are faced with the dilemma which surely ought never to be presented to us of either wasting tonnage or adding to our already insupportable liabilities. Further there are often cases in which it is desirable on grounds of efficiency to devote the resources of the British Empire to furnishing the allies with some particular class of supply and to draw from the U.S. some other class. But as it is, every move in the direction of pooling supplies, whether to save tonnage or to secure efficiency of production, has the effect of increasing the liabilities of the U.K. and of increasing the proportion of the assets of the U.S. Treasury in the form of British obligations though leaving unaffected the United States' total liabilities. For the more the British Empire supplies to the allies, the more must we draw from the U.S.

It seems to me to be plain that a financial arrangement which has such results is quite wrong. The division of financial liability between us and the U.S., whatever may be the most equitable principle of adjustment, certainly ought not to depend on such factors as the above. Unless considerations of self-interest are put entirely on one side by one party or by the other, which is counsel of perfection, such a system is bound to lead to disputes and suspicions which are unseemly in themselves and detrimental in their consequences to the common cause.

I believe, therefore, that we ought to explore with Mr McAdoo the possible alternatives.

5. Before passing to these alternatives, there is an important source of possible misunderstanding to be disposed of.

One important factor which has led to the present state of affairs has been, according to my understanding of the position, not an intention on the part of the U.S. Treasury to secure as large a proportion as possible of British obligations, a motive which probably was not present to their minds at all, but their preoccupation to avoid entanglement in the problems of international exchange operations and in the business of financing the purchases of the Allies *outside* the U.S. When Mr McAdoo obtained from Congress large assignments of money for the European allies, he assured Congress that the proceeds would be mainly expended within the U.S. He has been properly anxious to keep this undertaking to the letter and to avoid slipping into a position in which his advances were actually being expended in a manner which it would be difficult to explain and justify in the light of this undertaking.

I wish to make it perfectly plain that neither of the alternatives proposed below would have the effect of upsetting this arrangement. A principle of division of functions by which the primary responsibility for arranging finance outside North America (it is not easy to separate Canada from the U.S. for this purpose) remains with us while the responsibility of the U.S. Treasury is limited to North American finance is one which I accept as being on the whole the best arrangement in present conditions, although I hope that it will not be acted on too rigidly. What I want to avoid is that the effect of our incurring obligations to the world at large, on behalf of the Allies as a whole, on terms which are often excessively onerous, should not only be to load us with liabilities so early in maturity and so dangerous in character as to jeopardise our future financial security—that I am prepared to face—but also to load us with an increased aggregate of liabilities (inclusive of those incurred towards the U.S.) out of all proportion to our own requirements as distinguished from the requirements of the alliance as a whole.

6. The first alternative which I have to propose is of a very drastic character but one which I do most earnestly press on Mr McAdoo as by far the clearest and best solution of our present difficulties.

At the present time we are lending France about $75 million monthly and Italy about $43 million exclusive of what they owe us for interest which is about another $15 million monthly. My proposal is that the U.S. Treasury should take over all the future obligations of France and Italy exclusive of those issued in payment of what they owe us for interest. In this event the U.S. Treasury would lend monthly to France and Italy about $110 million more than they lend them at present and they would lend to us $110 million less than they lend us at present. Their total advances would remain unchanged. We should remain responsible for arranging the finance of such supplies to the allies from the world at large as we are responsible for at present. France and Italy would pay us for supplies so purchased through us in dollars obtained by them from the U.S. Treasury instead of in their own Treasury bills. We should use the dollars so received not for remittance outside U.S. but to meet part of our own approved American expenditures which we now meet out of loans received from the U.S. Treasury.

It would then become a matter of indifference to everybody whether we supplied France and Italy from outside U.S. and ourselves from within U.S., or whether they were supplied direct from U.S. The business of allied supply and of pooling resources could be conducted with a single eye to efficiency.

I believe that great moral and political gains might emerge from such an arrangement. Conflicting self-interest is the canker always eating at the efficiency of every association of nations even when they are associated for a supreme common cause. The present relation between the British and U.S. Treasuries as regards the assistance they are affording to France and Italy is from this standpoint profoundly unsatisfactory. The policies of purchase and supply which we continue to enforce and the advice we tender to one another must be absolutely above the suspicion of being influenced by interested financial motives. As things are at present, experience shows that this can never be entirely the case. But under the system I now recommend we could work together with absolute mutual confidence and an increasingly complete co-operation. British and American departments could get together on the infinitely complicated and difficult business of pooling resources without disturbance from the confused currents of self-interest which now darken counsel.

I therefore urge this change on Mr McAdoo as one likely to exert a real clarifying influence on the economic side of our joint effort, as one dispelling suspicion and promoting relations of true harmony and friendship between the two treasuries and as one capable of easy and candid explanation to the parliaments of the associated nations.

7. As the total advances of the U.S. Treasury would be left unchanged and as no addition would be made to their financial liabilities, I do not think that I am making an unfair request of them. But I recognise nevertheless that the substitution of French and Italian obligations for British obligations can be regarded as involving financial sacrifice. It is perhaps right, therefore, that we consider whether in the event of the U.S. Administration feeling unable to accept the above, which I much hope will not be the case, there is not open to us as an alternative some *pis aller* nevertheless preferable to the existing arrangements.

A possible compromise might be as follows. (1) We to remain responsible broadly speaking for the same supplies to France and Italy as at present; (2) a certain fixed monthly amount towards the cost of these to be repaid to us out of the dollar credits accorded to these two countries; (3) these dollars to be used by us to meet our approved U.S. expenses and for no other purpose and to be in diminution of the loans we should otherwise receive from U.S. Treasury; (4) the fixed monthly amounts to be somewhat but not much in excess of those we have received of late under the system of exchanges and dollar reimbursement.

I suggest that the amounts under (4) should be $50 million monthly from France in place of $40 million as hitherto, $40 million monthly from Italy in place of widely fluctuating amounts, $2 million monthly from Belgium. We should render monthly accounts as to the manner in which these sums had been expended, charging against them the same general types of expenditure as those for which we have lately claimed dollar reimbursement. These sums would however be regarded as agreed sums in advance. That is to say, we on our side should always restrict our claims to these sums while the U.S. Treasury would admit claims within these limits without dispute.

This arrangement would have the advantage, first, of slightly diminishing the extent to which we act as a conduit for U.S. Treasury advances, second, of avoiding wrangles between ourselves and the U.S. Treasury as to what may and may not be regarded as a proper claim for dollar reimbursement, a question on which it is almost impossible to establish clear and practical principles *a priori*. But its advantages would fall very far short of those of the first alternative.

8. In the absence from London of Mr Crosby, I have shown this cable to Mr Cravath. I suggest that you should send a copy of it to Mr McAdoo as a basis for subsequent discussion. To avoid the great labour of coding and paraphrase, this cable is being sent en clair.

Writing to Keynes from Washington 11 April 1918, Blackett emphasised that the governing factor was the attitude of Congress to the United States Treasury.

McAdoo is continually anticipating...[a] political attack on his administration...[he] has been far too clever for his foes so far, and indeed he has been far too statesmanlike in his actions and has taken far too broad a line in his defence of his department to be seriously in danger. But he believes in being forearmed...He does not want to be open to the particular accusation that he is lending money to France and Italy to spend outside the U.S., less still to spend in Great Britain, and he is not at present prepared to regard the fact that Great Britain spends a corresponding amount in the U.S.A. as a sufficient defence. He is certainly not yet out of the wood as regards support of sterling exchange (but for which our position would be unassailable), and above all he is in continual fear of being told that the British Treasury has out-manœuvred him . . .

I believe we shall get some advantage out of the argument [Keynes's]. The U.S. Treasury now recognises that Britain has a good case for dollar reimbursement, not merely up to the aggregate arrived at by using the principles of Lord Reading's letter of 17 September but up to some larger total. They are anxious to find arguments which will justify doing more than they have done but they must be arguments which are capable of explanation to Congress in each particular instance and not merely on broad lines.

As time went on other cases for reimbursement arose. A series of amicable letters between Keynes and Cravath show that Crosby left Europe for Washington to discuss the whole question, promising fair and equitable dealing to all parties, while in the meantime Britain continued to supply France and Italy. Eventually the allies adopted as a solution what was termed the 'theory of constructive delivery and redelivery', a formula which allowed, for example, wheat bought by Italy from a neutral country to be paid for with dollar credits by means of a three-cornered exchange—the United States selling wheat to Norway, to be paid for with fish supplied to Italy, leaving Italy debtor to the United States for the American wheat exported.

Keynes assisted French reimbursement himself when he attended the sale of Degas' personal collection in Paris 7 and 8 May 1918, in company with the director of the National Gallery. At his suggestion Bonar Law authorised him to spend up to £3,000 on behalf of the National Gallery; thirteen paintings and eleven drawings by French artists were bought. Keynes also bought a Cézanne painting and an Ingres drawing for himself.

Other discussions were going on in Washington at this time. The British Treasury wished to make use of capital obtained by loans from the Japanese and others to reduce the overdraft. The American Treasury insisted that these loans should be devoted to current expenditure in order that British borrowing from themselves should not be so high. The Chancellor of the Exchequer, in a telegram drafted by Keynes 26 April 1918 (T 172/445), agreed to the use of capital sums in this way on condition that the United

States Treasury would give a written undertaking to replace them. Reading refused to make such a condition with the Americans; in a personal telegram to Bonar Law 30 April (T 172/445) he said, '. . . I hope you will just accept it from me that the only possible course in your interest was the one I took.' This infuriated Keynes's colleague Andrew McFadyean who wrote, 'Lord Reading's courage seems to have forsaken him.' Keynes agreed, but conceded that 'in view of the major issues now approaching discussion, it is probably wiser to let this issue go for the present', and drafted a telegram which is more interesting for what was cut out of the draft—probably by Keynes— than for what was actually sent. The passage that follows is an excerpt from this cable from the Chancellor of the Exchequer to Lord Reading sent 8 May (T 172/445). The inconsistency of tone between what was deleted—shown in square brackets—and what remained reflects the impatience of Keynes and others on his side of the Atlantic with the day-to-day frustrations of dealing with the Americans, and the trust in their good intentions conveyed by the reassuring messages from British representatives in Washington, messages which were reinforced by Keynes's own growing contacts with Americans in London.

Personal and secret   Chancellor of Exchequer to Lord Reading

Your telegram No. 1009 and also private telegram of 30 April

I cannot but acquiesce in the course you have taken and trust that your concession will be a useful introduction to the major discussions you are about to initiate. If these discussions are successful we can afford to let go all the minor issues, although the action of the U.S. Treasury has been in my opinion [small-minded and] unreasonable. [Coupled with their action earlier in the year over subrogation and paying off our maturing obligations it almost looks as if they took a satisfaction in reducing us to a position of complete financial helplessness and dependence in which the call loan is a noose round our necks and whenever obligations of ours mature in future we shall have to submit to any conditions they may choose to impose. I resent also their habit of refusing all understandings in writing and telling us to accept vague oral assurances, especially in view of the frequently changing personnel of the U.S. Treasury and our Russian experience.]

I acquiesce because I agree with you [I say the above because between ourselves these feelings are better expressed than left unexpressed. But I am not at all sure] that the U.S. authorities will very likely combine smallmindedness over minor issues with generosity of outlook when a matter is brought to them as one of large policy. I attach therefore the greatest possible importance to the impending discussions on the finance of the allies. Our future relations with the U.S. Treasury very much depend on their treatment of this issue.

Keynes was always a vigilant watchdog of the Treasury interest. This can be observed in his response to a proposal to further more efficient allied co-operation by setting up inter-ally executive bodies for all war needs to establish requirements for the new joint finance and transport councils. The suggestion was made by Professor B. Attolico, an Italian member of the Inter-Ally Council for War Purchases and Finance, in a letter to Austen Chamberlain, leader of the British delegation, who circulated it to the War Cabinet. Keynes's reaction was a minute to Chalmers (18 April 1918), as follows:

Sir R. Chalmers

This memo which Mr Austen Chamberlain has recommended to the notice of the War Cabinet alarms me very much.

If the matter were limited to American supplies, there would be no objection.

But it is not.

If allocation is made by inter-ally executives, in spite of the fact that we and not the allies find the finance, the authority of Treasury control will be much impaired. It will be very difficult to refuse an allocation so made, although experience does not in fact justify confidence in such allocations.

Further, in cases where the goods to be allocated are derived wholly or mainly from the British Empire, it is not right that they should be divided up by an inter-ally body. And the post-bellum implications of a further multiplication of executives we have already agreed in disliking.

J.M.K.

18.4.18

On Chalmers' instruction Keynes expanded this into a letter to Chamberlain, dated 19 April, which Chamberlain included with other papers for the attention of the conference called to discuss the matter.

To AUSTEN CHAMBERLAIN, *19 April 1918*

Dear Mr Chamberlain,

I am a little alarmed at some of the proposals in the letter from Professor Attolico, which you have circulated to the War Cabinet. After discussing the question with Sir Robert Chalmers, he asks me to write to you as follows.

If Professor Attolico's proposals were limited to supplies to be paid for out of American credits the work of the Inter-Ally Council would undoubtedly be rationalised and facilitated. But it is not clear that they do not in effect go much further than this. If allocation is made to any greater extent than it is at present by inter-allied executives in cases in which the goods are financed out of British credits, the danger is lest the authority of Treasury control would be much impaired. Our experience is that where there is a serious limitation of supply of the article in question the recommendations of an Inter-Ally Council are a valuable guide to action. But where there is plenty of material to go round and the primary objection is financial, they are inclined to give each ally what they apply for.

There is also a further point which deserves attention. Hitherto inter-ally executives have been confined to cases where supply was drawn from important sources outside the British Empire as well as from sources within it. Where, on the other hand, the supply is mainly, or wholly, derived from sources within the Empire, the allocating body is in general a British authority and not an inter-ally authority. This seems to me to be the right arrangement and it is one which we have done our utmost jealously to guard. It is not right, for example, that an inter-ally body should sit in judgment on the international distribution of British Empire supplies of wool or jute or tin or rubber. The French, on the other hand, mainly with an eye, in our opinion, on postbellum developments have made strong efforts to establish inter-allied executives in just such cases as those which I have cited above. I am, therefore, a little afraid lest Professor Attolico's proposals may play into their hands and allow the control of British Empire supplies to pass out of our hands.

I much hope, therefore, that it may be possible to confine the doctrine laid down by Professor Attolico by the limiting principles that inter-ally executives are only applicable first to articles in which American, as well as British, credits are involved and second to those in which supplies are drawn from a variety of international sources.

Of course, if Mr McAdoo accepts our proposals for taking off our shoulders the burden of French and Italian finance the position will be greatly altered. The Americans can justly ask for an inter-ally body to pronounce on the propriety of allocations which they are expected to finance.

As regards these proposals you will have seen that Lord Reading's latest telegrams are more hopeful. Cravath is now doing his utmost for us. I understand that Mr Crosby leaves for America shortly, and it is probable on the whole and subject to some limitations that he will plead our case. The Chancellor of the Exchequer will see him before he leaves and will hand him copies of the principal papers which set forth our case.

Yours sincerely,

J.M.K.

Replying 21 April, Chamberlain said, 'The considerations set out in your letter of the 19th are important, but I think that we are in danger of arriving at the result which you deprecate by accident and without full consideration.' At the meeting of the conference 30 April Keynes emphasised the necessity for the United States to be represented on these executive bodies. After a second meeting the conference recommended that the bodies should be set up under the name of programme committees, indicating their advisory rather than executive function.

In another minute to Chalmers, 11 May 1918, Keynes called upon his long experience with the Wheat Committee and the exchange situation to outline a scheme to buy up the world wheat crop as a means of securing supplies of European currencies. Such a proposal to corner a major market was just the kind of thinking that Keynes himself suspected in the French.

Sir Robert Chalmers

I have discussed with Sir John Beale certain proposals by which the Wheat Commission should undertake to purchase cereals for neutral European countries against payment not in the country of origin but in the local currency of the European neutral to be supplied.

This would not, of course, involve any shipping obligation as the sales would always be made f.o.b.

The Argentine crop has proved so very abundant and the prospects for this year's harvest in North America are now so good that there is a prospect of abundant supply during the rest of this year. In these circumstances there may be considerable advantage from the point of view of our retention of control and of keeping prices as low as possible if the buying is all in our hands. This is the advantage from the point of view of the Wheat Commission. From the point of view of the Treasury the advantage is that we should thus secure very considerable amounts of local currency in the chief European countries and thus put ourselves in a stronger financial position.

The principal sources of supply are North America, Australia and the Argentine. The first two present no financial difficulty. The scheme is partly dependent on our securing an additional loan in the Argentine which would render our position secure in that country. The latest information points to a reasonable likelihood of our obtaining an additional loan in that country.

The countries which we should contemplate supplying are Scandinavia (including Iceland), Holland, Switzerland and Spain. We should induce these countries to come to terms with us by cutting them off from all facilities of purchase on their own account if they did not do so. This, I think, we are in a position to do, especially if the United States joins hands with us. By issuing an Order under the recent Defence of the Realm Regulation which Sir Adam Block has secured we can make it extremely difficult for neutral countries to secure Argentine currency for the purpose of financing cereals. In addition, the Wheat Commission are now so completely in possession of terminal and warehouse facilities that, although neutrals would have no difficulty in buying up–country, they are likely to find considerable obstacles in the way of getting the wheat on board ship except through the good offices of the Wheat Commission.

If these proposals are approved in principle I should propose to take the following steps:

(1) To secure a further loan of $50 million in the Argentine which would be available for purchases of Wheat for sale to all destinations.

(2) To issue an Order under the Defence of the Realm Act prohibiting bankers from financing purchases of cereals by neutrals.

(3) To explain the scheme to the United States government and to invite their co-operation, particularly as regards action similar to ourselves under (2) above which, I believe, they now have powers to take.

(4) To ask the Foreign Office to put an express clause in the Swedish agreement now in negotiation fixing a price in kronor at which we would undertake to deliver wheat f.o.b. Argentine or Australia as the case might be (we have already secured such a clause in the Icelandic agreement).

(5) To take steps to explain the situation to the Norwegian and Dutch governments and to point out to them the advantages of securing in the manner proposed the quantities of wheat already promised them under recent agreements. As regards Norway, there is some reason to think that purchase through the Wheat Commission is already laid down in the agreement, but a copy of the agreement is not yet to hand.

(6) It will also be necessary to instruct the cable censor to

stop cables relating to the purchase or finance of cereals on neutral account.

It would, of course, be understood that if the United States was financing the wheat sold to one of the neutrals they would be entitled to the local currency resulting from such sale, and that we should be entitled to it where the finance had been provided by us. In the event of France providing any part of the Argentine finance she would secure similar privileges.

I put forward this scheme mainly with a view to its immediate financial advantages in increasing our control over the neutral exchange position. But I think it also has some value as tending yet further to concentrate in London the whole business and distribution of the world's supplies of cereals.

J.M.K.

11.5.18

Some idea of Keynes's opinion of the Treasury while he was still a member of it may be gathered from a letter he wrote to Beatrice Webb, 11 March 1918, commenting upon a memorandum on the reform of the civil service that she had sent to him.

To BEATRICE WEBB, *11 March 1918*

Dear Mrs Webb,

I am ashamed of not having answered sooner your letter of the 11th Feb. But my time and energy for private correspondence is greatly reduced and I have not had lately the opportunity for dictating. I am sure that you will forgive me for this.

I have read your draft report with a great deal of interest and have also discussed it a little with Dudley Ward to whom you also sent a copy.

The chief comment I have to make is that your analysis of the Treasury system does not pay quite sufficient regard to its organisation into divisions, each division dealing with a certain group of government offices. According to present practice, the division which deals with the general work of a government department deals also with staff questions relating to that department. There is a good deal to be said for this, although I have sometimes thought that it would lead to greater efficiency if every question were relegated to a division solely occupied with this side of administration—the course in fact which you in effect recommend. The argument in favour of the present system is that those Treasury officials who are dealing with the general work of a department are in a much better position to judge of the reasonableness of additions to staff or alterations to salary than officials would be who dealt with a staff question *in vacuo* without knowledge of the particular kind of work which the staff in question was to perform.

I am also rather doubtful whether your costing department is not best operated in the form of branches of the principal buying departments. I believe the costing departments in the Admiralty and in the Ministry of Munitions would have a better chance of getting their way than an outside department, even if the latter is vested with prestige and authority. But here again there is a great deal to be said on both sides.

On the question of Treasury control over expenditure, my own opinion is that, given a strong Chancellor of the Exchequer and given a Cabinet which desires strict control of expenditure, the present system is well adapted for its work. The breakdown of Treasury control on important matters which has taken place to a large degree during the war is due, I strongly affirm, neither to any intrinsic impossibility in the task nor to any intrinsic inefficiency in the present system of control. The explanation is to be sought rather in a government which habitually put finance last of all the relevant considerations and believed that action however wasteful is preferable to caution and criticism however justified. My official superiors often remind me of the maxim traditional in the Treasury that no subordinate official can hope in the long run to be stronger than the Chancellor of the Exchequer. And in his turn I suppose it is true that no Chancellor of the Exchequer can in the long run enforce a policy which is opposite to the prevailing current in the Cabinet or contrary to the temperament of an autocratic Prime Minister.

There are a great many things in the form of public accounts and in the manner of keeping them which ought to be changed and simplified in the light of evolution of constitutional financial practice. It is also desirable that there should be an appearance of a new era in order to give the Treasury a chance of gaining its prestige. But the fundamental conception of the nature of Treasury control which has come down to us from Victorian times seems to me to be sound.

It is hard to over-emphasise the importance of *prestige* attaching to the Treasury. The activities of the Department are so far negative that it is bound to be unpopular. The scope in which it has to act is so wide that it must often be ill informed and can never hope to be as well informed as those whom it is its duty to criticise. Occasions for criticism have to be chosen in the light of general good judgment and common sense, and a bow must often be drawn at a venture. The possibility of this depends on prestige. If the departments know well by experience that an unpopular decision of the Treasury can invariably be appealed against with success in the Cabinet the authority of the Treasury is gone. Treasury officials lose heart, and a spirit of compromise sets in, in which they attempt to save what they can out of the wreck rather than to dictate to the whole administration the wisest and best policy in the interests of the whole.

Yours very truly,

J.M.K.

Keynes gave a more public account of his attitude towards the Treasury within a few years of the events of this chapter, in a lecture to the Society of Civil Servants on 'The State and Finance'. The talk was one of a series on the development of the civil service and Keynes was urged to allow it to appear with some of the other lectures in a published collection. He refused, for a reason that he often gave in answer to similar requests. A shorthand report had been sent to him, and although he wrote to E. F. Wise 26 July

1921 that it was 'excellently well done and doubtless reproduces verbatim what I said, it does not seem to me to be suitable for publication, except after substantial alteration and rearrangement. It is a great advantage of lecturing that one can say things in a less thought-out form than when one writes. But you ask too much of a professional writer in wishing to print in a bound book something which falls so very far short of what he considers his standards in printed matter. Very few lectures stand printing, and I am quite sure this one would not.'

Nevertheless, the shorthand version is given here because in its 'less thought-out form' it presents a very good impression of the attitude of the lecturer and the reaction of the audience, as well as the matter of the lecture.

THE CIVIL SERVICE AND FINANCIAL CONTROL

Our system of Treasury control in this country is, I think, unique, and it has been regarded as one of the most essential and one of the most splendid parts of our constitution. In France the institution of Treasury is a very different kind of thing and more or less a tax-collecting institution. Its influence and control over departments is secondary, and a great deal of the work which is done by our Treasury is nominally done in France by committees of the Chamber.

In the United States the Treasury has very little authority beyond looking after the collection of taxes. The function of the Secretary to the Treasury is to submit gross estimates he receives from other departments, and I think I am right in saying his duties are practically limited to putting them forward. He has no opportunity of criticising or reducing them before presentation. Public men in the United States have openly recognised the extreme weakness of their system, which permits of all kinds of demands coming forward and every new year there is great fluctuation in the financial arrangements of the State.

I do not know when it was exactly that the system of this country was finally perfected, but I suppose one might say roughly that it dates in its present form from the Exchequer Audit Act of 1866, which established Treasury control from the legal point of view more or less in its present form. But it belongs—whatever the exact date might be that it reached its final form—it belongs essentially to the age of efficiency and incorruptibility in the civil service which was introduced in the Gladstonian epoch. It belongs to the days of the civil service Commissioners and the modern civil service, with its traditions, on which the country has now for a considerable time prided itself.

The Treasury has been co-existent in its present form with the civil service in its present form, and it was the crown of the structure which under the Gladstonian epoch took the place of the old semi-corrupt patronage institutions which were the legacy of the eighteenth century.

Under the successive great chiefs of the Treasury, its prestige was built up. As it existed in the days previous to the war, while its legal authority was very considerable, its real force was derived, I should say, from its prestige which had been built up by the successive great chiefs under various Chancellors of the Exchequer and traditions of government of which it was so important a part. That prestige—and this perhaps is one of the points on which most criticism has arisen—was aided by ritual and for that ritual there was, in my judgment, very good reason.

In a sense there is nearly always a good case for expenditure. Sometimes, perhaps not infrequently, perfectly fatuous proposals are put forward, but more often quite serious proposals for expenditure as to which a good deal can be said for them, particularly if regarded in isolation. But that form of expenditure must be based on consideration of the other side of the account— what other expenditure will it render impossible, and what burden will it throw on the community? In arriving at decisions, therefore, any department whose business it is to deal with the proposals of other departments must be armed with every conceivable weapon which can be given to it. The Treasury thus came to adopt those weapons which are, perhaps, usual with an institution which depends to a great extent on prestige— precedent, formalism, aloofness, and even sometimes obstruction by the process of delay, and sometimes indefinite replies.

Behind all that there was a large measure of wisdom. You must not be subject to a really personal attack by all those who are criticising; you must be protected. The aloofness of the Treasury was not a piece of old-fashioned absurdity, but a real part of the ritualism for the preservation of the prestige of the department. My Lords had a long life; they could reasonably hope to outlive and outlast the whims of individual ministers and particular parties; and that long-livedness was aided by their impalpable and invisible character.

It was not for nothing that the Treasury was not called the Treasury, not yet the Chancellor of the Exchequer, but 'My Lords'. My Lords could exercise a real influence over the rest of the Civil Service, which could not have been preserved if the more human faces of particular persons had been substituted for the visionary bodies. They are symbolised, I suppose, by the great chair in the Board's room, which the Chancellor of the Exchequer does not occupy, and which is properly occupied by nobody at all, but is only the visible embodiment of 'My Lords' that exists in the place. At any rate in the old days [of] the Treasury, there was a very small body of persons living a kind of semi-nonexistent, purely spiritual entity, occupying non-existent space somewhere between the Scottish Education Department, the King's Proctor, and No. 10 Downing Street. But it was nevertheless that small body, thus entrenched, on which in great part the efficiency of the Gladstonian system of finance depended. Not only so, but the fact that the Treasury paid great attention to precedents, was influenced by precedents, not only by the merit of the individual case, gave it a traditional character largely independent of successive ministries. In many administrative matters, in many of the minor as well as more important questions upon which there was no great division between the parties, the Treasury stood for the continuity of the Civil Service, for the preservation of a uniform policy and for the handing down of traditional wisdom. In this structure there was inevitably a great deal that was only irritating to those who stand outside it. In some ways I think Treasury control might be compared to conventional morality. There is a great deal of it rather tiresome and absurd once you begin to look into it, yet nevertheless it is an essential bulwark against overwhelming wickedness. It is because in a way the Treasury is always fighting against odds that it is always necessary that it should have all the weapons proper to prestige. It called in even certain aesthetic elements to its aid, and the precise form of Treasury draft was one of the real weapons in its armoury. Things could only be done in a certain way, and that made a great many things impossible, which was the object aimed at. And supported by these various elements, it became an institution which came to possess attributes of institutions like a college or City company, or the Church of England. Indeed, I think it might have been defended on the same grounds on which the eighteenth-century sceptics were accustomed to make: 'A defence that would be as a bulwark against too much enthusiasm.' This frigid body by its coldness was a protection against ill-regulated enthusiasms such as a more accessible and more human body could not have been in the same measure.

[An example of the bulwark appearing among Keynes's papers is 'The Cost of Existing Policy in Persia: A Note by Mr J. M. Keynes', in which the War Cabinet's Eastern Committee, meeting 30 December 1918, was told, 'This expenditure seems out of proportion to the objects attained and will be difficult to defend.']

Individually, I think you could correctly describe it as very clever, very dry and in a certain sense very cynical; intellectually self-confident and not subject to the whims of people who feel that they are less hidden, and are not quite sure that they know their case. Recruited as it was, particularly in the nineties, from the great universities—and not least from the universities of Scotland—it tended to develop a certain cynical attitude, for the Treasury is not a place where one could attain an unduly exalted idea of human nature. The Secretary to the Treasury always tends to get a certain humorous cynicism. In this connection I always look upon the passage in the Memoirs of Bagehot referring to the Right Honourable James Wilson, who is regarded as an extraordinarily credulous and sentimental man whom nothing would reduce to cynicism. Bagehot, perhaps as final proof of the point I make, says that the Right Honourable James Wilson was Financial Secretary to the Treasury, and he did not leave it a disillusioned man.

So far we have discussed the pre-war Treasury. During the war great changes took place. Actually, they began in the years preceding the war. Some say that the present Prime Minister [Lloyd George] really did the foul deed. It is true, I think, that he had no aesthetic sense for the formalisms, and no feelings for its institutional aspects. It is true also that he never had the faintest idea of the meaning of money. But the real causes, I am sure, lay deeper. They lay in the change in our social philosophy which had been going on during the year preceding the war, a change in our ideas and methods of government. Economy was no longer worshipped as the ideal, and activities which would have greatly shocked an earlier generation had come to be practically accepted by all schools of opinion, as proper activities for a government. It was natural that in face of such a change of general opinion of that kind an established institution like the Treasury, depending on traditions and precedence, was playing a losing game; and the fact that it was playing a losing game was injurious to the prestige on which as an institution it had always depended.

Whatever had been the case before, the war, and more particularly the vote of credit, created a new position. During the war, it became less easy, if only out of consideration of time and the magnitude of the problems, for the Treasury to exercise the minute form of control it had previously and habitually practised. With the practical abolition of estimates and the institution of votes of credit, the old opportunity for rationing departments, for looking at expenditure as a whole, ceased to exist, and it was evident that all the Treasury could do during the war was to improvise as good a substitute for the detailed control it had previously possessed as it could do in the time.

But it was a very small department, and I think its old procedure was adapted to a different state of affairs. It had been the custom to spend an enormous amount of time on questions such as salaries of the personnel, whereas the big items of expenditure which had to be looked after during the war were, of course, mainly of a different kind. The result was that many departments got their heads pretty completely, and sometimes in my judgment with rather ruinous consequences. Indeed, in the later part of the war, or rather in the middle part of the war, immediately before the United States came to our assistance, the necessity of regulating the foreign exchange was one of the chief factors which kept the Treasury control a reality at all. When it was a matter of ordinary spending money, control by the Treasury almost ceased. It never ceased entirely so far as staff questions were concerned. So far as foreign purchases were concerned, after getting very weak it became very strong again, and in the later stages of the war was fairly effective in all cases of big expenditure. But undoubtedly the old system was swept away and nothing very definite was put in its place. What took place greatly depended upon individual Civil servants and individual ministers, and different practices were applied in different parts of the Treasury and the different outside departments of the government. The whole thing was of the nature of an improvisation. But even during the war, I believe, it would have been advantageous if a more systematic Treasury control had been visible. There were, of course, innumerable enthusiasts who believed they could win the war if only they could spend unlimited sums of money. While there was this spirit abroad the importance of husbanding resources was not appreciated as it might have been; when you had got several different departments each of them trying to get hold of those resources a balancing department to consider the claims of everybody was tremendously desirable.

The fact that during the war Treasury control was not systematic led in some cases to waste desperate beyond description. There are a certain number of cases with which the public is now familiar, but if I were to draw upon my memory I assure you I could recall many far worse cases than anything which has ever come out yet. Today, there is now some reaction. The need of Treasury control is realised; the importance of economy is, at any rate, on everybody's lips. A great many of the experimentalists who thought that they could make the fortune of the government if only they were allowed to enter into various speculations with Treasury funds have mostly come to grief, and it is wisely realised that changes from the war regime are necessary and that some sort of revised Treasury control is necessary. I understand that, in fact, the position of the Treasury is being considerably restored. But it is quite certain that the form of Treasury control can never again be quite what it was because the circumstances are so different and the nature of the activities of the government so much changed.

This is the moment, therefore, when everybody has to think rather carefully what revised form of Treasury control is wisest for the future. Well, there is one point about past Treasury practice where I agree with the critics—that is the over-emphasis in Treasury procedure on staff questions. I have no doubt that that was due in its origin to the fact that the Treasury system of the civil service commissioners took the place of the semi-corrupt system of patronage, and that in the earlier days it was in appointments that things were most liable to go wrong. People in those days had memories of the eighteenth-century methods which persisted some time after the eighteenth century, and it was extremely important from the point of view of the efficiency of the civil service as a whole that under no pretence whatever should those bad methods be allowed again when those old bad methods had been got rid of with so much difficulty.

But I do not believe that in these days so much attention to staff questions is one with which the Treasury should properly apply itself. I believe there has been already a very important reform by which staff questions are now all gathered together and dealt with by a single section or division of the Treasury. In the days when I first knew the Treasury the same division of the Treasury which dealt with the staff of, say the War Office, was the department which also dealt with the general War Office questions. There was Treasury control over War Office expenditure generally, and the personnel of the Army generally, but I think the same department dealt with the staff questions of the War Office. On the other hand, if there was any other department of state whose major questions were dealt with by a division of the Treasury that division also dealt with any staff questions that might arise. So you had every division going into a great many minor questions. That system has now ceased, and there is one division which deals with staff questions relating to other departments and all that sort of work. I think I would hand over the whole of that sort of detailed work to an outside department analogous to the civil service commissioners, and leave to the Treasury simply the general questions as a general policy throughout the civil service. Great questions of principle, such as the pay of various grades and so forth, must always remain under Treasury control, when questions of details of staff supervision are taken from it. One advantage of this would be that when there was a dispute between heads of the civil service, and staffs of the civil service, there would be a body in whom ultimately, the decision will rest. The Treasury is at present in a dual position as the body responsible for economy and also for looking after the welfare of the civil service. But on most other points my view on the whole is conservative, particularly on one point which is vital at the moment—that is, whether Treasury control is best exercised as a body as hitherto, or whether some of it should not be handed over to the finance sections in the other departments. No finance department could ever efficiently exercise control from within. In any big department a finance section or department is essential to secure economies in details of management. There is a great deal of accounting involved, proper methods must be employed, and there must be somebody in that department who is responsible for seeing that the various branches do exercise a proper financial oversight over everything they are doing and that from a financial point of view the business is conducted in a proper manner. But I am sure that real control on major issues must always come from outside and it must be exercised in the traditional Treasury way. You must have a Treasury which can say No, and one which must be strong enough to say No to certain forms of expenditure.

The sort of control the Treasury must exercise is a thing that cannot possibly be done inside any other department, because it involves the balancing of one department's claims against those of other departments, and consideration of the whole in relation to the demands on the taxpayers. Not only must it exercise financial control, but it must also see that there is no positive waste; that money is not drawn away on useless activities. It can also criticise proposals from a financial standpoint as being ill-judged, and that is a thing no department, however efficient, ought to do for itself. The task of the Treasury, and the thing which makes its task so difficult, is that part of its business which is also to turn down good proposals. Finance sections of other departments could turn down bad proposals, but they cannot be expected to turn down proposals for which there is a good deal to be said. The Treasury has to deal with proposals coming from many departments, some of them perfectly good proposals, and its business is to weigh good proposals against better proposals and to judge them in the aggregate, keeping the taxpayer in view all the time.

These are clearly things which can only be done by a central department, which knows what is going on in all quarters, and is a formidable authority. You need a much more formidable authority to deal with proposals which have merit than to turn down obviously wasteful and bad proposals. For every function I do not see any other substitute for a centralised department run on the lines on which the Treasury has been traditionally organised, essentially because its duty is the distribution of limited means over the best proposals out of all those which are coming forward. It is only the Treasury which can be cognisant day by day of the aggregate demands which are coming forward; and which are going to come forward in the next quarter. All this tends to make it an unpopular department. If it were merely getting rid of sheer inefficiency and waste nobody would mind, but it has to judge of the relative urgencies and relative pressure and to take everything into account that cannot be resisted. The more efficient and the more active a department is, the more it needs Treasury control; because the more energetic and push-ing forward it is, the more it will tend to get to itself a greater share of the national resources than is proper for that department to have. A Treasury official, criticising those proposals, cannot be expected to be an expert on particular things, but he must very often draw his bow to fight a particular scheme. That critic is naturally unpopular. All the same, if the Treasury official, although no expert, is very sharp at cross-examination, he is a valuable element in the total scheme of bureaucracy. It is inevitable that a department in proposing a scheme is sometimes hostile, but under clever cross-examination it fails. A great deal of such cross-examination may be irritating, but the mere fact that it has to meet such strong firm criticism will make a depart-ment more inclined to put forward only a scheme in which it has complete confidence. I do not think there is any fear of too much control, more especially in the present state of affairs. Treasury control is part of the necessary scheme of things if the whole machinery is to be efficient.

My own experience may, perhaps, be considered too much of the Treasury description. I was first of all in the India Office, in a department which exercised something like Treasury control over the spending departments in India. I was during the war in the Treasury, so I think I may be accused of being unduly Treasury-minded. Personally, I think one receives the highest possible praise in being described as Treasury-minded.

Very few people are as Treasury-minded in their own departments as perfect wisdom would dictate. Outside the department men cannot be expected to love the Treasury, but when coming forward with proposals for expenditure they ought to make a clean breast of it. They ought to tell the truth. There is a tendency, I am afraid, for both parties to play blind man's buff. That is hopeless, and it is a real danger in a modern bureaucratic system. I would like to take the instance of Germany, because I think it was one of the causes of the undoing of Germany in the later stages of the war. Germany possessed a more highly organised bureaucracy than this country. In pre-war days I think there was a struggle between the different departments; each department got into the habit of fighting for its own ends. From the many revelations I noted during and since the war, I concluded that one of the things that was wrong in the whole German war machine was that the departments got into the habit of fighting each other as much as the enemy. There was, in fact, a resort to the telling of lies. For instance, during the much-discussed controversy about restricted and unrestricted submarine warfare the German Admiralty sent messages out to each of its naval attachés abroad instructing them to send untrue messages back, in order that they could show these untrue messages to other departments.

In our own case I am sure it was beginning towards the end of the war. People would do it in perfectly good faith. Individuals in the civil service would be so convinced of the necessity of getting their own way that they were not above deceiving it. There were some cases in which we began to get tainted with the German spirit, and a department would give absolutely untrue or misleading information to the Treasury. It is a disease that every bureaucracy when highly organised becomes subject to. Once that sort of thing begins on an important scale, that bureaucracy is beginning to crack. It will eventually be overwhelmed with ruin, and will cease to be an efficient organ for the conduct of State affairs. I am sure there is no greater duty for a department than to be honest and candid with the Treasury, and to realise the extreme difficulties and responsibilities of an instrument of government which is charged with advising the Cabinet on the distribution of its resources, and that it should never hamper or mislead it, however irritating the control in question may be.

The Treasury is not only the head of the civil service in name, but it stands for the prestige of the whole body; and no bureaucracy can be efficient unless it is subject to the hourly castigation of a formidable Treasury.

20-2

PART II
THE PROBLEMS
OF THE PEACE

Chapter 4

PREPARATORY WORK ON PEACE
TERMS, 1916–1918

Keynes was drawn into the planning for the peace at what was still an early stage of the war when, at the request of the Board of Trade, he collaborated with Professor Sir W. J. Ashley in writing a 'Memorandum on the Effect of an Indemnity', dated 2 January 1916. In September 1918 he took part in a conference on the future development of the inter-allied economic organisation. From the time of the Armistice until the end of the year he was occupied with the Treasury's study of the whole question of reparations.

Ironically, the early document written with Ashley had an effect that could not have been to Keynes's liking. This, together with the Board of Trade memorandum on 'Economic Considerations Affecting the Terms of Peace' to which it was annexed, was produced for the use of the War Cabinet in November 1918, and the Hughes Committee, appointed to consider the feasibility of claiming an indemnity, had these two reports before them. When Lloyd George came to write *The Truth About the Peace Treaties* twenty years later, he attributed all schemes for extracting tribute from Germany over a long period of years to the inspiration of the Ashley–Keynes memorandum. Moreover, he wrote: 'Mr Keynes is the sole patentee and promoter of that method of extraction.'

According to Lloyd George,

All the extravagant estimates formulated after the war as to Germany's capacity to pay were based on this plan ... To the minds of City financiers and of all burdened taxpayers, the Keynes–Ashley plan of payment by instalments growing with the growth of Germany's wealth opened a vista of an expanding annual tribute which would ultimately cover the war taxes.

The prospect of keeping the German workers of all ranks in a condition of servitude for 40 years did not dim the prophetic vision or abate the zeal of these twin economists. They shared the natural feelings of the ordinary Briton that, as Germany made the war she must pay for it to the limit of her capacity ...

Lloyd George's own scepticism as to Germany's capacity to pay, he said, had been confirmed by the cautious estimate of the main Board of Trade report. He compared the Board of Trade document with a Treasury report

issued in December 1918, 'largely inspired by Mr Keynes', the chief difference between them being 'the emphasis placed by the latter on the levy of a
tribute on Germany's internal resources extending over a period of years'.

This skirmish against Keynes was merely a side-issue to Lloyd George's
principal attack on the bankers and financiers whom, and not the politicians,
he held to be responsible for the exaggerated expectations held by the public.
The chapter quoted gives his account of how his trust in the commonsense
realism of men of business was betrayed by the members of the Committee of
Indemnity (known by the name of its chairman, W. M. Hughes, the Prime
Minister of Australia) and by the British representatives on the Reparations
Commission in Paris, Hughes, Lord Cunliffe and Lord Sumner.

Early publication of this excerpt in the *Daily Telegraph and Morning Post*,
13 July 1938, before the appearance of the book, prompted Keynes to ask the
Treasury to trace the joint memorandum. 'I remember a document of
Ashley's, though not distinctly what part I played in it, but I thought it was
mainly confined to an historical account of previous occasions when reparations were imposed', he wrote to S. D. Waley [Principal Assistant Secretary
in the Treasury], 15 July 1938. When he was furnished with a copy of the
memorandum he protested in a letter to Sir Warren Fisher [Permanent
Secretary of the Treasury] that Lloyd George's description was 'a complete
travesty...

From a letter to SIR WARREN FISHER, *26 July 1938*

We were asked to report on the probable effect on our trade and
industry of an indemnity (whether in money or in kind) paid by
the enemy at the conclusion of the war or within a reasonable
time afterwards to make good damage in the territories over-run.
Most of the report is devoted to an historical survey. We then
divided our analysis into the effects of an indemnity 'at the
conclusion of the war' and one made 'within a reasonable time
afterwards'. We made no proposal in favour of an indemnity. We
made no estimate or recommendation as to its magnitude, and
there is no mention of forty years or any other period. Moreover,
the whole report is based on the assumption that no claim for
reparations would be made by this country, and that reparations
would solely be concerned (in accordance with our terms of
reference) 'to make good damage in the territories over-run'.

There is not the slightest foundation for any of the remarks which L. G. makes in the considerable passage which, very oddly, he devotes to this report.

There is no evidence in Keynes's papers or in the Treasury files to show what was his particular share in writing this memorandum. Two appendices initialled by Ashley, on 'German Investments Abroad' and 'Sales, During the War, of German Foreign Investments', which appeared when the paper was first circulated in 1916, have been omitted here, as they were from the 1918 memorandum.

MEMORANDUM ON THE EFFECT OF AN INDEMNITY

Introductory

1. A Memorandum has been desired by the Board of Trade 'concerning the probable economic effect on our trade and industry of an indemnity (whether in money or in kind) paid by the enemy at the conclusion of the war, or within a reasonable time afterwards, to make good damage in the territories overrun'.

It may be convenient to begin with a brief statement of the essential meaning of an indemnity payment; to pass next to a historical survey of previous indemnity experience; then to consider the forms in which wealth could be extracted from the enemy in the particular circumstances of the present case; and, finally, to examine the possible consequences of employing this wealth 'to make good damage in the territories over-run'.

2. The demand for an indemnity is a demand for the transference from the paying to the receiving country, either—

(1) of a quantity of existing property; or

(2) of a sum of immediate cash; or

(3) of a promise to transfer property or cash over a series of years.

So far as the transference of existing property between two countries is concerned, it would appear obvious that such a transference does not differ in essence from the transference of property between two individuals within the same country.

It is possible and it is advantageous in substantially the same sense and with the same qualifications. While the ownership of property is commonly and properly regarded as in itself an advantage, it is easy to imagine cases in which its acquisition may be indirectly harmful. In the case of a transaction between nations, the magnitude of the quantities involved and the intervention of governmental action create additional problems. But this does not destroy the presumption of unsophisticated common sense that a transference of property by any of the above modes is in itself a bad thing for the country surrendering it, and a good thing for the country receiving it.

No exception from the above need be made as regards an immediate transfer of cash; although in this case, cash being useless apart from its use as purchasing power, there is more particular danger of indirect ill-effects.

As regards the transference of wealth over a series of years, the effects would be practically identical with the effects of the receipt of interest from foreign investment. They would mean an increase of imports or of further foreign investments, or of both, and in special circumstances they might involve a reduction of exports.

Historical survey

3. The view that the reception of an indemnity is bound to do more harm than good finds its chief support in the economic evils which attended the financial crisis in Germany in 1873. These evils were, at the time, naturally enough attributed in France to the reception of 'the milliards'; a like opinion was expressed in Germany, though in a far more qualified sense, by certain opponents of Prince Bismarck[1]; and in recent years the contention has been revived in England. But, when the view was first put forward, economists had hardly come to realise the cyclical movement of trade, and the German crisis of 1873 was

[1] Bamberger, *Die fünf Milliarden* (1873); Soetbeer, *Die fünf Milliarden* (1874).

not put into its proper place in relation to similar phenomena before and since. The sounder opinion would seem to be that the German crisis of 1873 was not primarily caused by the indemnity, though it was certainly intensified and possibly hastened by it; and this is the view of those who have seriously studied the circumstances.[1] But the ways in which the indemnity, while exercising, on the whole, a favourable influence on Germany, contributed for a time to unwholesome influences already existing, can be pretty well ascertained; and the experience of Germany can thus be utilised to indicate the measures by which other countries may avoid like dangers.

4. The payment of the French indemnity of 1871–3 is the only precedent of any importance, and it took place at a time when the present mechanism of exchange, banking and currency was already in working order. It therefore furnishes a convenient means of approach to the consideration of indemnities in general. It is necessary to distinguish between (*a*) the means by which the French government obtained the necessary funds; (*b*) the forms in which the indemnity was actually transferred from one country to the other; (*c*) the ultimate sources of the payment.

5. As to (*a*), the French government obtained the necessary funds almost wholly by means of two great loans. The first, the 'two milliards' loan, issued on 27 June 1871, very soon after the suppression of the Commune, was taken up in one day, almost entirely by French subscribers. The second, the 'three milliards' loan, issued on 28 July 1872, was subscribed twelve times over, and more than half the amount offered was subscribed from abroad. The amount actually allotted to foreigners does not seem to have been more than a third of the whole, and practically all of it returned to France within a very short time. The interest on the loan became, of course, a permanent burden upon the French people in the shape of taxation, until the debt should be redeemed.

---

[1] Giffen, 'The Liquidations of 1873–76' in *Economic Inquiries*; Wagner, in *Jahrbuch für Gesetzgebung, 1874*; Schmoller, *Grundriss*, II, 482; Herkner, 'Krisen' in *Handwörterbuch der staatswissenschaften. Cf.* O'Farrell, *The Franco-German War Indemnity* (1913), ch. 3.

6. As to (*b*), the indemnity was actually paid over by

		£ millions
(i) The transference to the German government of the Alsace-Lorraine railways (for which the French government had to compensate the shareholders), allowed in the account as worth		13
(ii) A cash payment, in forms of currency allowed by the treaty, made up of		
German coin and notes collected in France	4·2	
French gold and silver coin	20·5	
French notes, accepted as a favour	5·0	
		29·7
(iii) Bills to the value of, approximately		170
		212·7

More than three-quarters of the indemnity payment, it will be seen, took the form of bills. These bills, it should be remarked, were not finally 'liberative' until they had matured and their value had been received by the German Treasury in German currency.

7. Much more vital is the question (*c*) as to the nature of the wealth on which these bills were ultimately drawn; in other words, of the ultimate sources from which the payment was derived. There is now general acquiescence among economists[1] in the conclusion expressed by M. Leon Say in his special Report of August 1874,[2] that a comparatively small portion of the bills represented commercial commodities exported from France in excess of imports. The statistics of French trade would hardly allow for a payment on this account of more, at most, than a quarter of one milliard, out of the five required. The main explanation M. Say found, not in the ordinary transactions of trade, but in the power of payment at the disposal of the French people in consequence of its very large holdings of foreign securities. How far France simply diverted to Germany the dividends and interests derivable from its holdings, how far it actually disposed of securities M. Say was unable to determine; but in all probability both processes took place on a very large

---

[1] E.g. Leroy-Beaulieu, *Science des Finances*, 4th ed. II, 239; H. C. Adams, *Public Debts* (1887), pp. 54 *seq.*

[2] Reprinted in his *Finances de la France sous la troisième République* (1898), I. On this is based the anonymous article in *Blackwood*, February 1875 (by Frederick Marshall), from which most subsequent English writers derive their information (reprinted in Rand, *Selections illustrating Economic History*).

scale. M. Say conjectured that the mere diversion of investment income between 1871 and 1873 could furnish from two to two and a half milliards of francs, 'if not more'; the actual sale of securities was variously estimated at from one and a half to two milliards, and may be largely accounted for by the desire of their owners to invest in the new and more attractive French Rentes. In neither case, it is important to observe, did the transaction involve the transference to Germany of a mass of material commodities either newly produced in excess of the world's previous output, or newly liberated from the world's previous consumption. The world's production could not have been increased in two years, or the consumption of the world outside Germany reduced, to an amount corresponding to the nominal value of the bills transferred. What was involved was simply the transference to Germany of already existing French claims on the world's production (or taxation), and the diversion to Germany of the right to receive (for particular years or in perpetuity, as the case might be) the income already being paid. This income might be, and no doubt largely was, received in the form of the commodities which the debtor countries had been in the habit of exporting; or it might be re-invested and left abroad, in which case the income in the form of commodities would be made perpetual in respect of duration but proportionately reduced in respect of amount.

8. Though the only French investments parted with to Germany which are considered by M. Leon Say as well as by Leroy Beaulieu and those who have followed him, were investments in *foreign* countries, Bamberger asserts that the transference, in the years immediately after the war, of many large mines, in the acquired territories, from French to German hands, 'served to balance many millions of the indemnity'. If this was so, the operation was similar in substance to the transference of the Alsace-Lorraine railway, though the transference in this case was to private ownership, and took place indirectly.

9. It is not necessary to deal here at any length with the general

question of the advantage accruing to Germany and the disadvantage to France in consequence of the indemnity. Even those
who were most critical at the time as to the German policy
recognised that it did, at any rate, enable Germany to dispense
with the taxation which would otherwise have been necessary,
and that it compelled France to burden itself still more heavily
in this respect. They recognised also, that the reception of a
certain quantity of gold directly from France, and of an additional supply purchased elsewhere with part of the proceeds of
the indemnity, greatly facilitated the adoption by Germany of a
gold standard. Those who share the opinion commonly entertained by financial and economic authorities, that the adoption of
a gold standard was advantageous to Germany, will regard the
assistance of the indemnity as beneficial. It may be remarked
that France was enabled to dispense for a time with part of its
previous stock of the precious metals, owing to its temporary
recourse to an irredeemable paper currency.

10. The indemnity, as already mentioned, while advantageous to Germany, did also hasten and intensify the speculative
movement which brought about the crisis of 1873. The economic
effects of that crisis were, it is true, greatly exaggerated at the
time. It was primarily a financial and not a commercial or
industrial depression; and it was one also from which the
country was not slow in recovering. On the whole, it did but
slightly interrupt the progress of Germany in trade and wealth.
Still, such as it was, it was harmful; and though a crisis of some
kind was probably inevitable after the German victory; inevitable indeed—though it would have come somewhat later—
had there been no war at all; it undoubtedly must be regarded as
unsatisfactory for Germany that the mischief should have been
to some extent increased by the indemnity. It becomes, therefore, necessary to point out that this additional mischief was
wrought not so much by the indemnity itself as by the methods
of its reception by the German government, and still more by
the methods of its expenditure.

11. A relatively small matter must first be mentioned, *viz.* the disturbance to the German money market, in the narrower sense of the term, due to an injudicious feature in the method of prescribed payment. The payments to the German government were permitted only at assigned periods. But during the intervals the banks were continuously receiving the proceeds of the bills paid in by the French government. They naturally sought to obtain interest on the accumulating funds and to lend them on short loans. There was, therefore, a relative plethora of 'money' on the market in the intervals between the dates of payment and a relative dearth immediately before and after;[1] and this want of adjustment to the needs of the money market was increased by the absence at this time (before the establishment of the Reichsbank) of a close connection between the banks and the government. But it is clear that this want of adjustment can be overcome in the case of similar cash payments in future by different arrangements as to the dates of payment, and by a prudent policy on the part of such establishments as the Bank of England or the Bank of France.

12. It is sometimes assumed that the payment of the French milliards, so far as it consisted in the transference from one country to the other of a quantity of the precious metals, inevitably sent up the prices of commodities and of services; and that this was necessarily an evil. A rise in prices—whether socially desirable or not—was, however, already taking place owing to quite other causes. So far, indeed, as the French gold was concerned which entered Germany direct in payment of the indemnity, this was not at once put into circulation, but reminted by the German government and issued at its discretion. Even in conjunction with the gold which reached Germany on private account, the whole of the gold lost by France was less than the amount coined by the government. If the German government put into circulation more gold than the state of trade called for, and allowed the number of silver coins circu-

---

[1] This point was especially emphasised by Bamberger.

lating in South-western Germany to be unduly swollen for a time by additional French 5-franc pieces, these were errors in policy which need not have been committed. It is clear that the rapid expansion of German trade called for an enlargement of the metallic currency; and the larger volume of the currency was rather a result than a cause of the rise of prices.

13. More serious was the stimulus to speculation and over-trading which was occasioned by the policy of the German government in its employment of the proceeds of the bills. One measure about which there is no doubt was the rapid repayment of a large mass of public debt contracted by the North German Federation and the larger States. This inevitably caused the previous State creditors to look round for other investments. So far as they acquired the foreign investments which French capitalists were parting with (in order to subscribe to the French loans)—and this we know happened to a large extent—the field of investment in Germany was not affected. But so far as the previous German owners of public debt now purchased German securities, their action would set free the capital of the previous owners of those securities who, on their part, would also seek new investments; and so on, through the whole range of investment. The prices of all securities would rise, and larger supplies of capital would be available for new undertakings, many of which were of a dubious character.[1] It should be remembered that the device of limited liability was still a comparatively new and untried form of financial organisation; and the statistics of company formation during the years immediately preceding the crash of 1873 clearly indicate an over-rapid and feverish develop-ment in that direction. A similar effect must have been produced by some other of the larger disbursements of the Government from the indemnity fund. For instance, the endowment of successful generals would send up the price both of landed estate and of gilt-edged securities. Moreover, it appears that the

---

[1] This was Soetbeer's main point; and his observations have been subsequently echoed in Germany, e.g., by Herkner.

administrators of various permanent funds which were created out of the indemnity payment (e.g., the pension fund for wounded soldiers) also placed some part of the available capital in various high-class German securities. These were probably wisely chosen for the purpose; and there is no reason to believe that the policy was not financially advantageous to the funds in question. But such action had the same effect of liberating, for investment elsewhere, the capital of the previous holders of the stock now purchased by the several administrations. In all these ways an excessive amount of capital was directed into the field of invest-ment; and this, as before remarked, hastened and intensified the financial crash which, in any case, was on its way.

14. An elaborate examination of the economic effects of the indemnity was made in 1874 by Professor Adolph Wagner of Berlin. Professor Wagner was regarded at the time as the most authoritative writer on financial subjects in Germany. His con-clusion, reached deductively by abstract reasoning, and con-firmed inductively by an appeal to trade statistics, was that the indemnity was, on the whole, greatly to the advantage of Germany and to the disadvantage of France. In his judgment it assisted to bring about a rise of real wages in Germany, and helped thus to improve the standard of living of the mass of the people. On the other hand, he argued that the loss to France, owing to the inequitable system of taxation, was specially in-jurious to the poorer classes. He recognised, however, that the indemnity, in the way in which its expenditure was actually managed, did have some effect in unduly stimulating specula-tion; and as to this he makes the following significant observation. 'These effects could, to a certain extent, have been avoided by spreading the payment of the indemnity over a *longer* period, by investing to a larger amount and for a longer period in *foreign* securities, and by enforcing payment to a larger extent in the form of *concrete use-values* and things other than money (e.g., navy, payments in kind, cession of colonies).'

15. The only other example of a considerable indemnity is

that to which China was compelled to agree in 1901 after the Boxer rising. In the method of payment there were some interesting features which may conceivably in the future be referred to as precedents. Regarding China, in the language of a director of the Russo-Chinese Bank as 'a solvent debtor but momentarily embarrassed',[1] it was agreed to spread the payment over a long term of years (39 years). The security for the payments was to be the revenues of the Customs, together with those of the salt tax—an arrangement which necessarily increased the already large measure of foreign control over Chinese finance. The total amount to be paid, however, was only some 65 million pounds sterling; it was to be divided between more than a dozen powers (Russia receiving about 19 million and Germany about 13); and it was largely expended in China itself. The episode would seem to cast no light upon the probable effects of an indemnity after the present war.

The possible forms of an indemnity to follow the present war[2]

16. The opinion of Professor Wagner already quoted (paragraph 14) that it would have been expedient to enforce the payment of the indemnity of 1871 to a large extent, in 'concrete use values', i.e., in forms of material property, was likely to carry great weight in Germany; and during the present war a policy of compulsory transfer from Britain to Germany of various concrete forms of wealth as part of the anticipated indemnity to be paid to the Central Powers, has been expounded by men of influence in the German business world.[3]

---

[1] Sargent, *Anglo-Chinese Trade and Diplomacy*, p. 294.

[2] The references in this memorandum cited as *D.N.* are the *Daily Notes from the Foreign Press on Economic Subjects*, issued by the War Trade Intelligence Department, and for some time marked *T.C.H.*

[3] E.g. Dr Riesser, President of the Hansa-Bund, an association of great commercial interests, and one of the leaders of the National Liberal Party, speaking in December 1915, mentioned, as possible forms of indemnity, 'securities, land, monopoly revenues, concessions, mines, railways and ships' (*Berliner Tageblatt* in *D.N.* [*T.C.H.*], 211, p. 11) Similarly, according to the *Neue Zürcher Zeitung* for 6 January 1916, 'the measures which

Such forms of indemnity are certainly free from some of the difficulties attendant upon the methods adopted in 1871; and it is proposed, therefore (following the classification indicated in paragraph 2), to deal with the subject of an indemnity to be paid by Germany after the present war by approaching it first on that side.

Transfer of Existing Property

17. (i) *German Ships.* The material property most obviously suitable for the purpose is the ships of the enemy navies and the ships of the enemy mercantile marine, beginning with those at present interned in neutral ports. The acquisition of a number of German warships would render it possible to restrict proportionately the shipbuilding programmes of the allied governments for some years to come, and to that extent to relieve the taxpayer. As to the mercantile marine of Germany, the value of its steam shipping before the war may be roughly estimated at about 61 millions sterling.[1] If credence can be given to the assertions loudly made by the leading representatives of German shipping interests, the losses of tonnage due to the war will have been completely repaired when peace returns.[2] It is generally believed in Germany that the shipping companies have received substantial financial assistance from the government, in accord-

are under consideration for meeting Germany's financial liabilities after the war include the exaction of war indemnities in the form of raw materials. For example, the whole yield of the Australian tin mines and the South African gold mines might be taken for ten years or so as part of the war indemnity. The surrender of accumulated stocks of indiarubber and copper might also be demanded' (*D.N.* [*T.C.H.*], 200, p. 3).

[1] Official German estimates of the value of German steam shipping were 12·6 millions sterling in 1895, 29 in 1900, 37·6 in 1905; *Entwicklung der deutschen Seeinteressen*, prepared in Reichs-Marine-Amt, p. 99. If the value increased in proportion to the tonnage (1,774,000 in 1905, *ibid.* p. 89; 2,877,800 in 1914, Harms, *Deutschlands Anteil*, etc., p. 159), it must, in 1914, have been well over 61 millions sterling.

[2] According to the *Berliner Tageblatt* (quoted in the *Daily Chronicle* for 18 July 1916), Herr Ballin, of the Hamburg-America line and Herr Heineken, of the North German Lloyd 'have declared that their building operations have known no cessation, and that their fleets, at the conclusion of the war, will resume their operations with perhaps a still higher tonnage than they possessed when war broke out'. For Herr Ballin's grandiose programme see *The Economist*, 19 August 1916. For statements as to ships already built, see the newspaper accounts in *D.N.* 312, 325, 383.

ance with a recommendation of the budget committee of the Reichstag in May 1916; and it is certain that a closer alliance has recently been effected between the shipping and the steel interests. On the other hand, the ambitious programmes of ship-building may be delayed by difficulties in the supply of steel and labour.

It will be possible for our government to obtain estimates of the value of German shipping in the hands of the Allies, as well as of those interned in United States and South American ports; and the transfer of these ships would be peculiarly easy. For the shipping belonging to companies and individuals the German government would have to compensate the owners by the issue to them of government bonds.

Though a mere transference of shipping from one country to another would not increase the total tonnage of the world, and, therefore, would have no effect on the general level of freights as soon as the shipping of the belligerent countries returned to commercial management, it would—so long as anything like the present control of tonnage is retained—enlarge the tonnage at the disposal of the recipient governments, and enable them, if they so chose, to increase the supply (and so reduce the price) of such imported foodstuffs and raw materials as they deemed of primary importance.

18. (ii) *Railways and Public Utilities in Ceded Colonies, etc.* Of the indemnity received by Germany from France in 1871–3, about one-sixteenth part, as was shown above (paragraph 6) took the form of the transfer of the Alsace-Lorraine railways. It may be assumed that in such annexations of enemy territory as may take place, similar transfer will be effected of railways and the fixed plant of transportation and communication and other public utilities in the ownership of the governments or subjects of the Central Powers—including docks, cables, telegraphs, lighting works, etc.—and that their assessed value will be included in the indemnity, the enemy governments being left to compensate private owners in such ways as they may think fit.

The equipment of the world with fixed capital of the kind indicated has been enormously extended since 1871; and the values to be transferred under this head may therefore be very considerable.[1] The annual income derivable from them— whether managed by a central or local government or leased to operating companies—may be used to relieve the taxation, either of the central government or of the colonial administrations.

19. (iii) *Railway rolling stock, machinery and live stock to replace that removed from Occupied Territories.* The replacement of rolling stock, machinery and livestock, removed by the enemy from Belgium, Serbia and Northern France, would be a form of reparation so visible and instructive that it might well be insisted upon to the utmost practicable extent. It would be the most expeditious method of enabling the countries in question to regain their pre-war economic conditions, and to resume their trade with allied countries and such other countries as they may wish to deal with in future.

20. (iv) *Foreign Securities in German Ownership.* Dr Von Helfferich has estimated the *net* foreign investments of Germany before the war as about 20 milliards of marks (1,000 millions sterling); and of these it would appear, from the calculations of which he has made use, that some four-fifths took the form of securities. The estimate is considerably below that previously current in Germany; and is intended to be less than the actual gross total by an amount equal to the investments of foreigners in Germany.

Considering how dominating a part the holding of foreign securities by France took in the transactions of 1871–3, it is of importance to ascertain to what extent the pre-war German holdings still remain in that country. And on this subject our evidence is scanty and contradictory.

But there is some reason to believe that the value of German investments abroad may, at the close of the war be at least 700

---

[1] The German Colonial Society estimates the value of the railways alone in the German colonies as over 400 million marks (20 millions sterling); according to the *Hamburgischer Correspondent* for 19 July 1916 (*D.N.* 370, p. 5).

millions sterling, including public debt of the Allies to the amount of perhaps 200 millions.

The payment of the French indemnity in 1871–3 was, as shown above (paragraph 7) *ultimately* effected, to the extent of from 1½ to 2 milliards, by the transference of securities. But that transference took place as the result of the voluntary action of their individual owners, who preferred to sell foreign securities in order to purchase the new French Rentes.

So far as German holdings of securities include parts of the public debt of the allied governments—Russian, Italian, Serbian, Belgian, Roumanian—the same end may be reached more certainly by simply requiring, as part of the indemnity, that the indebtedness shall be cancelled, leaving the German government to compensate its owners by the issue to them of German bonds. So far as this is done, it will either relieve the allied governments from the necessity of raising by taxation the annual interest on the amounts cancelled, or enable them to relieve the British tax-payer by a speedier settlement of their debts to this country. There should be no great difficulty in ascertaining the amounts involved.

21. According to a high financial authority in Hungary, the income derived by Austria from its foreign investments (including those in Hungary) was some 24·86 millions sterling, and the similar income of Hungary (including investments in Austria) was 7·4 millions sterling; while the income of the Dual Monarchy, as a whole, from countries outside, reached 16·36 millions sterling.[1] These incomes capitalised at 5 per cent[2] would represent an invested capital of 497, 148 and 327 millions sterling respectively. There is some reason to believe that a larger proportion of Austrian holdings of foreign securities remains unsold than is the case in Germany.[3]

[1] The calculation is that of Dr Fellner, Professor in the University of Budapest, and managing director of the Ungarische Agrar Bank, in a lecture before the Hungarian Academy of Science, reported in *Pester Lloyd*, 7 March 1916, D.N. (*T.C.H.*) 260, p. 8.

[2] According to Sir George Paish, the British income from foreign investments is about 5 per cent (*Journal of the Royal Statistical Society*, LXXIV, pt. 2).

[3] The *Frankfurter Zeitung* is quoted by *Vorwärts* for 19 December 1915 as complaining that 'in Austria the well-to-do persist in keeping their foreign stocks as a reserve against

Immediate Transfer of Cash

22. (i) *Gold in the Reischbank*. The gold holding of the Reichsbank has risen during the war to 126 millions sterling at the end of 1916.

Efforts are being made in Germany to extend the use of cheques and, by making it possible to reduce the note circulation, to lessen the amount of gold which the Reischsbank must hold as cover.[1] But it is hardly likely that these efforts will have early or large success.[2]

Supposing that, when the war ends, there are still at least £100 millions of gold in the vaults of the Reichsbank, there seems no conclusive reason why a considerable part of this should not be parted with in payment of an indemnity, and why Germany should not follow the precedent of France in 1871 in having recourse for a time to an irredeemable paper currency. This would, indeed, only be a prolongation of the situation already existing in the German Empire. It would not seem difficult to distribute the gold so paid between the Allied Powers and to determine its use by each in such a way that it

emergencies' (*D.N.* [*T.C.H.*] 185, p. 6). According to another statement (*Die Zeit* for 16 December 1916, in *D.N.* 495, p. 4), 'so far as these investments are in enemy securities, the documents are mostly in enemy countries'.

[1] The official communiqués on this subject are not free from contradiction. According to a statement in the *Reichsanzeiger* for 5 September 1916, as reported by *D.N.* 405, p. 6, 'the Reischbank is under the legal obligation to keep at least 100 marks in gold for every 300 marks of its notes which are in circulation'. This was indeed the legal minimum before the war; and it is probably still thought expedient not to fall below it; cf. F.O. *Report on the Economic Situation in Germany during September*, p. 6. But, according to a later official communiqué, published in the *Frankfurter Zeitung* (for 11 October 1916) and all the other papers, and reported in *D.N.* 438, p. 6, the present situation is more precisely as follows: 'According to law, the bank must have a covering for *one-third* of its note circulation, either in gold, silver, or Treasury notes. But the issue of the latter is limited, and the silver holding of the bank has fallen very low. Hence there is the more need for gold. True, the *Loan Bank Notes* are available as cover for bank notes, but, *in order to keep up the value of German bank notes abroad*, and *also to maintain the credit of the Empire*, gold is preferable to the Loan Bank Notes.'

[2] It may also be noticed that the opportunity for a further use of cheques in Germany is less extensive than might be supposed; and that the opinion of influential economists in favour of the present system, as opposed to one in which cheques should play as large a part as in England or America, may tend to hinder any very sweeping change. *See* Schumacher in *Entwicklung der deutschen Volkswirtschaftslehre I*, VII, 19 *seq.*, and in *Weltwirtschaftliche Studien* (1911), pp. 62 *seq.*

should have no large effect upon the level of prices. So far as Great Britain is concerned, any supply of gold that may come from that source will serve to replace the gold that has been borrowed by the United Kingdom from the reserves of the allies. This would be simply moving it from one hoard to other hoards, and would not produce the possibly injurious effect on prices and credit which might follow if Germany were left free to export it in exchange for raw materials.

23. (ii) *Loan in Neutral Countries.* If Germany could raise loans in the United States of America, Holland and Scandinavia, the proceeds could be used to discharge the short-period obligations of the allies in these countries, and so to lessen the burden of debt and the taxation it involves, without having any injurious indirect effects. The likelihood that Germany will be able to effect such loans will be variously judged. It may depend on the terms offered to investors, and especially on whether Germany is compelled to resort to the method of 'discount financeering', i.e., of issuing the loan so far below par as to create a large margin of possible profit and indefinitely postpone the risk to investors of conversion to a lower rate of interest.

Transfer of Wealth over a Period of Years

24. It will be seen from the foregoing paragraphs that the popular conception of an indemnity as consisting in a number of periodical payments of cash (mainly through bills of exchange) as the result of a voluntary loan, mainly internal—on the analogy of the Franco-German indemnity described above—by no means exhausts the possibilities of the situation. The actual payment of the loan may take place, as we have seen, to a greater or less extent by means of the immediate transference of various forms of property other than bills; and although it will be necessary for the German government to raise a loan in order to compensate the owners of private property transferred to the allies, that loan may be a compulsory one, i.e., the compensation may consist in an equivalent, determined by the state, in government bonds.

But when the fullest use has been made of the methods already mentioned, it will remain to be considered whether a part, even a considerable part, of the indemnity should not consist of a number of payments spread over a period of years. A demand of this latter kind would differ from those already suggested in two respects. In the first place, it would leave it to the indemnity-paying country to find the means of payment, instead of pre-scribing the transference of certain defined forms of wealth. In the second place, it would involve a charge not so much on wealth already accumulated as on future accumulations. The two methods are, therefore, in a sense, alternatives; and the method of prescribed forms of immediate payment has the advantage of enabling the indemnity-receiving country to guard against the danger inherent in the other method. On the other hand, the indemnity demand may be too large to be covered by the transference of immediately available wealth; and, if so, the methods will naturally be regarded as complementary.

The future accumulations on which an indemnity would draw would come from two sources: from the income from external investments, and from the savings from internal economic activity. What external investments will remain to Germany and Austria after the war (other than their share of the national debts of the allies, which, it has already been suggested, may be cancelled as part of the indemnity) we have made some attempt to conjecture in a preceding paragraph. Their amount may be so reduced as to strengthen the contention of Professor Wagner already noticed and based on other considerations, that it is wise to spread the reception of an indemnity over a longer period than that of 1871–3. For it might be only by means of a prolongation of the period that Germany (and Austria) would be able to accumulate considerable fresh quantities of wealth for indemnity purposes. It will be especially necessary to pay regard to this consideration if the productive capacity of Germany is seriously weakened by immediate transfers of property of the kind suggested earlier in this memorandum.

The possibility of enforcing a payment spread over a term of years depends on the assumption that the allies will retain in their hands during that protracted period adequate guarantees. The purpose served in 1871–3 by the occupation of French territory might be served by the retention of some German colony which it is intended ultimately to restore.

25. In recent discussion of the effect of indemnities the extent to which an indemnity must reach the recipient countries in the form of a stream of ordinary commercial commodities is often greatly exaggerated, as the previous paragraphs show. So far as it does so reach them, it has been objected that it must necessarily injure the working classes by depriving them of employment. But the fund which gives employment to labour is not something apart from the national income, but consists in that income itself. If that income is swollen for a time by the receipt of imported commodities unpaid for by visible or invisible exports, this means that there are more means of production (machinery and materials) on which the population can be set to work, or of consumable goods for their actual enjoyment than would otherwise have been available. The gain accrues to the benefit of the working people through the greater demand for their services which proceeds from the government or those to whom it distributes the indemnity. In Germany real wages rose in the years following its reception; and the effects of the crash in 1873 were speedily recovered from, especially in the industrial field. And, in any event, if the indemnity were purely an indemnity of reparation for territories overrun, there would be no net addition to the imports of this country.

26. In the terms of reference for this memorandum, a desire was expressed that attention should be paid to the question whether the results of the payment of an indemnity on our trade and industry would be appreciably affected by tariff arrangements in this country.

It is evident that the effect of the tariff arrangements of a recipient country must depend (*a*) on the shape in which the wealth transferred by the indemnity reaches that country, and (b) on the nature of the tariff.

Material wealth transferred from a paying to a recipient government would naturally be exempted from any impost which would have affected it had it been transferred on private account, since any payment by a receiving government would be a payment to itself, involving book-keeping and nothing else. A tariff could only affect the commodities which came to the recipient countries through the ordinary channels of commerce; and the amount of these would—as has been indicated above—be relatively small or great according to the conditions of the indemnity.

In the terms of reference 'three alternative hypotheses' were mentioned: '(1) tariff for revenue only; (2) a protective tariff; (3) entire prohibition of certain imports from enemy countries.' In the consideration of these hypotheses the probably limited scope of their application, as just explained, must not be lost sight of.

To take the third first. Entire prohibition of *certain* imports from enemy countries would compel the enemy to pay by means of other products or by means of the products of other countries. To the extent to which the paying country is caused thereby either to resort to other less profitable manufactures or to sell in other less profitable markets, the restriction would impose an additional burden upon it; and the recipient country, also, might itself receive a smaller quantity of immediately exchangeable wealth than would otherwise have been the case. But since such a prohibition would, presumably, be resorted to, not primarily to punish the enemy, but rather to benefit the recipient countries by enabling certain manufactures to be established or retained which are deemed to be in the national interest, the national advantage in the long run might be thought to outweigh the immediate loss. It would be going beyond the scope of this memorandum to do more than indicate the theoretical possibilities of the situation.

The same general principle applies to a high or 'protective' tariff. The dutiable foreign commodities which it allows to come in cost the consumer more, for the time, than he would otherwise have paid; and the consumer also pays, for a time, a higher price on the competing commodities of native production. That increase in cost may not amount to the whole of the duty imposed —in many cases the foreign producer or merchant will be compelled to bear some part of the burden. Still, a duty does involve some immediate loss to the recipient country; which again has to be balanced against the advantage which the duty is intended to produce in permitting the growth in the country of some manufacture which is deemed desirable on economic or political grounds.

It should be observed that since the payment by means of commodities may be largely indirect, through imports from other than the enemy country itself, the rate of duty to which the imported goods are subject will be that imposed on goods from the exporting country, which may or may not be the same as that on goods from enemy countries. This consideration will be especially pertinent if the payment of the subsidy means, to any notable extent, the mere diversion to the recipient countries of income previously received by the enemy from foreign investments. In this case it may be presumed that the stream of commodities will consist of those which the country of investment was previously in the habit of sending to the investing enemy country.

In the case of a tariff for revenue only, the disadvantage, such as it may be, of some loss in the amount of imported wealth must be balanced against the advantage to the state of raising revenue by that method rather than by a further recourse to direct taxation. It may be remarked that Germany in 1871–3 was a country with revenue duties; that the existence of such duties did not prevent a large increase in the importation of articles of consumption as part of the real payment of the indemnity; and that it was not asserted, in the controversies of the period, that the benefits of the indemnity were seriously lessened by the existence of the tariff.

The summary conclusion would seem to be that tariff measures will, to some extent, lessen the immediate benefit of an indemnity, though this loss must of course be weighed against the ultimate advantages, economic or political, which the tariff measures are intended to produce. The desirability of benefiting in the present to the fullest extent from an indemnity cannot, in itself, be a conclusive argument against a tariff policy aiming at objects other than immediate gain. The problem stated in this way raises large questions which are outside the present reference.

The employment of the proceeds of the indemnity 'to make good damage in the territories overrun'

27. The terms of our reference limit the character of the indemnity contemplated to that of an indemnity designed 'to make good damage in the territories overrun'. In this event, the functions of Great Britain, so far as indemnity payments were made to it, would be those of a trustee, receiving wealth to be passed on, in the same or other forms. Much of the foregoing argument, especially that of the last paragraph, being concerned with the consequences of a net accession of wealth, would, therefore, be irrelevant to this country. With an indemnity restricted to the restoration of the economic life of the occupied territories, the economic advantage to Great Britain would chiefly consist in the avoidance of that further taxation which will be necessary if Great Britain is to assist in the restoration of the ravaged countries without an adequate contribution to that purpose from the enemy.

28. If, however, the indemnity were to be taken, in whole or in part, in the form of material possessions, as suggested above, it would not necessarily be suitable or convenient that the ships or gold or railways or securities, as the case might be, should be transferred to the particular countries whose economic restoration was to be effected by means of the wealth so made available.

If an indemnity were sought to a certain amount, and were paid in part in material wealth, it would be necessary for a valuation to be made of the objects transferred, and for the particular ally which acquired them to make itself responsible for putting an equivalent amount of wealth at the disposal of the territory to be restored.

29. In conclusion, one or two connected points deserve special emphasis. When a question is raised as to the economic effects of an indemnity, the doubt in the mind of the questioner is sometimes suggested by the idea of a possible resultant stimulus to the trade of the defeated enemy and a corresponding hindrance to the trade of the victorious Alliance.

The restoration of the ravaged territories will clearly afford a large employment for trade and industry. If the indemnity takes the form of a steady stream of goods and services from the enemy's factories and fields to the countries he has injured, the stimulus will, indeed, be his, although it would not be easy to maintain that a stimulus resulting in trade which will bring no kind of return, present or future, can possibly be beneficial.

If, on the other hand, the principal allies were to receive concessions in kind from the capital wealth of the enemy, undertaking to supply the goods and services required for economic restoration, the stimulus would be theirs, and the doubt suggested above would lose whatever basis it may ever have possessed.

W. J. ASHLEY

2 January 1916   J. M. KEYNES

In his correspondence with the Treasury Keynes referred to the previous time when Lloyd George had attacked him for his part in the authorship of a secret document (p. 116). 'After considering the present occasion again in the light of last time, I still feel that I cannot quite leave the matter where it is', he wrote to Sir Warren Fisher, 9 August 1938. 'This is, I think, a greater outrage than the previous one, since Lloyd George alleges, so as to make it the basis of an attack, that I made certain proposals which I simply did not make at all. It is not merely a case of making an inference which I myself considered an unjustified one.' Accordingly he asked the Treasury's permission to make a statement and when the book was reviewed by R. C. K. Ensor in the *Sunday Times*, 23 October 1938, he addressed the following letter to the editor:

To the Editor of the Sunday Times, *30 October 1938*

Sir

In the review you published last Sunday of Mr Lloyd George's first volume on the peace treaties, Mr Ensor writes: 'Now and then he gets a blow in at a critic; as when he accuses Mr J. M. Keynes of having given a special stimulus to the piling-up of Reparations.' This is certainly the impression Mr Lloyd George tries to give in a quotation he makes from a memorandum marked 'Secret'. I am informed that, as an ex-Civil Servant, I am still precluded from quoting the actual terms of this document.

But I am allowed to say that the report prepared by the late Prof. W. J. Ashley and myself early in 1916 made no recommendations of any kind for a German indemnity and was, moreover, based throughout on the assumption that this country would make *no* claim for reparation. The Board of Trade had asked us to report on 'the probable economic effect' on British trade of an indemnity payable by Germany, not to this country, but to France and Belgium, 'to make good damage in the territories overrun'. Our report was limited to this specific issue.

It was indeed a bold, though scarcely a bright, idea on the part of Mr Lloyd George, in all the circumstances of which he is well aware, to attempt to represent my influence as having been the opposite of what he knows it to have been. But I can confirm his claim that he never honestly believed in the advice given him by Lord Cunliffe, Lord Sumner, and Mr Hughes, and that his acquiescence in it (as well as his appointment of these three, *after* he knew the opinions of two of them, as the sole British members of the Reparations Committee of the Peace Conferences was due, not to conviction, but to a supposed political expediency.

Mr Lloyd George does not explain why he appointed to this vitally important body two persons who held with fanatical conviction a view (to quote his words) which he 'regarded as a wild and fantastic chimera' and with which (so he states) no member of the Cabinet agreed, with one possible exception.

Yours etc.

Cambridge
J. M. KEYNES

This 'wild and fantastic chimera' was the offspring of the Committee of Indemnity. Their report, which was never published, came to the conclusion that Germany should pay the whole cost of the war to the allies, estimated at £24,000 million, and contemplated an annual payment of £1,200 million as interest and amortisation on that amount. They reached this judgment at a time when the Treasury's investigations were showing that Germany was capable of paying something between £2,000 million and £3,000 million in all. Lloyd George had hoped that the committee would damp down public expectations by calling attention to the consideration that it would be necessary to stimulate German industry and risk competition from her trade if a large sum was to be paid. On the contrary, fearful of the high tax burden of the war debt and alive to the fact that the British Empire would receive little if only reparation for physical damages was claimed, they allowed themselves to be dominated by a chairman who declared, 'Everything is practicable to the man who has strength enough to enforce his views, and we have that strength.' In the introduction to their report the committee stated that the Ashley–Keynes memorandum had 'proved of great value'. They took from it exactly what they wanted and no more: the point that receiving an indemnity was not in itself harmful to the creditor country, and the idea of spreading out its collection over a period of years.

Keynes was present at three meetings of the committee, 28 and 29 November and 2 December 1918, as the representative of the Treasury, his function being to answer questions. The minutes printed for the War Cabinet do not show him to have had the influence, baleful or otherwise, that Lloyd George claimed for his memorandum. At this time he was engaged on the official Treasury report. 'Our investigation is not yet complete, but so far, it looks very probable that the amount of reparation is larger than the amount that

Germany can pay', he tried to warn the committee. Germany could pay a certain amount in immediately transferable property and the rest in whatever yearly surplus she had for export abroad. To go beyond this surplus it would be necessary to stimulate her exports by furnishing her with raw materials and markets, thereby risking competition. Keynes thought that without stimulation of her exports Germany could pay £1,000 million of moveable property at once and £1,000 million additional tribute amortised over thirty years. To Hughes (who complained that 'those who know most about this matter are likely to be our worst advisers'—meaning that they were too easy on Germany) it seemed obvious that Germany could pay £4,000 million if the payment was only spread over a longer period.

The members of the committee themselves realised that the evidence that they had was, as Hughes admitted, 'of the vaguest character'. Two businessmen whom they interviewed had thought that Germany could pay only £60 million to £65 million a year and £125 million a year respectively; Hughes discounted their judgment because they had German trading connections. The figure of £1,200 million was produced by Lord Cunliffe as a result of talking the matter over in the City. Hughes agreed at the meeting of the War Cabinet that considered—and buried—the committee's report that it would not be possible to get the sum of £24,000 million or anything like it.

Keynes was in attendance at this meeting on 24 December, which also had before it the Treasury's indemnity memorandum. 'It is, of course, true that I played a considerable part in preparing this', Keynes wrote in his letter of protest to Fisher already mentioned. 'But my name appears nowhere, the memorandum was submitted to the Chancellor of the Exchequer by and on the responsibility of Bradbury, and was then passed on by the Chancellor of the Exchequer to the Cabinet. It is impossible for Lloyd George to know what changes may have been made in the original draft, either by Bradbury or by the Chancellor, or whether those who drafted it were giving their own private opinions or drafting it in accordance with instructions...'

Keynes's papers contain various memoranda by others on different aspects of the subject and he made use of some of this material, as, for example, estimates by O. T. Falk of British claims for damage or loss of property and of the value of German foreign trade. But the earliest version of the Treasury report, 'Notes on an Indemnity' marked 'First Memorandum Nov. 1918', appears to have been Keynes's work alone. Kept as a typed carbon, it has a note to Bradbury on the file cover: 'This is a copy of the document which I sent to the Chancellor of the Exchequer in your absence. JMK 2/11'. The paper itself carries Keynes's initials with the date 31 October 1918. (In a letter to his mother, 3 November, Keynes remarked that 'an exciting incident of the week was writing a memorandum on indemnities at top speed for an airman to fly to Versailles with'.)

NOTES ON AN INDEMNITY

1. The French Indemnity of 1870 was paid as follows:

(i) the transference to the German government of the Alsace-Lorraine railways (for which the French government had to compensate the shareholders) allowed in the account as worth

£ million

13

(ii) a cash payment made up of German coin and notes collected

in France	4·2	
French gold and silver coin	20·5	
French notes accepted as a favour	5·0	
		29·7

(iii) Bills (largely sterling bills on London) to the value of

170

Total £212,700,000

2. An indemnity might be for any or all of these purposes.

(i) to replace ships sunk by submarines;

(ii) to restore damage done in occupied territory;

(iii) towards the general war expenses of the allies.

3. An indemnity for (i) would naturally be effected by means of German ships, either those now in German ports, those abroad (many of which are already in the service of the allies),[1] or those to be built in German shipyards in the near future.

The value of German steam shipping before the war was roughly estimated at £61 million. Allowing for losses on the one hand and increased values on the other, perhaps the present

---

[1] Some, however, have been condemned and have passed out of German ownership, e.g. those in Portugal.

value might be guessed at upwards of £100 million. This is exclusive of warships. If losses of cargoes by submarine warfare be reckoned, as well as losses of hulls, the above sum would not go very far towards making good the aggregate loss. More than half the losses have been to British shipping and the British Treasury has paid for virtually the whole of the cost in respect of neutral vessels lost while in the service of the allies.

4. In considering an indemnity to restore damage done in occupied territory, it is natural to look first of all to (a) the value of assets in territory to be annexed by the allies (b) the value of moveable property the transference of which would liquidate the claim once for all.

As regards (a), just as the railways of Alsace-Lorraine figured as part of the indemnity from France to Germany, so these railways will naturally figure again in the reverse transaction. It would obviously be convenient and desirable to set off so far as possible any sums due to France for damage done, against assets obtained by her through the annexation of Alsace-Lorraine. The value of the railways must now stand at a far higher figure than that of 1870 and there is likely also to be a further considerable amount of state and municipal property. In addition, the mines (e.g.) might be transferred to the French government, the owners (assuming the mines to be privately owned by German citizens) being compensated by Germany. One way or another, Alsace-Lorraine ought to go far to compensate France for damage done.

Italy could obtain similar compensation for damage in territory to be ceded by Austria; the value of the docks etc. of Trieste is obviously large.

Apart from Alsace-Lorraine there are similar assets (on a much smaller scale) in the German colonies. The value of such assets should be contributed to the Indemnity Pool by whatever Power acquires these colonies, the enemy government being left to compensate private owners in such ways as it sees fit. The value of enemy property in German colonies in the occupation of His Majesty's Forces was roughly estimated a year ago at £25 million.

5. Other property, besides ships and assets in ceded territory, available for the immediate liquidation of sums due, consists chiefly of the following:

(*a*) About £120 million gold and £5 million silver in the Reichsbank. This is exclusive of the Russian gold which will presumably be returned quite separately. It is unlikely that there is any other important quantity of gold and silver which could be made available in Germany. The amount of gold and silver left in the Austrian State Bank is believed to be very small— say £10 million.

(*b*) Debts due to enemies from British citizens and enemy property in British territory amount to about £160 million. Similar enemy property in the United States has been estimated at from £80 million to £100 million. Including France and Italy, the total might fairly be put at £300 million at least. Austrian, Turkish and Bulgarian property is included in this, as well as German; but at least five-sixths is German.

As against this, there are debts due to British subjects and British property in enemy territory (including claims against enemy governments in respect of property requisitioned or sequestrated) amount to about £250 million.

There is, however, no necessary reason why the one need be set off against the other. Enemy claims here could be paid into the Indemnity Pool, the German creditors being compensated by the German government, while on the other hand British claims in Germany could be revived as live claims just as if war had not intervened.

(*c*) Foreign securities in German ownership not included in the above. The *net* foreign investments of Germany before the war were estimated at £1,000 million. Part of these are included in the above, and part, estimated at £300 million, has been sold during the war. The total also includes the public debt of the allies to an estimated amount of £200 million, which is dealt with separately below.

The amount, additional to (*b*) and (*d*), which could be rendered transferable, probably would not exceed £200 million at the outside.

(d) An amount of Russian, Italian, Serbian, Belgian and Roumanian debt is held in Germany, estimated, as above, at £200 million. This could be cancelled, the bondholders being compensated by the German government.

5. To sum up, immediately transferable property, exclusive of ships and assets in ceded territory, which could be got hold of in practice, probably does not exceed £500 million. Even this sum would involve results very crushing to German credit and to her recuperative power and might defeat its object by leading to a condition in which the allies would have to give her a loan to save her from starvation and general anarchy. On the other hand (say) £250 million could be obtained without such crushing results.

6. If France and Italy were mainly compensated by assets in coded territory, such a sum would probably be more than ample to cover damage done in Belgium. Belgium's total bill for indirect costs would, however, come to a much larger figure. For example we have lent Belgium £75 million; France has lent her £75 million; and the United States has lent her £40 million.

7. There remain contributions from Germany in machinery, livestock, rolling stock, coal, steel, etc.

The *value* of what could be made immediately available in this form without crushing Germany's productive power is probably not very large in comparison with the figures given above.

8. Contributions in the form of annual tribute from Germany might reach £100 million annually at the expense (if additional to the above) of crushing her future economic life; and perhaps £25 million without crushing her. But these are mere personal estimates.

At 5 per cent, £100 million represents a capital of £2,000 million, £25 million, a capital of £500 million.

9. The total assets available according to the above estimates are, therefore:

(i) Ships—value say £100 million.

(ii) Assets in ceded territory—amount substantial, but no estimate available.

(iii) Other immediately transferable property:

(*a*) without crushing Germany £250 million;

(*b*) with crushing Germany £500 million.

(iv) Capital value of sums transferable in kind and a cash tribute over a period of years:

(*a*) without crushing Germany £500 million;

(*b*) with crushing Germany £2,000 million.

In the aggregate, and calculating very roughly, the above indicates that (say) £1,000 million could be obtained without crushing Germany, half of it immediately under (i) (ii) and (iii) and half of it gradually under (iv).

10. Presumably the assets would have to be handed over to an inter-ally board to be valued and liquidated to the best advantage; claims to be met out of the indemnity would similarly be submitted to the board for examination by them.

Assuming this machinery, the practical proposal for an indemnity might be on the following lines:

(i) Payment by Germany for war damages to be fixed at £1,000 million.

(ii) The claims chargeable against this sum to be those following in order of priority:

(*a*) Actual physical damage inflicted in occupied territories.

(*b*) Indirect losses sustained by Belgium.

(*c*) Damage inflicted by submarine losses.

Any surplus, the existence of which is unlikely, to be devoted to setting on their feet the new independent States to be carved out of the Central Empires.

(iii) Assets in ceded territory to be first of all valued in satisfaction of this claim: next after this assets now in the hands of trustees in countries at war with Germany; next after this gold, foreign securities and ships at the option of Germany to such amount as may be necessary to bring the total to £500 million. In addition German bonds maturing evenly over thirty years and yielding five per cent interest, payable at par in each of the allied capitals, to the nominal value of £500 million.

(iv) The above assets to be transferred to an Indemnity Pool to be administered by an inter-allied board, this board also to consider and adjudicate upon claims under (ii) above.

11. The above applies primarily to Germany. Austria could not contribute any substantial sum in immediately transferable property—say £50 million at the most under the various heads discussed in the case of Germany. Perhaps Austria's contribution could be best effected by holding her constituent parts (or some of them) to their shares of the debt which Austria-Hungary has incurred towards Germany. That is to say, Germany's £1,000 million would be on behalf of herself and her allies, the share of the allies being represented by actually paying to Germany the interest they already owe her.

12. The question whether Bulgaria is to be allowed to repudiate her debts to Austria and Germany remains to be considered.

13. As regards Turkey it is suggested:

(a) that Germany be held to her guarantee of Turkey's note issue;

(b) that Turkey submit to international organisation and control of her finances;

(c) that Turkish bonds, payment of interest on which would be guaranteed by the international board controlling her finances, to an amount equal to the debt owing from Turkey to Germany, both war and pre-war debt, be transferred from Germany to the Indemnity Pool as a contribution to the general funds of the Indemnity Board.[1]

31.10.18   J.M.K.

There is nothing in Bradbury's papers to show what part he took in framing the final memorandum. On the evidence of Lloyd George, Bonar Law must have had some influence in determining the estimate of Germany's

[1] This sum might be deducted from the £500 million bonds to be furnished by Germany herself as proposed above.

capacity to pay. In his book Lloyd George said that Bonar Law thought the Board of Trade maximum figure of £2,000 million was too low. As we have seen, Keynes's first estimate of what could be obtained 'without crushing Germany' was £1,000 million. The Treasury's final estimate was a figure 'not exceeding £3,000 million'.

This padding of the estimate for political expediency apart, it is clear from the manner in which both questions and criticisms were handed over to Keynes that he was regarded as the Treasury expert on the indemnity. It is also evident that he felt the final version of the memorandum to be enough his own work to incorporate whole parts of it into *The Economic Consequences of the Peace*. The section on Germany's capacity to pay in the 'Reparation' chapter of the book (pp. 106–31, *JMK*, vol. II) contains paragraphs lifted, often *verbatim*, from the similar section of the memorandum. The very phrase 'economic consequences' occurs in the title of Part V of the memorandum, 'The Economic Consequences of an Indemnity'; the argument of this section is the argument that Keynes tried to put to the Hughes Committee, including a comparison with the size of the tribute levied by the Germans on the French in 1871.

As it seems entirely likely that Keynes was the author of the memorandum, give or take minor changes, as well as being in charge of its preparation, the main text is given here. The seven appendices which were part of this memorandum have been omitted. They were 'Notes on the Method of Calculation of the British Reparation Claim Account', 'Estimates of German National Wealth', 'Estimates of Germany's Foreign Investments', 'Estimated Value of the German Colonies', 'Effect on Germany's Economic Resources of Cession of Poland, Upper Silesia, and Alsace-Lorraine', 'The Financial Position of the German Government after the War', and 'German Foreign Trade'.

MEMORANDUM BY THE TREASURY ON THE INDEMNITY PAYABLE BY THE ENEMY POWERS FOR REPARATION AND OTHER CLAIMS

The existing pronouncements of President Wilson and the allied governments

The items in respect of which the Allies are entitled to ask for repayment in the form of an indemnity are presumably governed by the relevant paragraphs in (1) President Wilson's Fourteen

Points, (2) his essential subsequent pronouncements, (3) the modification of his terms agreed upon by him and the allied governments and (4) the armistice conditions. The terms of these pronouncements are, however, neither detailed nor unambiguous, and are likely to be interpreted differently by the different governments concerned. It is important, therefore, that His Majesty's Government should have determined beforehand what interpretation they place upon them.

The relevant passages are as follows:

(1) *Paragraph* 7. 'Belgium, the whole world will agree, must be evacuated and restored . . .'
Paragraph 8. 'All French territory should be freed, and the invaded portions restored, and the wrong done to France by Prussia in 1871 in the matter of Alsace-Lorraine, which has unsettled the peace of the world for nearly fifty years, should be righted . . .'
Paragraph 11. 'Roumania, Serbia, and Montenegro should be evacuated and occupied territories restored . . .'

(2) There is nothing specially relevant in these pronouncements.

(3) *Paragraph* 2. 'Further, in the conditions of peace laid down in his address to Congress on 8 January 1918, the President declared that invaded territories must be restored as well as evacuated and made free. The allied governments feel that no doubt ought to be allowed to exist as to what this provision implies. By it they understand that compensation will be made by Germany for all damage done to the civilian population of the allies and to their property by the aggression of Germany by land, by sea, and from the air.'

(4) *Paragraph* 6. 'It is stipulated that in all territory evacuated by the enemy, military establishments of all kinds shall be

delivered intact, as well as military stores of food, munitions, and equipment, and also that stores of food of all kinds for the civilian population, cattle, etc., shall be left *in situ*.'

Paragraph 7. '5,000 locomotives, 150,000 waggons, and 10,000 motor lorries in good working order with all necessary spare parts and fittings shall be delivered to the Associated Powers within the period fixed for the evacuation of Belgium and Luxemburg. The railways of Alsace-Lorraine shall be handed over within the same period, together with all pre-war personnel and material. Further, material necessary for the working of railways in the country on the left bank of the Rhine shall be left *in situ*. All stores of coal, and materials for the upkeep of the permanent way, signals, and repair shops shall be left *in situ* and kept in an efficient state by Germany during the whole period of the armistice. All barges taken from the allies shall be restored to them.'

Paragraph 19. 'With reservation that any future claims and demands of the allies and the United States of America remain unaffected, the following financial conditions are required:

Reparation for damage done.

Whilst armistice lasts, no public securities shall be removed by the enemy which can serve as a pledge to the allies for recovery or reparation of war losses.

Immediate restitution of cash deposit in National Bank of Belgium, and, in general, immediate return of all documents of specie, stock, shares, paper money, together with plant for issue thereof, touching public or private interests in invaded countries.

Restitution of Russian and Roumanian gold yielded to Germany or taken by that power.

This gold to be delivered in trust to the allies until signature of peace.'

Paragraph 28. 'In evacuating the Belgian coasts and ports, Germany shall abandon all merchant ships, tugs, lighters, cranes, and all other harbour materials, all materials for inland

346

navigation, all aircraft and air material and stores, all arms and armaments, and all stores and apparatus of all kinds.'

Paragraph 29. 'All Black Sea ports are to be evacuated by Germany; all Russian warships of all descriptions seized by Germany in Black Sea are to be handed over to allies and United States of America; all neutral merchant ships seized are to be released; all warlike and other materials of all kinds seized in those ports are to be returned, and German materials as specified in clause 28 are to be abandoned.'

There are corresponding articles as to leaving material *in situ* in the armistice terms with Austria, Turkey, and Bulgaria.

For what can compensation be claimed?

The question of what can be claimed from the Central Powers in the form of pecuniary or material compensation is governed in the main by the statement (in modification of President Wilson's original terms) agreed upon by him and the allied governments and communicated by the President to the government of Germany shortly before the armistice negotiations. That is to say, 'compensation will be made by Germany for all damage done to the civilian population of the Allies and to their property by the aggression of Germany by land, by sea, and from the air'. The reservation quoted above in paragraph 19 of the armistice terms, 'that any future claims and demands of the allies and the United States of America remain unaffected', was presumably intended to reaffirm and safeguard the above statement, and to make it clear that the property handed over under the armistice terms was in no sense in final settlement.

It may be maintained in some quarters that the term 'damage done to the civilian population of the allies and to their property by the aggression of Germany' could be held to cover all expenditure of whatever description due to the war. But if so, this could have been stated in more explicit language and there would be no force in the apparent emphasis on damage done to *civilians*.

It must also be remembered that the context of the term is simply in elucidation of the meaning of the term 'restoration' in the President's Fourteen Points. It is very unlikely, therefore, that the United States would agree to any such extension of the interpretation of the term. In what follows, therefore, the terms of reference are taken to exclude any claim for repayment of the general costs of the war.[1] Subject to this as wide a field is covered as is possible within the limits of fair interpretation.

The claim seems further limited not only to damage done to the *civilian* population and their property, but to damage done *directly* to them. That is to say, to take an example, it would not include compensation to the widow of a soldier or to a civilian who had lost his employment in consequence of the war or had been run over by a motor-bus through the darkening of the streets—or indeed to a ship lost at sea through the rules of navigation imposed by the Admiralty as a result of submarine warfare.

While, however, the damage done should be limited to direct damage, it is necessary to include damage inflicted by the allied armies in the course of operations of war as well as damage so inflicted by the enemy. It would, indeed, be impossible in battle areas to distinguish between the damage done by the respective armies.[2]

In any event, there is no object in endeavouring to strain the interpretation of the above phrases, if the conclusion reached below is correct that, without any straining, it is possible to arrive at a total in excess of what Germany can pay. There is, that is to say, no inconsistency between the limitation of the allies' claims to 'reparation' and the exaction of payment from Germany up to the full limit of her capacity. If this fact is established it is advisable that the allies should be very careful to

[1] The French proposals for the preliminaries of peace with Germany, communicated by the French ambassador on 26 November 1918, ignore the above altogether, and propose that the total costs of the war should be paid by Germany in fifty-six annual instalments.

[2] The allied governments should be asked to agree that their reparation claims are to be so interpreted and that they entirely waive any claims against the British army for damage attributable to that army's military acts.

draw up their claims on the most unexceptionable lines, in order that the enemy may have no opportunity to draw off the discussion on to ground where we might find ourselves doubtfully placed or fail to obtain the support of the United States.

There is, however, nothing in the formula to limit the damage to damage inflicted contrary to the recognised rules of warfare. That is to say, it would be proper to include loss due to legitimate capture of a merchantman at sea, as well as the costs of illegal submarine warfare.

It might, nevertheless, be fairly urged that as between the various claims of the different allies priority should be given to compensation for illegal acts, of which the chief would be the invasion of Belgium and unrestricted submarine warfare. This would be specially necessary and important if the total bill presented turns out to be in excess of what the enemy can pay, and the dividend received by the claimants is consequently less than 100 per cent. In this event Belgium would not be fully indemnified unless she received priority. Priority for illegal damage would also be greatly to the advantage of this country, since probably 93 per cent of the damage we have suffered under the above heads has been illegal, whereas in the case of France the proportion is relatively small.

In the case of the United Kingdom, therefore, the bill would cover the following items:

(*a*) Damage to British life and property by the acts of an enemy government, including *inter alia* damage by air-raids, naval bombardments, submarine warfare, and mines.

(*b*) Compensation for improper treatment of interned civilians. It would not include the general costs of the war or (e.g.) indirect damage due to loss of trade.

The French claim would include, as well as items corresponding to the above—

(*c*) Damage done to the property and persons of civilians in the war area, whatever army may have been directly responsible for the destruction, and by aerial warfare behind the enemy lines.

(*d*) Compensation for loot of food, raw materials, live stock, machinery, household effects, timber, and the like by the enemy governments or their nationals in territory occupied by them.

(*e*) Repayment of fines and requisitions levied by the enemy governments or their officers on French municipalities or nationals.

(*f*) Compensation to French nationals deported or compelled to do forced labour.

In addition to the above there is a further item of more doubtful character, for which a claim should be made, though it might not be possible to sustain it, namely:

(*g*) The expenses of the Relief Commission in providing necessary food and clothing to maintain the civilian French population in the enemy-occupied districts.

Lastly, it might be argued that, under section 8 of President Wilson's Fourteen Points as regards righting the wrong done to Alsace-Lorraine, it would be legitimate for France to claim back—

(*h*) The indemnity paid by them after the Franco-German War.[1]

The Belgian claim would include items corresponding to (*a*) to (*g*) above. But in the case of Belgium it is probable that certain special claims might find a place, as, for example, book debts due from Germany in connection with their dealings with the National Bank of Belgium and the Société Générale.[2] It is also arguable that in the case of Belgium something more resembling an indemnity for general war costs might be justified.

In particular a claim might be made—

---

[1] The French government propose that, in addition to repayment of the capital, they should also receive compound interest for the period 1871 to 1919, this payment to be discharged in fifty annual instalments.

[2] Mark paper or mark credits owned in ex-occupied territory by allied nationals should be included in the settlement of enemy debts, along with other sums owed to allied nationals, and not in connection with reparation.

(*i*) For loss arising through the non-collection of taxes by the Belgian government, which otherwise would have supported the normal expenses of the Government as distinct from war expenses.

The cost of Belgian relief under (*g*) and the normal expenses of Government under (*i*) having been met already by advances from the British, French, and United States governments, any payment received in compensation for these sums should be used by Belgium in part discharge of her debt to these governments. As the whole of the war expenses of Belgium has been met by loans from the British, French, and United States governments, it would be the case here also that any compensation received should be utilised by Belgium to repay these governments.

As regards Russia, it is presumed that no claim for compensation of any kind will be raised by the allies. If the aggregate claims exceed what Germany can pay, the effect of including such a claim would only be to diminish the dividend payable to the other claimants. The only principle on which it would be to our interest to include a claim would be one by which any proceeds due to Russia would be distributed to the various allies who have lent Russia money in part satisfaction of the loans which have been repudiated. But this would raise many difficult questions which had better be avoided. It might, however, be thought desirable to prefer a claim, for damage done and for fines inflicted, on behalf of Poland.

So far the argument has been developed on the assumption that the enemy power which is to pay will be Germany, or at least primarily Germany. But when we come to the claims of Italy, Serbia, Montenegro, and Roumania, the question has to be faced as to how far Austria is to be made responsible. If the capacity of Austria to pay be put at its highest, it is probable that the dividend would be a small one. The best course will therefore be to establish a principle of joint and several responsibility, and to treat on the one side the claims against the Central Powers (including Bulgaria and Turkey) as a whole, and on the other side their assets as a whole, so that the assets of Germany will be available against damage to Serbia on precisely the same terms as against damage to France, and correspondingly any assets which can be contributed by the other members of the enemy alliance will be thrown into the general pool.

On this basis the Italian claim would include items corresponding to (*a*) to (*f*) above.

The Serbian claim would be on the same lines as the Belgian claim, except that there has been no Relief Commission in Serbia (see (*g*)), and since the invasion of Serbia was not contrary to international agreement, there would be no claim for priority.

Roumania raises special considerations, for the solution of which no adequate material is yet available. It has to be decided whether and how far the separate peace entered into by Roumania affects the matter. The destruction of the oil-wells by the British authorities, in anticipation of the German invasion, raises a special question on which a separate note will be prepared.

It is suggested that the committee of the conference which deals with indemnities should be asked to determine first of all the questions of principle raised above, and that a questionnaire should be prepared for submission to them on the basis of the above, outlining in a clear manner the specific questions on which the committee's recommendations are required.

Estimated Amount of the Claim of the Allied Governments against the German and other Enemy Governments for Reparation

British Claim

The table below gives a preliminary estimate of the amount due from the enemy governments on British account for direct

352

losses to civilians and their property through hostile action, both legal and illegal. It represents the account of the whole Empire, and is drawn up on the basis of the definition of 'reparation' discussed in the second section above. An attempt has been made to separate the amounts due for legal and illegal action respectively, in view of the possibility of losses due to illegal action being given priority. It will be observed that the claim is composed almost entirely of losses in respect of ships, and that of these losses nearly all were due to illegal action, with the result that of the whole British account about 93 per cent represents losses due to illegal action.

All the items in the account are necessarily only approximate estimates, but with a few minor exceptions it is almost certain that the estimates are on the low side. It may be possible to obtain more accurate figures at a later date, but a really exact estimate could only be obtained as the result of a prolonged examination of details.

It has not been practicable to enter a claim in respect of the improper treatment of prisoners of war and interned civilians, as no estimate of sufficient value has yet been secured. At the same time some idea can be formed as to the order of magnitude of this claim, and it is probable that it would not exceed £10 million. This omission cannot therefore much affect the final figure.

The manner in which the following estimates have been compiled is explained in Appendix 1.

Claims of other allied governments

It is of course impossible to prepare an estimate on the same lines as the above for the other governments. They will doubtless present their own figures when the time comes. At the present stage it is only possible to give rough forecasts of what these claims are likely to be, based on such information as is available, or such reports as have come to hand.

In the case of Belgium, the cost of actual physical damage and

British Reparation Claim Account

(ooo's omitted)

	Losses due to German action			Losses due to Austrian, Turkish, and Bulgarian action			Total losses due to enemy action
Estimated loss in respect of the property of British subjects in	Illegal action £	Legal action £	Total illegal and legal £	Illegal action £	Legal action £	Total illegal and legal £	Illegal and legal £
1							
(a) Belgium	15,993	Nil	15,993	Nil	Nil	Nil	15,993
(b) France	2,364	Nil	2,364	Nil	Nil	Nil	2,364
(c) Italy	—	—	—	—	—	—	—
(d) Poland	144	Nil	144	144	Nil	144	288
(e) Other Russian territory	25	Nil	25	24	Nil	24	49
(f) Roumania	179	Nil	179	180	Nil	180	359
(g) Serbia	33	Nil	33	32	Nil	32	65
(h) Montenegro	—	—	—	—	—	—	—
(i) Greece	100	Nil	100	100	Nil	100	200
(j) Luxemburg	7	Nil	7	Nil	Nil	Nil	7
	18,845	Nil	18,845	480	Nil	480	19,325

II Estimated loss in respect of ships and their cargoes directly destroyed by enemy action							
(a) Value of hulls of British ships sunk	205,065	15,435	220,500	22,785	1,715	24,500	245,000
(b) Interest on value of hulls of British ships sunk from date of sinking to end of the war	20,507	1,543	22,050	2,279	171	2,450	24,500
(c) Value of British fishing vessels and their gear sunk	2,850	715	3,565	Nil	Nil	Nil	3,565
(d) Interest on value of British fishing vessels and their gear sunk	285	72	357	Nil	Nil	Nil	357
(e) Value of British-owned cargoes sunk	156,519	11,781	168,300	17,391	1,309	18,700	187,000
(f) Interest on value of British-owned cargoes sunk and damaged	16,908	1,272	18,180	1,878	142	2,020	20,200
(g) Cost of repairs to hulls damaged	16,238	1,222	17,460	1,804	136	1,940	19,400
(h) Damage to cargoes	12,555	945	13,500	1,395	105	1,500	15,000
(i) Value of compensation in respect of lives of passengers and crews lost	16,740	1,260	18,000	1,860	140	2,000	20,000
(j) Value of passengers' and crews' effects lost	1,256	94	1,350	139	11	150	1,500
(k) Losses of allied and neutral vessels in British service	12,555	945	13,500	1,395	105	1,500	15,000
	461,478	35,284	496,762	50,926	3,834	54,760	551,522
III Estimated loss in respect of ships detained before the war	2,500	Nil	2,500	250	Nil	250	2,750
IV Estimated loss in respect of bombardment (air and naval)	4,700	Nil	4,700	Nil	Nil	Nil	4,700
Total	487,523	35,284	522,807	51,656	3,834	55,490	578,297

loss of material property is probably much less than is popularly supposed. Apart from destruction effected in the first weeks of the war, the area of Belgian soil which has been the scene of hostilities is of comparatively small extent, and in addition the battle area was restricted by the almost stationary character of the battle line in Belgium throughout the war. It has been suggested that the actual damage to, and loss of property in, Belgium through enemy action may not exceed £100 million. Nevertheless the claim presented in the first instance by the Belgian authorities will be on a substantially more liberal scale than this, and the first inquiry by the Central Industrial Committee of Belgium is reported to estimate the damage caused by military operations, and the removal of important machinery and raw material, at £262,400,000.

In addition, the Belgian government will claim substantial sums for amounts due by the Reichsbank in connection with banking and currency arrangements in Belgium during the occupation, for the repayment of fines and requisitions levied on Belgian municipalities, loss of trade and employment, and for many other items consequential on a prolonged enemy occupation of an entire country. It has been reported that the approximate magnitude of the total Belgian account is about £600 million, but figures widely discrepant from this have also been mentioned.

In the case of France the physical damage effected is on an enormously larger scale than in Belgium, proportionately to the immensely greater length of the battle-front and the greater depth of country over which the front has swayed from time to time. There will also doubtless be other claims corresponding to the Belgian claims mentioned above, and, in addition, the demand for the repayment of the indemnity of 1871, together with interest. The figure reported as representing the French claim, at any rate at one stage of their investigations, exclusive of the repayment of the indemnity, is £2,500 million (63 milliard fr.).

The Italian claim must evidently be on a far lower scale. But the Italian Treasury are believed to entertain hopes of reaching a figure of £100 million.

As regards other countries, for example, Poland, Roumania, Serbia, and Montenegro, no forecasts or estimates are available. If, however, the uncriticised claims of the major Allies are put at £600 million for the British Empire, £600 million for Belgium, £2,500 million for France, and £100 million for Italy, a total is reached of £3,800 million. It appears, therefore, that, as a very rough estimate, a round figure of £4,000 million might be taken as representing the preliminary claim of the Allies under the head of 'reparation'. This total may suffer some diminution under criticism. It is uncertain whether any claim will be presented on behalf of the United States. Mr Lansing has, however, issued a notice to American nationals to lodge with the State Department within thirty days details of any losses they may have sustained 'through German submarine warfare whether to cargoes or personal property and effects, whether the goods were not insured or only partially insured, and regardless of whether they were carried in American or foreign vessels'. The amount is not likely to be significant compared with the claims of the other governments.

The French government have suggested that neutral States should be allowed to claim reparation on the same basis as the allies. This is surely inadmissible both in principle and in relation to the interests of the allies.

If it is proposed to claim an indemnity beyond the scope of reparation, it would seem impossible to stop short of a complete claim for all the expenses of the war, including the capital charge in respect of war pensions. In the case of the United Kingdom the estimated cost of the war up to 31 March 1919 is put at £8,850 million. To this must be added about £500 million expended by the Dominions and India otherwise than by loans from the home government, already included in the figure of

£8,850 million. The capital charge in respect of war pensions is very roughly estimated at £1,125 million, making a total cost of the war to the British Empire of £10,500 million.[1]

Before this can be added to the war costs of other allies, however, it is necessary, in order to avoid double entry, to deduct the amount of the above, which consists of loans to them, namely, £1,550 million, which reduces the net total to £8,950 million.

The cost of the war to the various allies up to 1 November 1918 (excluding loans made by each ally to other allies and also the cost of pensions), may be estimated at approximately:

	£ million
British Empire	6,660
United States	2,150
France	4,100
Italy	2,100
Russia	3,500
Belgium	200
Serbia	50
Roumania	50
Greece	30
Portugal	10
or, say, a total of	18,850

The capital charge in respect of war pensions might amount to a further £3,000 million, and costs subsequent to 1 November 1918, for demobilisation, etc., to a further £2,500 million, making a grand total of £24,350 million; or in round figures £25,000 million.[2]

In the following section the capacity of Germany to pay is discussed. While it is impossible to arrive at a precise conclusion, the general result of this discussion is to show that Germany

[1] This figure is up to 31 March 1919.

[2] The corresponding figure of the cost of the war to Germany may be put at about £8,000 million, of which £1,250 million is for pensions.

cannot pay an amount exceeding the £4,000 million required for reparation. If this is correct, and if reparation is to receive priority of payment, the question of an indemnity to meet the general costs of the war, namely, £25,000 million, need not arise.

Germany's Capacity to Pay

The methods by which Germany can pay the sum which the associated governments decide to exact from her fall into four groups:

1. Immediately transferable wealth in the form of gold, ships, and foreign securities.

2. Raw materials, substantial quantities of which can be obtained over a comparatively short period, say three years, such as coal, timber, potash and dyes.

3. The value of property in ceded territory.

4. An annual payment spread over a term of years.

There are excluded from the above two minor categories which must not be forgotten, but the money value of which is probably unimportant as compared with the above, namely:

(*a*) The actual restitution of property removed from territory occupied by the enemy, as for example, Russian gold, Belgian and French securities and works of art. In so far as the actual goods taken can be returned, these ought obviously so to be returned to the rightful owners, and could not be brought into the general indemnity pool.

In the French proposals an attempt is made widely to extend this category. In their scheme a distinction is made between 'restitution' and 'reparation', according to whether repayment *in pari materia* is or is not substantially possible, and priority is given to the former. Under 'restitution' there is included (1) the repayment of the indemnity of 1871, (2) the repurchase of mark currency in the hands of French nationals, (3) the repayment of taxes, dues, and requisitions in kind or in forced labour in occupied territory, (4) the restitution of material equivalent to the raw materials, ships, plant, manufactured articles, or works of art destroyed or removed; as well as the return in original of bullion, securities, archives, and works of art. If ships are covered by restitution, we should have nothing to lose by giving priority to restitution over reparation. But there seems no reason in equity or in logic for giving such items priority of compensation over damage done to buildings; and it would be almost impossible in practice to draw a line between the two classes.

(b) The value of military and naval material handed over under the armistice terms including rolling-stock and men of war. There are probably good precedents for regarding such cessions of material as legitimate prize to the armies capturing it. If, however, other German assets are not sufficient to meet the bill in full, such property ought hardly to be retained by the particular ally into whose hands it may have chanced to fall, but should, rather, be brought into the general indemnity pool. This item is not likely to be large enough to disturb the general character of the rough estimate now to be made.

In making estimates under each of the above heads we are faced, firstly, with the difficulty that the only available material is information published in Germany, for the most part prior to the war, and, secondly, with the difficulty of framing a clear hypothesis as to the position in which Germany will find herself as regards the integrity of her territories and their physical condition after the signature of peace. The following estimates are, therefore, put forward very tentatively and may prove to be substantially inaccurate. Some of the evidence on which they are based is shown separately in appendices. An attempt has been made throughout to make the estimate on the high rather than on the low side, so that the resulting total may be regarded as a maximum.

Immediately Transferable Wealth

(a) *Gold*. After deduction of the gold to be returned to Russia, the official holding of gold as shown in the Reichsbank's return of 30 November 1918 amounted to £115,417,900. This is a very much larger amount than appeared in the Reichsbank's return prior to the war,[1] and is a result of the vigorous campaign which has been continuously conducted in Germany for the surrender to the Reichsbank not only of gold coin but of gold ornaments of every kind. Private hoards doubtless still exist but, in view of the great efforts already made, it is unlikely that either the German government or the allies will be able to unearth them. It is not known whether the Reichsbank or the government possess a secret hoard but, as every effort has been made throughout the war to counteract the effect of a largely increased note issue by showing as much gold as possible in the Reichsbank's return, it is extremely unlikely that any substantial amount is held by the government outside this return. The return should therefore be taken as probably representing the maximum amount which the German government have been able to extract from their people.

In addition to gold there is a sum of about £1 million in silver in the Reichsbank. There is, however, a further substantial amount in circulation, the holdings of the Reichsbank having been as high as £9,100,000 on 31 December 1917, and having stood at about £6 million up to the latter part of October 1918, when the internal run began on currency of every kind. We may, therefore, take a total of (say) £125 million for gold and silver together.[2]

(b) *Shipping*. Exact statistics are not yet available, but on the present estimate that about 4,500,000 gross tons of German shipping are available to be taken over, the total value of this would represent, at the price of £40 per ton suggested by the Ministry of Shipping, a sum of £180 million.

(c) *Foreign Securities*. No official return of foreign investments has ever been called for in Germany, and the various unofficial estimates are confessedly based on insufficient data, such as the

---

[1] On 23 July 1914 the amount was £67,800,000.

[2] The French government have proposed that the indemnity of 1871 should be returned to them to the extent of £80 million in gold within a month of the signature of peace. If this demand is acceded to, there is not much left for other purposes.

admission of foreign securities to the German stock exchanges, the receipts of the stamp duties, consular reports, etc. An additional error is also introduced by the fact that almost all the estimates, having been made for the purpose of estimating national wealth, represent *net* foreign investments; that is to say, after deducting the value of property in Germany itself owned outside Germany.

The principal estimates which have been made are given in Appendix 3. This shows a general consensus of opinion among German authorities that their net foreign investments stood before the war at about £1,000 million. It is proposed to take for the basis of the present calculation the highest estimate made by any authority, namely, £1,250 million, and to add to this a further £250 million to correct the omissions referred to above, making a grand total of £1,500 million.

From this total several deductions have to be made. In the first place we ought to exclude for the present purpose the greater part of investments estimated in Austria-Hungary at £200 million, and in Russia at £200 million, bringing down the pre-war total for investments elsewhere to £1,100 million. In the second place, practically all Germany's holding of Scandinavian, Dutch, and Swiss securities have been returned to their countries of origin, and it is supposed that at least two-thirds of Germany's North and South American securities have also been sold. It is estimated that a deduction of £400 million[1] should be made on this head, bringing down the total of £700 million. In the third place, German assets in allied territory, amounting to upwards of £200 million, have already been seized by the associated governments, which it is proposed to use as an offset to the commercial and other claims of allied nationals under the 'clearing house' scheme for enemy debts and claims. Not the whole of these consist of securities, but a deduction of at least £100 million must be made on this head. Of the remaining investments, the greater part were in fixed-interest-bearing

---

[1] This figure may well be too high.

securities, which have suffered a depreciation in value of from 15 to 20 per cent due to the general rise in the rate of interest. Furthermore, investments in Turkey, Roumania, and Bulgaria are of doubtful value. If a further deduction of £50 million is made to cover these factors, we are left with a total of £550 million.

These securities, it must be remembered, are not in the hands of the German government, but in the hands of private persons. The securities held in Germany are mainly bearer securities, which it is easy to conceal or to withdraw from the country. They must consist of a vast variety of small items, the existence of many of which would escape any official enquiry. Further, an exodus to other parts of the world of the class of Germans who chiefly hold these securities is to be anticipated, and will be extremely difficult to prevent, especially as holders of the securities, even if they were prevented from leaving the country immediately might conceal their securities with the idea that in the course of years escape from Germany will be ultimately practicable. Indeed a certain proportion may be already held in safe custody in the adjacent neutral countries. It would therefore be very optimistic to believe that the allies, or the German government acting for them, could actually secure title to more than two-thirds of the theoretical maximum, which would reduce our maximum below £400 million.

We are left, therefore, with a total of immediately transferable property of about £700 million, made up of gold and silver £125 million, shipping £180 million, and securities (say) £400 million. In order, however, to be on the safe side and to allow for various possible errors in the above investigation, it is suggested that this figure of £700 million, should be arbitrarily increased by £100 million, and that the argument should proceed on the basis of its being possible to secure immediately transferable property to the value of £800 million. It would be for the German government to prove that this total cannot, in fact, be reached.

Raw Materials Obtainable in the Near Future

(*a*) *Potash*. The economic aspect of this demand has been dealt with in the memorandum submitted by the Board of Trade, where it is suggested that 1,300,000 tons of pure potash, roughly the equivalent of three years' peace requirements of the allies, should be demanded. According to German estimates the total annual requirements of the world for German potash will be about 1,500,000 tons. There seems, therefore, no reason why the allies should not demand an annual amount of potash equivalent to this total over a period of three years, leaving to the allies the disposal to neutrals of any surplus over their own requirements. In 1913 the average home price per ton was about £6 8s, and the average price for sales abroad about £11 5s. Taking a middle price of say, £8 per ton, the delivery of 4,500,000 tons as above might be accepted as the equivalent of £36 million.

(*b*) *Coal*. The Board of Trade estimate an annual deficit in the coal supply of France and Belgium immediately after the war of about 30 million tons,[1] which unless it is obtained from Germany, will have to be supplied so far as possible by the United Kingdom, thus diverting British coal from other remunerative markets. A large demand for coal may also be expected from Italy, which it will be difficult to satisfy. It might therefore be desirable, if it were possible, to secure deliveries of, say, 40 million tons annually to these three countries over a period of three years. This, on an estimate of £11 per ton, may be taken as the equivalent of £120 million. This supply would amount to about 20 per cent of Germany's aggregate coal production in 1913, namely, 190 million metric tons, and is substantially in excess of her net coal exports in the same year, namely, 24 million metric tons of coal *plus* coke to the equivalent of 7,500,000 metric tons. So large a demand as 40 million tons would therefore

---

[1] If, however, France gets the Saar Valley, 16 million tons a year should be available from this source.

have a very damaging effect on German industry in general, which would be accentuated if, as is proposed, the rich coalfields of Upper Silesia are added to Poland, and the less important fields of the Saar Valley to France. Before the war the coalfields of the Saar and of Upper Silesia accounted for nearly one-third of the total output of Germany. If, therefore, Germany loses these fields and is compelled at the same time to increase her exports to 40 million tons, the amount left for home consumption will be reduced from about 160 million tons to about 90 million tons. Output might be increased somewhat, but such a reduction would be hardly compatible with the maintenance of Germany as a great exporting industrial country, and would react on her capacity to pay an annual tribute as well as the above.

(c) *Timber*. The need for timber for reconstruction purposes needs no emphasis, and the policy pursued by Germany during the war of stripping the forests of all occupied territory gives a sufficient justification for a drastic demand for replacement. The views of the expert allied authorities on this question are summarised in an extract from the minutes of a meeting of the Commission internationale d'Achats de Bois, held on 9 November last:

> Considering that the quantities immediately available in Europe during the first year following the war are barely 50 per cent of the yearly pre-war European requirements, it is suggested that timber from Austria-Hungary might be made available to assist the Italian and Egyptian demands, while timber from Germany would be available to meet the demands of destroyed areas in Northern France and Belgium. As a further means of protection, the enemy countries should be prohibited from acquiring standing timber or making purchases of timber in the countries from which the allies will have to draw their supplies for a period until the supply is more on a level with the demand, as is now the case, and at least until normal conditions reassert themselves. Prior to the war, the enemy countries had enormous forests at their disposal

which should suffice to meet their own internal demands during that period, as well as to give large supplies to the allies.

On the assumption that timber is cut with due regard to forestry principles, the last sentence in the above extract may be incorrect. Before the war, the total production of timber in Germany only sufficed to meet two-thirds of her own internal demands, while Austria's pre-war exports to all destinations were not more than sufficient to cover half of the German deficit. It is evident, therefore, that if timber is to be taken in part payment from Germany on any important scale, a ruthless exploitation of the forests both of Germany and of Austria will be necessary.

On an extremely rough estimate the total demands of the European allies immediately after the war are placed at 250,000 standards per month, or about 500 million cubic feet per year for soft wood, and 50 million cubic feet for hard wood or, over a period of three years, 1,500 million cubic feet of soft wood, and 150 million cubic feet of hard wood. If the whole of this amount were demanded from Germany the value, taking soft wood at 2s per cubic foot, and hard wood at 4s, would amount to £180 million in all.

Part of the allied demand for timber might be transferred to Austria-Hungary, which, as distinguished from Germany, has an exportable surplus in normal times. On the other hand, however, a very large part of the timber land in Austria-Hungary will be transferred to one or other of the new States.

(d) *Dyes.* The Board of Trade recommend (see their separate memorandum) that dyes to the value of £10 million, or at the outside £20 million, might be requisitioned and handed over to the allies subject to certain safeguards specified by them.

On the above very high estimates, therefore, the total value of potash, coal, timber and dyes which could be handed over within three years would amount to a total of about £350 million, namely, £36 million for potash, £120 million for coal, £180 million for timber and £20 million for dyes. For the purpose of an outside estimate this figure may be used, but it would be imprudent to base a practical policy upon it.

The Value of Property in Ceded Territory

There are various ways in which the value of Alsace-Lorraine and the German colonies can be estimated. We have—

(*a*) the value of the territory measured not in respect of its immediate wealth, but by its potential resources;

(*b*) the aggregate present value of property in the territory, private and governmental;

(*c*) the value of governmental property.

If there were no question of exacting payments from the enemy for reparation, and only a transfer of territory were in question, it would be arguable that the power annexing the territory should credit the ceding government only with the value of private property taken over by the annexing government, for which the private owner was compensated by the ceding government, no allowance being made either for potential resources or for governmental property. For example, when Alsace-Lorraine was ceded to Germany by France, the indemnity took account of the value of the railways of the country which the German government took over from the private shareholders, who had owned them, against compensation from the French government, but of nothing else.

In present circumstances, however, such a treatment of the properties of Alsace-Lorraine would be very inequitable to the allies other than France. The value of the governmental property taken over is substantial, and undoubtedly should constitute a set-off to France's claim for reparation. While it would not be reasonable to take account of potential resources, the value of governmental property in ceded territory, as well as the value of private property expropriated in return for compensation paid by the German government, should be contributed to the indemnity pool, and should be deducted from any payments due to France out of that pool.

At the present time the capital value of the railways of Alsace-Lorraine is officially stated at about £50 million. The value of state forests is estimated at £12 million, and of other state enterprises at about £500,000, while the value of the post and telegraph systems, of government buildings, etc., might be put very roughly indeed at about £15 million, making in all a total of about £78 million.

To this there is to be added compensation for the expropriation of German holdings in iron mines, potash, oil fields, textile industries, etc., for which compensation will be paid by the German government to its dispossessed subjects. With these additions we may take perhaps the very arbitrary figure of £100 million as the total German off-set in respect of the cession of properties in Alsace-Lorraine.

For the Polish provinces of Prussia, all details are lacking, but a rough estimate of £75 million, or two-thirds that of Alsace-Lorraine may, perhaps, be put forward tentatively.

As regards the German colonies there have been several recent estimates of total value ranging from £125 million to £225 million. These estimates, however, are based upon the potential value of mineral wealth, trade development, etc., and it would, therefore, be out of the question to accept even the lower of these estimates, unless France was willing to accept a comparable basis in respect of Alsace-Lorraine.

The total value of government buildings, land, etc., in the colonies has recently been estimated on a very generous scale at £10 million, to which must be added a figure of perhaps as much as £10 million for capital sunk by the government in the railways. Private German capital invested in the colonies is estimated, again very generously, at £25 million. Assuming the expropriation of the whole of these, we have the figure of £45 million. Further particulars of the potential wealth of the German colonies are given in Appendix 4.

On the assumption that the reparation claim includes a charge on behalf of Poland, the value of property in Prussian

Poland may reasonably be included in the available assets. On this assumption, the total estimate for ceded territory amounts to £220 million.

Exclusive, therefore, of tribute payable over a long term of years, we have now reached a total of £1,370 million, made up of £800 million for immediately transferable property, £350 million for raw materials transferred over a period of three years, and £220 million in respect of ceded territory, all these figures being maxima.

An Annual Payment Spread over a Term of Years

In dealing with this question we are on even less firm ground than in the estimates given above, since not only are the statistical data inadequate, but the assumptions on which we are to proceed are doubtful. It must, however, be pointed out at the outset that the method of tribute over a period of years is, broadly, alternative to, and not additional to, the exaction of the maximum amount already discussed. This is particularly the case as regards supplies of coal and timber. In so far as proposals for the supply of raw materials over three years represent abnormal production calculated to exhaust German resources, they would immensely reduce the capacity of Germany to furnish other exports or to continue these exports subsequently. In so far as they represent trade which can be continued, they will be allowed for in estimating the maximum annual payment. Furthermore, if the whole of Germany's gold, ships, and foreign securities be taken from her, her capacity to pay for raw materials to set her industry going and her means of obtaining foreign credits will be gravely impaired if not destroyed. It is not practicable both to impoverish Germany by the methods already outlined and also to exact tribute on the basis of her pre-war productive capacity. The extent of the allowance to be made on these heads it is, however, almost impossible to estimate.

Turning to the general question, it is evident that an annual payment can only be made by Germany over a series of years by diminishing her imports and increasing her exports, thus increasing the balance in her favour available for making payments abroad. The most solid basis for estimating the extent to which this process could be carried is to be found, therefore, in an analysis of her trade returns before the war. On the basis of such an analysis, supplemented by some general data as to the aggregate wealth-producing capacity of the country, a guess may be made as to the maximum extent to which the exports of Germany could be stimulated to exceed her imports.

In the year 1913 Germany's imports amounted to £538 million and her exports to £505 million, exclusive of transit trade and bullion. That is to say, imports exceeded exports by about £33 million. On the average of the five years ending 1913, however, her imports exceeded her exports by a substantially larger amount, namely £74 million. It follows, therefore, that the whole of Germany's pre-war balance for new foreign investment was derived from the interest on her existing foreign securities, and from the profits of her shipping, foreign banking, etc. If the whole of her foreign securities and shipping are taken from her this source of revenue external to the country comes to an end and she will have no source from which to meet an annual tribute, except by an excess of exports over imports. Our problem, therefore, is to estimate the extent to which it might be practicable to increase exports and diminish imports. The balance of trade in Germany's favour resulting from this is the measure of the annual sum which it is within her capacity to pay. In the following investigation a continuance of pre-war price is assumed in the first instance and a rough allowance is then made for the change which has taken place in price levels.

A further very important factor, however, for which it is first necessary to make allowance is the diminution of Germany's capacity through the loss of territory to be ceded. This is shown in a very striking manner in Appendix 5, from which it appears that the loss of Poland, Upper Silesia, and Alsace-Lorraine will have a shattering effect on Germany's economic system and on her capacity to export. In cereals and potatoes these regions produce a substantial surplus over their consumption. They comprise 32·7 per cent of the coal output of Germany, 72·4 per cent of the iron ore, 74·7 per cent of the zinc, and 37·8 per cent of the blast furnaces. The loss of these districts will be specially disastrous to those export trades in which Germany has been fairly independent hitherto of the importation of raw materials.

Two-thirds of Germany's import and export trade is enumerated under separate headings in Appendix 7, only one-third being left unenumerated. The considerations applying to the enumerated portions may be assumed to be more or less the same as regards the unenumerated portions.

The table of exports shows that the most important exports consist of:
(1) iron goods, including tin plates (13·2 per cent),
(2) machinery, etc. (7·5 per cent),
(3) coal, coke, and briquettes (7 per cent),
(4) woollen goods, including raw and combed wool (5·9 per cent), and
(5) cotton goods, including cotton yarn and thread, and raw cotton (5·6 per cent),

these five classes of exports between them accounting for 39·2 per cent of the total exports. It will be observed that all these goods are of a kind in which before the war competition between Germany and the United Kingdom was very severe. If, therefore, the volume of such exports to overseas or European destinations is very largely increased the effect upon British export trade must be correspondingly serious. As regards two of the categories, namely, cotton and woollen goods, the increase of an export trade is dependent upon an increase of the import of the raw material, since Germany produces no cotton and practically no wool. These trades are therefore incapable of stimulation unless in the distribution of the raw materials Germany receives a preference over other countries beyond the previous standard of consumption, and even then the effective increase is not the gross value of the exports, but only the difference between the value of the manufactured exports and of the imported raw material. As regards the other three categories, namely, machinery, iron goods, and coal, Germany's capacity to increase her exports will be greatly diminished, if not rendered impossible, by the proposed cessions of territory in Poland, Upper Silesia, and Alsace-Lorraine. As has been pointed out above, these districts accounted for nearly one-third of Germany's production of coal and double her aggregate pre-war exports of this article. But they also accounted for no less than three-quarters of Germany's iron ore production,[1] for 38 per cent of her blast furnaces, and for 9.5 per cent of her iron and steel foundries. Unless, therefore, Alsace-Lorraine and Upper Silesia send their iron ore to Germany proper, to be worked up, which in any case would involve an increase in the imports for which she will have to find payment, so far from any increase in export trade being possible a decrease must be anticipated.[2]

Next on the list come cereals, leather goods, sugar, paper, furs, electrical goods, silk goods, and dyes. Cereals are not a net export and are far more than compensated by imports of the same commodities. As regards sugar, nearly 90 per cent of Germany's pre-war exports came to the United Kingdom.[3] An increase in this trade might be stimulated by a grant of a preference in this country to German sugar or by an arrangement by which sugar was taken in part payment for the indemnity on the same lines as has been proposed for coal, timber, etc., above.

---

[1] A less proportion in value, as the ore from these districts is relatively low priced.

[2] The Inter-Ally Steel Committee have lately estimated that the cession of territory to France, apart from the loss of Upper Silesia, will reduce Germany's annual pre-war production of steel ingots from 20 million tons to 14 million tons, and increase France's capacity from 5 million tons to 11 million tons. If these forecasts are correct, Germany will cease to be an important exporting country for iron and steel products.

[3] Germany's exports of sugar in 1913 amounted to 1,110,073 tons of the value of £13,094,300, of which 838,583 tons were exported to the United Kingdom at a value of £9,050,800. These figures were in excess of the normal, the average for the five years ending 1913 being about £10 million.

Paper exports also might be capable of some increase. Leather goods, furs, and silks depend upon corresponding imports on the other side of the account. Silk goods are largely in competition with the trade of France and Italy. The remaining items are individually very small—potash, for example, only contributes 0·6 per cent of Germany's total exports—and a glance down the list shows that, generally speaking, the same sort of considerations apply as to the above.

An examination of the import list shows that by far the greater part falls into two categories, namely, raw materials for manufacture and food. The chief items comprising the former, namely, cotton, wool, copper, hides, iron ore, furs, silk, rubber, and tin, could not be reduced without reacting on the export trade, and would evidently have to be largely increased if the export trade was to be largely increased. Imports of food, namely, wheat, barley, coffee, eggs, rice, maize, and the like, present a different problem. It is unlikely that, apart from certain comforts, the consumption of food by the German population as a whole before the war was in excess of what was required for maximum efficiency; indeed, it probably fell short of that amount. Any substantial increase in the imports of food would therefore react on the efficiency of the industrial population, and consequently on the volume of surplus exports which they could be forced to produce. It is hardly possible to insist on an increased productivity of German industry if the workmen are to be underfed. It might be urged, however, that the above is not true of barley, coffee, eggs, and tobacco. If, therefore, it were possible to enforce a régime in which for the future no German drank beer or coffee, or smoked tobacco at all, a saving of from £40 million to £50 million a year at least could be effected. Otherwise there seems little room for any significant reduction.

An analysis of German exports and imports according to destination and origin (see Appendix 7) is also relevant. From this it appears that of Germany's exports in 1913, 18 per cent went to the British Empire, 17 per cent to France, Italy, and

Belgium, 10 per cent to Russia and Roumania, and 7 per cent to the United States; that is to say, more than half of the exports found their market in the countries of the *Entente* nations. Of the balance, 12 per cent went to Austria-Hungary, Turkey, and Bulgaria, and 35 per cent elsewhere. Unless, therefore, the present allies are prepared to encourage the importation of German products, a substantial increase in total volume can only be effected by the wholesale swamping of neutral markets.

It is obviously impossible on these data to make a forecast of any great value as to the maximum modification of Germany's export balance under the conditions presumed to exist after peace. But the above analysis affords, nevertheless, some indication of its possible magnitude. On the assumptions (1) that we do not specially favour Germany over ourselves in supplies of such raw materials as cotton and wool, (2) that France and Poland, having secured the iron ore deposits, seek to secure the blast furnaces and the steel trade also, (3) that Germany is not encouraged to undercut the iron trade of the allies in overseas markets, (4) that a preference is not given to German goods in the British Empire generally, it is evident by examination of the other items that not much is practicable. Let us guess that, after making some allowance for the increase of prices since 1913, imports could be reduced by £75 million per annum, and exports increased by £100 million per annum (although it is impossible to explain how on the above assumption this could be done); the pre-war average adverse trade balance of about £75 million would then be converted into a favourable balance of £100 million. In order to be on the safe side, let us add 25 per cent to this figure. We then reach as our conclusion an annual payment of £125 million which, spread over thirty years, represents, at 5 per cent, a capital sum of a little less than £2,000 million.

If the Allies were to 'nurse' the trade and industry of Germany for a period of (say) five years, supplying her with loans and with ample raw materials during that period, a substantially larger sum than the above could probably be extracted thereafter; for Germany is capable of very great productivity. If this process is considered too dangerous, then the fact must be faced that the break-up of Germany's economic system by the cession of her coal and iron fields, the destruction of her overseas trade by the liquidation of her foreign businesses and of her credit by the seizure of all her gold, ships, and securities, the rationing of her supplies of raw materials, and the closing of allied markets to her exports is incompatible with a vastly increased trade and an international balance in her favour many times greater than before the war. If Germany is to be 'milked', she must not first of all be ruined.

It is also worth while, however, to examine the question from another standpoint. A critic of the above estimate might base his argument on Germany's total surplus annual productivity as distinct from her export surplus. Helfferich's estimate of Germany's annual increment of wealth quoted in Appendix 2 is £400 million to £425 million.[1] Before the war Germany spent between £50 million and £100 million on armaments, which can now be dispensed with. Why, therefore, should she not pay over to the Allies an annual sum of £500 million? This puts the crude argument in its strongest and most plausible form. But it overlooks the following:

(1) Appendix 6 on the financial position of the German government after the war puts the annual charge for pensions at £100 million. This represents a loss of productivity which more than cancels the gain through reduction of armaments. Indeed, the real loss of productive capacity as a result of Germany's total casualties must be for some years to come very much in excess of £100 million annually.

(2) Putting on one side the burden of the internal debt, which is a question of internal distribution rather than productivity, we must still allow for the foreign debt incurred by Germany

[1] Exclusive of increased value of existing land and property, the increased increment of which Helfferich estimated at £75 million.

during the war, for the exhaustion of her stocks of raw materials, for the depletion of her livestock, for the impaired productivity of her soil through lack of manures, and for the diminution in her wealth by reason of the failure to keep up repairs and renewals for four years. Germany is not as rich as she was before the war, and the diminution in her future savings for this reason could not be put at less than £50 million annually.

(3) Germany is supposed to have profited about £100 million per annum from her ships, her foreign investments, and her foreign banking and connections. If these are taken from her, this sum must be deducted from her surplus.

(4) The loss of Alsace-Lorraine, Poland, and Upper Silesia could not be assessed at less than £50 million annually.

We are left, therefore, with a figure of £200 million. Adding an arbitrary 25 per cent to this to cover omissions and contingencies, we have £250 million. The reconciliation of this with the previous estimate of £125 million takes account of two further factors somewhat different in kind from those discussed so far:

(1) An annual surplus available for home investment can only be converted into a surplus available for export abroad by a radical change in the kind of work performed. Labour, while it may be available and efficient for building in Germany, may yet be able to find no outlet in foreign trade. We are back on the same question which faced us in our examination of the export trade—in *what* export trade is German labour going to find a greatly increased outlet? It is probable that labour could only be diverted into quite different channels with some loss of efficiency; and it is certain that it could not be so diverted except with a large expenditure of capital. You cannot set up a new industry or increase an old one without such capital. If the whole annual surplus is to be absorbed by the tribute, where is this capital to come from?

(2) We are without experience of a modern nation under the lash. The psychology of a white race under conditions of servi-

tude has been the subject of no recent experiment. It is, however, generally supposed that if the whole of a man's surplus production is taken from him, his efficiency and his industry are diminished. The entrepreneur and the inventor will not contrive, the trader and shopkeeper will not save, the labourer will not sweat and hasten, if the fruits of their industry are set aside, not for the benefit of their children, their old age, their pride, or their status, but for the enjoyment of a foreign conqueror.

One other basis of calculation has been canvassed in the press. Sir Sidney Low, in a letter published in *The Times* of 3 December criticising certain utterances of the Prime Minister and Sir Eric Geddes, writes as follows: 'I have seen authoritative estimates which place the gross value of Germany's mineral and chemical resources as high as £250,000 million sterling or even more; and the Ruhr basin mines alone are said to be worth over £45,000 million. It is certain, at any rate, that the capital value of these natural supplies is much greater than the total war debts of all the allied states. Why should not some portion of this wealth be diverted for a sufficient period from its present owners and assigned to the peoples whom Germany has assailed, deported, and injured? The allied governments might justly require Germany to surrender to them the use of such of her mines and mineral deposits as would yield, say, from 100 to 200 millions annually for the next 30, 40 or 50 years. By this means we could obtain sufficient compensation from Germany without unduly stimulating her manufactures and export trade to our detriment.'

It is not clear why, if Germany has wealth exceeding £250,000 million, Sir Sidney Low is content with the trifling sum of 100 to 200 millions annually. But his letter is worth quoting as a *reductio ad absurdum* of a certain line of thought. While a mode of calculation which estimates the value of coal miles deep in the bowels of the earth as high as in a coal scuttle, of an annual lease of £1,000 for 999 years at £999,000, and of a field (presumably) at the value of all the crops it will grow to the end of recorded time, opens up great possibilities, it is also double-

377

edged. If Germany's total resources are worth £250,000 million, those she will part with in the cession of Alsace-Lorraine and Upper Silesia should be more than sufficient to pay the entire costs of the war and reparation together.

In point of fact the *present* market value of all the mines in Germany of every kind has been estimated at £300 million,[1] or a little more than one-thousandth part of Mr Low's expectations.

Germany's capacity to pay is, therefore, measured as follows:
(1) Immediately transferable property, £800 million.
(2) Raw materials transferable over a period of three years, £350 million.
(3) The value of ceded territory, £220 million.
(4) Tribute spread over a period of thirty years, about £1,900 million.

(2) and (4) are alternative, and cannot both be counted; (1) and (4) are also largely alternative.

We thus reach a grand total not exceeding £3,000 million. As maxima have been taken throughout, this result is in excess of what could in fact be obtained. Some political and economic considerations also come in, which are discussed in the next section. An actual payment of £2,000 million, if effected without evil indirect consequences, would be a very satisfactory achievement in all the circumstances.

That is no reason, however, why less than the full cost of reparation should be asked of the enemy in the first instance, and the burden of proving incapacity should be thrown on them.

The above calculation allows nothing for the contributions of Austria-Hungary, Bulgaria, and Turkey, which it is indeed impossible to estimate. It would be necessary to know how far the dismemberment of these empires is to proceed, and the distribution of responsibility between the parts, before even a beginning could be made in the estimation. Nor have we adequate

[1] Before the war the value *at the mine* of Germany's total annual output of iron ore was valued at £5,500,000.

data as to the present economic condition of these countries. If the finances and revenues of what territory remains to Turkey are administered by an Inter-Ally Commission, some contribution should be obtained large enough to deserve attention. But at the best the contribution obtainable cannot be large compared with the figures discussed in relation to Germany. While, therefore, the above omission must not be overlooked, and some rough addition made to cover it, the omission is unlikely to modify any general conclusions derived from restricting attention to Germany. A subsequent memorandum will be prepared dealing with these countries, if adequate material is obtainable.

The Economic Consequences of an Indemnity

It has been maintained that the payment of the French indemnity to Germany in 1871 did Germany more harm than good, and that this is likely to be true of indemnities in general. This view is contrary to common sense, and is not more tenable on close examination. It must be advantageous to a country to receive imports without having to work or pay for them, and the process is correspondingly disadvantageous to the country paying the indemnity.

While this is scarcely worth arguing, it does not, however, entirely dispose of the present case. Two eventualities have to be sharply distinguished; the first, in which the usual course of trade is not gravely disturbed by the payment, the amount of it being approximately equal to the sum which would accrue to the paying country abroad in any case, and would have been invested abroad if it were not for the indemnity; the second, in which the amount involved is so large that it cannot be paid without a drastic disturbance of the course of trade and a far-reaching stimulation of the exports of the paying country.

In the first case, it would be far-fetched to see in it any serious economic inconveniences. No trade would be interfered with, and the broad result would be that, instead of Germany's employ-

379

ing her annual foreign surplus to build up for herself a strong financial position internationally, the whole of this surplus would be available instead for strengthening the position of the allies.

But in the second case the position is altogether different. An indemnity so high that it can only be paid by means of a great expansion of Germany's export trade must necessarily interfere with the export trade of other countries. It might be to the advantage of this country, as a whole, to receive the bulk of her iron goods and machinery from Germany without having to pay for them; but it would not be to the advantage of our iron trade. Nor would the position be substantially different if Germany were prevented from marketing her goods in this country, and were limited to neutral markets; for this might mean the destruction by German undercutting of our export trade in those markets. If Germany were prevented from undercutting everywhere, she would be prevented from paying the indemnity at all. It would be held, therefore, by those who oppose 'dumping' —and on the same grounds—that it would be disadvantageous for this country to receive from Germany a tribute, directly or indirectly, in the form of iron goods and machinery if this were ruinous to the corresponding British industries.

There is, however, a further difficulty. The whole of the indemnity is not to be received by this country. There are several other participants, and so far as reparation is concerned, the British share is only about 15 per cent. It will be very disadvantageous to this country artificially to stimulate German exports in order that the proceeds of these exports may be paid over (e.g.) to France. The fact is well known, and is also confirmed by the analysis made above of Germany's exports, that her export trade before the war showed a strong tendency to compete with British trade. Broadly speaking, her great staple industries are the same as ours. Without a great diversion of productivity from industries now working for the home market in Germany into the export industries, Germany cannot even pay for reparation, far less the general cost of the war. These export industries cannot enjoy a great expansion without injuring ours. In so far as this country receives the indemnity, there is a heavy off-set to this injury. But, in so far as the indemnity goes into other hands, there is no such off-set.

Our conclusion is, therefore, that it must be disadvantageous to the staple industries of this country if Germany is forced and enabled (for she cannot be forced unless she is enabled) to pay in full even for reparation. An indemnity high enough to absorb the whole of Germany's normal surplus, for investment abroad and for building up foreign business and connections, must certainly be advantageous to this country and correspondingly injurious to the enemy. We can safely take the profits of the trade she will transact in any case. But this total is soon reached. Anything beyond that means building up her export trade largely at the expense of our own. The limit of what we can safely exact, having regard to our own selfish interests only, may therefore be as low as £2,000 million.

In dealing with general economic consequences, there are two other points which must not be entirely overlooked, although they belong to the political at least as much as to the economic sphere.

If the German government have to find a very large annual sum in addition to the service of their own war debt, they will be set an impossible fiscal problem. It may be assumed, therefore, that the repudiation of their internal debt will probably result from the exaction of a high annual tribute. If all war debts east of the Rhine have been repudiated, the proletariat of Western Europe may object to be shut out from the supposed advantages of such a situation. Repudiation is a contagious disease, and each breach in the opposite convention brings it nearer everywhere.

In the second place, if the central government of Germany has engaged itself to hand over to foreigners the whole of the national surplus, the possession of a central government becomes a very expensive luxury, and separatism a plausible way out. An indemnity so large as to leave the German population without hope is liable to defeat itself. Why should they pay it?

An occupation of a part of Germany is no answer to separatism. The occupation of the left bank of the Rhine will be no inducement to an independent Republic of Saxony to pay up; and the cost of even a partial occupation may be so great as to exceed what extra it brings in as tribute. The forests and railways and state domains are useless as a security. If they could be carried away bodily their value is totally inadequate.[1]

Conclusions

Summarising the argument, we find:

1. The capacity of the enemy to pay falls short of the probable reparation claim (though possibly not of the claim finally justified after examination and criticism).

2. It is, nevertheless, of comparable magnitude with this claim, that is to say, 50 to 75 per cent of it.

3. A claim for the general costs of the war, in addition to reparation, could not be met even in part.

Two alternative lines of policy are open:

1. To obtain *all* the property which can be transferred immediately or over a period of three years, levying this contribution ruthlessly and completely, so as to ruin entirely for many years to come Germany's overseas development and her international credit; but, having done this (which would yield more than £1,000 million, but less than £2,000 million), to ask only a small tribute over a term of years, and to leave Germany to do the best she can for the future with the internal resources remaining to her.

---

[1] If every house and factory and cultivated field, every road and railway and canal, every mine and forest in the German Empire could be carried away and expropriated and sold at a good price to a ready buyer, it would not pay for half the cost of the war and of reparation added together.

2. To levy less ruthlessly in the immediate future, and to supply Germany with considerable quantities of raw material, with a view to her developing for the benefit of the allies an export trade on a far greater scale than hitherto; and having thus nursed her back into a condition of high productivity, to compel her to exploit this productivity under conditions of servitude for a long period of years.

The effect of the argument of this memorandum is to prefer the first of these alternatives to the second, which can only be carried out to the detriment of our own export trade, with great technical difficulty, and under political conditions of a dangerous description, and even then will not be *very* productive.

An annual levy on a relatively small scale could, as indicated above, be added to a contribution under (1) without giving rise to the objections which are associated with an annual levy of large amount.

The wealth of France in 1871 was estimated at a little less than half that of Germany in 1913. An indemnity from Germany of £500 million would, therefore, be about comparable to the sum paid by France in 1871. The real burden of an indemnity in excess of this would increase more than in proportion to its amount, and the payment of £2,000 million by Germany would have an effect immeasurably severer than the £212 million paid by France in 1871.

Both the report of the Hughes Committee and the Treasury memorandum were criticised by L. S. Amery, Parliamentary Secretary to the Colonies, in 'Notes on Indemnity', a paper circulated to the War Cabinet 31 December 1918 (CAB 24/72). 'They seem both of them to exaggerate the position in two opposite directions', Amery wrote to Bonar Law, 26 December,

and . . . leave out of account what seems to me almost the most important aspect of the whole matter, namely how whatever sum Germany and her allies are capable of paying is to be distributed as between ourselves and our allies. Unless we address ourselves very seriously to that side of the question I am very much afraid we may get done in the eye by our various pushful allies.

Bonar Law passed Amery's paper on to Keynes who, in the character of author, put his comments in a personal letter. (The whole exchange is to be found in the Chancellor of the Exchequer's papers, T 172/905.)

Letter to L. S. AMERY, *6 January 1919*

My dear Amery,

I have just read with very great interest your paper on indemnities and you may like to see the following notes on points which have occurred to me during its perusal.

1. As a minor point, by the way, what you say of the indemnity of 1871, while no doubt it substantially represents the facts, requires to be supplemented by the following. In the course of the negotiations Thiers urged that the war should not be regarded by Prussia as a kind of financial speculation and that no more than the actual war expenditure should be exacted. Bismarck accepted this view and endeavoured to justify a sum of frs. 5,000 million, specifying the items by which it was made up, namely, frs. 2,000 million for war expenditure proper and frs. 3,000 million for various indirect losses to Germany and German subjects. This calculation was questioned by the French negotiators but in vain.

2. I am very much alive to the point you emphasise as to the small dividend which this country would receive from 'reparation', having regard to our total effort, as compared with what certain other allies would receive. But I believe we should have a much better chance of obtaining some adjustment on this whole question by a different route. In the first place I doubt if your method is politically possible. The doctrine has been already accepted that 'reparation' must be a first charge on any indemnity received. Your object would not be attained except by upsetting this principle, which would be very difficult and would be heavily contested by France[1] and Belgium who would almost

[1] M. Ribot has already demanded that the priority you claim for us should be conceded to the French.

certainly secure the support of the United States. We should in fact be fighting on our weakest ground if we sought recompense for our greater financial sacrifice on these lines. In the second place the real disparity between expenditure and relative resources is not as between ourselves and France but as between ourselves and France on the one hand and the United States on the other. By the invasion of her country France has suffered a wholly exceptional kind of damage from which we have been free; and I should not care to have to argue that in proportion to resources our net expenditure and indirect loss has been greater than that of France. Your method of approach, however, makes the controversy primarily one between us on the one hand and France and Belgium on the other, whereas the United States would be left exactly where she is. There is good reason to think that France intends at the Peace Conference to raise the whole question of adjustment of financial burden as between the United States and the allies. We should prejudice our position in this important discussion if we were to adopt the line you advocate in the matter of indemnities.[1]

3. I rate higher than you do the practical difficulties of securing any agreed estimate of 'real' loss as contrasted with gross expenditure.

4. You rightly point out that the Treasury memorandum dealt rather cursorily with the question of evaluating territories transferred. I agree that this subject needs much further consideration. But I gave some thought to the general principles involved and was averse to insert a large figure on this head on the following grounds. It would be impossible to get France to admit that the acquisition of Alsace-Lorraine must reckon as an annexation and I do not believe she would agree to the evaluation of this territory on the kind of basis which she might very likely accept as applicable, e.g. to the Saar Valley, if she gets it. If this view is correct, it seems to me that we have much to lose and little

---

[1] Our best alternative would be to claim, on the basis of the Paris Resolutions, that illegal damage should have priority, which would put Belgium's claim and ours for U-Boat losses in front of France's general damage claims.

to gain by setting a high money value on annexations. Such a principle would certainly apply to any German colonies left in our hands and as far as I can see to very little else having a counterbalancing effect in our favour.[1] Before expressing a final opinion upon this it would be necessary to have before one a statement of all the principal territories which are in fact to be transferred. Pending this it would be rash, I think, to adopt any basis of valuation higher than that suggested in the Treasury memorandum.

5. As regards your main criticism of our estimate of the maximum annual payment, I daresay some further weight should have been given to possible reductions in internal consumption. I did not, however, overlook this element and did in fact make some considerable allowance for it, suggesting that an amount of, perhaps, £50 million annually might be saved by a reduction in the consumption of 'comforts'. I doubt, however, if it is possible to go very far in this direction consistently with efficiency and I should have thought that in the particular case you cite, namely clothing, the economy possible was not an important one in relation to the big figures at issue. I certainly do not see any possibility of doubling the figures suggested in the Treasury Memorandum by means of additional allowances for factors of this kind.

Sincerely yours,

J.M.K.

---

[1] I see that you value the Jugoslav provinces at £500 million. If this estimate is correct and if Italy obtain this territory Italy would be in the position of owing money to other claimants on the 'reparation' pool. But how could she possibly pay it? The same applies to Poland.

Chapter 5

THE PEACE CONFERENCE, 1919

Keynes attended the Peace Conference in Paris as the senior Treasury member of the British delegation and was the official representative of the British Empire on the Supreme Economic Council. He resigned from the Treasury and left the conference when he became disheartened and disillusioned by the terms of the resulting treaty. In the course of time he published three accounts based upon his experiences—*The Economic Consequences of the Peace* (*JMK*, vol. II), which appeared in December 1919; 'Mr Lloyd George: a Fragment', written as part of *The Economic Consequences* but suppressed by the author until 1933 when he included it in *Essays in Biography* (*JMK*, vol. X), and 'Dr Melchior: a Defeated Enemy', published posthumously in *Two Memoirs* (*JMK*, vol. XIV). Most of the documents following in this section were written immediately after the events that they describe took place, and Keynes drew upon them for what he published later.

Keynes arrived in Paris for the conference on 10 January 1919. His first discussions were with Norman Davis, chief representative of the United States Treasury, and one of his early communications to Sir John Bradbury concerned their relations. Officially American financial credits were to come to an end with the close of hostilities, foreign loans only being constitutional for war purposes, but the British had already received a credit of $250 million to tide them over the first post-war months and were seeking an additional $500 million—which had been refused both by the Assistant Secretary of the Treasury, Albert Rathbone, and by the Secretary, Carter Glass. Keynes however was confident that the Americans would see Britain safely through, in spite of 'Mr Rathbone's habit of writing what can only be described as solicitors' letters and the threatening and lawyer-like language that he seems sometimes to use'—as he put it in a letter to Sir Hardman Lever drafted for Bonar Law, 31 December 1918 (T 172/447). This was his minute to Bradbury, 14 January 1919:

Sir John Bradbury

I have had several important conversations with Mr Norman Davis as to the relations between ourselves and the American Treasury. He is very much in disagreement with the attitude which Mr Rathbone has taken up and is doing what he can to counteract it. He is now proposing that Mr Rathbone should be invited over here for a short time in order that his conversion may be effected on the spot, and I am strongly urging him to take this course.

The atmosphere here is of course very different from that of Washington. The Washington attitude is that the war is over and that the most strenuous efforts possible must be made to secure economy and bring advances to an end by whatever means at the earliest possible date. That is to say Mr Rathbone's policy is directed by strictly Treasury considerations and has nothing whatever to do with high policy on the part of the President or anyone else.

It is in fact directly opposed to policy as it presents itself to the Americans here. In the first place Hoover [Herbert Hoover, Director-General of the Inter-Allied Supreme Council for Relief and Supply], as you already know, will be very gravely embarrassed if we are cut off from the means of buying his products, and in the second place the Americans here appreciate that our participation in relief operations is absolutely dependent on the continuance of assistance from them. And they see that if Washington is pressing us to adopt such expedients as to issue more dollar Treasury bills we shall draw in our horns obstinately and leave them unassisted in the various projects they have in view. Thirdly, and perhaps most important of all, co-operation between ouselves and the Americans here is proceeding at a great pace. In all the meetings I have been to so far Norman Davis and I privately concerted our policy together beforehand and I hear that this sort of thing is going on in other quarters also. The last thing therefore that they want to do is to quarrel with us prematurely over money. In certain unlikely but conceivable circumstances all this might be reversed. But in the meantime I am confirmed in the view I had formed before I left London that we may for the next two or three months go on very unconcernedly as regards our American finance irrespective of the letter Mr Rathbone may address to Sir Hardman Lever. I learn privately that the President has appointed a committee to advise him here during the Peace Conference consisting of himself as chairman, House as deputy, Hoover, [Vance] McCormick, [Bernard M.] Baruch, [Edward N.] Hurley and Norman Davis as members. Davis has been formally appointed by Mr Carter Glass as his representative on this committee. He has also been appointed United States Treasury Commissioner in Europe. He is the United States delegate to Treves and Mr Hoover's colleague for financial purposes on the Supreme Council of Relief and Supply. The whole authority of the United States Treasury on this side of the Atlantic is therefore vested in him. While he will always drive with us as hard a bargain as he can, I am sure notwithstanding that it is possible to work with him in close intimacy and that on essentials our policies need not come into conflict.

In the event of the United States Treasury maintaining their present attitude in an unmodified form Mr Davis tells me confidentially that he believes he can persuade the above committee, who in the aggregate are extremely powerful, to put up a joint memorandum to the President advising him that the Treasury be overruled. I think it unlikely, however, that matters will come to this pass, and I believe that a compromise can be effected sufficiently satisfactory to Davis, though not so satisfactory to us, by which on the one hand the United States Treasury give no guarantees or assurances on specific grounds of hope, yet do in fact enable us to live from hand to mouth at least during the period of the conference.

J.M.K.

14.1.19

Keynes's hopes were justified; Davis persuaded Secretary Glass to allow the additional loan. The Americans at the conference plainly needed Britain's co-operation in the handling of relief, as Keynes explained in a second message to Bradbury the same day, 14 January. In this minute he asked for instructions from the Chancellor of the Exchequer—who, in Lloyd George's coalition cabinet formed January 1919, was Austen Chamberlain. At the same time he took into account the opinion of Bonar Law, the new Lord Privy Seal, who was attending the conference. The minute follows.

Sir John Bradbury

The Supreme Council of Supply and Relief, of which Lord Reading and Sir John Beale are the British representatives, have, after discussion, referred to representatives of the four treasuries the question of the financial constitution of the Council.

In accordance with these instructions, I have prepared the attached draft which has been circulated to the American, French and Italian representatives. It will not come before the Council for final examination until after my return from Trèves at the end of the week. May I therefore receive *by telegram* the instructions of the Chancellor of the Exchequer as to whether he desires any modifications, and in particular as to what financial liability he is prepared for this country to undertake?

In this last connection you will observe that the *proportions* in which the financial burden is to be distributed is left blank. Up to now the conversations have been on the basis of 40 per cent for the United States, 25 per cent for the United Kingdom, 25 per cent for France and 10 per cent for Italy. Mr Bonar Law, however, is inclined to think that we should not take up so large a share as 25 per cent in view of the fact that the bulk of the produce to be sold to the countries relieved will be American. On this I submit the following observations:

(1) Last week Mr Hoover endeavoured to get through Congress an appropriation of $100 million to be absolutely at the free disposal of the President for relief purposes over and above what might be obtainable under the recognised arrangements for loans to allies. Congress has, however, held up this application pending information as to the share in the expenses which is to be supported by the other allies. The Americans are therefore very anxious that they should be able to announce that we and

France are taking a quarter each. I am inclined to think that it might be good policy to meet them in the matter, the amount of money available not being very considerable.

(2) If, however, the Chancellor of the Exchequer directs, I believe I could, armed with this decision, persuade the Americans to take a 50 per cent share, leaving 20 per cent each for France and ourselves.

(3) It is to be observed that in no event do we have to find cash for American expenditure. If the cost of British produce furnished falls short of our 25 per cent share, we shall be entitled to pay the balance to the Americans in obligations and not in cash. Our cash position is, therefore, fully protected.

(4) The sum of £12,500,000 which we should have to find on a 25 per cent basis between now and the end of next August is by no means wholly additional to our present expenditure. In particular the whole of our outgoings on Belgian relief will be absorbed in this figure as well as the minor assistance which we are according to Serbia and to Roumania.

The whole position is rather an extraordinary one as the immense surplus of the pig products for which the Americans have to find a market makes them unusually willing to take a larger share than other people, and exposes them to pressure from us if we think it wise to exert it to the full extent. I am inclined to think, however, that if for the present we can dispose of the whole question of European relief for a sum of £12,500,000, we shall have done very well indeed.

J.M.K.

14.1.19

'Dr Melchior: a Defeated Enemy' is the story of Keynes's relationship with Carl Melchior, the head of the German financial delegation; the background is an account of the negotiations to provide food for Germany. The decision to furnish the food, conditional on the handing over of German ships, was made by the Supreme Council of Supply and Relief meeting 12 January. The method of payment was discussed the following day at two meetings which Keynes described for Bradbury in a third minute written 14 January. Here, as in 'Dr Melchior', the French Finance Minister, L. L. Klotz, emerges as the villain.

Sir John Bradbury

The appended paper shows broadly the conditions on which food supplies are to be furnished to Germany. Clause 5 as to the means of payment was the subject of much controversy. The principle at stake was of course whether payment by Germany for necessary food should be a first charge on her resources or whether the most liquid resources available should be reserved for indemnity purposes.

At the Council for Relief and Supply the text as drafted was accepted after discussion by the French representatives. At the Armistice Commission, however, under the chairmanship of Marshall Foch, Monsieur Klotz took the most violent exception to it and declared that he was quite unable to accept the formula. He agreed that Germany should pay for the food supplied. But he was not prepared to agree that the cash so received should necessarily be paid over to the ally furnishing the food. He contended that the debt from Germany so created was to be reckoned as one amongst the many debts from Germany to the associated governments and that while this debt should take a high rank it should not necessarily rank first and its exact position should be the subject of subsequent discussion between the allies.

At the Armistice Commission I refused to give way on this point and was strongly supported by the Americans who were indeed the party chiefly interested, and were exceedingly angry at Klotz's attitude. Finally the matter was referred to the Supreme War Council which was meeting in the afternoon.

At this meeting Mr Bonar Law, supported by the Prime Minister and President Wilson, uncompromisingly opposed Monsieur Klotz's view and Monsieur Klotz, after attempting various compromises, was finally overruled, the clause being adopted as originally drafted and the only concession he obtained being the right to reopen the discussion two months hence should the French government then desire to do so.

It may be taken, however, that the Supreme War Council has definitely established the principle that payment for essential supplies to the enemy must take priority over other claims.

It will be impossible to determine the most convenient method of payment until we have ascertained from the Germans what their resources actually are.

Mr Ward and I, together with Mr Norman Davis for America and the Comte de Lasteyrie for France, are proceeding to Trèves this afternoon where we shall meet the President of the Reichsbank and do our best to ascertain from him his exact position.

I anticipate that credits of minor amounts may be available in the Argentine and other neutral countries. But I doubt whether very much will be available in these sources. The advantage of our position will be that the Germans will be presumably so anxious to secure the cereals and fats which we are in a position to offer in return for payment that they will do their best to meet us. A further source of funds is to come from freights earned by the German mercantile marine which they are to place at our disposal in return for the food supplies.

As regards bacon, it has been suggested by the Americans that we unload on Germany the large stocks of rather low-grade bacon which we now hold and replace these by fresher stocks from America which would be more readily saleable. From the food point of view this would clearly be a good deal for us. But it would only be convenient financially if we can sell our bacon stocks to Germany in return for cash which is convertible into dollars for the purpose of paying for the supplies we should purchase in America in replacement. It may therefore, be worth considering whether the most convenient manner in which Germany should pay is not out of the very large amounts of German property held by the public trustee in New York.

The situation is a curious one. The blockade on fats to neutral countries is being raised and Germany is to receive fat supplies on a very generous scale. Bolshevism is to be defeated and the new era to begin. At the Supreme War Council President Wilson was very eloquent on the subject of instant action on these lines. But really the underlying motive of the whole thing is Mr Hoover's abundant stocks of low-grade pig products at high prices which must at all costs be unloaded on someone, enemies failing allies. When Mr Hoover sleeps at night visions of pigs float across his bedclothes and he frankly admits that at all hazards the nightmare must be dissipated.

J.M.K.

14.1.19

According to plan, on the afternoon of 14 January Keynes, with the other allied representatives, departed on Marshal Foch's special train for Trèves to discuss these food and financial arrangements with the German delegates. 'Dr Melchior' gives the personal details and flavour of the encounter; the document reproduced here is Keynes's official report to the Treasury, signed 20 January 1919.

REPORT ON FINANCIAL CONVERSATIONS AT TRÈVES
15–16 JANUARY 1919

The German delegates present were Dr Kaufmann, President of the Reichsbank, Dr Melchior of the firm of Messrs Warburg, Dr Ratjen, the German financial representative at Spa and three representatives of the German Foreign Office. Dr Melchior was their spokesman almost throughout.

Mr Norman Davis, the American representative presided, the Comte de Lasteyrie, Professor Attolico and myself representing the French, Italian and British treasuries respectively.

The proceedings were in English, a shorthand report being taken of the greater part of them, and were very imperfectly interpreted into French. Without losing a formal character, they became somewhat freer and more in the nature of an inter-change of views and information as time went on, particularly on the afternoon of the second day when the main difficulties had been disposed of. There was, however, no conversation with the German delegates of any kind outside the formal con-ferences except to a certain extent on the part of the American representatives (see below).

The following were the principal questions discussed:

(1) Inquiries were made of the German delegates as to the safety of the Reichsbank's gold and note-issuing plant in view of the Spartacus disturbances and they were pressed to agree to a movement of these further west, and if possible to Frankfort. After telephonic communication with Berlin they were able to tell us that the aggregate gold reserve amounted to about £112,500,000 of which only £45,000,000 was held in Berlin, the balance being distributed between no less than 95 pro-vincial branches, the most important of these provincial reserves being £7,350,000 at Nuremburg, £6,750,000 at Munich, £4,850,000 at Frankfort-on-Main, £3,300,000 at Magdeburg, £2,450,000 at Wurzburg and £2,350,000 at Ulm. They added that the Deutsche Bank held no gold stock in Berlin and that the amounts of gold outside the Reichsbank branches were in-appreciable. The gold at Berlin is protected by armed guards, machine guns and gas contrivances, and while the German delegates could not pretend to be free from anxiety, they believed that they had taken all the precautions possible in the circum-stances. They agreed that it would be better, if it were possible, to move the gold further west, and undertook to take steps in this direction at the first convenient opportunity. They declared, however, that to do anything at the present moment would be dangerous in the extreme.

As regards the note-printing plant, they had to admit that owing to the treachery of the guard, the Spartacus group had been in possession of the premises for two days during the recent disturbances. They also admitted that owing to transport and other difficulties the Reichsbank was now holding unusually large quantities of unissued notes. They stated, however, that the removal of the plant would present great technical difficulties, and they believed that in case of need the plates could be rapidly defaced. (This however seems to presume the loyalty of the employees of the printing office.) They added further that the numerators (for numbering the notes) could be easily removed, and would be difficult to restore, so that notes issued irregularly could be easily distinguished from the regular issues. They promised to consider the technical possibility of arranging for the numbering of the notes to be effected away from Berlin.

The German delegates showed no reluctance to disclose any facts for which they were asked, and after we had clearly explained to them that the associated governments had no intention by the present proposal to take their gold away from them and only wished to co-operate in obtaining security against possible action by the Bolshevik elements, they seemed anxious to adopt any practical suggestions which were made to them. In reply to an inquiry as to whether a formal demand from the associated governments as to the gold and note-issue plant might not strengthen their hands in taking the necessary action, they agreed that this might be so at the appropriate time. They insisted, however, that at the present moment it would be extremely dangerous and begged that the fact of our proposals might be kept absolutely secret, a report of them being liable to provoke the very danger we were seeking to avert. They pointed out that they themselves as 'bourgeois elements' ran the risk of being suspected of conspiring with the associated governments for the protection of their own private interests.

In view of the declarations of the German delegates, the financial representatives of the associated governments were unanimously of opinion that no further action was either necessary or desirable.

(2) The discussion of payment for foodstuffs was hampered by the fact that the German shipping delegates had not arrived and that the German financial delegates were consequently not in possession of the precise proposals which were about to be made to their colleagues. On the first day we informed the financial delegates that certain foodstuffs would be supplied subject to conditions as to shipping, and invited proposals as to how these should be paid for. After insisting that it was of the utmost importance for even a partial recovery of Germany that their liquid resources should not be taken from them for this purpose, they earnestly and repeatedly requested that they might be allowed to effect payment by means of a mark credit, the decision as to the final liquidation of credit being postponed for settlement at the Peace Conference along with other financial claims against Germany. This proposal was not in effect very different from the proposal of M. Klotz at the Supreme War Council, except that he would have taken immediate assets as a pledge in advance of the ultimate settlement. The associated delegates at once explained in the firmest possible manner that this really involved a loan and that any devices for postponement of payment were quite out of the question. At a later stage after communication with Berlin Dr Melchior again repeated his proposal and urged on the associated delegates the importance from their point of view as well as from Germany's of allowing them at least a certain measure of economic recovery, pointing out that this would be rendered quite impossible if liquid resources were exhausted by immediate requirements for foodstuffs. The associated delegates again replied that this opened up far wider questions than they were in any way authorised to discuss. They were not there to enter into questions of the general supply of Germany or of her future economic position. The War Council had decided that it was in the general interests of the world that immediate supplies of food should be offered to Germany within certain limits of amount and against payment for cash, and the sole duty of the associated delegates was to ascertain from the

German representatives in what degree and form they were in a position to accept this offer. Dr Melchior replied that the political and economic situation rendered it quite impossible for the German government to reject an offer of food and that they were therefore in our hands as regards the means of payment. At the same time he again begged us that the circumstances to which he had drawn attention might be fully communicated to the associated governments.

He then proceeded to outline the offer of immediate resources, which he had been authorised to make by telephone from Berlin, where the ministers concerned had held a meeting the night before, in payment for food. This consisted of marks 100 million in gold: marks 25 million in Dutch florins, Swiss francs and Scandinavian kroners, and 50,000 tons of potash for immediate delivery. He also concurred in the suggestion of the associated delegates that the freight earnings of the German mercantile marine to be operated by the associated governments might be devoted to food payments. In reply the associated delegates pointed out they were at present authorised definitely to accept in payment only the marks 25 million in neutral currencies, that they would report to their governments for further instructions the rest of the German offer, but that in any case the total sum of money now offered was inadequate to pay for more than about half of the foodstuffs which the associated governments were prepared to supply.

On the last point Dr Melchior stated that the meeting of ministers in Berlin had unfortunately not had before them a precise statement of the food offer of the associated governments, and that the sum in question had been arrived at as representing the approximate value of certain supplies for immediate delivery which the German government required, a list of which he gave us. (This list was received by the food representatives and to a considerable extent it coincided with the offer of the associated governments, including, however, certain quantities of other articles which had not previously been considered, especially supplies of condensed milk and medical stores. This list is being examined by the food representatives and will be reported upon by them.

In the circumstances there seemed no course to adopt except to receive over the signature of the German representatives a statement of their offer as outlined above, and to request them to return to their government with a view to making further inquiries as to additional funds. This the German representatives agreed to do, but Dr Melchior took the opportunity of pointing out that while we were in a position to enforce payment in gold if we chose, such a course would react most painfully on the whole credit and currency system of his country. The German delegates expressed their willingness to meet the associated delegates again in ten days' or a fortnight's time with fuller information, with a view to a more definite settlement.

In conclusion Dr Melchior expressed a strong hope on the part of himself and his colleagues that some means might be adopted whereby, for such discussions as the present, economic and financial delegates might be in a position to meet and discuss otherwise than under the auspices of the military authorities and the armistice negotiations. For their own part they attached importance to being independent of their own military authorities and to possessing a definite civilian status. The associated delegates undertook to report to their governments accordingly.

(3) The third subject of discussion arose out of the financial clauses added to the armistice at the previous meeting at Trèves. On this occasion the German government agreed not to give any authorisation for the export of securities possessed by individuals or by institutions without previous approval by the allies. The French representative now reported, however, that this engagement had been made a dead letter by what was in effect a trick on the part of the German government, who had taken up the attitude that since German legislation did not in fact require an authorisation on their part for the export of securities, it was not

open to them to make the above clause effective. That is to say they made a distinction between agreeing not to issue an authorisation and agreeing to prohibit. They held that as no authorisation was required, an engagement not to issue an authorisation was of no effect. I associated myself very strongly with the protests of the French against such action, and in reply the German delegates could only say that at the time of the signature of the clause in question, they had made it quite clear to the French representatives what the position was, and that they had expressly stated that they were not binding themselves in signing the clause to take any measures to alter the legislative position. It was clear, however, that the French representatives, whether by their own fault or not, had not understood how valueless was the engagement which they were obtaining.

In the circumstances it was difficult to see what positive action was open to us. I contented myself therefore by stating in the coldest possible tones that an incident such as this must make a most unfortunate impression and would not facilitate the conduct of future negotiations on a basis of fairness and equity; also that it would make it necessary to scrutinise very precisely the exact wording of any future engagement; and that such an incident seemed particularly unnecessary in a case where what we were asking did not appear to be injurious to the interests of the German government themselves, who were equally interested with us in preventing private individuals from exporting their fortunes abroad; but that in the circumstances we had no option but to leave matters where they were, reserving to ourselves the right to take what steps might seem good to us in the event of its coming to our notice that securities were being exported to an important extent. This attitude on my part gave great satisfaction to M. de Lasteyrie, and apparently it produced the necessary effect on the Germans. They telephoned later in the day to the effect that they deeply regretted the incident and were telegraphing to Berlin for authority voluntarily to make new arrangements which would, they thought, be satisfactory to us.

They had not yet received a reply when we left and promised to send their specific proposals to us in writing from Spa.

The precise tone to be adopted towards the German delegates was naturally a matter of some difficulty. A slightly unfortunate position arose through the marked disparity between the tone of the French and American representatives, a disparity which was not overlooked by the German representatives. Apart also from the tone adopted during the discussions, several of the American representatives sought opportunities for personal and private discussion with the German delegates outside the formal meetings. These informal discussions were in themselves very useful and valuable information and impressions were obtained from them. But this did not serve to lessen the awkwardness of the situation. The Comte de Lasteyrie, the French government representative, made some angry complaints to me as to the tone adopted by Mr Norman Davis, and stated that he intended to report the matter to his government, the general grounds of his complaints being, first that Mr Davis had not associated himself fully with some of M. de Lasteyrie's protests against statements made by the German delegates, and secondly, that Mr Davis seemed sometimes to set himself up as an arbiter between the French and German views. I do not think that M. de Lasteyrie's complaints were by any means sufficiently well founded, and I did my best to soothe him. His dissatisfaction was partly due, I think, to his bad knowledge of English, and the imperfections of the French interpreter who often omitted significant words, or gave a slightly different turn to what was passing. M. de Lasteyrie's own protests also were in my opinion often rather uncalled for: whenever the German delegates pleaded for the possibility of some measure of economic recovery for their country he thought it necessary to talk a little rhetorically about sufferings elsewhere. The difference of tone which was perhaps the real basis of his annoyance was however undoubted. My own practice was to maintain a courteous but cold attitude, to make no protests, merely taking note of the observations of the Germans and to support the French government's point of view whenever possible.

In my opinion Mr Norman Davis's attitude was in essentials perfectly correct. I cannot however say the same of Mr Hurley, who, in the course of the shipping negotiations, proved himself an impossible chairman, and was guilty of serious indiscretions. If Mr Anderson of our Ministry of Shipping had not taken the matter in hand with the most admirable skill and firmness, the shipping negotiations would have been seriously mishandled. Their ultimate success was entirely due to Mr Anderson.

The general demeanour of the German representatives was strikingly conciliatory and even submissive. They made no complaints, refused no information for which they were asked, were perfectly clear and business-like, seemed to indicate their willingness to do almost whatever was told them, and only allowed themselves by way of reply to make what were in effect veiled pleas for mercy. Dr Melchior himself showed great ability in the conduct of the proceedings. Personally they seemed strained, anxious and depressed in a high degree, and Dr Kaufmann, the elderly director of the Reichsbank, was without vitality. Their sense of strain and intense seriousness made a strong impression on all of us.

The above report is confined to a description of the actual discussions. The following substantial issues requiring decision arise out of them:

(1) The amount which the Germans offered us in neutral currency was trifling, in part because the balances they were dealing with were confined to those of the Reichsbank and did not include the currencies of other German banks or individuals. The reason for this was one of great importance. Various German institutions have made engagements to meet in neutral countries at an early date, and if we compel the German government to impound private foreign balances, we may be compelling private

German creditors to repudiate their engagements abroad. The effect of this on German credit might, in the long run, be as bad for us as for them. I formed the impression that the German authorities intend to make a very strong stand in protection of the inviolability of private German property abroad, and I doubt if it will be possible to move them from this attitude at any rate prior to the peace negotiations. The matter must be carried further; but I believe that the upshot of the enquiry will be that the amount of foreign balances which we can wisely take in payment for supplies will prove to be extremely small.

(2) In this event, the question of an alternative means of payment will arise in an acute form. It will be observed that the Germans themselves were prepared to pay to a certain extent in actual gold. There are, however, obvious objections to accepting payment in this form. The German authorities will naturally do all they can to utilise in payment for supplies their most tangible and obvious assets, on the ground that these are the most likely assets for them to lose anyhow as reparation payment, and to withhold their more secret resources in the hope that these may escape observation permanently.

(3) In any event the problem of sending to Germany the necessary supplies under conditions of blockade otherwise than on credit and without unduly trenching on reparation resources presents an almost insoluble problem. The import requirements of Germany in the near future necessary even for a moderate economic recovery must amount to upwards of a hundred million sterling. In this connection see the appended recommendations of the financial delegates to the Relief Council.

(4) The request of the German authorities for some recognised means of communication on financial and economic matters otherwise than through the military organisation entrusted with the armistice is one which it would be in our interest as well as theirs to meet. It will certainly be necessary for the financial delegates to meet again in about a fortnight's time with a view to completing the negotiations already initiated. But apart from

this it is altogether impossible to carry on the elaborate and detailed business of dealing with German supplies through the present channel. We shall in effect be entering upon trade relations upon a very large scale, an enterprise which is impossible with no regular means of communication between civilians.

The experiences of the Shipping Commission with Marshal Foch, which they will doubtless report separately, emphasise the importance of the above.

J. M. KEYNES

20 January 1919

Keynes was ill with influenza when he came back from Trèves and escaped for two weeks convalescence on the Riviera. He made a second trip to Trèves to meet the Germans 13–15 February and on his return addressed a plea for additional staff to Bradbury. This letter is one of several revealing the very limited size of the Treasury organisation in Paris and the great pressure on Keynes and others.

To SIR JOHN BRADBURY, *17 February 1919*

Dear Bradbury,

I returned from Trèves this morning to find the staff question still acute.

On the plus side I have been able to make arrangements as follows:

(1) A clerk has been secured for Falk from the general pool here.

(2) I am in a position, I think, to secure a lady secretary for Ward from the staff of the Ministry of Food here for the same salary as she is receiving from the Ministry of Food. I have not yet exact information as to what this is, but it is probably £200 a year, and a living allowance of frs. 25 a day so long as she is not housed in the Majestic. She has already been working for Ward some days and is indispensable. May I have your approval for this step?

(3) McKinnon Wood of whom I spoke in my previous letter has been working for us for some days, and I am about to formalise the arrangement with the Foreign Office. The proposal

is that he should remain nominally with them and be seconded to us.

(4) J. R. M. Butler, Fellow of Trinity and a nephew of Ramsay's has arrived here for some temporary work. I propose to get in touch with him and endeavour to secure his services as soon as this work has come to an end.

On the minus side, however, there is the following:

(1) I have had a letter from Davidson asking that Fry may be released to return to London to help him, Davidson, with the House of Commons work. In view of the fact that the health of Fry's wife really requires his presence in London I can hardly resist this proposal, although it is impossible to spare him until a substitute has been found. I am making preliminary inquiries as to obtaining Captain Russell Cooke of the War Office whose services might, I think, be available. If I find he is able to come may I engage him?

(2) Falk is getting extremely anxious to return to his business, and obviously cannot be relied on to stop here much longer. I feel sure from what he has said that I ought to be in a position to dispense with his services at a fairly early date.

There is no diminution in the amount of work which still keeps us employed from breakfast to midnight. Even if all the above proposals come off therefore, I must still beg of you to let me have one more Treasury junior.

It is, I think, highly desirable that I should come back to London towards the end of this week to report on various matters which cannot well be dealt with in correspondence, and to obtain the instructions of the Chancellor of the Exchequer on a number of points. It is at the moment very difficult to get away, but I shall do my best to come over the first day subsequent to Wednesday on which flying is possible.

Yours sincerely,

J.M.K.

Wednesday was 19 February 1919, the date of a meeting with the French at which Keynes, representing the British Treasury, formally refused them further financial assistance. On 25 February he was in London to explain the situation to the War Cabinet, according to the official minutes (CAB 23/15) as follows:

From the Minutes of the War Cabinet, 25 February 1919

Mr Keynes stated that the French were asking for 650 million dollars from the United States and 100 million pounds from Great Britain, partly in payment for goods supplied and partly to support their credit with the rest of the world. The Americans were firm that they would make no loan for French expenditure on purchases made outside the United States of America. The French wanted to get credit from Great Britain and would accept it even if it were limited to the purchase of produce from the British Empire, but that would not relieve our exchange difficulties and would merely tend to swell the burden of French debt to us. The 100 million pounds was partly made up in money owed to Great Britain, partly for raw meatials, and partly for restoring the general trade balance. The French government were keeping the franc artificially at 26 francs to the pound, though owing to the local inflation of prices if an article worth one pound were imported it could be sold for anything up to 130 francs. If the exchange were allowed free play the value of the franc would fall to an unknown extent, certainly to 30 possibly even to 50 francs to the pound. There was certain assistance we must render to the French, the point of doubt was whether we should give assistance for general commercial purposes and for restoring their trade balance in the world. It was not worth doing on a small scale and on a large scale we could not afford it. The American exchange had turned against us in the last ten days and was now running at the rate of 2 million dollars a day against us.

The cabinet decided that the Chancellor of the Exchequer would go to Paris to discuss these matters with the French and the Americans (who had championed the French cause with the British and now were themselves to be urged to help the French). In the meantime an advance of £2 million was authorised to enable France to carry on.

A somewhat different account of the events of this period was presented by Klotz in his book *De la Guerre à la Paix* published in 1924, which accused the British Treasury, in the person of Keynes, of causing the fall of the franc, among other crimes. With the approval of the Treasury and Austen Chamberlain Keynes replied to these allegations in an article in *The Times*, 27 February 1924 (the headings and cross-headings are those of *The Times*).

From The Times, *27 February 1924*

FRANCE AND THE TREASURY
M. KLOTZ'S CHARGES REFUTED

M. Klotz, the author of 'De la Guerre à la Paix' (Paris: Payot, 1924), was Finance Minister of France in the administration of M. Clemenceau. His chief object in writing it has been to attack the financial policy of the British Treasury towards France during the later stages of the war and afterwards, this attack being chiefly associated with the names of the then Chancellor of the Exchequer, Mr Austen Chamberlain, and of myself, who was in charge of the department of the Treasury concerned. The French public probably knows by now how much importance to attach to what M. Klotz says. Nevertheless, his statements have been widely quoted and cannot be allowed to pass without correction. As I am permitted to use information which I acquired in an official capacity, this opportunity can be taken to make a small addition to the history of that period.

M. Klotz alleges (chapter XIII, 'Finance Interalliée):

1. That, apart from 'very limited' sums, Great Britain cut short her financial assistance to France on 3 January 1919.

2. That the excuse alleged was the refusal of the United States to continue advances to Great Britain, and that the excuse was untrue.

3. That this action was the cause of the depreciation of the franc.

The outline of his story is as follows. The first indication of a possible breach in 'the financial co-operation' (this is M. Klotz's invariable phrase for borrowing money) between France and Great Britain was shown by the attitude of the Bank of England and of Sir John Bradbury ('déjà sir John se révèle') in November 1918. On 3 January 1919, in the midst of negotiations, credits were suddenly cut off. On French representations in London the previous *modus vivendi* was temporarily renewed. The British Treasury's urgent need for dollars had been the ground of this agitation. But in February Mr Rathbone, Assistant Secretary of the United States Treasury, informed the French delegate that the United States had never manifested an intention of withdrawing their financial support from the British Treasury, that the latter still had large funds in New York, that they could not conceive how the British Treasury could use their situation at Washington as a ground for refusing credits to France, and that they considered, generally speaking, that there was a moral obligation on each country to finance the expenditure of its allies in its own country. ('Excellent language', comments M. Klotz.)

British Attitude

A little delay, M. Klotz thinks, would have led to a general agreement. But the British Treasury made its assistance entirely dependent on what could be obtained in the United States. At a Conference on 19 February, Mr Keynes, representing the British Treasury, refused any arrangement, and left for London ('attitude atroce'). The United States representatives put pressure on Mr Lloyd George to continue assistance to France pending a further conference. Finally, Mr Austen Chamberlain came to Paris himself. He agreed to continue his assistance up to a very limited amount, but absolutely refused to abandon his policy of no longer meeting the entirety of the French requirements ('l'intégralité des besoins'). M. Klotz again brought in the Americans to put pressure on him with suggestions that the United States would continue to lend to Great Britain if Great Britain would lend to France. They could, however, make no impression on Mr Chamberlain, who stood absolutely firm. It is on this action of Mr Chamberlain's that M. Klotz puts the blame for the subsequent fall of the French franc. This 'defection' made it impossible for the French Treasury to continue, as they had intended, the support of the French exchange. It was the prelude to the general rupture of the equilibrium of the exchanges and the collapse of the franc, which was the preponderating cause of the economic disorder into which the whole world found itself plunged from the end of the year 1919 onwards, and which has increased in intensity down to the present day. Thus all our troubles are due to the defeat of M. Klotz's plan for a continuing inter-ally 'financial co-operation', which meant, apparently, that the British taxpayer was to be more or less permanently responsible for maintaining the franc at par.

M. Klotz's state of mind, as exhibited in his own account, is enough to show the difficulties of the British Treasury at that time. But the following *résumé* of what really happened during those months will show how misleading are his statements of fact and how unjust his comments.

Control of Expenditure

By the end of 1918 the British Treasury had furnished France with funds to the amount of £418 million. For two years before that we had no longer been possessed of any net surplus assets, and it was necessary for us to borrow in our turn from the United States the full equivalent of all that we lent to France. If we had given France everything she asked for we should have been bankrupted and perhaps have lost the war before ever the United States came in. (December 1916 was the date of our extremest financial distress.) It had been necessary, therefore, for the British Treasury, first under the directions of Mr McKenna and afterwards under those of Mr Bonar Law, to undertake the burdensome and thankless task of 'Treasury control' not only over British government departments, but also—since we were in effect financially responsible for its results—over the expenditure of all the allies, France included, outside their own territories. After the United States came in we shared the task with them, with the further difficulty, inevitably added, of constant debates as to which of us should finance any given piece of expenditure. The European demands seemed to the American government so enormous that they insisted, soon after entering the war, on the establishment of an Inter-Allied Committee on War Purchases and Finance under American presidency to scrutinise the claims that were put forward. This body mainly depended on the organisation for criticism and control which the British Treasury had already established. It is a phase of the conduct of the war of which the history has never been written in full and, perhaps, is not likely to be. It is enough to say here that the business was got through without much unnecessary friction and, although a good deal of money was wasted, some measure of economy was imposed without loss of efficiency to the war departments. M. Klotz who, according to the famous saying of a great authority, had no knowledge of finance, seldom apprehended the details; but his faithful officials did, and we in the British Treasury maintained happy relations in our daily intercourse, lasting over years, with our opposite numbers in the French Treasury.

Thus the relations of the British and French treasuries had been governed throughout the war by a series of agreements designed to secure to France the assistance which was essential to her, without loading the already overstrained British Treasury with any unnecessary burden. In the course of 1918, however, an important change came over the situation. The British and American governments had to buy from the French government the francs needed in France to meet the local expenditure of their ever-growing armies. During the latter part of that year France was receiving from this source such large sums in sterling and in dollars, particularly the latter (the American army spent altogether more than a thousand million dollars' worth of francs inside France), that she had but little need of any other resources.

M. Klotz's Claim

This led to a new controversy. M. Klotz held that he had a prescriptive right for all his expenditure outside France to be paid for by Great Britain and the United States; and that, if he were getting, as he was getting, a windfall from an external source available to meet this expenditure, it was very unfair that he should be forced to use his own money instead of other people's. For his policy was to put the windfall aside for use at some later date when the war and the armistice would be over and allied loans at an end. (He did, in fact, succeed in locking away a substantial dollar balance for later use.) We, obviously, could not accept this view. Accordingly, at the end of November 1918, *after* the armistice, Mr Bonar Law warned France that in such circumstances the arrangements, under which she might call for further loans from us, could not be continued indefinitely. At that date, M. Klotz had undrawn credits in the United States amounting to no less than $435 million. We asked urgently for a revised arrangement to be made whereby France would utilise her own resources, so as to free the British Treasury from a burden which events were proving to be unnecessary. Repeated requests having failed to obtain any satisfactory reply from M. Klotz, he was at last notified on 3 January 1919 that advances would have to be stopped forthwith. This step at once produced a reopening of the negotiations, pending which some further advances were immediately made, M. Klotz duly expressing his gratitude. This is the first incident, which M. Klotz represents as a gross act of calculated treachery on the part of the British Treasury.

As regards the attitude of the United States, those who were familiar with the situation will remember that the gravest doubts existed as to the powers of the United States Treasury to make any advances at all after the armistice, inasmuch as loans to foreign governments were only permissible for the purposes of American national security and defence and the prosecution of the war. On 31 December 1918 the British government was, in fact, officially informed by the United States Treasury that no new advances could be made. Thus it was strictly true in January 1919 that Great Britain had received definite warning as to the cessation of American financial assistance—a warning which she was bound to pass on to her allies. This position was modified subsequently. It was this modification alone that rendered possible the further substantial advances to France which we actually made. But never at any time was there a possibility of America's agreeing to finance our future requirements, on the condition of our agreeing to finance those of France; and if, indeed, this had been done, our debt to America would have been swollen by the amount of these loans to France, and at this moment we should be paying interest and sinking fund upon them without any corresponding recoveries from the French Treasury.

'Unpegging' the Exchange

We come now to the conference of March 1919. There were two separate questions before this conference—the question of financing the commitments left behind by the war and the question of continuing advances for the purpose of 'pegging' the exchanges. At that date Mr Austen Chamberlain had reached the decision that the continued maintenance of the exchanges on an artificial level, after the war was over, was radically unsound and must end sooner or later in the bankruptcy of any government attempting it. For these reasons he determined to 'unpeg', i.e., withdraw artificial support from, our own dollar-sterling exchange. All subsequent experience has justified and all authorities have applauded the undoubted wisdom of this decision, which was actually carried into effect on 20 March 1919. In such circumstances the proposal that we should continue to support the franc exchange, whilst withdrawing support from our own, was preposterous. M. Klotz's demands amounted to throwing upon the British taxpayer all future deficits in the French budget.

On the question, however, of financing outstanding French commitments Mr Chamberlain made a proposal of considerable generosity which was embodied in the Anglo-French Financial Agreement of 13 March 1919. The funds made available under this agreement were in fact so ample that a portion of them was never utilised. It is a sufficient reply to M. Klotz's statements about credits being cut off that, subsequently to January 1919 we advanced to France more than £70 million, exclusive of interest, accruing after that date, which amounted to another £110 million.

Not content with our having lent his country over £600 million, M. Klotz thinks it suitable, at a time when not a penny of capital or of interest has been paid, to abuse Great Britain for not continuing for an indefinite period, months after the war was over, to lend him vast additional sums, which we did not ourselves possess, but would have had to re-borrow from a third party, for the purpose of supporting the French exchange when we were not supporting our own.

M. Klotz's book is full of many other inaccuracies if it was worth sparing the space to expose them—as, for example, the episode of the oil supplies, on which he lays great stress. And, if Mr Lloyd George remembers as vividly as I do the cruel discomfiture which M. Klotz suffered at his hands in the Supreme Council on 8 March 1919, ending not only in the complete defeat of the latter's proposals, but in his being beaten, almost literally, to the ground by the violence and vivacity of the British Prime Minister's exposure of his folly and incompetence, he will smile to read M. Klotz's version, mellowed by time and forgetfulness, of the afternoon's proceedings.

Chamberlain complimented Keynes on the article, writing 4 March 1924: 'You have told the substance of the story with an accuracy and detail that I could not have reproduced from any papers that I have kept, and still less from memory at this distance of time.' Klotz was spurred to reply in a two-column letter to *The Times*, published 11 March 1924, in which he set upon Keynes for his 'swollen vanity . . . a hypertrophy of self which is akin to megalomania' in thinking that he personified the British Treasury and indeed England.

It is Mr Keynes whom I accused and whom I continue to accuse. I said, and I repeat—and proofs abound—that Mr Keynes committed towards

France an *acte atroce* on 19 February 1919, when he assured the triumph of his monetary megalomania which remains the true cause of the financial catastrophe which has fallen on the whole world . . .

Keynes brought about the disaster, Klotz said, by refusing to listen to the advice of Colonel House at an 'historic conversation' in March 1919 when House had predicted 'commercial crises and unemployment in countries with a high exchange'. If the Anglo-French agreement had not been cancelled, the pounds that would have been put at the disposal of France would have reacted favourably on British trade and employment in the same way as French expenditure in England during the war had produced war profits.

The truth is, as Mr Keynes elsewhere recognizes, that Great Britain no longer wished either to lend or to borrow—a policy for which something could be said but which was adopted prematurely under the influence of Mr Keynes, who was haunted by the idea that the return to the free play of the economic laws could alone hasten the return to proper relationship between expenditure and real resources. Between illness and a state of health comes convalescence, always painful, but needing to be guided with care and patience. Mr Keynes wished to abolish the stage of convalescence; the patient has therefore, owing to his rash treatment, suffered a dangerous relapse. At the moment when Mr Keynes showed most obstinacy was he not inspired by his idea of the system of compensation of debts which he dramatically but inopportunely put forward a little later—ask the Americans!—and was he not convinced that, the darker the situation appeared the more his plan would seem, against the black sky, like a flash of genius? . . .

The last sentence referred to the 'Keynes Plan' for the rehabilitation of European credit, adopted as Treasury policy for a brief time in April 1919 (pp. 429–36). The letter concluded with Klotz's version of the meeting of the Supreme War Council, 8 March 1919, alluded to by Keynes in the last paragraph of his article and fully recounted in 'Dr Melchior'. According to his own interpretation Klotz succeeded in salvaging for a bruised and ravaged France and Belgium nine-tenths of the amount of German gold and foreign securities which Keynes's 'clients—the profiteers of peace' had intended to apply to provisioning Germany.

This diatribe provoked a reaction from Chamberlain in a letter to *The Times*, published 12 March. Loth, he said, to break his abstention from public reference to Klotz's book—'in which I appear, not indeed as the principal villain of the piece, but as the weak and subservient mouthpiece of Mr Keynes's atrocities'—he contented himself with declaring 'as emphatically as possible' that Klotz's account of the private, and as he understood it, confidential conversation with Colonel House 'bears no resemblance to the facts. Either M. Klotz is betrayed by his memory or—as is, perhaps, more probable—he never understood what was said.'

There followed an exchange of letters between the two former finance ministers, the upshot of which was an agreement to submit the controversy to the memory and judgment of Colonel House. In an amused editorial the *Spectator* remarked that Colonel House had the reputation of being 'the most discreet and cautious man in the world'—so discreet and cautious, indeed, that no verdict was recorded in *The Times*, nor in his published papers.

Chamberlain's duties as Chancellor of the Exchequer did not allow him ordinarily to be present at the peace conference and he designated Keynes as his representative on the Supreme Economic Council. In a letter (24 February 1919) to Lord Robert Cecil, who presided at the Council, he nominated Keynes,

> on the understanding that in my absence he will be received on the same footing as I should be if I were present, namely, that of a full member with full rights of speech and decision. I shall endeavour to keep him sufficiently informed to enable him to assume the responsibility in my name of all such decisions as I should be prepared to take were I present in person. It will, I think, be obvious to you that even if I were present questions might arise on which I should feel it necessary to consult His Majesty's Government before committing them . . .

Besides being the principal Treasury representative and deputising for Chamberlain Keynes was one of the two British Empire members on the conference financial committee. He was also chairman of the financial delegates in the armistice negotiations with Germany.

A deadlock over finance and the surrender of ships delayed the settling of food supplies for Germany until 14 March, after three more meetings with the Germans and high drama in the Supreme War Council, as related in 'Dr Melchior'. In the memoir Keynes tells how he eventually arranged for the German financial delegates to stay in France at the Chateau de Villette near Paris. In 1942 Dr E. Rosenbaum, who had been a member of the German delegation at Versailles, was rearranging some papers in the library of the London School of Economics and came across some of the German minutes of these meetings which he sent to Keynes.

To DR E. ROSENBAUM, *11 April 1942*

My dear Rosenbaum,

Thank you so much for sending me those fascinating reminders of old days in the shape of the Protokolls of the Chateau de Villette. It brings back matters which had completely escaped my memory. If you seriously intend to throw these into the waste-paper basket if I return them to you, may I keep them to put with other mementoes of those days? This is in fact an episode on which I wrote shortly afterwards some elaborate memoirs, which have never yet been published. It is amusing to have a report from the German end. How on earth did you get hold of these documents?

The history of the meetings at the Chateau de Villette was as follows:

During the early months of 1919 we had to have fairly frequent conferences with the German representatives, and for this purpose we used to make journeys to Trier [Trèves] and Spa and elsewhere. When the peace negotiations began to take up too much time, it was very difficult to get away for these periodic conferences. I thought, therefore, that it would save a great deal of trouble to get a deputation from Germany to come permanently to the neighbourhood of Paris available for discussions with us whenever we wanted them. I succeeded in getting a telegram through the Armistice Commission, extending the invitation. I remember that I got into a great row about this with Foch because I got it through without his knowledge, and I was formally reprimanded, though with a twinkle of the eye, by General Sir Henry Wilson. In fact we got the German delegates there for very little purpose. Shortly after they arrived there was a general slowing up, and I do not believe I visited the Chateau de Villette more than a couple of times, though I fancy the German representatives must have stayed there until eventually they went to their quarters in Versailles for the discussion of the Peace Treaty itself. Some of the lists you sent me remind me of the distinguished neutral and other financiers whom I collected in Paris with a view to discussing a general project of international financial reconstruction, which, in the event, never came off. How much subsequent evil might have been avoided if only they had!

They were the most distinguished financiers of each country that I could get track of. Yet of those concerned in these negotiations no less than four ultimately ended in prison on well-justified charges of fraud—Rydbeck, Glückstadt, Manzi-Fê and Klotz.

Yours sincerely,

J.M.K.

The minutes of the British Empire Economic Committee, meeting 4 April 1919, mention that Keynes, in reporting a conversation with the Germans at the Chateau de Villette, said that he had been impressed by the extreme depression of the delegates. 'He urged the necessity of not weakening the present German government and suggested that this should be borne in mind in the conduct of negotiations.'

Max Warburg, a business partner of Melchior, was a member of the German group. Writing his memoirs some twenty years later (*Aus meinem Aufzeichnungen*), Warburg recalled Keynes as an attentive listener, quiet voiced, saying little but speaking always to the point. The impression that he gave was of one trying very hard to understand the difficulties and arrive at the truth. It was impossible, Warburg remarked, to detect any feeling from the expression of his face; only from his manner of putting questions could his sympathy be sensed.

Food for Austria had to be arranged as well as food for Germany. The British Director of Relief, Sir William Goode, writing in his *Report on Economic Conditions in Central Europe*, a government White Paper, stated that only because of Keynes's initiative in the Supreme Economic Council in arranging a joint loan was famine averted in Austria early in 1919. 'Without his resourceful vision of an England humane, although victorious, it would have been almost impossible to carry out the finance in connection with British relief.'

At about the same time that Keynes was working on the Treasury indemnity memorandum with all its tabulations of the cost of the war, he also produced a proposal for the all-round cancellation of inter-ally debt. This was an idea that was in the air; for example, it turned up in a Foreign Office discussion on the future of Europe in which Keynes was involved. He embodied it in a paper entitled 'The Treatment of Inter-Ally Debt Arising out of the War':

FROM 'MEMORANDUM ON THE TREATMENT OF INTER-ALLIED DEBT ARISING OUT OF THE WAR'

It is therefore suggested that at the opening of the peace conference, this country should propose to the United States that all debts incurred between the governments of the associated countries...should be cancelled; and furthermore, that Great Britain is prepared...to forgo the whole of her share of the indemnity, *not as against the enemy* from whom it would be claimed, but for herself, placing this sum at the disposal of the peace conference to be applied...either to set up the new states to be carved out of the enemy empires or for any purpose.

Keynes summarised the advantages.

While, however, the sums which we should forgo must be regarded as to some extent paper claims, the sums we ourselves owe to the United States must undoubtedly be regarded as very real debts, the repayment of which, failing such an arrangement as the present, must be faced within no very long period of years. If we continue to owe to the American Treasury and to the American public a sum approaching £1,000 million, we ought to be prepared to find annually something approaching £100 million for interest and repayment of capital. Such a burden will cripple our foreign development in other parts of the world, and will lay us open to future pressure by the United States of the most objectionable description. It will also materially complicate the problem of future taxation at home. Lastly, we should escape the obligation of returning to the allies the gold we have borrowed from them, an obligation which may otherwise prove gravely embarrassing, and which they should certainly be asked to forgo in the event of the above arrangement, and in the event of their securing an adequate share of indemnity payment from the enemy in German gold.

In short, the general liquidation of the financial position and the clearing up of all sorts of difficult and embarrassing problems which the proposed clean cut would ensure would make up from a financial standpoint for the sacrifice of paper claims which would be called for.

The United States government would be asked to make a larger sacrifice than Britain; Keynes thought that they could hardly refuse in view of the far smaller sacrifice they had made hitherto. But he remarked that the settlement was probably not one which would commend itself to the officials of the United States Treasury. It would have to be justified to the Americans 'on the general rather than on financial considerations, and would probably be settled in the main on the judgment of the President'.

The version of the paper from which these quotations are taken is undated, but a note from Keynes to Bradbury attached to the copy in Keynes's files is dated 29 November 1918. In the note Keynes asked if he might submit the memorandum to General Smuts, who was a member of the War Cabinet, as representing the views of the Treasury. Bradbury passed the question on to Bonar Law who wrote that he would be glad for Smuts to see the memorandum but that 'such a proposal would need to be discussed by the Cabinet and I should not be prepared to pin myself to it. It seems to me too altruistic at all events till we see more clearly than at present what total sum it would be possible for Germany to pay.'

Keynes revived the memorandum four months later in a second version addressed to the new Chancellor of the Exchequer (Chamberlain). In its earlier form the paper led off with a recital of Britain's greater sacrifices as compared with those of the United States; the second version, intended for American consumption, tucked in these comparisons more tactfully near the end. A note, dated 28 March, in Keynes's handwriting on the printed copy in the Treasury files (T 172/988) reads: 'A copy of this will be conveyed confidentially to the President, through Col. House, in accordance with a proposal of which the Chancellor of the Exchequer is aware.'

The revised memorandum links the cancellation of debts to Keynes's credit rehabilitation scheme. It is the revised version, signed by Keynes and dated Paris, March 1919, that is given here.

THE TREATMENT OF INTER-ALLY DEBT ARISING OUT OF THE WAR

The loans advanced by the allies[1] to one another are approximately as follows:

Loans to	By United States	By United Kingdom	By France	Total
	£ million	£ million	£ million	£ million
United Kingdom	800	—	—	800
France	485	390[2]	—	875
Italy	275	390[2]	35	700
Russia	38	520[2,3]	160	718
Belgium	56	90[4]	90	236
Serbia	4	20[4]	30	54
Roumania	2	16	35	53
Greece	8	15	15	38
Portugal	—	10	—	10
Totals	1,668	1,451	365	3,484

[1] Excluding loans raised by the United Kingdom on the market in the United States, and loans raised by France on the market in the United Kingdom or from the Bank of England.

[2] *After* deducting loans of gold to the United Kingdom, from France £50 million, from Italy £22 million, and from Russia £60 million, which are returnable when the counter loans are repaid.

[3] This allows nothing for interest on the debt since the Bolshevik Revolution.

[4] No interest has been charged on the advances made to these countries.

Thus the total inter-ally indebtedness amounts to about £3,500 million without setting off loans from one ally against loans to another. Since the United States of America came into the war, the United Kingdom has borrowed £800 million from the United States for expenditure in the United States and for support of the sterling exchange, and has at the same time lent £750 million to her other allies for expenditure in various parts of the world, including a certain amount in the United States, and for support of their exchanges; so that almost the whole of our indebtedness to the United States was incurred not on our own account, but to enable us to assist the rest of our allies, who were for various reasons not in a position to draw their assistance from the United States direct.

If all the above inter-ally indebtedness were mutually forgiven, the net result on paper (i.e., assuming one loan to be as good as any other) would be as follows:

	Net loss	Net gain
	£ million	£ million
United States	1,668	—
United Kingdom	651	—
France	—	510
Italy	—	700
Russia	—	718
Belgium	—	236
Serbia	—	54
Roumania	—	53
Greece	—	38
Portugal	—	10

In the light of these figures a proposal for an entire cancellation of inter-ally indebtedness is put forward as being likely to promote the well-being of this country and of the world. The following are the chief arguments in favour of it:

1. Failing such a settlement the war will end with a network of heavy tribute payable from one ally to another. The total amount of this tribute may even exceed the amount obtainable from the enemy; and the war will have ended in the allies paying indemnities to one another instead of receiving indemnities from the enemy, which would be an intolerable end, justifying cynical conclusions.

2. For this reason the question of inter-allied indebtedness is closely bound up with the intense popular feeling amongst the European allies on the question of indemnities—a feeling which is based not on any reasonable calculation of what Germany can, in fact, pay, but on a well-founded appreciation of the intolerable financial situation in which these countries will find themselves *unless* she pays.

Take Italy as an extreme example. If Italy can reasonably be expected to pay £700 million, surely Germany can and ought to pay an immeasurably higher figure. Or if Italy can only claim against Austria, and it is decided (as it must be) that Austria can pay next to nothing, is it not an intolerable conclusion that Italy should be loaded with a crushing tribute, while Austria escapes? Or, to put it slightly differently, how can Italy be expected to submit to payment of this great sum and to see Czecho-Slovakia pay nothing?

At the other end of the scale there is the United Kingdom. Here the financial position is different, since to ask us to pay £800 million is a very different proposition from asking Italy to pay £700 million. But the sentiment is much the same. If we have to be satisfied without full compensation from Germany, how bitter will be the protests against paying it to the United States. *We*, it will be said, have to be content with a claim against the bankrupt estates of Germany, France, Italy and Russia, whereas the United States has secured a first mortgage upon *us*.

The case of France is at least as overwhelming. She cannot secure from Germany even the measure of the destruction of her countryside. Yet victorious France must pay her friends and allies more than four times the indemnity which in the defeat of 1870 she paid Germany. The hand of Bismarck was light compared with that of an ally or of an associate.

A settlement of inter-ally indebtedness is, therefore, an indispensable preliminary to the peoples of the allied countries facing with other than a maddened and exasperated heart the inevitable truth about the prospects of an indemnity from the enemy.

3. It might be an exaggeration to say that it is impossible for the European allies to pay the capital and interest due from them on these debts, but to make them do so would certainly be to impose a crushing burden. They may be expected, therefore, to make constant attempts to evade or escape payment, and these attempts will be a constant source of international friction and ill-will for many years to come. A debtor nation does not love its

creditor, and it is fruitless to expect feelings of goodwill from France, Italy and Russia towards this country or towards America, if their future development is stifled for many years to come by the annual tribute which they must pay us. There will be a great incentive to them to seek their friends in other directions, and any future rupture of peaceable relations will always carry with it the enormous advantage of escaping the payment of external debts. If, on the other hand, these great debts are forgiven, a stimulus will be given to the solidarity and true friendliness of the nations now associated.

4. The existence of the great war debts is a menace to financial stability everywhere. There is no European country in which repudiation may not soon become an important political issue. In the case of internal debt, however, there are interested parties on both sides, and the question is one of the internal distribution of wealth. With external debts this is not so, and the creditor nations may soon find their interest inconveniently bound up with the maintenance of a particular type of government or economic organisation in the debtor countries. Entangling alliances or entangling leagues are nothing to the entaglements of cash owing.

5. This consideration is of special importance in relation to the settlement of the Russian question. While the Bolsheviks have made some offer, the good faith of which I doubt, to recognise the war debts of the Czar, it is hard to believe, if the recognition of any future Russian government by the allies is to be made dependent on the assumption by that government of the foreign debts of Russia, that any government really fulfilling this condition could possibly establish itself. To get immediate supplies, Russia might promise anything, but there would be no performance. A general settlement of the kind now proposed would enable the allies to write off the Russian debt (which they will have to do anyhow) without making any exception in favour

of Russia, or appearing to countenance or yield to Bolshevik doctrine.

6. If the loans are to be met, a serious obstacle will exist to future trade relations between the allies. We shall, of course, be ready to encourage imports from our European debtors and exports to our American creditor, but we must necessarily discourage the reverse. The fact that our European allies would be incapable of paying both their interest charges and also for imports means that one or the other must be sacrificed; and the same applies equally as between ourselves and America. If we are to be repaid, we can only be repaid in goods; if we are to repay, we can only repay in goods; which means that trade must be mainly one way. On the other hand, if—as I think, the United States Treasury contemplate—the position is adjusted without detriment to trade by the grant of further loans (preferably through private and not through governmental channels), this merely means that we fool ourselves by piling up obligations at compound interest until the mounting billions produce a final *reductio ad absurdum*, and banker and Bolshevik become of one mind as to the propriety of going on. The only real escape would be found (and this is no better than a veiled repudiation), if the units of the currency in which the debts are expressed were to fall so far in value that the nominal debt no longer represented a significant quota of human effort.

7. The main financial sacrifice involved in this proposal will fall on the United States, not only as regards nominal amount, but also because the policy of the United States Treasury has had the result that they have lent mainly to the countries whose credit is relatively good, namely, ourselves and France, leaving us to re-lend to the poorer debtors.[1]

But while this greater financial sacrifice is one which the

---

[1] Even after the United States came into the war the bulk of Russian expenditure, even in the United States itself, had to be paid for by the British Treasury.

United States would be fully entitled to refuse, it is right to point out that the relative financial burdens supported so far by the United States on the one hand, and by ourselves on the other, are such as to justify a redistribution. The position may be summarised as follows:

(i) The United Kingdom has exported during the war about £400 million of actual gold, including about £156 million of gold borrowed by the British Treasury or the Bank of England from France, Russia and Italy under promise to repay in actual gold. Of this total no less than £300 million was shipped to the United States (an appreciable part *after* the entry of the United States into the war) to meet the obligations of ourselves and our allies in that country. As a result of these exports, British gold reserves now stand at about £110 million and the United States gold reserves at about £600 million and if we were to repay to our allies what we have borrowed from them our reserves would be less than nothing.

(ii) The United Kingdom has disposed of about £1,000 million worth of her foreign securities and in addition has incurred foreign debt to the amount of about £1,200 million. The United States, so far from selling, has bought back upwards of £1,000 million and has incurred practically no foreign debt.

(iii) The United States has made a substantial financial sacrifice since she came into the war, but, inasmuch as she has not, like the rest of us, incurred foreign indebtedness, and before her entry into the war profited out of it largely, even now she is actually richer than she was in 1914. The United States Treasury has a fiscal problem of considerable dimensions, but the American people as a whole have no financial problem whatever; their resources are unimpaired.

(iv) The population of the United Kingdom is about one-half that of the United States, the income about one-third, and the accumulated wealth between one-half and one-third. The financial *capacity* of the United Kingdom may therefore be put at about two-fifths that of the United States. This figure enables us to make the following comparison: excluding loans to allies in each case (as is right on the assumption that these loans are to be repaid), the war expenditure of the United Kingdom has been about three times that of the United States, or in proportion to capacity between seven and eight times.

8. The relation of the present proposal to a satisfactory settlement of the indemnity problem has been pointed out already. But it might also facilitate other problems of the Peace Conference. There is no reason why these great financial concessions should not be made conditional on the powers to receive them moderating their territorial aspirations.

9. According to present plans Germany will owe a large sum, e.g., to France, France will owe a large sum to Great Britain, and Great Britain will owe a large sum to the United States. If all these sums were to be paid for certain, doubts and anxieties would be allayed. But it would serve, as an alternative method to that proposed above, if the allied and associated governments were to agree to accept German government reparation bonds in final discharge of debts incurred between themselves. In some respects this might provide a solution more readily acceptable to the public, especially in the United States. I will prepare a further paper in amplification of it.

The above is the argument under heads. But anyone's attitude to the proposal must be coloured at least as much by his view as to the future place in the world's progress of these vast paper entanglements as by immediate considerations of detail. Assume that a tribute is laid for thirty years upon all the enemy countries, heavy to the limit of possibility; assume that the allies are really to pay to one another and to America the figures named above, and suppose that in some quarter repudiation begins to break out (it has begun already), can this financial network last a day? Before the middle of the nineteenth century no nation owed

426

payments to a foreign nation on any considerable scale, except such tributes as were exacted under the compulsion of actual occupation in force and, at one time, by absentee princes under the sanctions of feudalism. It is true that the need for European capitalism to find an outlet in the New World has led during the past fifty years, though even now on a relatively modest scale, to such countries as Argentine owing an annual sum to such countries as England. But the system is fragile; and it has only survived because its burden on the paying countries has not so far been oppressive, because this burden is represented by real assets and is bound up with the property system generally, and because the sums already lent are not unduly large in relation to those which it is still hoped to borrow.

Bankers are used to this system, and believe it to be a necessary part of the permanent order of society. They therefore believe, by analogy from it, that a comparable system between governments, on a far vaster and definitely oppressive scale, represented by no real assets, and less closely associated with the property system, is natural and reasonable and in conformity with human nature.

I doubt this view of the world. Even capitalism at home, which engages many local sympathies, which plays a real part in the daily process of production, and upon the security of which the present organisation of society largely depends, is not very safe. But, however this may be, will the discontented peoples of Europe be willing for a generation to come so to order their lives that an appreciable part of their daily produce may be available to meet a foreign payment, the reason of which, whether as between Europe and America, or as between Germany and the rest of Europe, does not spring compellingly from their sense of justice or duty?

On the one hand, Europe must depend in the long run on her own daily labour and not on the largesse of America; but, on the other hand, she will not pinch herself in order that the fruit of her daily labour may go elsewhere.

In short, I do not believe that any of these tributes will continue to be paid, at the best, for more than a very few years. They do not square with human nature or march with the spirit of the age.

If there is any force in this mode of thought, expediency and generosity agree together, and the policy which will best promote immediate friendship between nations will not conflict with the permanent interests of the benefactor.

None of these considerations are likely to meet with any lack of sympathy from the representatives of the United States. Their objections will arise not from themselves but from the less-formed opinions of their distant public. Our best course, therefore, is not to agitate or complain, or stir the waters of controversy, but to take intimate counsel with them what to do next.

J. M. KEYNES

Paris, March 1919

The Americans in Paris, however, did not take to the idea of debt cancellation. Within two weeks Keynes produced a second plan, the joint guarantee of reparation bonds—or, as he italicised it in a letter to his mother, '*a grand scheme for the rehabilitation of Europe*' (17 April 1919). It was one of several credit proposals, the others unofficial, which were current at the time. Keynes visited London for its presentation to the cabinet. Chamberlain vigorously commended the plan in a letter to Lloyd George (17 April) as being 'marked by all Mr Keynes's characteristic ability and fertility of resource'.

It provides the stricken countries of Europe, whether allied or enemy, with the means of re-equipping themselves and restarting on a sound basis the trade and industry of the world; it provides equally for the new nations which the conference is calling into existence, and it offers hope to the enemy powers and provides them with the means by which, whilst accepting the arduous conditions of the peace which will be imposed upon them, they can restart their industrial life and put themselves in a position to meet their onerous obligations. Finally, it does this by means of an international agreement placed under the auspices of the League of Nations and thus makes the rehabilitation of the world the first task of the new League.

The Chancellor of the Exchequer's letter accompanied a copy of the bond scheme and a covering explanation which Keynes had written himself for its presentation to the American, French and Italian heads of state. Chamberlain asked Lloyd George to discuss the plan privately with President Wilson and announce it formally to the conference as the policy of the British government. He suggested that when the President received the document Keynes should be authorised to hand a copy of it to Norman Davis and give him any necessary explanation.

The text of Keynes's bond scheme with its explanatory memorandum, dated April 1919, follows.

SCHEME FOR THE REHABILITATION OF EUROPEAN CREDIT AND FOR FINANCING RELIEF AND RECONSTRUCTION

1. (i) German bonds to be issued to a *present* value of £1,000 million and to a *face* value of £1,200 million, carrying interest at the rate of 4 per cent per annum and sinking fund at the rate of 1 per cent per annum as from 1 January 1925, these payments to have priority over all other German obligations whatever, including additional claims for reparation not covered out of the above, the difference between the face value and the present value representing the funding of interest from 1 January 1920, up to 1 January 1925.

(ii) Austrian, Hungarian and Bulgarian bonds to be issued to the present value of £125 million, £170 million and £50 million respectively on similar conditions. (N.B.—Turkey to be dealt with separately.)

(iii) Roumanian,[1] Polish, Czecho-Slovakian, Jugo-Slav[1] and Baltic States bonds to be issued to the present value of £15 million, £40 million, £20 million, £15 million and £10 million respectively on similar conditions.

2. Interest on each of the issues of enemy bonds under 1 (i) and (ii) above to be guaranteed jointly and severally by the other enemy states, in the event of any one of them failing to provide the payments due.

3. In the event of the failure of the above guarantees, interest

---

[1] Roumania and Serbia also to receive a share of reparation.

at 4 per cent on all the above bonds to the aggregate present value of £1,500 million (or £1,800 million as from 1 January 1925), to be guaranteed by the principal allied and associated governments, by the three Scandinavian governments and by the governments of Holland and Switzerland.

4. In the event of the guarantee under (3) becoming operative, the guaranteeing governments to be responsible in proportions determined in advance, as set forth in the accompanying Schedule A.

5. In the event of any of the guaranteeing governments failing to meet their guarantee, the remaining guaranteeing governments to make good this failure in the same proportions amongst themselves as under (4).

6. A failure of any government to meet its guarantee under the above clauses to be considered by the financial section of the League of Nations, and if judged by them to have been avoidable shall be punished by such penalty or forfeiture of a financial, economic or commercial character as the League of Nations may determine.

7. The bonds to be free of all taxation in all the issuing or guaranteeing states.

8. Of the £1,000 million bonds to be issued by the German government £724 million shall be paid over to the allied and associated governments on account of sums due for reparation; £76 million shall be utilised for the discharge of existing debts to the three Scandinavian countries, Holland and Switzerland, and the remaining one-fifth of the total, namely, £200 million, shall be left in the hands of the German government to be made available for the purchase of food and raw materials.

9. Of the bonds amounting to £345 million in all to be issued by the Austrian, Hungarian and Bulgarian governments, four-fifths in each case shall be paid over to the allied and associated governments on account of sums due for reparation, the remaining one-fifth being left in the hands of these governments for the purchase of food and raw materials.

10. The bonds amounting in all to a present value of £1,000 million to be received by the allied and associated governments on account of reparation to be divided between them in the proportions determined upon by them for the division of reparation receipts generally.

11. The bonds to be accepted at their par value plus accrued interest in payment of all indebtedness between any of the allied and associated governments.

12. The bonds to be acceptable as first-class collateral for loans at the central banks of all the issuing or guaranteeing states, subject to such terms and limitations as may be in force with these institutions from time to time.

Schedule A

	Per cent
United Kingdom	20
United States	20
France	20
Italy	10
Japan	10
Belgium	5
Norway	
Sweden	
Denmark	15
Holland	
Switzerland	

DRAFT FOR AN EXPLANATORY LETTER TO BE ADDRESSED BY THE PRIME MINISTER TO THE PRESIDENT, M. CLEMENCEAU, AND SIGNOR ORLANDO

The Chancellor of the Exchequer and Lord Robert Cecil, on behalf of the British representatives on the Supreme Economic Council, have forcibly urged on the notice of His Majesty's Government the necessity of some bolder solution for the rehabilitation of the credit and economic life of Europe than is now available. For the time being the United States is providing on a generous scale for the urgent food requirements of the non-enemy countries of Europe. We, on our part, are furnishing assistance on a more modest scale. But these measures, which are primarily directed to the relief of immediate distress, are inadequate, as Mr Hoover himself is the first to recognise, to the solution of the whole economic problem. On the one hand, the United States may not be able to continue indefinitely her present assistance; on the other hand, this assistance does not touch the problem of supplying raw materials to any of the countries concerned, and does not apply to the enemy countries at all.

The position as it is reported by the British representatives on the Supreme Economic Council is as follows: In the case of Germany the existing financial provision is not expected to look after food supplies alone much beyond June, and for raw materials there is no provision at all, which, in view of the existing unemployment, are not less necessary if order is to be preserved in that country, peace to be signed and the obligations of the peace to be fulfilled. The other enemy countries are at a complete economic standstill and there is at present no plan whatever for dealing with them or for preserving their social and economic organisation from disruption and decay. The condition of the new states, of Serbia and of Roumania is hardly better. Mr Hoover is meeting their immediate food requirements, but their economic and commercial fabric cannot be created or re-created unless they can be put in the possession of purchasing power with which to enter the markets of the world. France, Italy and Belgium present a different problem. But here also the external financial position has been represented to the Chancellor of the Exchequer by the Finance Ministers of these countries to be little short of desperate, and the need of outside assistance to be essential if they are to restore their countries and re-commence the normal activities of peace. The United Kingdom enters upon the peace in a somewhat less unfavourable condition, with the question as to how we are to pay what we owe to the United States Treasury as the chief problem of our external finance; but we are in no position to give assistance to others on anything approaching the scale that they require. I may add this, however, that the difference between the position in England and the complete economic prostration of some of the other countries named above is so enormous, that our own serious difficulties in gett'ng the wheels of industry going may be some index to the appalling magnitude of the problem in these other countries. In short, the economic mechanism of Europe is jammed. Before the war, as Mr Hoover has said, 400 million Europeans by working their hardest just managed to feed, clothe and house themselves, and perhaps amass six months' capital on which to live. That capital has vanished; the complicated machinery of internal and external production is more or less smashed; production has to a great extent ceased. The largely increasing population of Europe has only been maintained by the increasing development and inter-connection of world industry and finance. If this is not only checked, but for the time being destroyed, it is difficult to see how the population can be maintained, at any rate during the very painful period of drastic readjustment. If free movement were possible and other countries could absorb it, there would inevitably be a vast emigration from Europe, until an equilibrium were established between the numbers of the population and the means of livelihood. As that is not possible this equilibrium must be reached in some other way. In Russia it is being reached, it appears, by reduction of population by starvation, and by drastic changes of occupation, e.g., by the town population being forced out on to the land as labourers.

To what extent the same conditions spread over the rest of Europe must depend largely on whether or not the obstacles to the resumption of production can be rapidly overcome.

What, in such circumstances, are the alternatives before us? In some quarters the hope is entertained that with the early removal of obstacles in the form of the blockade and similar measures to free international intercourse, private enterprise may be safely entrusted with the task of finding the solution. I am in accord with the view that an early removal of such obstacles is an essential measure, and that in the long run we must mainly look for our salvation to the renewed life of private enterprise and of private initiative. Indeed, so far as trading and manufacture is concerned, as distinct from finance, no other measures should be necessary from the outset. Nevertheless, in the financial sphere, the problem of restoring Europe is almost certainly too great for private enterprise alone, and every delay puts this solution further out of court. There are two main obstacles: (*a*) the risks are too great; (*b*) the amounts are too big and the credit required too long. The more prostrate a country is and the nearer to Bolshevism the more presumably it requires assistance. But the less likely is private enterprise to give it. To a small extent and with a great margin some trade will be done and some barter. But not enough to meet the situation.

Apart from private enterprise His Majesty's Government see only two possible courses—direct assistance and various forms of guaranteed finance, on a very much larger scale than is at present contemplated, by the more prosperous of the Allied and Associated Countries, which probably means, to an extent of not less than 90 per cent., the United States; or an attempt to recreate the credit system of Europe and by some form of world-wide co-operation to enable the countries whose individual credit is temporarily destroyed to trade on their prospects of reparation from the enemy states or to capitalise their future prospects of production. Every consideration of policy and interest indicates the superiority of the second. The people of Europe will have to live on the fruits of their own daily labour and not upon the bounty of another continent.

His Majesty's Government therefore desire to lay before the governments of the United States, of France and of Italy the concrete proposal contained in the paper annexed to this letter as their constructive contribution to the solution of the greatest financial problem ever set to the modern world. They are prepared to commit themselves immediately to participation in such a scheme, subject to the legislative sanction which it will presumably require in all countries; and they invite your observations and your criticisms.

I do not propose to enter upon any detailed explanation or justification of this proposal until it has been examined in outline by yourself and your advisers. There are many points in it which will require very careful discussions between our experts, and it is doubtless capable of much modification and improvement without detriment to the main ideas which underlie it. But these ideas I recommend to your judgment.

I may, however, at the present stage say this much. The scheme is an attempt to deal simultaneously in as simple a way as possible with several distinct problems. The countries which have been the victims of devastation are enabled to convert the bonds of the enemy into immediate purchasing power for the purpose of early restoration. France is probably the greatest gainer from the scheme and is offered a way out from her almost overwhelming financial difficulties. The acute problem of the liquidation of inter-ally indebtedness, while not disposed of, is sensibly ameliorated. The governments of the new states are enabled to prepare definite economic programmes which will consolidate their at present precarious positions and inspire confidence in their peoples. The neutrals are shown that their claims against the estate of the enemy will not be overlooked, in spite of the circumstances of these claims' origin, provided they are prepared to play their part in a world-wide scheme for the preservation of the credit of Europe. The enemy peoples are shown a way of discharging a part of their obligations and are given a reasonable measure of security for their economic existence in the immediate future. The good faith of the world as a whole is pledged, for the carrying out of a scheme the sole object of which is to set on its feet the new Europe. On the other hand it opens prospects of a renewal of trade to those countries, primarily the United States and secondarily the British Empire, who have surplus goods to export or a favourable balance of trade to liquidate. It cannot be supposed that two great continents, America and Europe, the one destitute and on the point of collapse and the other overflowing with goods which it wishes to dispose of, can continue to face one another for long without attempting to frame some plan of mutual advantage. And if it be admitted, as it must be, that trade can only recommence on the basis of credit of some kind, what better security can the lenders hope to secure than is herein proposed? But chief of all perhaps, only a scheme of large and broad dimensions, which can be announced to and understood by the whole world, can inspire that sentiment of hope which is the greatest need of Europe at this moment. A proposal which unfolds future prospects and shows the peoples of Europe a road by which food and employment and orderly existence can once again come their way, will be a more powerful weapon than any other for the preservation from the dangers of Bolshevism of that order of human society which we believe to be the best starting-point for future improvement and greater well-being.

I suggest that the relation of this scheme to the reparation terms which we are about to place before the German government might be as follows. In these terms as at present drafted we demand an immediate payment of £1,000 million, from which sum is first to be deducted the cost of the armies of occupation and of approved supplies of food and raw material to the enemy. I suggest that if the present proposal is adopted the initial payment might be £1,000 million, *exclusive* of the cost of the armies of occupation and of approved supplies, and that the enemy might be permitted to pay £724 million out of this sum in the special bonds thus to be created, providing the balance and also the cost of the armies by the transfer of ships, gold, securities and so forth.

Sir Robert Cecil forwarded Chamberlain a criticism of Keynes's plan by R. H. Brand, who was a member of the British delegation (T 172/988). Brand objected that the proposal did not solve the problem of the indebtedness of France and Italy to the United States and Britain, that it extended government borrowing (Keynes admitted the tendency towards inflationism in a paragraph deleted from the final version of the scheme's explanatory letter), and that the principle of joint liability raised problems of risk and politics. He himself favoured cancellation coupled with measures to restore internal stability.

Chamberlain replied to Cecil 22 April 1919:

No doubt it would be a very good thing if the United States would propose or support a universal cancellation of debt, but my information from Paris is that they show no inclination to do anything of the kind, and even such a scheme as that would leave the new states without credit to set them going. At any rate I feel strongly that the time has come for us to put forward a constructive policy. To propose the mere cancellation of debt looks as if we were trying to shift the whole burden on to America: to take part in a large scheme like the one proposed by Keynes is to show readiness to help shoulder the common burden ... But at least the Prime Minister now has two alternatives, either of which he can submit to the President, one, the mutual cancellation of debts and the other the scheme of mutual guarantee proposed by Keynes.

Keynes related the outcome in a discouraged minute to Bradbury and Chamberlain written 4 May 1919.

Sir John Bradbury
Chancellor of the Exchequer

As I have already reported the scheme for the relief of the financial credit of Europe was transmitted by the Prime Minister to President Wilson and to Monsieur Clemenceau. The objects of it were sympathetically looked upon by the Americans including, I think, the President, and I had one or two quite satisfactory conversations with Mr Norman Davis and Mr Hoover. Owing, however, to the extreme publicity which surrounds everything which happens at the Crillon Hotel [headquarters of the United States delegation], Mr Davis found it necessary to cable a copy of the proposals to his Treasury, before he was authorised to pass any definite comment upon them, lest a copy should first of all reach them through some other source.

The result of this has been immediate and violent opposition on the part of Washington. I am informed that they have cabled many thousand words of criticisms and horror and have formally interdicted Mr Davis and Mr Lamont from discussing any such question with me even in private conversation. Amongst other objections Mr Leffingwell has discovered that the scheme would require an alteration of the constitution of the United States.

As a result the American representatives here have crept to heel and the next communication which we received on the subject was the attached article in the *New York Herald* of 3 May. This article was followed up by a moderate and sensible leader in the *Temps* (also attached) the same evening. I am told that a letter has gone or is going from the President to the Prime Minister objecting to the scheme, but indicating the possibility of the Americans making some counter proposal. At the moment, however, the most exact information to hand is the article in the *New York Herald*. In view of the incomplete account of our proposals given by the Americans to the Press I think it deserves consideration whether we should not put on record publicly exactly what our proposals were. May I have your instructions?

So much for the official position. Unofficial conversations continue in spite of the prohibition of the United States Treasury, and Mr Davis and Mr Lamont dined last night with General Smuts and myself. As nearly as I can make out their present state of mind it is as follows:

They divide the problem into three heads: (1) the finance of new countries such as Poland; (2) the finance of enemy countries, particularly Germany; and (3) the finance of France and Italy. They are inclined to deal with these three questions separately rather than in one comprehensive plan. As regards (1) they are disposed to do something, and it is on this head that we may expect counter proposals. They estimate the total amount of loans required for such countries at £100 million which is, in my judgment, about right. Their counter proposal will, I think, take the form either of asking us to give some guarantee in connection with the loans or that a certain percentage of the loan should be our responsibility. In any event the form of assistance will be that of a straight loan to these countries. It is, I think, quite possible that the counter proposal may represent a genuine effort to meet the position in the new countries. Much will depend on what proportion of the burden they are prepared to take up and what limitations they put upon the expenditure of the money.

As regards (2), assistance to Germany, they find themselves in a dilemma. On the one hand they are aware of the necessity of doing something and are not at all averse on general grounds to giving assistance towards putting Germany on her legs. They see on the other hand that any assistance they give Germany will enable us to extract more reparation, and this they are determined they will not assist. They point out, with some justice, that our reparation proposals will take away from Germany her working capital, and that we are in effect asking them to restore the working capital to Germany which we have thus unnecessarily taken away. They suggest that the right solution is for us to abandon our reparation proposals, at least in their present form, and to leave to Germany her working capital intact. The feeling of the Americans, I may add, over the whole of our reparation policy is extremely adverse and will colour all their dealings with us in any proposal in which reparation is directly or indirectly involved. While, however, the above American criticism has a good deal of foundation, it is by no means a complete answer. The difficulty of the German position arises not so much out of the fact that we are to take away part of her moveable property, but out of the fact that she has practically no liquid capital. The greater part of what we are taking from her can by no means be regarded as liquid capital, and even if we were to leave it to her the problem of her immediate future would not be solved. At the moment therefore the Americans are vainly trying to solve the problem of assisting Germany without assisting us, and they have not yet been able to alight on any method of doing this.

As regards (3) they are determined to do nothing. Their annoyance both with France and Italy is at the present time intense and there is nothing less likely than that at the present juncture the President will give any financial assistance to either of them.

In short Washington rejects my proposals by reason of their strong desire to clear out of European responsibility (without however realising what this will mean to Europe), while the sympathy which might be expected from the Americans here by reason of their greater acquaintance of the European situation, is diminished by their dissatisfaction with the course of the peace negotiations. They do, however, intend to assist the new countries. They would like to assist Germany if they saw a way to do it without helping our reparation schemes; but France and Italy they would like to see punished.

The whole position is disappointing and depressing. I do not expect very much from the American counter proposal as regards the wider problems in the situation. But we have to remember that the position, in spite of all appearances to the contrary, is still exceedingly fluid. It cannot be supposed likely that the reparation proposals will ever be signed in their present form. The whole situation may change profoundly in the course of the next month. And only then can we say for certain what is practicable and what is not.

In this connection please see my separate note on the prospects of the peace conference as a whole.

J. M. KEYNES

4 May 1919

President Wilson stated his reasons for turning down the bond scheme in a letter to Lloyd George, 3 May. The President was convinced, he said,

that it would not be possible for me to secure from the Congress of the United States authority to place a Federal guarantee upon bonds of

European origin. Whatever aid the Congress may see fit to authorise should, in my judgment, be rendered along independent lines . . . Your Treasury, I understand, and certainly ours believes it wise to retire at the earliest possible moment from 'the banking business'.

But the crux of the letter for Keynes was in the last paragraph.

You have suggested that we all address ourselves to the problem of helping to put Germany on her feet, but how can your experts or ours be expected to work out a *new* plan to furnish working capital to Germany when we deliberately start out by taking away all Germany's *present* capital? How can anyone expect America to turn over to Germany in any considerable measure new working capital to take the place of that which the European nations have determined to take from her? Such questions would appear to answer themselves, but I cannot refrain from stating them, because they so essentially belong to a candid consideration of the whole difficult problem to which we are addressing ourselves . . .

Keynes recorded his reaction to the President's letter in a minute to the Prime Minister's private secretary, Philip Kerr, 10 May. The committee mentioned in the first paragraph was specially set up at the President's suggestion to find a constructive solution to the problems of Europe. Keynes and Lord Robert Cecil were the British members.

Mr Kerr

The committee set up at the instance of the President at yesterday's meeting of the Four obviates, I think, the necessity of any very detailed reply to the President's letter. At this committee, which met for the first time this morning, we hope to be able to discuss orally the principal difficulties which otherwise it might have been necessary to elaborate in writing.

The President's letter, as it stands however, indicates a spirit far too harsh for the human situation facing us. In particular it is surely impossible for the Americans to disclaim responsibility for the Peace Treaty to which, wisely or not, they have put their name equally with the other governments. The President, beginning with his Fourteen Points, has declared the necessity of reparation for the devastations of war. He cannot therefore dissociate himself from attempts to put this into practical execution. It is also worth remembering that while the Americans greatly criticised the aggregate of the indemnity they did not, so far as I remember, oppose the initial £1,000 million. Yet the force of the President's letter entirely turns on the inadvisability of exacting this sum of £1,000 million. In this I entirely agree with him. The sum of £1,000 million exists nowhere outside the imagination of certain people, and an attempt to secure it in hard cash cannot be successful. But one of the advantages of my proposal was precisely the point that by counting the guaranteed bonds to be issued as part of the £1,000 million we were able to meet the immediate requirements of the devastated countries *without* taking away from Germany the whole of her working assets. It was an attempt to avoid the otherwise awkward consequences of our having demanded, and of our having paraded the demand, for an impossible sum. And it is not open for the President, who was a party to this demand equally with everyone else, to speak as he does of such an attempt.

Nevertheless controversy on the above lines would be vain. There is a substantial truth in the President's standpoint, and we can only look for fruitful results out of the discussions of the new Committee.

J. M. KEYNES

10 May 1919

Keynes described the evolution of the new committee in a minute to Bradbury on the day that it was established, 9 May.

Sir John Bradbury

The following is an extract from the minutes of the British Empire Committee for Friday, 2 May:

It was resolved

(1) That sales of raw materials from the war stocks in the possession of the British government should be made on credit to the German government; and to the governments of the countries receiving relief.

(2) That pending the coming into operation of a scheme for

financing the supply of raw materials by private trade, further credits beyond the $12\frac{1}{2}$ million sterling already approved should be granted by the British Treasury and should be employed for selling to Germany and to the countries receiving relief raw materials.

Mr Keynes dissented from the above resolutions. He further stated that a vote of the House of Commons would be necessary.

The resolution was not really intended to be more than pious. But I promised to forward it to the Treasury. The view which I expressed in the discussion was to the effect that I sympathised and agreed with the general view of the situation held by the drafters of the resolution, but that we had already made a constructive suggestion towards the solution of the problem and that there was little for us to do until either this scheme had been accepted or some alternative had been put forward. I added that as everyone knew, it was financially impossible for us to solve the problem by ourselves, and that a supplementary estimate for financial assistance to Germany would present great parliamentary difficulties. The resolution was nevertheless carried unanimously apart from my dissent, partly for reasons with which it is impossible not to sympathise, and partly because several of our departmental officials here, having become professional suppliers of Germany, are now as eager to carry out their task at the expense of the British Treasury as they used to be when they were professional suppliers of our allies. I never cease to be astonished at the undeviating devotion of the British civil servant to the immediate objective entrusted to him.

At a meeting of the Supreme Economic Council on 5 May, the following resolution was accepted for transmission to the Council of Heads of States:

The Raw Materials Section desire to represent the extreme urgency of supplying raw materials to Europe. Without the supply of raw materials there is no hope for the peace of Europe. The Section therefore recommends that the matter should be immediately laid before the Council of the Heads of States with a request that they will give such directions to the financial authorities of the associated governments as will make possible a solution of this question.

It was agreed that the resolution should be accompanied by a copy of the report which should be revised as regards financial detail by the Chairman of the Finance Section before despatch.

The American delegates stated that their government was not in a position to accept the financial proposals outlined in the report.

As a consequence of this resolution a meeting of the Council of Four was held this morning which was attended by Lord Robert Cecil and myself. After Lord Robert had made a brief exposition of the general situation in Europe, including the enemy countries, the President stated that in his opinion the matter was too technical and difficult for useful discussion between the Four themselves at that moment and proposed that a committee should be appointed immediately, composed of two representatives of each of the Great Powers, to prepare a constructive scheme and report as soon as possible. This proposal was immediately accepted, and the first meeting will be held tomorrow at which Lord Robert and I, with Mr Brand, will represent the British government. This proposal on the part of the President marks a distinct step forward. But I am not yet very optimistic as to whether anything definite will result.

At the same meeting of the Four the question of food supplies for Germany was also discussed. So far the Germans have furnished funds to the extent of about £24,500,000. They have promised a further £10 million, which would make a total of £34,500,000. On the other hand by tomorrow we shall have delivered food up to the full extent of the £24,500,000 already provided; the further £10 million will not cover deliveries up

444

to the end of the month; and the aggregate of supplies already delivered or definitely arranged for amounts to £68,500,000, that is to say, £34 million in excess of any finance that is in sight. In short, the financial arrangements for the German food supply have broken down completely without making any allowance for their requirements of raw materials. This has been partly inevitable, but has been aggravated by our complete failure to get German exports going—a consequence of the attitude of the French, and also to the comparative failure of the German scheme for requisitioning the securities, on which I am sending you a separate note.

The difficulties of the position are added to by the Germans procrastinating in every way possible, doubtless with the object of being as little as possible committed to us in the event of a failure in the peace negotiations. It has been decided that no course is open to us except to notify the Germans on Monday that in view of their failure to furnish funds, all further shipments of food to Germany are being entirely suspended. But this is hardly calculated to have a favourable influence on the peace negotiations.

J.M.K.

9 May 1919

Keynes was not at all hopeful that this committee would accomplish anything concrete, as can be seen in a subsequent minute to Bradbury written 22 May. In fact, the report produced was never discussed by the Council of Four. Keynes had to be content with writing his plan for the rehabilitation of Europe into *The Economic Consequences of the Peace*, where it appears in the final chapter, 'Remedies'.

Sir John Bradbury

As I reported to you some ten days ago a small confidential committee has been appointed by the Council of Four to report to them on the general question of the rehabilitation of European credit. This committee arose out of the refusal of the President to consider the financial proposition put forward to him by the

445

Prime Minister on the recommendation of the Chancellor of the Exchequer.

A preliminary sub-committee prepared the attached memorandum 'A' which was presented to the second meeting of the committee itself in the middle of last week. At this meeting I stated that so far as the United Kingdom was concerned we hoped to scrape along on the basis of our own credit, public and private, provided we did not have to lend to others. M. Clementel [Georges Clementel, French Minister of Commerce] and M. Loucheur then made long speeches to the effect that France required a loan of £800 million spread over two years, half from the United Kingdom and half from the United States. Repayment would have to be spread over 30 to 40 years.

Signor Crespi stated that Italy required a loan of £600 million spread over three years, not including her requirements for payment of interest. The Italian position is set out in more detail in the attached memorandum 'B'.

According to the representatives of these countries the French annual rate of adverse balance of trade at this moment was estimated at £600 million and the Italian adverse balance on the basis of the 1918 figures at £300 million.

Mr Davis, with the preface that he was not in a position to be as constructive as he had hoped, then handed in the attached memorandum 'C'. It was evident to the committee that this was a quite futile document which took the matter no further. In subsequent conversation, however, the American representatives went a little further than what they had written down.

After the meeting Mr Brand drew up memorandum 'D' as representing a possible solution of the position which the course of the discussion indicated as possible. At the end of the meeting Mr Davis promised to seek the approval of the President for something more constructive and it was agreed that he and I should prepare a draft report.

I append this draft report in its latest form as memorandum 'E'. This report has not yet been passed by the committee

beyond paragraph 4 and its further consideration has been postponed until Saturday owing to the absence from Paris of Lord
Robert Cecil. The whole of the document is substantially agreed
by the British and Americans and I think by the Italians. But
there is little prospect that the paragraphs about reparation will
be agreed to by the French. These paragraphs aim at giving a
truthful picture of the situation and are consequently at complete
variance with the proposals of the reparation chapter of the draft
treaty of peace. Nevertheless the British and American representatives are unanimously of the opinion that we cannot shut our
eyes to the facts for more than another two or three weeks or that
if we do the problem of putting forward any sound financial
proposals becomes quite impossible.

Apart from this, however, I do not attach much importance to
the document, and I do not believe that it will come to anything.
The proposals about currency reform are very virtuous but are
unlikely ever to come into effective operation. The same is true
of the proposals for facilitating trade. I fear that I take but little
interest in the document, which is chiefly to be looked on as a
sort of smokescreen for the purpose of allowing all of us to
evacuate Paris without too much discredit or leaving the problem
too obviously unsolved. The Americans do not really intend to do
anything; and even apart from that no concrete proposal capable
of being put into force can come into existence in the unreal
atmosphere of Paris.

You will observe that the report does not commit any particular power to make any particular contribution, but limits
itself to giving a rough estimate of how much will be required.
So far as we are concerned I anticipate that we may have to make
some small addition to the £12,500,000 and that having done that
we shall be well advised to clear out of all further responsibility
for a situation of which it is impossible for us to make a good
job.

I have, however, one cheerful item of news to convey. The
concluding passage of the draft report was written by Mr Davis

447

and is intended to foreshadow a recommendation which he has promised me to make to the President, to the effect that the interest on all inter-allied debt should be remitted for a period of three years. This proposal, if it could be carried out, would be of the greatest utility to us and to all concerned and would be a real contribution to the problem, both by relieving the British, French and Italian treasuries of an immediate anxiety and by making it more possible for us to take our part in any comprehensive scheme which may be put forward. This proposal, however, must be regarded at the present stage as being no more than a very confidential communication between Mr Davis and myself and we ought not to reckon on its coming to anything.

I take this opportunity of adding that of the £12,500,000 which I have been administering here, from £1,000,000 to £1,500,000 is still intact and unallotted. This credit has therefore gone a very long way and has proved sufficient to meet really essential demands for a very satisfactorily long time. While the demands actually made on me have been very large and incessant the credit of £12,500,000 has given me just sufficient latitude to enable me to temper firmness with concessions in every case in which a strong case for concessions had really been established.

J.M.K.

22 May 1919

Keynes's papers from the conference are a welter of proposals, counter-proposals and compromises, drafts and re-draftings of the delegates' search for a settlement. He was known as a liberal and Lloyd George made use of him to balance off the reactionary Hughes, Cunliffe and Sumner. When these three drew up their own plan of payments from Germany rising to £600 million a year, to run until 1961, Lloyd George asked Keynes for something more moderate. Keynes's scheme of 22 March, which he drafted with the assistance of Brand, also failed to please, but it is interesting for the provision it made to restore to Germany any physical assets from the prescribed list of what should be handed over that would affect her future capacity to pay.

A minute that Keynes wrote to Lloyd George 28 March, about the wrangle with the French over the division of the spoils, breathes the atmosphere of tired exasperation that was settling into the conference.

Prime Minister

Mr Lamont tells me that this afternoon M. Loucheur gave him a reply to the compromise proposed by the Americans.

This reply was an absolute refusal. After consulting M. Clemenceau, M. Loucheur declares that the proportion of 2·24 to 1 (i.e. 56 to 25) is his final and lowest offer and that M. Clemenceau cannot contemplate any figure less favourable to France. He adds that he is prepared to contest the whole question of proportions due, on the basis of the Fourteen Points; that these, omitting pensions, yield at least four to one in favour of France, and including pensions at least three to one; and that he is in a mood to be very combative indeed on the whole subject.

Lord Sumner is of opinion that in view of this no purpose is served by further discussion except between the principals—yourself, the President and M. Clemenceau. The Americans will, I think, continue to give support to the proposal of 2 to 1, but not combative support.

I only add the following:

(1) The appended note shows that M. Loucheur's statement, as to the taxable capacity of the devastated areas, was at least as unveracious as his other statements. These figures include (for example) the *whole* of the Pas de Calais, and allowing for such over-inclusion entirely substantiate your estimate of 5 to 10 per cent as being very *generous*.

(2) If you have any disposition to make a further concession, I suggest that it might be in the following form:

The proportion of 2 to 1 to remain, on the assumption of 16 per cent to the minor Allies; if this 16 per cent proves insufficient, then any addition *up to* 19 per cent which may be necessary shall be at *our* expense alone; beyond that at France's expense and ours in the proportion 2 to 1.

	France	U.K.	Others
That is to say, we start at	56	28	16
which is your offer and if necessary, having regard to the claims of minor allies,			
adjust to	56	25	19
which is Loucheur's offer.			

So little, really, is there between us.

28 March 1918

'Keynes carries a great load of responsibility', Chamberlain wrote to the Prime Minister, 17 April, 'and you will understand that there are times when he feels that the right of access to a minister on the spot is really necessary for the discharge of his duties.' In the absence of any minister of the government in Paris at that particular time, it was arranged at Chamberlain's request that Keynes might consult General Smuts when he was in need of guidance.

Throughout April while the financial clauses of the treaty were being hammered out Keynes was frequently in attendance at the meetings of the Council of Four in Lloyd George's flat and President Wilson's house in Paris. From this close acquaintance with developments he arrived at a disillusioned view of the future prospects of the conference which he summarised for Bradbury and Chamberlain, 4 May, the same day that he reported the failure of his credit scheme.

Sir John Bradbury
The Chancellor of the Exchequer
On the eve of the completion of the draft treaty of peace I send you some general impressions on the situation.

First, as regards reparation some important changes have been made since I sent you the last printed text. The principal of these are the three following:

1. The Council of Three [the Italians had left the conference temporarily] have decided that the claim against Germany is to

cover only actual damage by Germans and that she is to have no joint responsibility for damage done by her allies. In the case of fronts in which Germany's allies have taken the major part, the extent of Germany's liability for damage done is to be measured by the proportion of her naval and military effort in that field of operation to the effort of the enemy belligerents as a whole. This latter proportion is to be estimated by the Reparation Commission, but how no one knows.

2. The division between the allies of the sums received from Germany in respect of reparation are to be divided in proportion to the actual proved claims of each for the Reparation Commission. A secret agreement to this effect has been signed by the Prime Minister, the President, and Monsieur Clemenceau of which I attach a copy.

3. As a result of bitter complaints on the part of Belgium as to her treatment, two important concessions have been made to her. In the first place she is to receive towards her claims the first £100 million reparation receipts. In the second place the allies who have lent money to Belgium during the war are to be entitled to claim this amount from Germany as an additional category of claim under Annex 1 of the reparation chapter. In respect of this claim Germany is to hand over a special series of bonds to the allies in question, and on receipt of these bonds the indebtedness of Belgium is to be cancelled. Thus Belgium alone amongst the allies will start the peace with no war debt whatever and will also receive the first £100 million of real money.

The effect of the first change recorded above is far-reaching, especially when it is considered in conjunction with the second decision as to the basis of division of the receipts. The effect of the two decisions between them is to cut out from the reparation receipts almost entirely Italy, Serbia and Roumania. These countries will be able to claim on Austria but will not benefit to any appreciable extent from reparation receipts from Germany.

Up to the present the decision is secret and has been chiefly made, I imagine, as a reprisal against Italy. Italy's absence from the conference will have cost her dear and her rage when she discovers what has happened during her absence will be correspondingly great. Opinions differ as to whether the effect on Italy will be to bring her to heel in the hope of obtaining a concession, or whether it will only serve to stiffen her further in her present attitude. So long, however, as the above decision remains secret this question is academic. Incidentally Serbia and Roumania are cut out also—which as regards Serbia at least is surely hardly a tenable position on our part. These countries also are at present in ignorance of the decision and we are all wondering whether the few minutes which these countries will have for examination of the treaty before it is presented to the Germans will suffice for the discovery by them of what has happened and, if they do find out in time, what they will do.

Another decision lately taken is to the effect that Poland is to be excluded from claims for reparation receipts and the text has been amended accordingly. This also is at present unknown to the party affected.

As matters now stand my guess as to the out-turn of the claims of the several countries under Annex 1 of the reparation chapter is as follows:

	£ millions	Per cent
United Kingdom	2,000	30
France	4,000	60
Belgium	500	7½
Others¹	200	2½
Total	6,700	100

¹ Assuming U.S. makes no pension claim.

You will notice that we come out exceedingly well on paper and, while the aggregate claim against the Germans is now much lower than it used to be, the proportion to be received by us has gone up.

I cannot however for one moment believe that the reparation chapter as it now stands can possibly persist as a solution of the problem showing indeed as it does a high degree of unwisdom in almost every direction. Stiff though it is I doubt if it will satisfy those who have illusions about indemnities. On the other hand there are many provisions in it which one can hardly imagine accepted by the Germans. The machinery of the scheme, working through the Reparation Commission is a mere paper solution which could not possibly work in practice. If the commission ever gets going, which I doubt, an early and complete breakdown must be certain. Not only so but the reparation chapter in its present form has left the whole of the American delegation with the bitterest feelings towards their principal European associates. In fighting week after week preposterous demands on the part of ourselves and the French they have got into a habit of arguing and working in the interests of the enemy which is not likely to disappear in the future. So far as finance goes it is no exaggeration to say that the sympathies of the Americans are now much more with the enemy than with any of us. But this is not the end. The protests from Italy, Serbia, Roumania and Poland when they discover what has happened are likely to be overwhelming.

The financial clauses are, I think, innocent and the territorial clauses are no more than what everyone expects, although they are likely in some respects, more particularly as regards Silesia, to provoke tremendous opposition from the Germans. The military and naval clauses are justifiably stiff, but in their detailed provisions go beyond what any self-respecting country would submit to.

Some of the most objectionable features, however, are to be found in the chapters which lie outside the grand issues. The economic chapters contain nothing very important, but consisting of a long series of pinpricks insisting upon innumerable small concessions without reciprocity which in the aggregate will diminish to an appreciable extent the sovereignty of Germany as an independent country.

The transit and inland transport chapters contain a further

453

series of humiliating and interfering provisions including the internationalisation of a considerable part of the river system of Germany.

There remain two chapters of high political importance. The chapter on punishment provides that the German government shall hand over to us such persons at present unnamed as we may choose to charge with offences against humane practice in war. This clause has been eloquently opposed by General Botha in the British Empire Committee where he pointed out that the Boers had prolonged the war for an additional eighteen months in order to escape such a condition and in his opinion no honourable country could sign such a term. The other chapter is that dealing with the occupation of Germany. For five years the Allies will be entitled to occupy what they are now occupying. At the end of five years the northern sector will be vacated, at the end of five years more the middle sector, and at the end of fifteen years the remaining portion. If, however, Germany fails in any way to keep the provisions of the treaty including reparation payments occupation of the country will be at once resumed up to the full extent. This chapter, unlike most of the treaty, has been kept fairly confidential and a few persons have been aware of it. From the financial point of view it will have serious consequences. There is believed to be some understanding between President Wilson and Monsieur Clemenceau that the French government will not in fact keep large numbers of troops in the areas occupied by her, but there is no limiting provision in the treaty. As the whole of the cost of occupation is to be met by Germany as a prior charge in front of reparation payments, it will be open to the French government to keep the whole of their army in German territory and thus to meet the whole expenses of it at the cost of Germany or, rather it should be said, at the cost of ourselves, inasmuch as the sums so paid over will correspondingly diminish what is available for reparation. The whole of this chapter indeed would appear to lend itself to the most terrible abuse.

I have of course picked out in the above the least satisfactory features of the draft treaty. I am now so familiar with those parts of it with which I have been more closely concerned that it is difficult to say what effect the draft as a whole will produce on those who see it for the first time. But I am sure that apart from other difficulties it cannot be regarded as workable. The settlement is a paper settlement which even if it is accepted cannot possibly be expected to last. Practically no one here has seen the treaty as a whole until the last few days. No considered judgment has ever been passed on it as a whole. We await the judgment of the world in perplexity.

What the attitude of the Germans is to be is naturally a subject of much speculation here. The financial representatives whom I visited a few days ago are quite different creatures from the nervous and broken-spirited men whom I met three months ago at Trèves. At that time they were manifestly suffering in body and mind from their experiences. They were defeated and depressed without a plan or much hope of one and prepared for almost anything. Now, however, they have a backbone again. Their spirits are good and they have an air of being at ease with themselves, as though their internal crisis was over (the crisis I mean internal to their own mind and spirit) and they were prepared for what the future might have in store for them. Reports on the political position of Germany all indicate that Spartacism is for the moment, at any rate, under control and is no longer the danger that it was, but that orderly political forces are much more advanced in opinion in the leftward direction than the present government. In this connection I append an interesting report from Capt. Gibson.

I still believe that the Germans would like to sign if the terms make this possible for them and that they do not intend to go home without attempting a prolonged discussion both of principles and details. But that they will sign the treaty in the form in which it now stands I cannot for one moment believe. Why should they? What worse fate have we in store for them in the event of refusal? Even if they know that they must yield in the end we have reached the time of the year when the food position is no longer immediately desperate and they could afford passive resistance for a few months if it were only for bluff in the chance of seeing what result this would produce on the world and on the populations of the allied countries.

No one here seems to have any clear idea as to what the procedure is to be. The draft will be presented to the Germans in a few days. At any time in the course of the fifteen days following they can send written communications asking questions etc. These questions will be referred to a series of inter-allied committees, on which each chief ally has one representative, who will prepare written answers. At the end of the fifteen days the Germans are to make their considered reply in writing. What is to happen next remains to be seen.

Indeed I and most of us here are exceedingly pessimistic. The conference has led us into a bog which it will take more statesmanship to lead us out of than it has taken adroitness to lead us in.

Perhaps after all we shall get a solution by throwing overboard without too much fuss a very considerable part of the present complicated production, thus getting back to the simple form of peace which is alone possible. The chief difficulty about this will be, of course, that our original terms will have been published, apparently in their entirety, to the world. It looks very much, therefore, as if the choice lay between a disastrous breakdown and a diplomatic triumph for Germany. As the President and the Prime Minister are undoubtedly bent on peace it may be the case that the second is the more probable.

4 May 1919   J. M. KEYNES

Yet, while Keynes despaired of the conference and was indignant on behalf of the Germans, he was alert where British interests were at stake. He wrote the following minute to the Prime Minister on the same day as the foregoing, 4 May.

The Prime Minister

A final proposal to Belgium was made on Saturday afternoon to M. Hymans and the other Belgian representatives. They expressed themselves as willing to do their best to get their government to agree to a settlement on these lines. Monsieur Hymans left for Brussels accordingly last night carrying the draft proposals with him to lay before the Belgian government. He promised a definite reply in the course of today.

The only point of importance which arose was the exact degree of priority to be attached to the first £100 million to be received by Belgium. The Three decided on Friday that this sum was to be paid out of the first *cash* receipts and was not to be reckoned in front of such concessions as ships. The Belgians would have raised no objection to this. But the Americans and M. Loucheur insisted upon pressing that the payment of this sum to Belgium should be a priority at least to the extent indicated in the second draft of paragraph 1 below even in front of ships ceded under the ton-for-ton arrangement. If the second draft of clause 1 is accepted as it now stands we may on 1 January 1921 be in the position of having ourselves to pay out to Belgium part of the value of the ships we shall have received.

This does not seem to me right, and I suggest that we should only accept the second draft of clause 1 with the following words added, 'exclusive of the value of the restitutions and also of restorations under Annexes 3 and 4 of this chapter'. (Annex 3 deals with ships and Annex 4 with certain restitutions in similar but not in identical material.)

May I have your instructions? No final draft of the first clause has yet been communicated to the Belgians.

J.M.K.

4 May 1919

Ten days later Keynes wrote to his mother that he had decided to resign from the Treasury.

From a letter to MRS KEYNES, *14 May 1919*

It must be weeks since I've written a letter to anyone—but I've been utterly worn out, partly by work partly by depression at the evil round me. I've never been so miserable as for the last two or three weeks; the Peace is outrageous and impossible and can bring nothing but misfortune behind it. Personally I do not believe the Germans will sign, though the general view is to the contrary (i.e. that after a few moans and complaints they will sign anything). But if they do sign this will be in many ways the worse alternative; for it is out of the question that they should keep the terms (which are incapable of being kept) and nothing but general disorder and unrest could result. Certainly if I was in the Germans' place I'd rather die than sign such a peace.

Well, I suppose I've been an accomplice in all this wickedness and folly, but the end is now at hand. I am writing to the Treasury to be relieved of my duties by 1 June if possible and not later than 15 June in any event. So I may just be back in time for the tail end of the May Term.

Apart from any other reasons, I am quite at the end of my tether and must have a holiday.

I've a letter lying unanswered inquiring if I will be a candidate for the directorship of the London School of Economics—pay £1500 or perhaps more. I shall ask a few questions about it, but have no intention of accepting. I hope Father agrees.

I am supposed to be sitting to [Augustus] John for my portrait for his Peace Conference set; but there has been no time so far.

There is no copy of Keynes's letter to the Treasury among his papers or in the Treasury files, but Chamberlain, writing to him on 21 May, referred to a letter by Keynes to Bradbury dated the 19th. Chamberlain wrote:

My dear Keynes

Bradbury has just shown me your letter of the 19th. I know how great a sacrifice of personal inclination, and even more, you have made in continuing your work for us in Paris. On your side I think you know how much I have valued and appreciated the enormous assistance which you have given to us. I know that you want to be set free as soon as possible and that the obligations of your present position are very irksome to you, but until things are more settled I could not replace you satisfactorily and I do most earnestly beg that you will consent to continue for a time the public work in which you have been engaged. You yourself truly say that the character and amount of that work may very probably change greatly within a short time, but the immediate future is full of uncertainty and until we can see a little more clearly what course events will take it is impossible to formulate a plan for a permanent organisation, and the maxim against swapping horses in the middle of a stream applies with full force.

Bradbury will write to you as to the other members of the staff but I could not leave to him the expression of my strong feeling that a continuation of your services is for the present of great importance in the public interest, nor can I refrain from making my personal appeal to you to continue your help until the situation is more clearly defined.

Yours sincerely,

AUSTEN CHAMBERLAIN

Keynes replied:

To AUSTEN CHAMBERLAIN, *26 May 1919*

Dear Chancellor of the Exchequer

I appreciate your letter very much, just as I have had good reason to appreciate my treatment by the Treasury all through; and if my only grounds for leaving were the need of a rest and the desire to get back to my own work, I could not resist your appeal. But that is not the position. I was so anxious to leave this conference on general grounds that I did not like to make too much fuss about my reasons arising out of disagreement with the policy which is being pursued here. But I stated them in my previous letter and to me they are very real and important. We have presented a draft treaty to the Germans which contains in it much that is unjust and much more that is inexpedient. Until the last moment no one could appreciate its full bearing. It is now right and necessary to discuss it with the Germans and to be ready to make substantial concessions. If this policy is not pursued, the consequences will be disastrous in the extreme.

If, therefore, the decision is taken to discuss the treaty with the Germans with a view to substantial changes and if our policy is such that it looks as if I can be of real use, I am ready to stay another two or three weeks. But if the decision is otherwise, I fear that I must resign immediately. I cannot express how strongly I feel as to the gravity of what is in front of us, and I must have my hands quite free. I wish I could talk to you about the whole miserable business. The Prime Minister is leading us all into a morass of destruction. The settlement which he is proposing for Europe disrupts it economically and must depopulate it by millions of persons. The new states we are setting up cannot survive in such surroundings. Nor can the peace be kept or the League of Nations live. How can you expect me to assist at this tragic farce any longer, seeking to lay the foundations, as a Frenchman puts it, 'd'une guerre juste et durable'?

The Prime Minister's present Austrian policy puts me in an equal difficulty. Lords Sumner and Cunliffe have produced a reparation draft of which I have already sent you a copy. Now General Smuts and I are invited to join their deliberations. But the British representation cannot be fundamentally divided against itself, and it is necessary to choose. I append a letter which General Smuts has written to the Prime Minister about this. I also enclose two of Sir F. Oppenheimer's latest telegrams.

I am writing separately to Bradbury on staff questions.

Sincerely yours,

J.M.K.

It was a copy of Smuts's letter of resignation from the Austrian Reparations Commission that Keynes had enclosed. In it Smuts said that the imposition of reparation 'on a broken, bankrupt, economically impossible state like Austria, or a new friendly allied state like Czecho-Slovakia . . .

seems to me a hopeless policy, which could only lead to the most mischievous results'. He added: 'I have discussed the matter with Keynes who appears to be exactly in the same position as myself.'

Keynes had protested about the Austrian terms in a minute to Sir Maurice Hankey (Secretary to the War Cabinet), of 22 May.

Sir Maurice Hankey

The draft reparation chapter of the treaty with Austria is verbatim the same as that with Germany except where there is special reason for variation. The result of this in many cases is to include provisions which in the case of Austria are rather absurd and are bound to remain a dead letter—in fact the whole document is so drafted as to give ample opportunity for it to be treated as a dead letter for practical purposes. There is evidently no very serious intention in the minds of the authors actually to take any appreciable indemnity from Austria. For the purpose of immediate public consumption it is concocted, I suppose, to taste.

The more interesting and important features of it are the following:

(1) The third paragraph of Article 2 is, I think, a suitable and ingenious way of dealing with the drafting difficulty.

(2) Assuming that reparation payments are to be exacted from Austria I agree that the remarkable provisions of Article 3 by which these charges are to be spread over the whole of the territory of the former Austro-Hungarian empire are logical. It would be impossible and unreasonable to fix on the small remnant of population of Austria proper the whole of the charges falling to the former empire. But the proposal that Czecho-Slovakia, Poland, Jugo-Slavia and the parts of Austria ceded to Italy should also pay reparation is not going to be popular or furnish good propaganda in those countries. In point of fact, of course, the whole proceeding is pure humbug and there are various provisions, particularly in Article 14, which make it clear to anyone who reads between the lines that in

461

practice no actual cash payments will be exacted from those countries and that the whole account will wash out. But it would require much tact and cleverness to explain to each section of the European public precisely which parts of this document are to be taken as humbug and which are not.

(3) No sum is fixed in Article 5 for payments during the first two years, which is a wise course and tacitly recognises the impossibility of such payments. Annex 2 will allow the newspapers to say that Austria is to pay an indemnity of ten milliard gold crowns, that is to say rather more than £400 million, but there are suitable provisions providing for the remission of this sum.

(4) The reparation commission set up to deal with Austria is to be the same commission as that which is to deal with Germany. Altogether this commission will be the largest government office in the world and will have to employ thousands of persons. Indeed theoretically the government of the greater part of Europe so far as it relates to financial and economic affairs will be in its hands. I should imagine that the reparation commission will come to be one of the most hated instruments of foreign domination ever invented.

(5) Annex 3, page 9. I suggest that the drafting might make it a little clearer that we are seizing all shipping entitled to fly the Austrian flag before or during the war as well as at this moment. In view of the Italian claim as regards the ships at Trieste there should be no possible ambiguity in the drafting.

(6) Annex 4, page 10 is absurd having regard to the present known position of Austria. In particular, paragraph 6 providing for the surrender of milch cows to Italy, Serbia and Roumania is a cruel and foolish provision at a time when the children of Austria are dying in such numbers for want of milk that the allied and associated governments are doing all in their power to rail condensed milk into the country.

The whole document strikes me as a purely academic effort having no relation whatever to the actual appalling condition of

Austria, as it must appear to anyone who has access to the information coming to the Supreme Economic Council. Austria is now a country of about 6 million population of whom $2\frac{1}{2}$ million live in the capital. The principal materials on which it depended now lie outside its frontiers. The factories are not at work because they have no coal and no prospects of coal. No one can conceive any way by which the population of the country can be permanently maintained at anything approaching its present level. At the same time no passports are permitted for anyone to leave the country. They therefore remain there without food, clothes, coal or employment. For example one-third of the children of Vienna now remain constantly indoors as they are naked. As distinct from the case of other countries which are in a bad way no one sees any coherent plan for the future of the country. Our problem is to find means for the emigration of at least half the inhabitants in order that Austria may continue as a small agricultural state. Pending this we have, at great financial cost to ourselves, to endeavour to keep the population alive. At present we are spending about £2 million a month in keeping the inhabitants of Vienna just this side of the grave. In the light of these facts the draft reparation chapter appears [a] frivolous and unreal document. But it is so unlikely to come into force that it must, I suppose, be considered harmless.

J.M.K.

22 May 1919

I append a telegram just received from Sir F. Oppenheimer. I am sure that he is right and that, if we had enough energy left, we ought to try and work out with the Austrians financial and economic provisions suited to their country. To take the German treaty and write Austria for Germany, more or less regardless of the vast variation of conditions, appeals to the mentality of this tired-out conference but leads to meaningless and inoperative conclusions.

J.M.K.

Keynes prepared Bradbury for his leaving.

To SIR JOHN BRADBURY, *27 May 1919*

I have written to the Chancellor direct about my own personal position. But the general position here as regards getting the necessary work done is much more serious than you think. As soon as the various Treaties of Peace are signed, I agree of course that then direct Treasury representation in Paris can come to an end immediately. But this is not going to happen at once, and I should expect that things may easily drag on here for another two months. Even the Economic Council is likely to be here for 3 or 4 weeks longer. In the meantime a strong Treasury representation is essential. Before deciding otherwise, I hope you will come out here for a day or two to see for yourself what goes on.

Armitage Smith, if he could stay, could replace Falk. But he and Ward will not be equal by themselves to the whole of the work. And I still press for someone else from the Treasury.

If I stay on for two or three weeks more, I must have proper personal assistance as I am now so worn out as to be quite unable to get along otherwise. In the much more probable event of my clearing out within a week from today, it will be all the more necessary to strengthen the staff.

The position is quite uncertain; but, so far as I can judge, the Prime Minister is in a bad mood,—partly from a desire to be *through* with the business however badly and disastrously.

At any rate I am so sick at what goes on that I am near breaking point; and you must be prepared for my resignation by telegram at any moment.

J.M.K.

Yet Keynes continued watchful for British interests, writing this minute the same day, 27 May.

Sir John Bradbury

At the committee appointed by the four Heads of States to consider the provision of finance for Europe, Mr Norman Davis definitely stated that the President had decided to propose to Congress that the interest on loans due from the allies to the American Treasury should be remitted for three years.

He also stated that the President would recommend some relaxation of the present conditions governing the use of the $1,000 million already placed at the disposal of the War Finance Corporation for the purpose of extending aid to American exporters. This relaxation will probably take the form of enabling exporters to discount bills drawn by foreign importers without recourse up to say 75 per cent of the value of the bill.

The United States Treasury will also have a small balance out of the sums already voted for advances to allies for the purchase of wheat during the cereal year 1919–20.

Mr Norman Davis added, however, that he thought the prospect of the United States Congress being prepared to do anything whatever for the finance of Europe, beyond the above measures, was exceedingly remote.

The above is to be treated as very confidential, Mr Norman Davis laying great stress on the importance of no rumours being current in advance of the President's own statement to the Congress.

The proposal as regards interest is a very solid and important concession to us. As regards the rest I do not much blame the United States representatives having regard to the hopelessly unsatisfactory character of the situation they are asked to remedy. But it means, I think, that we ourselves will have to go very slowly in the matter of making any advance beyond the £12,500,000 and not allow ourselves to be manœuvred into taking the place of the United States.

J.M.K.

27 May 1919

A clause in the Austrian treaty for the delivery in payment of reparations of a number of milch cows made Keynes so indignant that he asked the Prime Minister, through Philip Kerr, to have it withdrawn. Lloyd George did indeed raise the matter in the Council of Four, but finding that the other members were not anxious to make any changes, he let it drop.

To PHILIP KERR, *30 May 1919*

My dear Kerr,

I attended this afternoon a meeting of the Austrian reparation commission to put my case for a substantial modification of the present draft document.

At this meeting one important alteration was secured by which the figure of 10,000 milliards gold crowns put forward as the amount of Austrian bonds to be delivered, corresponding to the 100 milliards of gold marks in the German treaty, was deleted, and the actual figure of reparation to be exacted from Austria was left vague.

This is a great improvement, though not enough, in my opinion, to make the document a wise one.

In particular there is still one provision left in about which I feel great indignation, and I should be very grateful if you would draw the Prime Minister's attention to this. In Article 6 of Annex 4 Austria is to undertake to deliver within three months after the signature of the treaty certain quantities of milch cows and other cattle.

In view of what we know as to the desperate condition of Austria, especially as regards infant mortality—these conditions being reported to be worse than in any other part of Europe except perhaps Petrograd—this seems to me to be [a] cruel and unwise demand. Unlike all the other demands on Austria, it is not subject to modification at the hands of the Reparation Commission, but must be fulfilled forthwith.

I protested formally against this clause, which is one that we in Paris, sitting remote from the actual conditions of Austria, have no right to enforce. The actual sum of money involved is, of course, relatively trifling.

I understand that the reparation proposals for Austria are to come before the Four tomorrow morning. As I am rather unwell

466

I shall not be able to attend the meeting myself, but I do most earnestly hope that the Prime Minister will cut out the provision about the cattle.

As regards the rest of the document, it is, as I have said, slightly improved, but is still very unwise. Much the best plan, in my opinion, would be to present the draft treaty to the Austrians without the reparation chapter, reserving this until the position with Germany is more settled.

The argument which chiefly weighed at this afternoon's meeting was that any changes in the form of the reparation chapter presented to Austria as compared with the chapter presented to Germany would prejudice our negotiations with the latter. Hence a document which, in relation to the realities of the Austrian position, is altogether wide of the mark.

Yours sincerely,

J. M. KEYNES

On the day that the preceding letter was written Keynes gave way to exhaustion and retired to bed. But he rallied in a few days when Lloyd George, still seeking to get a fixed sum into the treaty with Germany, asked him to submit a memorandum on alternative reparation proposals. Keynes noted that two alternative methods were 'Handed by Ll. G. to Clemenceau' on either 2 or 3 June. The second was to give the Germans themselves three months to fix a cash sum to settle all claims; if their offer was not satisfactory, the present reparations clauses would stand. Keynes's brief memorandum concerned the first. A carbon copy in his papers is annotated 'Handed to the P.M. / June 2, 1919 / JMK' in pencil in his own hand. Writing to Bradbury 6 June, Keynes said that he prepared the memorandum 'on Tuesday'— although Tuesday in that week was in fact 3 June. Whatever day it was written, it was Keynes's last try. Nothing came of it; Lloyd George also asked Cunliffe and Sumner for a memorandum and adopted neither.

The first of the proposed alternative methods of dealing with reparation, namely, that the Germans should undertake as a contract the whole task of the physical restoration of France and Belgium and that a sum should be fixed in the treaty of peace

467

for all other items in the categories of damage, might be made the basis of a specific proposal on the following lines:

Under the categories of damage as at present proposed, the aggregate claim against Germany (as distinguished from claims against her allies) might be estimated—as a guess—at £6,300 millions.[1]

If the Austrian precedent is to be followed a certain deduction should be made from this sum in respect of the share of reparation and of war debt attributable to territory to be ceded under the treaty of peace. As this territory amounts to about 10 per cent in Germany, this allowance for reparation and war debt together could be roughly put at £1,300 millions, leaving £5,000 millions as the sum due from Germany. There would be great advantages in taking this sum as the basis of any arrangement, first because it is the sum provisionally proposed in the draft treaty of peace, and secondly because it is an amount which the Germans have pretended to accept (though really offering by reason of numerous deductions which they propose, a far inferior sum), and one, therefore, which it may be rather difficult for them to refuse.

Starting out from this figure of £5,000 millions it is suggested that Germany be required to undertake as a contract the whole task of the physical restoration of France and Belgium and that she be allowed a deduction of £2,000 millions in respect of this contract.

Payment of the balance of £3,000 millions should be required in cash or its equivalent and safeguards should be taken that the payment of it is not spread unduly over too long a period, but no interest should be required pending payment.[2]

---

[1] *Note:* In any case it is probable that the claims would not be less than £6,000 millions and not more than £7,000 millions.

[2] *Note:* The effect of interest payments at 5 per cent in swelling the total bill may be illustrated as follows:

Interest at 5 per cent on £5,000 millions is £250 millions per annum. If during each of the ten years Germany was to pay the very considerable amount of £150 millions annually —beyond which she could hardly go pending her restoration as one of the greatest industrial nations of the world—she would nevertheless be falling into arrears on interest alone at the rate of £100 millions a year and would owe at the end of the ten years £1,000 millions more than she owed at the beginning of the ten years.

This sum of £3,000 millions should be divided up between the allies in proportions determined upon now.

In assigning Great Britain's share account must of course be taken of the fact that the restoration of France and Belgium has been provided for outside this sum.

Subject to the above, none of the other German claims should be admitted; that is to say they should be allowed no further deduction from the sum of £5,000 millions in respect of ceded territory; nor should they receive any allowance in respect of the colonies; nor should they be given any credit for surrenders under the armistice, other than those already proposed in the draft treaty of peace.

With the fixation of a definite sum as above a great many of the present powers of the Reparation Commission would be unnecessary and some concessions could, therefore, be made to the German objections against the present dictatorial and far-reaching powers of that body over the internal economy of Germany.

Keynes left Lloyd George to 'the twins', Lords Cunliffe and Sumner.

To DAVID LLOYD GEORGE, *5 June 1919*

Dear Prime Minister,

I ought to let you know that on Saturday I am slipping away from this scene of nightmare. I can do no more good here. I've gone on hoping even through these last dreadful weeks that you'd find some way to make of the treaty a just and expedient document. But now it's apparently too late. The battle is lost. I leave the twins to gloat over the devastation of Europe and to assess to taste what remains for the British taxpayer.

Yours sincerely,

J. M. KEYNES

Mr Dudley Ward will remain to carry on the work of the Treasury representation.

Keynes wrote two letters to his mother.

To MRS KEYNES, *1 June 1919*

Partly out of misery for all that's happening, and partly from prolonged overwork, I gave way last Friday and took to my bed suffering from sheer nervous exhaustion. There I've remained more or less ever since, rising only for really important interviews and for a daily stroll in the Bois, with the result that I'm already much better. My first idea was to return to England immediately, but General Smuts, with whom I've been working very intimately for changes in this damned treaty, persuaded me that it was my duty to stay on and be available if necessary for the important discussions of these present days, declaring that one can only leave the field of battle *dead*. However the business will soon be determined and then, I hope in two or three days at latest, I return to England forever, bar certain very improbable changes in the possibilities of the case.

I dragged myself out of bed on Friday to make a final protest before the Reparation Commission against murdering Vienna, and did achieve some improvement.

The German reply is of unequal merit but remains an unanswerable exposure of all our wickedness.

Don't think me more broken down than I am. I eat and sleep well and there's nothing whatever the matter except fatigue.

I have left the Majestic and am living in a flat on the edge of the Bois, which is quiet and where I am very well tended.

To MRS KEYNES, *3 June 1919*

I am living alone in a flat, which has been lent to me, on the edge of the Bois with an excellent French cook and a soldier servant to valet me, and am getting on splendidly—otherwise I would most certainly have sent for you at once. I spend more than half of my time in bed and only rise for interviews with the Chancellor of the Exchequer, Smuts, the Prime Minister

and such. Dudley Ward comes down twice a day with the news.
I am indeed so much better that only extreme prudence in
matters of health keeps me secluded at all. But I distinctly
looked over the edge last week, and, not liking the prospect at
all, took to my bed instantly.

The P.M., poor man, would like now at the eleventh hour to
alter the damned treaty, for which no one has a word of defence,
but it's too late in my belief and for all his wrigglings Fate must
now march on to its conclusion. I feel it my duty to stay on here
so long as there is any chance of a scheme for a real change
being in demand. But I don't expect any such thing. Anyhow it
will soon be settled and I bound for home.

Norman Davis was one of the first persons whom Keynes had seen when he
arrived in Paris and one of whom he took special leave before his departure.

To NORMAN DAVIS, *5 June 1919*

Dear Davis,

I am slipping away on Saturday from this scene of nightmare.
I can do no more good here. You Americans are broken reeds,
and I have no anticipation of any real improvement in the state
of affairs.

But I should very much like to have one last talk with you.
Can you lunch with me here tomorrow (Friday) at 1.15—82,
Boulevard Flandrin. This boulevard is at the bottom of the
Avenue du Bois. When you arrive ask for Colonel Peel's flat.
It is the second entrance to the left on the second floor. I will
assume you can come unless I hear to the contrary.

As I shall not be able to await the arrival of May, I hope that
after lunch we may be able to talk about the settlement of
French dollar reimbursement. With my departure there will be
no one left who knows the history of the subject.

Yours sincerely,

J.M.K.

471

Keynes's final tidying-up letter from Paris was to Bradbury.

To SIR JOHN BRADBURY, *6 June 1919*

Dear Bradbury,

I am slipping off home on Saturday. I can do no more good here. On Wednesday I went to a meeting of the Council of Four on Austrian reparation, but had no success. The reparation chapter for Austria is to be the same as for Germany except that no definite figures are mentioned and there is more provision for letting her off later.

On Tuesday I prepared a memorandum for the Prime Minister at his request on possible modifications of our reparation proposals. I append a copy of this. Lord Cunliffe and Lord Sumner also prepared a memorandum. I think that the Prime Minister disliked both equally and was unable to get anyone to recommend to him the middle course which he wanted. As a result he has himself in person gone on the small committee which is to consider whether any change is to be made. I anticipate that something will result but nothing that is the least good.

I also append a copy of the report which we have made to the Council of Four on financial assistance for Europe. You have already seen an earlier draft of this. I doubt if much will come of it. You will see from a communication from the usual source, that the Americans intend to make it a condition of remitting interest that we should make a large loan of new money to France for the purchase of wool. In my opinion, the only condition of such remission, which can be fairly asked of us, is that we shall ourselves remit to an equal extent. This we ought to do. It might also be urged that remission will put us in a better position for assisting in the currency re-organisation and other assistance proposed for the new states, but to suggest that we should pay for the concession three times over by remitting interest ourselves, by helping the new states, and also by a loan of new money to France is a proposition which ought not to be made, and if made, not entertained.

I am very grateful that you have been able to send out Waley. He and Ward together ought to be able to carry on. If, as seems probable, the Economic Council moves to London at an early date (Lord Robert Cecil himself is returning on Tuesday) Waley's stay here may not have to be a very prolonged one.

On reaching England I propose to go direct to Cambridge, where letters will reach me at King's College; later in the week I shall be coming up to London and will come and see you at the Treasury.

Yours sincerely,

J.M.K.

There was a final minute, written the same day (6 June) to Frank Nixon and Bradbury, the last thoughts of a Treasury man.

Mr Nixon
Sir John Bradbury

This paper raises an important question of policy. In my judgment the proposal that we should continue to furnish the Serbian army with supplies for the purpose of keeping it mobilised after 30 June would be a mistake in itself and would raise a dangerous precedent. There must be some limit to the extent to which the money of the British taxpayer is used for military ventures in which they have no concern.

The suggestion is that we should pay to keep the Serbian army in an efficient condition against Bolshevism. The use of the Serbian army for this purpose is surely a very remote contingency. The real reason why the Serbian army is kept mobilised is very different and it is astonishing that the War Office should purport to be unaware of it.

It is generally believed here that the militarist party in Italy has designs against the new Jugo-Slav kingdom, before that kingdom can consolidate itself. The Jugo-Slavs on their side wish to be in a position to maintain themselves by force of arms; there is also the possibility of hostilities between the Serbians and Roumanians, as the result of an attempt to buy off Serbian

473

ambitions on the Adriatic by giving them territory at the expense of Roumania. Lastly, it is currently reported that the Italians are secretly arming the Bulgarians (and also according to some accounts the Roumanians) with a view to embarrassing the Serbians.

Part of the above is rumour, but even though it is not all well founded, it is with a view to these considerations that future Serbian policy in the matter of the use of its army will surely develop.

Serbia knows that its real danger is an encirclement by Italy, Roumania and Bulgaria, and they are not going to despatch their army on ventures against Bolsheviks.

In any case I submit that in so complex a situation there is no case for our giving assistance of the kind proposed. We are already sending arms to Roumania and we have not ceased to assist Italy. If we also arm Serbia, it is true that the position will cancel out. But it would be much cheaper to arm no one.

J.M.K.

6 June 1919

DOCUMENTS REPRODUCED
IN THIS VOLUME

MINUTES

PUBLISHED LETTERS

479

INDEX

INDEX